HQ 1064 U5 P65 1996	Pollard, Leslie James. Complaint to the Lord	

DATE DUE

AUDREY COHEN COLLEGE LIBRARY
75 Varick St. 12th Floor
New York, NY 10013

Complaint to the Lord

Complaint to the Lord

Historical Perspectives on the African American Elderly

HQ
1064
U5
P65
1996

Leslie J. Pollard

SUP

Selinsgrove: Susquehanna University Press
London: Associated University Presses

© 1996 by Associated University Presses, Inc.

All rights reserved. Authorization to photocopy items for internal or personal use, or the internal or personal use of specific clients, is granted by the copyright owner, provided that a base fee of $10.00, plus eight cents per page per copy is paid directly to the Copyright Clearance Center, 222 Rosewood Drive, Danvers, Massachusetts 01923. [0-945636-80-6/96 $10.00+8¢ pp, pc.]

Associated University Presses
440 Forsgate Drive
Cranbury, NJ 08512

Associated University Presses
16 Barter Street
London WC1A 2AH, England

Associated University Presses
P.O. Box 338, Port Credit
Mississauga, Ontario
Canada L5G 4L8

The paper used in this publication meets the requirements
of the American National Standard for Permanence of Paper
for Printed Library Materials Z39.48-1984.

Library of Congress Cataloging-in-Publication Data

Pollard, Leslie James.
    Complaint to the Lord : historical perspectives on the African American elderly / Leslie J. Pollard.
      p. cm.
    Includes bibliographical references and index.
    ISBN 0-945636-80-6 (alk. paper)
    1. Afro-American aged—History. 2. Afro-American aged—Institutional care—History. 3. Home for Aged and Infirm Colored Persons (Philadelphia, Pa.)—History. I. Title.
HQ1064.U5P65 1996
305.26—dc20   95-38952
                                                                       CIP

PRINTED IN THE UNITED STATES OF AMERICA

To the memory of Vanessa Choice
and Michael Bennett,

For most of us it takes a lifetime to achieve what you managed to accomplish in a short time. The intensity of your being helps us to live with the brevity of your lives.

Contents

Preface	9
Acknowledgments	11
Timeline: Black Aging History	13
Introduction	19
1. "Massa . . . you can't make me work no more": Old Age and Slavery	31
2. "What charity more pure and sweet": The Development of African American Old-Age Homes with Special Emphasis on the Home for Aged and Infirm Colored Persons (HAICP)	59
3. "Better off than poor white people": The Beneficial Society, the HAICP, and the Black Elderly	87
4. "But she was white": Race, Gender, and Residency in the HAICP	110
5. "Complaint to the Lord": Social Structure in the HAICP	138
6. "The rugged path of faltering age": Health Care in the HAICP	163
7. Hobart Jackson: The Father of Black Gerontology	186
8. Epilogue: A Word to Gerontologists	202
Appendix 1. Bylaws: 1864	206
Appendix 2. Rules and Regulations: 1864	209
Appendix 3. Organizational Structure	213
Notes	214
Note on Sources and Selected Bibliography	269
Selected Bibliography	271
Index	280

Preface

Complaint to the Lord provides historical perspectives on the African American elderly. Based on the assumption that Black history and culture should inform old-age policy formulation, it combines the macroperspective of the community taking care of its own needy elderly with the micro-perspective of the examination of the Home for Aged and Infirm Colored Persons (HAICP). Issues raised in the introduction are derived from this premise and pursued in the chapters that follow. The thrust of the study is the examination of the HAICP founded in Philadelphia in 1864 by Blacks and Quakers. It is necessary to analyze the African American cultural heritage as it relates to the aged before moving the investigation into the Home.

At the root of the African American heritage was a supportive tradition that sought in a variety of ways to solve gerontological problems. The core of this tradition was mutual care via kinship and respect patterns derived from West Africa and nurtured in the crucible of slavery. Thus, chapter 1 is an investigation of aging during slavery, where a supportive cultural tradition developed in the slave community. This mutual care tradition carried over into organized structures such as the development of Homes for the elderly, the most important of which was the Home for Aged and Infirm Colored Persons. These Homes, western in origin, offered a refuge from the public almshouse and, through time and usage, took on their own tradition in the African American community. Chapter 2 describes the founding of the HAICP as well as the development of other facilities. Beneficial associations were also formal methods derived from the multifaceted tradition of taking care of the elderly, but unlike Homes for the aged, these societies had African roots and provided psychological and economic security that held out the possibility of independence in one's own home. Beneficial associations are the subject of chapter 3.

The administration of the HAICP is described in chapter 4 as the study shifts from the external occurrences that shaped the broader historical perspectives of Black aging to an analysis of solutions to gerontological problems in a particular setting. Social structure in the Home is the subject of chapter 5, and health care is discussed in chapter 6. These chapters illuminate the lessons learned from an examination of how an institution, indeed a Home biracial in management and African American in residential population, during an earlier era dealt with gerontological problems and issues. The chapters address how HAICP mirrored the racial and old-age assumptions of the day and analyzes how a custodial philosophy and these assumptions defined the quality of life in the Home.

The administration of Hobart Jackson (chapter 7) discards the old philosophy and brings the HAICP (which became the Stephen Smith Home in 1953 and received its first White residents in 1954) into the modern era in the context of the ferment of the modern gerontology movement. Serving as HAICP administrator from 1948 to 1978, Hobart Jackson used this position as a springboard to become the nation's chief advocate for the African American elderly and, in this writer's opinion, the Father of Black Gerontology.

Chapter 8, "A Word to Gerontologists," reiterates issues for gerontologists and brings synthesis to the study. In both the examination of the larger occurrences outside the HAICP and the analysis of its internal operations, the intent is to enhance the understanding of the history of the African American elderly. That Black Americans were flexible in their solutions to old-age care and inspired by their heritage to seek those solutions concurrent with the family unit are salient facts to be remembered by those seeking solutions to the gerontological problems today.

Acknowledgments

No one writes a book without assistance from others. In the case of *Complaint to the Lord* I have incurred numerous obligations. Two individuals deserve special appreciation for providing assistance and encouragement that enabled me to complete this project. My mentor, Otey M. Scruggs of Syracuse University, contributed much needed guidance at all stages of this project. The late Hobart Jackson, administrator of the Stephen Smith Home from 1948 to 1978, opened up the records of the Home, wrote a brief biography for my use, and shared many insights on Black aging with me. I am forever indebted to them.

Several colleagues at colleges and universities across the country provided assistance along the way. My appreciation is extended to Dave Dennard, Frank Sisya, Robert Hall, Lester Pollard, Harry Morgan, and Alfred Young. I owe a special word of thanks to Todd Savitt of East Carolina Medical School who sent me items of information as he carried out his research on medical history. I would like to thank James Wilson, President of the Mercy-Douglass Corporation, for his kind responses to my requests for information.

I am grateful to my Paine College colleagues (present and former) for their help during the preparation of this manuscript: Kathy F. Bond, Millie Parker, Lewis Greenstein, Marva Stewart, Julius S. Scott Jr., William H. Harris, Shirley Lewis, Lee Ann Caldwell, Peggy G. Hargis and Alice M. Simpkins. Our gerontologist in residence, Purna Mohanty, was especially thoughtful and helpful.

The United Negro College Fund (UNCF) supported several proposals that enabled me to continue work on this project. The staffs of the libraries and collections at The Pennsylvania Historical Society, Library Company of Philadelphia, Temple University, Lincoln University, Syracuse University, University of Georgia, Swarthmore College, Haverford College, Clark-Atlanta University, and Lancaster County Historical Society also deserve a word of appreciation. Of course, all shortcomings are of my own doing.

As always, I appreciate the patience and understanding of my wife Brenda, my son Leslie Jr. and my daughter Melody (Flapsing).

Timeline: Black Aging History

Date	Occurrence
1619	Arrival of African Americans from their West African homeland where respect and kinship patterns were strong, the old were valued for their age, and they performed important community functions.
1661	First slave law passed in Virginia. All thirteen original colonies legalized slavery. Drawing upon their West African heritage, slaves developed a supportive tradition of caring for the elderly and needy family members.
1780	Free African Union Society (FAUS) formed in Providence, Rhode Island. First beneficial/benevolent society among African Americans. Eventually hundreds of such organizations helped old people directly or helped families provide for the elderly.
1781	Pennsylvania abolished slavery and all northern states eventually followed suit. In the upper South, it was made easier to manumit slaves, but slaveholders used the laws to get rid of old slaves. States passed new laws prohibiting the emancipation of slaves usually after the age of forty-five.
1787	Free African Society (FAS) formed in Philadelphia by Richard Allen and Absalom Jones. Beginning of Independent Black Church Movement. The Black Church spawned burial societies, cemetery companies, and benevolent societies and helped the old through poor collections as well.
1793	The Female Benevolent Society of St. Thomas was founded in Philadelphia. The first for African American Women.
1848	First Home for African American aged founded in New Orleans by a Catholic Congregation, the Sisters of the Holy Family.

1860	Home for Aged Colored Women established in Boston.
1864	Home for Aged and Infirm Colored Persons (HAICP) founded by Blacks and Quakers in Philadelphia. Now the Stephen Smith Geriatric Center, it became the leader in institutional care for the Black aged.
1865	Slavery ended and Reconstruction began. African Americans brought under federal protection. Old slaves lost support, efforts made over the years to provide pensions for them.
1868	The Little Sisters of the Poor, a White Catholic order founded its first Home in 1868. It operated thirteen Homes for the aged by 1874, all accessible to elderly Black people.
1880	The period of accelerated self help began, institutional facilities for the African American elderly developed, including old-age Homes, hospitals, insurance companies and so on.
1888	South Carolina Congressman Thomas Miller introduced a bill in the House of Representatives to establish old folks Home for elderly ex-slaves.
1896	Segregation became the legal pattern of race relations that the Black elderly today grew up under. They developed coping mechanisms, avoidance of interracial contacts and so on.
1910	Du Bois's survey at Atlanta University showed sixty-two Homes for Aged Blacks. During the decade a major migration began that left a majority of elderly Blacks in the South. Today about 61 percent of the African American elderly still reside in the South.
1929	The Bureau of Labor Statistics published the "care of the aged" study which included a survey of Homes for elderly Blacks.
1935	Social Security Act provided old-age assistance and insurance. Some Blacks thought long fight for pensions for old slaves had come to fruition. Farm and domestic employment, where most Blacks worked, were originally excluded from Social Security participation.
1940	Bureau of Labor Statistics included Homes for the Black aged in its *Monthly Labor Review* publication on caring for the aged.
1948	Hobart Jackson became administrator of the HAICP. Jackson later became America's chief advocate for the African American elderly and Father of Black gerontology.

Year	Event
1952	Hobart Jackson became first Black Fellow of the Washington-based Gerontological Society of America founded in 1945.
1954	Agricultural, domestic and migrant workers brought under Social Security Act.
1957	Milton Barrow published "Minority Status Theory" as conceptual framework for understanding the elderly.
1958	T. L. Smith published one of the earliest articles on the Black aged. Published in *Phylon,* the study was entitled "The Changing Number and Distribution of the Negro Population in the U.S."
1960	In one of the few articles dealing with Aged African Americans, Walter Beattie calls for an end to the tendency to lump all aged together and make uniform social policy.
1961	Cummings and Bennett posed disengagement theory as first major theory to understand aging and society.
1964	The Urban League published *Double Jeopardy* which greatly stimulated interest in Black aged as a distinct group within the aged population. The Civil Rights Bill passed.
1967	Jacquelyne Jackson began to establish herself as the foremost authority on the Black elderly. She lamented the paucity of research on Black aged in her now famous review of the literature in the *Gerontologist*.
1970	The National Caucus on Black Aged (NCBA) was founded in Philadelphia at the HAICP. Hobart Jackson, its first president, was the prime mover.
1971	This year was recognized as turning point in the study of the Black elderly. (1) Special issues on African American elderly appeared in the *Gerontologist* and *Aging and Human Development.* (2) "The Multiple Hazards of Age and Race: The Situation of Aged Blacks in the U.S." was edited by Inabel Lindsay. (3) White House Conference on Aging included special concerns session on Black aged. (4) Urban League founded Project Advocacy: In Support of Black Aged.

1972   Robert Atchley published first college textbook for courses in gerontology. Pointed out gap in Black aged research. The fourth edition in 1980 included section on history of aging.

1973   The National Center on Black Aged was founded in Washington, D.C. It was brainchild of Jacquelyne Jackson. Hobart Jackson became director.

1975   *Journal of Minority Aging* published originally as *Black Aging.* Jacquelyne Jackson was editor.

1977   Robert Dancy's, *The Black Elderly: A Guide to Practitioners* published, which focused on survival and coping skills of old Black folks.

1978–90   Histories of aging now included Andrew Achenbaum's *Old Age in the New Land,* David Fischer's *Growing Old in America* and several others, but little on the Black aged.

1979   Donald Gelfand and Alfred Kutzik published *Ethnicity and Aging,* which included Kutzik's history of social provisions for the elderly.

1980   Jacquelyne Jackson published *Minorities and Aging,* first textbook devoted to this subject for gerontology classes.

1982   Association for Gerontology and Human Development at Historically Black colleges and universities (AGHD/HBCU) founded.

1986   The Gerontological Society of America sponsored first history interest group at its annual meeting.

1988   Arnold Parks, *Black Elderly in Rural America: A Comprehensive Study* and James S. Jackson (ed.) *The Black American Elderly: Research on Physical and Psychosocial Health* published.

1989   Iris Carlton-Laney published article "Old Folks Homes for Blacks during the Progressive Era," one of the few historical pieces in existence.

1990   M. Harper edited *Minority Aging: Essential Curricula Content for Selected Health and Allied Health Professions* (DHHS) publication No. HCS (P-DV-90-4).

Zev Harel, et al. *Black Aged: Understanding Diversity and Service Needs* was published.

2000	Last of the elderly with any significant connection to slavery. Dropping off of attitudes and behaviors associated with segregation. Increased institutionalization of the Black aged
2030	First elderly cohort born after the Civil Rights Act and the Voting Rights Act. First of the African American old who were not products of *de jure* segregation.

Introduction: Black Aging History and Conventional Wisdom

> We come, but not to celebrate,
> Amid the flight and whirl of years
> The deeds of heroes, on whose brows
> Are laurels, drenched with blood and tears.[1]
> —Frances E. W. Harper, 1894

Historical perspectives must inform gerontological thought in order to formulate appropriate old-age policy. In his influential history of aging in America, Andrew Achenbaum concluded that historical perspectives are needed not only "to assess the elderly's current conditions," but also to evaluate expectations regarding older Americans' situation in the future. In addition:

> Historians . . . must convince experts in other disciplines, policy makers, and legislators that the temporal aspects of all policy discussions and decisions affecting the aged are just as important as demographic, socioeconomic, political, and ideological considerations.[2]

In summary, those who work with the aged or seek solutions to their problems need a historical framework for understanding the research, interpretations, and theories regarding the aged.[3]

This approach is particularly true for the African American elderly who have a unique cultural heritage and peculiar problems that stem from decades of social injustice and indignity. The tendency in gerontology to lump all aged together negates the evolution of the African American's particular social attitudes and their unique cultural characteristics. As early as 1960, gerontologist Walter Beattie noted the tendency toward homogeneity in the field of aging and warned that recognition of racial and socioeconomic differences must be made among the aged population. "If we do not," he wrote, "we will be creating community programs for older persons in the image of those groups and interests with which we have the most acquaintance. This, certainly, is a bias which social welfare programs must avoid if they are to truly relate to the interests and concerns of all of our communities."[4]

The Urban League was one of the earliest organizations to address the need for racial differentiation among the aged population. Its study in 1964, *Double Jeopardy,* concluded:

> Today's aged Negro is different from today's aged white because he *is* Negro . . . and this alone should be enough basis for differential treatment. For he has indeed been placed in double jeopardy: first, by being Negro and second by being aged. Age merely compounded those hardships accrued to him as a result of being Negro.[5]

The objective of the Urban League's report was to analyze problems African Americans faced in old age and to bring public attention to their specific needs as they resulted from their peculiar history. So it is that the objective of Black aging history is to provide the building blocks for understanding the African American elderly.

Jacquelyne Jackson, Duke University medical sociologist and the foremost authority on African American aging, does not dismiss the value of history, but she has concluded that "recent data are more important for evaluating current and developing new policies and programs pertaining to aging . . . we know that slavery existed and had a profoundly negative impact upon Black Americans. But slavery *per se* is currently an insufficient explanation for most of the problems associated with aging of contemporary Black Americans."[6] Jackson's statement is essentially true, but more emphasis needs to be placed on the history of Black aging, including slavery, not to make direct causal connections, but as the crucible where African values and beliefs were transformed into American realities. To understand the Black elderly, one must consider their cultural heritage—their philosophies, values, attitudes, and worldview—which was molded by slavery, segregation, and other forms of oppression. Noting that the elderly today are the grandchildren and the great-grandchildren of former slaves, E. Percil Stanford, another authority on Black aging, wrote in 1987 in reference to slavery: "The distance between the reality of that cultural experience and that [with] which one is faced in today's world is not exceptionally great."[7]

If slavery is easily dismissed, then can the same be said for other historical experiences? What about segregation, that system of de facto and de jure racial separation based on the same philosophical underpinning as slavery in which today's elderly endured for forty or fifty years? Can the present situation of old Black people be understood without examining their employment in nonpensioned jobs with low wages, labor union exclusion, differential social security participation, sporadic work histories, and the institutional patterns of exclusion? What about behavioral patterns (coping mechanisms, accommodationism, deference to White people, avoidance of interracial contact), dietary patterns (pork consumption, salt intake, fried foods, and so on), health care (attitudes toward doctors, home health practices), and religious attitudes (which have sustained Blacks in so many troubled times)? Should they too be easily dismissed without reliable historical perspectives?

Are not historical perspectives on the African American family critical to understanding the elderly? "Throughout human history," wrote Leo Simmons in his classic study of cross-cultural aging, "the family has been the safest haven for the aged; it is just here, in the home and circle of kinship, that the old have always found their greatest security during the closing years of life."[8] This statement is certainly accurate for the African American family, rooted in West African culture with its tenacious respect patterns, strong kinship bonds, and esteemed elderly who play a vital role in the social structure of the community. Concomitant with its African heritage the Black American family has also faced the challenge of its members' survival in an oppressive new environment. During slavery African Americans developed a mutual care or supportive tradition at the basis of which has been an adaptive family unit that took care of its old members' needs whether in the form of short-term or long-term care for the disabled, emotional support for the burdened down, or financial assistance for the indigent.[9] The strength of the African American family has been its flexibility, absorbing children as well as the old, and protecting them in a cohesive familial environment. As a result of its roots and this challenge, the Black family, extended and augmented, has developed an adaptive and supportive family system that provides care and support for its old, infirm, and dependent members. Robert Wylie concluded: "No matter how crowded the home there was always room for an orphaned child, an elderly grandmother, an indigent aunt or homeless friend."[10]

The care the elderly have received from younger family members has been matched to some extent by the elderly's performance of vital family functions. As we shall see, during slavery the old advised the young on such matters as love and religion, protected abused slaves, named and socialized children, served as role models, and acted as "social service agents." Later, they cared for the children while parents worked, took in children in cases of illegitimacy, desertion, or divorce, and contributed to the emotional and financial support of families. It has been the old, particularly Black grandmothers, who have provided a stabilizing force in the Black heritage by passing on traditions and values.[11] In low-income African American families, Joyce Ladner found that the elderly played an even more significant role than they did in middle-class families, enjoyed greater respect, and provided the young with folk knowledge and medical advice that is more readily dismissed in middle-class families.[12] About the grandmother Lee Rainwater has written:

> A grandmother may provide a home for her daughters, their children, and sometimes their children's children, and yet receive very little in a material way from them; but one of the things she does receive is a sense of human involvement, a sense that although life may have passed her by she is not completely isolated from it."[13]

From slavery to the present, young and old African American family members have shared responsibility for creating a reciprocal supportive environment to meet instrumental and expressive needs. The Black elderly, after years of self-reliance and independence and the enjoyment of a family environment, look forward to continuing that status in old age. It is crucial that they maintain family ties. Jacquelyne Jackson, Wilbur Watson, and other experts have warned that those who have the responsibility for making policy decisions about the African American aged should seek to preserve the help-relationships that exist between the young and old in Black communities. Compensatory care can do damage to these relationships by destroying effective support systems that allow the old to make a meaningful family contribution and to maintain self-respect and dignity. In Professor Jackson's words, "[Old Blacks] may suffer significant familial role losses if society does not intervene in black lives carefully."[14]

According to conventional wisdom, African Americans "took care of [their] own," and sending the old to nursing or long-term care facilities was considered only in very extreme circumstances or not at all. As Dickerson has observed: "For the Black who has experienced the indifference of the welfare service providers, the prospect of spending the remaining years of life away from family in an institution where they are considered totally useless is far worse than being at home where one is of some use even if it is the task of being a live-in sitter."[15] Elmer and Joanne Martin concluded in their important study of the African American extended family that, "it is taboo even to think of displacing [old Blacks], leaving them alone, or putting them in a nursing home."[16] To many, institutionalization is an indication that the extended family has broken down and can no longer live up to its expected obligations.[17] This position is not confined to members of the family but undergirds the assumptions made by staff and administrators of institutions. As one practitioner explained, "We usually assume that people would not be utilizing our services if the family were responsible and had resources. Therefore, we either rule the family out or look at them as if they had deficits."[18] Since fewer than 3 percent of the Black elderly are in nursing Homes, there is prima facie evidence that the Black American family, extended and augmented, continues to act on the conventional wisdom.

When Black families do choose to institutionalize their elderly, family members are beset by guilt. According to Lillian Stokes: "[B]ecause of the tradition of the [Black] extended family, the necessity of sending the elderly to a nursing home often creates guilt feelings."[19] Race, class, and family structure notwithstanding, guilt is characteristic of such decisions; however, there is increased guilt in African American families because there is a perception that institutionalization is an indication of family failure and because conventional wisdom claims there is an absence of a tradition of institutional care. Undoubtedly, this guilt adds to the trauma of those elderly who must use institutional facilities. To avoid such guilt and trauma, Black families usually attempt to care for their old, obviating or ignoring the care provided outside of or in conjunction with the home.

More to the point, the elderly do not always enjoy the dignity or quality of life that children hope to preserve for them by keeping them home at extreme sacrifices. Even after making heroic efforts—rotating shifts of relatives who take turns visiting the old person, taking the elderly person into one's home, or hiring someone to move in with the family to take care of the elderly member—dignity may still be more elusive than real. According to Chatters and Taylor, the conventional wisdom may lead to the "blind assumption that the Black elderly do not need formal agencies."[20] Eighty percent of the care that all old people receive is still at home, and the emphasis on keeping them there with dignity is appropriate. However, tensions or strains in households where older parents live with children may add unnecessary stress that may come, as Davis has observed, "at an age when the older person's health is poorest, energies lowest, and the need for less stress is greatest."[21] Disrupting normal family patterns may result in a diminution of guilt on the part of younger family members, but perhaps more often leads to stress that may irreparably damage marriages and children-parent or children-grandparent relationships. Elderly African American people, born in the early twentieth century at the height of anti-Negro thought and behavior, who have experienced years of discrimination, undergone much physical and psychological abuse, yet maintained their self-reliance and self-respect despite it all, are unlikely to find dignity when they are burdens to their families.

The unidimensionalists, those who contend that care outside the family is nontraditional, defy historical fact, ignore changing trends, obscure the social realities that Black families face, and negate the social and economic forces that have limited African Americans' access to institutional care. This myopic view fails to explain what has happened historically to those who have had no families and few resources. Therefore, African

Americans in general and gerontologists in particular must get beyond the conventional wisdom and come to understand the important historical perspective that institutional care is also a traditional means of caring for the African American elderly, though that tradition, of historical necessity, began later than that of keeping the elderly in family settings.

The reasons for nonutilization of old-age Homes are more complex than the unidimensionalists position concedes. Poverty and discrimination, rather than family tradition, noted the late Hobart Jackson, have historically kept Blacks out of existing institutional facilities for the elderly.[22] Today, 38 percent of the Black elderly are poor compared with 12 percent of the White aged. In 1976, 35 percent of the elderly in public housing, not designed for the old, were African American. Moreover, half (53 percent) of the Black elderly live in central cities and about 60 percent live in the South where social services have been historically underdeveloped. In 1981 Freida Butler found at least five reasons that have kept African Americans out of nursing Homes. Those reasons were high costs, racial discrimination, low-quality community Homes, mistrust of service providers, and negative attitudes toward institutional care.[23] A 1987 report by the National Caucus and National Center on Black Aged (NC/NCBA) prepared for the House of Representatives Select Committee on Aging, reiterated these findings, adding that facilities serving African American people are often unable to meet federal and state codes and to meet fire and safety standards. Also, the report commented that negative news stories exacerbated suspicions of bad treatment of residents in institutions.[24]

The major point here is that a balanced historical perspective is needed for two reasons. First, it would augur well for the needed acceptance of institutionalization when no alternative is available to African American families: second, it would contribute to the understanding of the Black American's historical provision of moorings outside the family designed to care for the old. As the number of Black elderly grow, accompanied by the dissolution of respect patterns and diminution of traditional roles, experts agree that institutionalization of the Black elderly will increase. Some observers believe that in the future institutionalization will become more acceptable to the Black American family. According to Huling:

> Retirement homes have not been especially desirable to older Blacks who were highly integrated into their family systems. However, with the current move among contemporary African Americans toward individuality and personal freedom from the system of extended families, there is a possibility that in future generations retirement homes may become palatable to them.[25]

Moreover, Huling projects that when the younger population becomes elderly, they may adjust to Homes more readily and even develop friendships in institutions.[26]

The need then is to find ways to get Blacks into good, affordable facilities when they can no longer care for themselves. The answer may lie in what Hobart Jackson called "a strong and viable system of nursing Home care in the Black communities" rather than in the unilateral focus on institutional alternatives geared to meeting the needs of elderly Whites. Since old Blacks are in their own homes, often without available services, Jacquelyne Jackson identified the problem as being essentially not "how to keep the older Black person out of an institution; it is rather how to get him or her into a good one."[27]

Nursing Homes are not always available in the Black community. Becoming increasingly associated with for-profit hospitals, when opened they fail because of undercapitalization and the poverty of their patient population. The 1987 report by the National Caucus and National Center, mentioned previously, claimed that what is needed to get Blacks into institutions is "strict enforcement of civil rights legislation" and increased oversight by the nursing Home ombudsman under the Older Americans Act. Moreover, long-term care policies, the report contends, must reflect increased nursing Home accessibility for older Blacks as a "fundamental objective" rather than the present emphasis on institutional alternatives or deinstitutionalization.[28]

Shorter life expectancy is another often-cited reason that Blacks are not in nursing Homes in significant numbers. In 1982 the life expectancy of White females was seventy-nine compared with seventy-four for Black females and seventy-two for White males and only sixty-five for Black males. Black Americans constitute 12 percent of the general population but only about 8 percent of the elderly population. However, there is a point in actuarial tables at age seventy to seventy-five, that Blacks can expect to outlive their White counterparts.[29] Although the mortality crossover, as it is commonly called, has generated much discussion, it will be shown in the next chapter that it is not new. As African Americans age beyond sixty-five, they become more equivalent to their numbers in the general population. For example, Blacks make up only 8 percent of the elderly population, but they made up over 12 percent of centenarians receiving Social Security in 1977.[30] The racial crossover in life expectancy is particularly worth noting in light of the fact that the oldest old (eighty-five and older) are the greatest users of long-term care facilities and among the Black population is expected to increase from about 257,000 in 1990 to 412,000 by the year 2000. Those blacks who survive into old age then seem to be a particularly robust group. Nathaniel Calloway has offered an explanation:

> Probably the most useful explanatory factor for this crossover is the elimination through neglect and discrimination of those non-whites who were highly sus-

Table 1. Racial Crossover

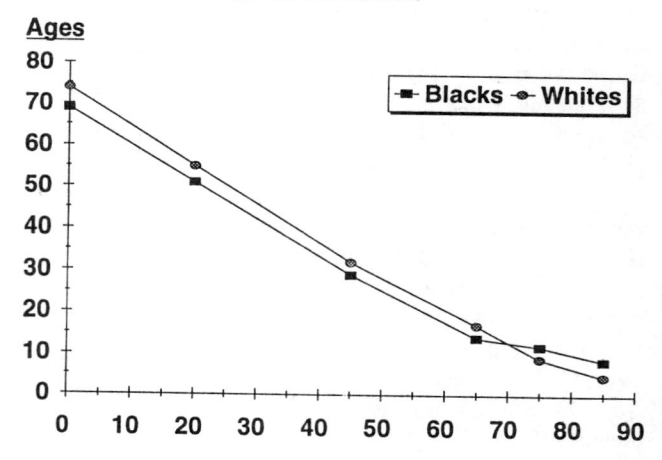

[Chart showing life expectancy at ages 0–90 for Blacks and Whites, with lines crossing around age 70-75]

Life expectancy at: 0, 10, 20, 30, 40, 50, 60, 70, 80, 90

ceptible to various diseases so that the aged survivor represented a selected group biologically superior in adapting to their circumstances and environment. The environmental adaptation also represents an interesting phenomenon of an underprivileged group adapting to their [sic] deprivation.[31]

Abandonment is generally associated with institutional care, but the African American family tradition may operate against this phenomenon. Wilber Watson has found that institutions and families may complement one another, as the Black elderly continue with family, friends, and church after going to a nursing Home. Even when severe disability and economic hardship have required placement of the elderly in a long-term care institution, frequent visits by family, friends, and members of the church have helped immeasurably to sustain the disabled elderly person despite infirmities.[32] This is clear historically, as we shall see in our examination in later chapters of the Home for Aged and Infirm Colored Persons (HAICP), which is a credit to the African American family and its traditions rather than to policies developed by institutions. Relatives proved to be important assets for the HAICP residents—visiting them, inquiring about proper treatment, engaging physicians, and withdrawing the mentally ill. In addition, in the HAICP, the relatives and benefactors, not unlike the present-day ombudsman programs, served to provide outside support as a countervailing force to the potentially despotic control of the Home.

A change in attitudes toward institutional care is much needed and will come in part from trustworthy historical perspectives. Those who foresee that the Black elderly must have greater access to nursing facilities, personal care Homes, and boarding facilities are not iconoclasts working against the grain of African American culture. To contend that Homes for the aged, for example, have been a historical way of dealing with problems of the Black elderly is not to impose a procrustean view but to correct one. When viewed from the vantage point of history, institutional care is not dichotomous and incongruent but complementary with African American family and culture. Any other view is not only at variance with African-American history, but also dangerous, for unless attitudes toward such care are changed, those elderly African Americans who use such services will continue to be regarded as discarded, their families viewed as unresponsive, and relatives burdened with unnecessary guilt.

Complaint to the Lord is based on the premise that Black aging history will enhance the understanding of the current cohort of elderly African Americans. It argues in the following chapters that cultural traditions of West Africa were maintained in a supportive tradition during the slave experience, not intact but flavoring African American lives in an oppressive environment. In freedom African American people, drawing upon West African frames of reference, developed a multidimensional tradition of resolving gerontological problems, including Homes for the Black aged as traditional mechanisms of support. While a comprehensive historical examination is beyond the scope of *Complaint to the Lord,* the study delineates themes that constitute the basis for an introductory history.

Complaint to the Lord

1
"Massa . . . you can't make me work no more": Old Age and Slavery

> When dey gits old and gray
> when dey gits old and gray
> white folks look like monkeys
> when dey gits old and gray.[1]
> —Slave Saying

> I have been writing of late of my thoughts and recollections of slavery. Old men, you know, are much in the habit, not only of talking about themselves, but of talking about the past. Things which occurred yesterday fade and vanish from their minds very quickly, but incidents of their childhood and youth follow them to the verge of the grave.[2]
> —Frederick Douglass to John Dancy
> 17 December 1894

Historical perspectives on old age and slavery are useful for two reasons. First, they are relevant for analyzing issues, problems, and concerns addressed later in chapters on the Home for Aged and Infirm Colored Persons (HAICP). Second, historical perspectives are provided that directly shed light on the contemporary conditions of the African American aged. In both instances the goal is to provide a better understanding of the Black elderly in today's society. The dual focus of this chapter is on the place of elderly slaves in the slave system and their role in the slave community. The African American supportive tradition—mutual aid, communal activity, respect for the elderly, kinship patterns, extended family—had its origin in the matrix of slavery and the West African heritage. It exists today, not as the result of a continuous historical process, but through the nexus of an ongoing response to changing, often oppressive, American conditions. A discussion of slavery and gerontological theories at the conclusion of the chapter is designed to point out the need to reformulate aging theory to accommodate variant patterns of aging.

To the extent that slavery can be judged by the treatment of its most vulnerable members, slave obsolescence held the key to understanding the peculiar institution. As an agricultural system, slavery allowed for tasks that could be matched with a myriad of abilities and strengths, allowing elderly slaves to maintain their usefulness by either performing intrinsically productive tasks or doing minor work that freed the robust to do the more physically demanding jobs. There were also superannuated slaves, incapable of performing either intrinsically or extrinsically productive tasks, who resided outside the hierarchy of work. The maintenance of old and superannuated slaves could drain vital funds from the coffers of age-conscious masters and strain the last thread of humanity from a production-based system. Nowhere did the capitalist and paternalist notions of slaveholders collide more dramatically than in the arenas of old age and superannuation.

It was in the slave quarter community, however, not in laws to protect slaves, plantation management, or in the paternalism of slaveholders, that the old found refuge from a degraded system. The slave community was a communal and familial network that provided comfort to the elderly and an opportunity for them to provide valuable services to family, friends, and community members. It provided slaves the cultural framework—in religion, folktales, spirituals, values, and philosophical orientation—for defining and assessing individual self-worth. Here, old and infirm slaves were venerated by the young and derived status from their roles as well as their age. Full understanding of elderly slaves then depends on comprehension of their dual existence in the slave system and in the slave quarters that stood in contradistinction to each another.

The Slave System

By contemporary definition (sixty-five years old and older) there were never many elderly slaves. During most of the antebellum period the average age of slaves was around twenty while the average age of slaveholders was over forty.[3] In 1850 the average age was about twenty-one for Blacks and twenty-six for Whites. At the next census, fewer than 10 percent of the slaves were over fifty years of age and only 3.5 percent (compared with 4.4 percent for Whites) exceeded the age of sixty, and only 1.2 percent were over seventy. Kenneth Stampp concluded:

> These statistics discredit one of the traditions about slavery days; that a substantial number of "aunties" and "uncles" spent their declining years as pensioners living leisurely and comfortably on their master's bounty. A few did, of course, but not enough reached retirement age to be more than a negligible expense to the average owner.[4]

The slave population suffered from a high rate of mortality because of improper or neglected health care, insufficient diet, and abusive physical labor as well as other things. Although some scholars have put slave life expectancies much lower, most data show a life expectancy range from low thirties for males to mid-thirties for females. In her 1982 study of senescent slaves and life course theory on Mt. Airy Plantations in Virginia (Richmond County), Janet Barber estimated that a slave woman who had reached age forty-five could expect to live to age sixty-four, and a male slave could expect to live to age fifty-nine.[5] In 1930 Charles Sydnor identified the crossover phenomenon among slaves. He argued that at age twenty a slave could expect to live another twenty-two years while a White person could expect to live to about age forty-four, but after age sixty, concluded Sydnor, the Black's "chance of living to one of the higher ages was greater than that of the White person."[6] To the extent that the mortality crossover, discussed in chapter 1, is an indication that Blacks and Whites age differently physiologically today, that was also the case during slavery.

Sixty-five is a modern chronological definition of old age. Preindustrial societies considered their members old as early as age thirty-five and sometimes even younger, and neither the slave system nor the slave quarters recognized a chronological demarcation between middle age and old age. State laws against manumitting aged slaves ranged from about age thirty to forty-five. Scholars of slavery have used ages forty-five to fifty as the onset of old age. Janet Barber decided on forty-five, basing her decision on the convergence of Virginia law, the decline of market values, the commencement of grandparenthood (thirty-nine for women, forty-four for men), and the beginning of empty-nest syndrome, which seems to this author a patently inappropriate concept to apply to those who constantly faced separation from their children.[7]

There were certain individuals who became designated as old by such labels as "uncle" or "aunt" or "old Tom" or "old Mary" because of their long life in the "peculiar institution." Others who were referred to as "granny" or "mammy" were old women who had been on the plantation for several generations and were respected by Blacks and Whites, often wielding authority that neither dared to challenge and enjoying social privilege outside the system's accepted code of etiquette.[8] Emily Burke, a New Englander, observed on her visit to a Savannah plantation that one old Black woman who was not a house servant sat and talked at will in the presence of White people and had free access to the house and was consulted on important matters and "reverenced by the whole family as a sort of "mother."[9] These elderly individuals were often accorded a place of dignity in the slave system as well as the slave community.

Elderly Whites during the antebellum period enjoyed high status, as did Black slaves, but for somewhat different reasons, though both were exalted for their knowledge, wisdom, and age. Agrarian elderly men knew the seasons, farming, woodcraft, and cooking, and old women knew cooking, quilting, knitting, and gardening. Their "opinions were respected because skill and wisdom came from experience."[10] Their veneration was also derived from their control over the land, politics, and the opportunity for social mobility—areas denied to the Black slave. In this regard, says Fischer, "youth was the hostage of age."[11] However, militating against this economic coercion was the western "escape valve" that demanded a delicate balance between respect and discipline. The Civil War ushered in the industrial revolution, which brought the "obsolescence of old age" and the loss of status and disesteem of the old.[12]

Although it is accurate to say that chronological definitions played no major role in the day-to-day affairs of antebellum people, it can be demonstrated in decisions about insurance coverages, tax assessments, marketing, and manumission laws that the cognitive makeup of slaveholders was not devoid of chronological content. Slave masters convinced lawmakers—slaveholders themselves wielded political power far out of proportion to their numbers—that tax exemption should be allowed on both ends of the slaves' life cycle. Generally, taxes on slave property began at about ten years of age and ended at age fifty or sixty. In Alabama, for example, capitation taxes on slaves ranged from about $1.10 for slaves between fifteen and twenty years of age to about $.20 for those between age fifty and sixty, relieving masters of the tax burden on old and superannuated property.[13] One ex-slave thought that the ages of slaves were conveniently inaccurate for this reason. "De white folks was s'pose to keep de ages of de slaves in order to know when dey was s'pose to start paying taxes on 'em. Guess you kin see now why de warn' so anxious 'bout keepin' close tract of de ages of niggers."[14]

About 3 percent of industrial slaves were covered by insurance, primarily skilled slaves and those who worked on dangerous jobs such as mining and water projects. Not many old slaves were employed by industrial firms. For example, of the slaves leased or owned by the salt firms of Kanawha County, Virginia, in 1850 only 29 (19 males, 10 females) out of 1,497 slaves were sixty and over.[15] Even fewer plantation slaves were insured, though insurance interests were increasing as demonstrated by the fact that sixteen insurance companies were founded between 1840 and 1860. Because masters had virtual life and death control over their slaves, insurance companies sought to protect themselves by restricting policy values to less than eight hundred dollars, limiting the term of coverage, charging exorbitant rates, inserting broad exclusionary clauses into the policies, and requiring comprehensive physical examinations (rejecting examinations performed by Homeopaths, Thomsonians, and Hydropaths). Nevertheless, insurance companies refused to cover old slaves. For example, the Franklin Slaughter Insurance Company insured slaves up to age sixty-two, while the North Carolina Mutual Life Company limited insurance to those under sixty.[16]

It was in the marketplace that the slave's chronological age and mental and physical condition combined with economic realities to determine the value of human chattel. If a buyer was to be found for aging slaves, it was necessary to draw a clear dichotomy between old age and superannuation. William and Ellen Craft recalled that their parents and other aged slaves were sold because "they were getting old and would soon become valueless in the market."[17] Another ex-slave recalled that when slaves "Got ter be old' and couldn't work much longer, their master would sell um to keep from buryin' um."[18] Of course, another remembered that the master "done got his worth outen um long before he bury um."[19] But some masters were not so astute at determining the right time to market their property. One ex-slave recalled that her father was "old" and at "every auction sale all the young niggers be sold; everybody pass old pappy by."[20] Another ex-slave was more to the point: "ya see, nobody wanted ol' slaves."[21]

The law required physicians to certify to a slave's "soundness" at the time property was transferred from one owner to another to protect buyers from fraud, preexisting disease, and disability, but slaveholders were not above palming off an old or infirm slave on an unsuspecting buyer. Helen Catterall has studied legal cases involving slaves and provides many examples of fraud. In one Georgia case a slave suffering from dropsy was sold to an unsuspecting buyer, and the seller had "used every artifice in his power to conceal [the slave's] true situation."[22] In a Missouri case a witness testified that he overheard a buyer instruct the seller "to put the age of the Negro at about fifty or fifty-five years, and not make her too damned old, as he might want to sell her again."[23] According to ex-slave John Brown of Georgia, gray hair was dyed or plucked from the head of old slaves who were scheduled for the auction block. Furthermore, he claimed that "slaves were instructed not to tell their ages when they are getting past the active period of life."[24] Former slave William Brown had the job of preparing old slaves for market. He wrote in reference to his preparation of slaves for a market in New Orleans:

> There was in this lot a number of old men and women, some of them with gray locks . . . I was ordered to have the old men's whiskers shaved off, and the gray hairs plucked out where they were not too numerous, in which case he had a preparation of blacking to color it, and with a blacking-brush we would put it on . . . they looked ten to 15 years younger.[25]

It seems that such practices were commonplace, even a source of pride, when an old or infirm slave was successfully palmed off on a Negro trader. But the elderly slave was often the loser in all this. Charity, according to the account of Emily Burke, was a woman who had performed many tasks on a Georgia plantation, including working as a nurse, but she was sold in her old age as a field slave. Unable to pick the required amount of cotton because she was then very aged and unaccustomed to that kind of labor, she was like the rest "cruelly beaten" and later killed.[26] Charity was evidently not one who benefitted from the master's paternalism despite her longevity in the system.

While paternalism has been credited with a key role in master-slave relationships, it is not clear how the concept operated in the day-to-day affairs of old slaves. Kenneth Stampp has described the paternalistic attitude as "a form of leisure class indulgence," which can be likened to the motivation that prompts one to join the Society for the Prevention of Cruelty to Animals.[27] On the other hand, Eugene Genovese has maintained that paternalism was the mediator between master and slave; the axis on which their relationships turned, mitigating the cruelest tendencies of the slave system and involving slave and master in a web of bilateral and reciprocal responsibilities. Yet, professor Genovese has conceded, the behavior toward the aged ran the whole gamut from cruelty and neglect to kindness and security.[28] In his discussion of slavery in the Black belt, characterized by high productivity and absentee ownership, W. E. B. Du Bois concluded that paternalism was nonexistent and the aged slave was "shamefully treated and neglected."[29] In his study of slaveholders, James Oakes concluded that paternalism could not have alleviated the dehumanization of slavery that had a racial base and "carried no implication of especially kind treatment of slaves."[30] On small plantations where masters managed their own slaves, paternalism was broader based, but on large plantations with overseers and drivers, paternalism operated in cases involving favorite slaves, usually house servants. Field hands who served a master for many years or grew old in the service of a single family could also benefit from the owner's noblesse oblige. In the final analysis, paternalism probably provided little comfort to the aging slave.

Slave apologists, however, were quick to point to the care of the elderly as an indication of the benevolence of the peculiar institution. Slavery defender Edward Pollard provides several descriptions of old slaves who were benefactors of the patriarchal institution. Uncle George was one of them: "He had grown old gently; he had never seen any hard service; and now in his old age was he not only required to do any work, but with regard commonly exhibited toward the slave when stricken with age, he had every attention paid him in the evening of life."[31] A southern physician concurred with this opinion: "no class of people in the world [is] better cared for than the southern slave—and in childhood or old age there is no difference shown."[32] It was said that the slave was not only freed from the anxiety of growing old, but also assured of a proper burial and care for his children. "When [the slave] is old, he knows that his wants will be supplied him in his small cottage . . . the man looks even beyond death and knows that when he shall have died he will be decently buried and his children after him provided for."[33]

The testimony of the slave himself is ambivalent about this and serves to confirm Genovese's observation that the treatment varied from kindness to cruelty. Bill Sims, a ninety-seven-year-old ex-slave recalled that on his plantation "when a slave got too old to work they would give him a small cabin on the plantation and have the other slaves to wait on him. They furnish him clothes and victuals until he died."[34] About an old slave Harriet Jacobs recalled: "When he hobbled up to get his piece of meat, the mistress said he was too old to have any allowance; that when niggers were too old to work, they ought to be fed on grass!"[35] Some elderly slaves were simply forced to eke out whatever living they could from the cabins provided for them. Frederick Douglass was particularly incensed over the treatment of his grandmother:

> If any one thing in my experience, more than another, served to deepen my conviction of the infernal character of slavery, and to fill me with unutterable loathing of slaveholders, it was their base ingratitude to my poor old grandmother. She had served my old master faithfully, from youth to old age; she had been the source of all his wealth; she had peopled his plantation with slaves; she had become a great grandmother in his service. She had rocked him in infancy, attended him in childhood, served him through life and at his death wiped from his icy brow the cold death-sweat, and closed his eyes forever. She was nevertheless left a slave—a slave for life—a slave in the hands of strangers; and in their hands she saw her children, her grandchildren, divided, like so many sheep . . . and to cap the climax of their base ingratitude and fiendish barbarity, my grandmother, who was now very old . . . took her off to the woods, built her a little hut, put up a little mud chimney, and then made her welcome to the privilege of supporting herself there in perfect loneliness; thus virtually turning her out to die![36]

Many years ago southern historian Ulrich Phillips painted a rosy picture of elderly slave life where large numbers of old slaves maintained a leisurely existence in a patriarchal institution. Phillips claimed that when a slave "lived to three score and ten, he would be worth substantially less than nothing, for he could render no service of worth, and his master must maintain him indefinitely on a pensioner's dole."[37] According to Phillips, this was necessary to placate family members and stabilize the workforce. "The Aged and infirm must be cared for along with the young and able-bodied, to maintain the good will of their kinsmen among the workers."[38] Certainly slave families were concerned for their members, but it is not known whether Phillips was correct that this concern translated into better treatment.

Despite numerous references to the care of old slaves as the best example of patriarchal practices, little evidence exists to indicate that most masters paid more than the minimum attention to caring for the old and infirm. No specific or comprehensive old-age policy emerged from the underbrush of slave management. When specific decisions were made, they involved such things as cutting off rations to reflect the elderly's lack of productive capacity, stronger slaves receiving larger portions than weaker or older ones received, or reducing workloads for elderly slaves.

In their journals masters shared their thoughts and practices on many aspects of slave life—medical care, punishments, rations, child care, harvesting, breeding of slaves and animals—but developed no consistent managerial theories or practices regarding elderly or superannuated slaves. James Breeden has studied slave management and concluded in his two-page chapter on "Old Age and Death":

> The protection of the slave in old age was one of the aspects of slavery frequently pointed to by the institution's defenders. But this chapter's shockingly small contents make clear that old age benefits did not command more than the incidental attention of the writers on slave management."[39]

Although it seems ironic that defenders of the institution made so much of the care for old and infirm slaves while so little developed in practice, a body of management procedure was perhaps too much to expect when aging demanded little attention in the larger society.

Masters' instructions to overseers also reflected the general absence of management policy regarding superannuated and elderly slaves. This point is important because overseers, like slaves, had their livelihood depend on their productivity and, unlike masters, lacked the property interests in human chattel. Typically, overseers were given a set of written instructions—a kind of "constitution" observed Bertram Doyle[40]—regarding the care and punishment of slaves as well as a list of rules regarding the effective management of the plantation. The instructions given a Yazoo, Mississippi, master in 1840, which Scarborough claimed to be typical, contained seventeen rules; six of them had to do with the welfare of slaves. About children one rule was clear: "The children must be very particularly attended to, for rearing them is not only a Duty, but also the most profitable part of plantation business."[41] But there was no mention of care for old slaves; their economic worth quite simply did not warrant a separate managerial statement.

Many masters agreed that overseers treated Black slaves harshly. As one master observed: "He don't work himself, but has more done than any man I ever had . . . but my dear sir, he is hell upon a Negro."[42] The slave's opinion ran almost unanimously in that direction. Ex-slave James Lucas spoke for most when he opined:

> Tweren't de masters what was so mean. 'Twas dem poor white trash overseers and agents. Dey was mean; dey was meaner dan bulldogs.[43]

Recognizing this fact, some masters put a favorite slave outside the "constitutional" jurisdiction of overseers. A Georgia master, for example, provided in his will "that my faithful old servant, Brit, shall not be put under any overseer, but remain on my plantation, to care of [sic] my stock, and that he be favored by my executor as far as may be expedient."[44] Elizabeth Green, a Mississippi planter, also provided that her senescent slave, Lem, not be put "under control of an overseer" and that others who had reached old age or were infirm be "paid a reasonable compensation for their services in whatever capacity they may see proper to serve."[45] A South Carolina master provided that "Silla and the rest of the family with old Jack, old Phebe and old Flora, remain on the place where my family shall live; and that the said old Negroes be treated humanely by my executors during their lives, but more particularly in old age."[46] A Virginia master provided in his will that his heirs keep "the young as well as the old [slaves] in order that by the labor of such as were profitable they might maintain those who were chargeable."[47] What is unusual about this request is that profits from physically capable slaves were tied to the maintenance of those who were not. Perhaps humanitarian motives were more easily written into wills than carried out in day-to-day affairs.

Such examples could be multiplied many times over but would only further demonstrate that what masters recognized in life—that elderly slaves needed special care—was sometimes implemented after their death. Of course, some masters recognized the value of experience and did not use overseers. "There was never an overseer on the whole plantation," W. L. Best recalled. "The oldest colored man always looked after the niggers."[48] Ex-slave Lindsey Faucette remembered that when the overseer was fired for beating a slave, the master "made Uncle Whitted de overseer 'cause he was one of the oldest slaves he had."[49] If the treatment of old slaves was the index to the humanity of slavery, it speaks volumes that slaveholders did not develop management practices or provide instructions to overseers that constituted a vortex of guidelines that helped to care for elderly slaves, pulling extreme masters to a central concept of care.

As stated previously, agricultural systems can accommodate a myriad of abilities and strengths, and it is difficult to be certain when a slave was no longer useful. It seems clear that senescent slaves performed less demanding tasks than younger slaves performed, but there is little evidence, at least on cotton plantations, that they modulated from rigorous to less rigorous tasks as part of a planned or predetermined program. That is, no master decided at the onset of a certain chronological age or condition that tasks would vary in accordance with predetermined rules. One was expected to do what one was physically capable of doing. Fogel and Engerman argued in their controversial study, *Time on the Cross,* that "planters solved the problem of old age by varying tasks to capacities of slaves," and that the earnings of those sixty-five and over were comparable with the earnings of young slaves in their midteens, offsetting the financial costs of maintaining the infirm and incapacitated. Furthermore, they contended, it was generally not until slaves became octogenarians that their maintenance costs exceeded their contribution. There was no reason then for masters "to work their slaves to death at early ages in order to avoid the burden of maintenance at late ages."[50] Charles Joyner, in his study of rice plantations of South Carolina, found that on the Waccamaw plantation in South Carolina slaves worked at lighter jobs throughout their sixties and retired around age seventy, a practice that reflected the elderly's "enhanced knowledge and diminished physical capacity."[51] Some on cotton plantations even acquired skills that were turned into useful functions in old age. An ex-slave explained:

> The old men usually had acquired some skill which they turned into useful service when they became too old to work in the fields. Their work was to make baskets for the cotton and shuck collars for the teams. During the cultivating season, one or more of the old men would go along to the field with the other hands to file, sharpen the hoes, thus making it necessary for any of the laborers to cease work to sharpen hoes. It was their duty also to keep the plow points, hoes and sweeps bright and ready for use by rubbing the rust with brick bats after pouring kerosene upon them.[52]

Physical condition and strength were the determinants of the work assignments of slaves rather than of preconceived notions about gender or age. Therefore, adult women and men often performed the same tasks in the master's field. There is general agreement that tasks for elderly men included polishing tools, gardening, watering and feeding animals, shucking corn, hunting, and driving wagons, while old women cooked, sewed, knitted, weaved, nursed children, and attended the sick; but there is no consensus that these tasks were the exclusive province of a particular sex. Children went to the fields between eight and ten years of age, but younger children worked alongside the elderly, the slave system providing the opportunity to solidify age relationships cherished and nurtured in the slave quarter community. While keeping children was usually reserved for old women, an ex-slave recalled that her "Grandpa Slafford" was an old man who "set by the fire all day with a switch in his hand and 'tend the chillun whilst their mammies was at work."[53] Into the loom house on a Mississippi plantation to make clothes or shoes went men and women, "antiquated or crippled" as long as they were not capable of field work."[54] Emily Burke observed on her visit to a Georgia plantation "that among southern field hands, the women can hoe as well as the men and the men can sew as well as the women, and they engage in all departments of labor according to the necessity of the case without regard to sex."[55] With the parity of strength between males and females in childhood and old age, gender distinctions in occupations were even more blurred at both ends of the life cycle.[56]

Retirement—withdrawal from work—is a modern practice instituted by an industrial society to replace obsolescent workers with younger, more "capable" ones. Although slavery had some aspects of an industrial system, its agricultural character obtruded. Farmers in pre–Civil War America did not retire, and if the idea was part of the cognitive makeup of slaveholders, then it was derived from physical incapacity rather than from some notion about chronological age. According to Hushbeck: "Certainly, mandatory or induced retirement because of age was unheard of in antebellum America, because the notion was not yet widespread that an aging worker was an obsolescent one."[57] Slave masters quite simply expected slaves to wear out, that is, to use every ounce of their physical energy in the furtherance of the masters' economic well-being. This expectation sometimes surpassed the slave's physical capacity, according to Todd Savitt, and "some slaveholders failed to or refused to recognize the signs of aging in their slaves and expected a level of work far in excess of capabilities."[58]

No one understood the connection between physical disability and retirement better than the slave. Complaints about feigning illness were ubiquitous as women pretended long pregnancies, and both sexes frequently complained of rheumatism, paralysis, and the loss of the use of limbs. Slave masters and overseers had quite a time discerning a real illness from an imagined one.[59] Those too sick to work as slaves were often rejuvenated by freedom. One ex-slave recalled that a slave who "done been par'lyzed fo' years" heard about freedom amidst the celebration of other slaves and 'got out de baid, hobbled on out de do', and stood dere praying Gawd for his mercy."[60] When slaves on her plantation were informed of their freedom, eighty-nine-year-old Lucretia Alexander recalled that "old colored folks, old as I am now, that was on sticks, throwed them sticks away and shouted."[61] In 1866 former planter Frederick Eustis complained to a government investigative committee that during "forty years of plantation life" he had never seen so little sickness. "There are twenty people whom I know who were considered worn out and too old to work under the slave system," he informed them, "who are now working cotton as well as their two acres of provisions; and their crops look very well. I have an old woman who has taken six tasks (that is, an acre and a half) and last year she would do nothing."[62]

Some slaves were unwilling to accept the slave master's linkage of retirement with physical disability and felt that longevity justified withdrawal from work. Jake was such a slave: Confronting his master, Jake proclaimed: "Just come to tell you massa, that I've labored for you for forty years now. And I done earned my keep. You can sell me, lash me or kill me. I ain't caring which, you can't make me work no more." Some masters, no doubt, would have exercised one of the options laid out to him, but Jake's master was obliging. "All right, Jake. I'm retiring you, for God's sake don't say anything to the other niggers."[63] In 1986 the Age Discrimination in Employment Act (ADEA) was amended to outlaw mandatory retirement in companies employing twenty or more workers, and the National Caucus and Center on Black Aged (NCBA) called for a universal ban on retirement. "It will help to assure that functional capacity will determine whether any person is hired, fined or demoted," the NCBA explained.[64] Jake would not have been impressed.

The kind of medical care slaves received was also important to their livelihood. The folly of refusing to give proper medical attention to or neglecting illnesses of valuable field hands was probably clear to slaveholders, but the high costs of treating chronic illnesses of old slaves threatened to drive the last thread of humanity from the slave system. In light of modern experience—which shows that high medical expenses may strain even the strongest family relationships—it is not difficult to understand Todd Savitt's contention that the "master, who, unless he had a strong affection for a particular slave, might easily grow to resent frequent outlays of cash on useless chattel and withdraw medical treatment altogether."[65] Viewed from today's vantage point, and given the state of medical practice during the antebellum period, leaving a chronically ill slave to his own devices or to the folk remedies of the quarters might well have been a more humane act than subjecting him to persistent cathartics and bloodletting.[66] Of course, some medical theorists and practitioners felt that slaves, because of their alleged immunities from and susceptibilities to particular diseases and because of their "peculiar resistance" to pain as well as their so-called anatomical differences, should or could not be treated with venesection and massive dosing and called for a separate branch of medicine. There was no call for separate medical treatment of slaves because they were elderly or elderly nonslaves for that matter, but slaves themselves often preferred the ministrations of Black "doctors" who as one slave noted, were not about "diz hur cuttin."[67]

Black healers, whom slaveholders used to reduce the cost of treating senescent slaves, were frequently old slaves themselves who over the years had acquired an extensive knowledge of the herbal arts. Their prescriptions included those that could be taken orally to cure disease as well as those to be worn around the neck or wrist to ward off an ailment. Ex-slave Elise Davis recalled:

> Massa, he look after us slaves when us sick 'cause us worth too much money to let die, just like you do a mule. He got a doctor or nigger mammy. She make tea out of weeds better'n quinine. She put string around our neck for chills and fever, with camphor on it. That sure keep off disease.[68]

Most diseases could be cured with the right herbs, but God's intervention was sometime needed. "Dere's a root for every disease . . . but you have to talk to God and ask him to help out," a Virginia slave recalled.[69] The old were the most skillful practitioners, and age was a key requirement for practicing medicine because it brought experiences that were handed down through oral tradition, but gender was also important as one ex-slave observed "most all de old women could get medicine out de woods."[70] Some medical treatments were practiced so extensively by old women that a regular physician complained that "old age [should not] be their only qualifications."[71]

Sixty percent of the Black elderly population still reside in the South, particularly Georgia, Alabama, South Carolina, Mississippi, and Louisiana, and according to scholars and practitioners such as Wilbur Watson, Wilbert Jordan, and James Carter, there is evidence that these treatments and remedies as well as the attitudes and beliefs that accompany them are still around. Wilbert Jordan observed that the old lady who is knowledgeable of herbal medicine "is in essence the first line of health in the traditional rural south."[72] An understanding of this cultural practice needs to be a part of the training received by present-day gerontologists who work with or study the Black elderly.

Perhaps another reason slaves preferred their own doctors was the fear of being used for experimental purposes. Although slaves were not educated, they were not immune to the reputation of hospitals, medical schools, and White physicians.[73] While scholars reject the idea that there was a conspiracy to steal slave bodies, most agree that the graves of the poor and helpless provided many cadavers for anatomical examination. Slaves were at the bottom of the vulnerable heap and became easy victims of what Richard Shyrock accurately called "the interplay between medical science and its social environment."[74] It was not without irony that as slaves grew older and their need for medical attention increased, their decrease in value concomitantly reduced their chances of obtaining proper care from their owners, perhaps exacerbating a fear of old age and a deepening sense of dependency.

The mental health of slaves, however, was not of special concern to masters. During the antebellum period, senile dementia had not been isolated, medically or socially, as a malady peculiar to the elderly, and mental disease, some of the leading authorities claimed, attacked the young who had not reached the protection of old age.[75] Also protected, some maintained, were slaves because slavery provided for their wants and needs and freed them from the anxieties concomitant with citizenship and independence, which proslavery supporters felt Blacks were not equipped to handle. Indeed the 1840 census seemed to provide "conclusive evidence" that slavery was conducive to good mental health since free African Americans seemed the worst victims of mental disease. According to census data, as one moved from the slave states to the free states, the incidence of insanity increased, for example, 1 out of 4,310 in Louisiana, 1 out of 1,309 in Virginia, 1 out of 257 in Pennsylvania, and 1 out of 14 in Maine.[76]

Discredited for its inaccuracies, such as the inclusion of dozens of insane Blacks in towns where no African Americans resided, the 1840 census continued to provide grist for the proslavery mill. William Postell, combining the census with probate court records, estimated that the ratio of slaves suffering from mental illness was about one in eighty-six in 1840. The undercount in the 1840 census was due to the fact that many mentally ill slaves "could be taught a simple routine and thus could be profitably employed" as well as rehabilitated by such methods.[77] If masters worried about mental affliction, it was because they might be deprived of a slave's labor because of institutionalization, or they might be subjected to a lawsuit because of the mischief of a mentally afflicted slave. To the extent that slaveholders imbibed the proslavery rhetoric and kept abreast of medical doctrine in antebellum America, there was little or no anxiety about the mental disease among slaves, for they enjoyed the double protection of chattelism and old age.

Laws were passed to protect communities from the cost of maintaining elderly slaves who might be freed by profit-motivated masters. Following the American Revolution, northern states, motivated by humanitarian impulse and economic expediency, freed their slave labor by gradual abolition—Pennsylvania (1780), Rhode Island and Connecticut (1784), Massachusetts (1780), New York (1799), and New Jersey, (1804). In these states care for elderly slaves was a difficult item of negotiation. Children could be apprenticed, but masters demonstrated a marked unwillingness to hold on to their superannuated property, and in most cases, New York and New Jersey, for example, they were relieved of their "obligations."[78] While manumission was never seriously considered in the lower South, where Blacks were more densely concentrated and slavery was more profitable, the upper South states such as Delaware (1782), Virginia (1782), and Maryland (1780) passed laws allowing masters to manumit slaves. Would-be humanitarians by the opening of the nineteenth century were using these laws to rid themselves of aged and infirmed slaves. To protect the public from having to care for pauperized elderly slaves, the states began to restrict freedom to younger slaves. Virginia in 1782 had restricted manumission of slaves to those under forty-five, and Maryland in 1796 followed suit; Delaware restricted freedom to those under thirty in 1819; Missouri, Arkansas, and Louisiana, following Virginia's 1782 statute, in 1804 restricted freedom to female slaves between the ages of eighteen and forty-five and male slaves between twenty-one and forty-five, discouraging indigency on both ends of the life cycle.[79]

The Kentucky Constitution (1794) required slave masters to care for elderly and infirm slaves, and subsequent statutes protected the communities from indigent freedmen, but in 1841 the state required a bond to set free any slave regardless of age or condition. In 1800 South Carolina required a certificate from a magistrate attesting to a potential freedmen's ability to provide for himself as well as a statement certifying to his good character. Georgia (1801), Mississippi and Alabama (1805), and South Carolina (1820) passed legislation denying manumission except by the approval of the state legislature. Tennessee and North Carolina (1801), Florida (1820), and Louisiana (1830) required securities for manumission if the slave became pauperized.[80]

As the events of the sectional period unfolded, particularly increased political debate, the growing militancy of the abolitionists, and the cataclysm of Nat Turner, laws against liberation became even more stringent. They reflected the South's growing defensiveness of its peculiar institution and its fear of the anomalous free Black in a dyadic system built for Black slaves and White masters. Therefore, the earlier laws just described were replaced by a body of legislation that called for removal of all freed slaves and later by prohibition of manumission altogether. Virginia had required removal in 1806, but between 1829 and 1836, Florida, North Carolina, Louisiana, Tennessee, Mississippi, Alabama, and Texas had followed her example. Louisiana in 1852 and Tennessee in 1854 required that slaves freed within their borders had to leave the country unless they were too old or too sick to travel. Louisiana (1857), Alabama (1859), and Maryland (1860) passed legislation prohibiting manumission altogether.[81]

The purpose of slave laws was not to protect the interest of the slave, but to protect communities from paupers. The abolitionists, William Lloyd Garrison in particular, accused the American Colonization Society, founded in 1815 to colonize Blacks outside the United States (particularly in Liberia, which it founded in 1820) of strengthening slavery by offering slave masters the opportunity to rid themselves of useless slaves by sending them to Liberia. Of course, the officers of the corporation denied the charge, and Garrison could not prove it.[82] Tom Schick in 1971 compiled figures to show that about 3,900 emigrants went to Liberia between 1820 and 1843. The ages of these ex-slaves showed that about 9 percent to 10 percent fell between forty-six and ninety-eight, about their numbers in the general population.[83]

Many states like North Carolina, Delaware, Virginia, and South Carolina specifically required that Overseers of the Poor, county officials entrusted with caring for the poor, charge masters for care of their pauperized property, and in all slave states the masters could be sued or the slave could be sold back into slavery unless they were of no value.[84] But the breakdown in the enforcement of this legislation allowed masters to rid themselves of senescent slaves with impunity. Leslie Owens found that "aged slaves sometimes drifted aimlessly, winding up in cities where urbanites thought them burdensome additions to the population."[85] Ira Berlin also claimed that slave masters found it to their benefit to rid themselves of the sick and infirm and that Baltimore officials, for example, had difficult times trying to force masters to support their aged charge.[86] Benjamin Klebaner cites several cases involving the Overseers of the Poor in Delaware, North Carolina, and Virginia in their efforts to get owners to live up to their responsibilities.[87] Emily Burke noted that in Georgia an asylum had been provided because numerous old and infirm slaves were left homeless and without subsistence, but she observed:

> I have known poor old men almost bent to the ground by hard labor, with locks which age had bleached as white a newly washed wool, rather than go to this asylum travel from one plantation to another, begging a potato from one slave and a morsel of hominy from another, sleeping at night in some corner of an old out-house or in the woods, till they were finally compelled by those who thought themselves doing a deed of mercy to take up residence in a place as much dreaded by these unfortunate creatures as the almshouse is at the North by poor people.[88]

An Alexandria, Virginia, woman sought the help of the mayor on behalf of a slave woman who had been burned in the service of her master, and as she put it, "was the greatest object of misery I have ever beheld." She pleaded: "She is now lothsome to every beholder, without a change of clothing, or one single necessity of life or comfort. Can you compel the savage creature who owns her to do something for her?"[89]

Viewed from the historical perspective of the slave system, the elderly slave lived a precarious existence as a nonproductive individual in a production-based system. Laws did not protect old slaves, paternalism benefitted few favorites, and unlike children, no specific management practices were designed to care for or protect them from overseers. What protection, security, and emotional well-being the old and superannuated slaves received from the vicissitudes of slavery was provided by the slave community. The observations of Edward Magdol are appropriate: "Whether masters were benign paternalists or rapacious brutes, Afro-American slaves in their quarters fashioned a culture that sustained them as individuals and informed their creation of a community for their survival."[90]

THE SLAVE COMMUNITY

Traditional West African societies strongly respected the elderly because of their age as well as their continued usefulness in the communities. Studies of a variety of ethnic groups (Ibo, Kpelle, Akan, Mali, Hausa, Bambara, Yoruba, and others) in Liberia, Ghana, Mali, Nigeria, and the Ivory Coast show a strong veneration for the old. In predominantly agricultural societies kin networks took care of the dependent (old, handicapped, indigent, sick, and others) in the absence of formal organizations found in modern societies. The word *old* translated to *wisdom,* and the language flattered the elderly as people of knowledge and vision. Even an enthroned child chief among the Akan of Ghana was called "the elder." Those who died still interacted with their communities because the worship of ancestors was widespread in West Africa, a religious practice that "established the elderly as the cultural link between the living and the dead."[91]

The old performed the society's rituals, presided at ceremonies such as birth, marriage, and funerals, ruled through "Councils of Elders," cared for and socialized children, and served as advisors and teachers. Many West African proverbs reflect the importance of the old. The Ibo say "a man may be born to wealth but wisdom comes only with length of days." An Ashanti saying stresses the obligation to elders: "My parents took care of me when I had no teeth, I will care for them when they have no teeth." This Mali proverb depicts the knowledge of the elderly: "A young man's gait is rapid, but he does not know the way. An old man's gait is slow, but it made the way." An Akan proverb reflects the reciprocal relationship between children and the old: "The hand of the child cannot reach the shelf, nor can the hand of the elder get through the gourd on the shelf."[92]

From their West African homeland, slaves brought a cultural heritage that influenced their lives in the New World. They brought their beliefs about the universe, conceptions of human existence, views on death and dying, and a tenacious reverence for the old. These intangibles were never jettisoned, always there to flavor the slaves' lives in an oppressive environment.[93] The veneration of ancestors survived, though not wholecloth, among Blacks in America who recognized no dichotomy between the temporal and the spiritual in a hierarchical relationship among God, the ancestors, and the aged. Approaching ghosthood, the aged were closest to the ancestors. They therefore occupied a favorable position with God and could avenge disrespect from the young or reward them for exemplifying the proper demeanor.[94] Africans everywhere in slavery, claims Sterling Stuckey, "had an overarching conceptual concern to be in good terms with ancestral spirits."[95] A prerequisite for which was to be in good with the old folks. But veneration for the elderly slave was not purely a function of religious-cultural beliefs; the young had a deep respect for the old because they performed duties in slavery not unlike those in West African societies.

Bereft of the opportunity to own land, acquire property, or otherwise experience social mobility, the African American slave derived status from within his community, and slave system functions were not those from which the slave derived his self-definition or his community status. The slave community constituted the primary environment, the crucible that shaped the slave's ethical system, defined the areas of interpersonal relationships, and fostered Black unity.[96] Here slaves derived their self-esteem from their own cultural references—religion, folktales, spirituals, and philosophical orientations. Status in the slave community was based on criteria of power or authority derived from religious beliefs, based on the amount of independence from the slave system and culled from the wisdom that came with age. High status on the plantation's social ladder, as Blassingame has demonstrated, seldomly provided ipso facto status in the quarters. The key to social standing in the slave community converged on whether one used his or her position in the plantation system for the benefit of those in the slave community. The driver who pretended to whip a slave, the house servant who provided bits and pieces of foodstuffs from the master's kitchen or information regarding sales or separation of families, and the artisan who made goods for the community were highly regarded in the quarters. Those who used these positions only for personal gain were not favored.[97]

In his study of slave class structure, Blassingame lists the members of the upper class in the following order of social importance: conjurors, physicians-midwives, preachers, elderly, teachers, carriers of culture, entertainers, and rebels.[98] one should note that those who held these important positions were frequently elderly; the literature is replete with "old midwives," "old preachers," "old conjurors," and "old doctors." Why then is there a separate category for the "elderly" when old people served in these valuable roles throughout the social hierarchy? Evidently, the elderly also enjoyed an ascribed status, that is, a social worth independent of their function. Robert Achenbaum has written: "Ideas about the worth and function of the elderly have a life of their own."[99] Perhaps the dynamics of the slave community were such that the old were esteemed independent of their function while the service of those who provided for the community reinforced and sustained the abstract idealism.

Where the onset of old age brought the gradual reduction of work load came more time for engagement with the slave community. A question for further study is whether the old slave actually improved his diet, quantitatively or qualitatively, because his reduced work load provided leisure to hunt, fish, or raise gardens. Since "retirement" was a function of physical disability, it is doubtful whether those who had reduced work load could take advantage of their leisure. Professor Boles claims that slaves with "leisure" time added variety as well as nutritional benefits to their diet but does not address the question of elderly slaves.[100] The point here is that as old slaves withdrew from the masters field to perform minor tasks, they became increasingly and commensurately engaged in the slave quarters. This involvement included sustaining those punished, protecting the abused, harboring runaways, mediating with masters in times of crisis, and comforting those separated from families. Old people were responsible for socializing all the plantation youth into slave culture and inculcating slave quarter values into children. The performance of related tasks for the system allowed reinforcement of this community responsibility. "In dem days de ole folks learned the chillun sumpin. . . . De ole folks learn us all a chile orter know," an ex slave remembered.[101] Old slaves advised young people on religion (Nat Turner learned his religious ideals from his grandmother) and love affairs, told stories of Africa (maintaining the oral tradition), and served as conduits of the cultural heritage. Almost all plantations had an old mystic or conjuror, thought to have the power of progress, growth, and evil, who sometimes exerted tremendous power and influence over slaves.[102]

Joanne Rhone has made the point that there was an informal social service delivery system that developed among slaves that provided "protection, cooperation, and mutual support." Old slaves she described as "social service agents" who "had the time, knowledge, and skill to be helpful to other slaves." In the slave community, "an environment that socially, economically, and politically separated them from the white community," Rhone claims, "it was clearly understood and accepted that older slaves would carry major duties in the area of human services."[103]

The old, infirm, or superannuated slaves were fortunate to have family or friends to care for them in times of need or masters' indifference. Herbert Gutman has shown that most families were strong, durable (only one in six was broken), and responsive to the individuals needs as viable units and has laid bare many of the myths and misconceptions that characterize Black family history.[104] Slave families reflected the exigencies of the institution of slavery but in function and structure often reached back to the cultural tradition of Western Africa. According to Sudarkasa, the African extended family was essentially an American transplant that:

> Had served on that continent, in various environments and different political contexts, as a unit of production and distribution, of socialization, education, and social control; and of emotional and material support for the aged and infirm as well as the hale and hearty.[105]

Moreover, slave families were not mirror images of White southern families. For example, despite the southern Whites' practice of marrying cousins, the slave family held to an exogamous exclusion of cousins as marriage partners. Separation of families, or the threat of it, did not destroy the bonds of family members, but strengthened and broadened kinship ties beyond the immediate family. Indeed, the kinship system, which acted as a kind of social insurance, subsumed individuals who shared no blood relationships and bound them together in a pattern of symbiotic fictive kinship as a buffer to withstand death, separation, and other exigencies. According to Herbert Gutman: "Scant but nevertheless suggestive evidence hints that making children address adult blacks as either aunt or uncle socialized them into the enlarged slave community and also invested non-kin slave relationships with symbolic kin meaning."[106] This practice of referring to nonkin by these titles was also effective in "binding together slave adults (fictive aunts and uncles) in networks of mutual obligation that extended beyond formal kin obligations dictated by blood and marriage," and in "preparing slaves in the event that sale or death, separated them from parents and blood relatives."[107] This practice of fictive kin or parakin (imbuing unrelated individuals with kinship status), developed during slavery, still exists and is observed by scholars in Black families today, particularly those who have no spouses or children. According to Chatters and Taylor: "Friend relationships are sometimes regarded in kinship terms ["brother George" or "sister Taylor"], which serves to solidify feelings of mutual obligation and to extend the rights and responsibilities of kin status to support participants."[108]

The West African relationship between grandparents and children was one of the strongest of bonds.[109] Herbert Gutman, Andrew Billingsley, and others have suggested that the elderly, most notably grandparents, had the important function of naming slave children, a function widespread in West Africa, especially in cases of third and fourth generation blood relatives, thereby providing the historical continuity of Black families so often ignored in the literature. Since fathers experienced a greater likelihood of being sold from the family, the boys born to a family were named for their fathers.[110] These practices bound together past and present and rooted the African American in his environment.

The slave family and community felt strong obligations toward one another, especially the weak, blind, and aged who needed care. Old folks served as patriarchal and matriarchal heads of extended families and generally stayed at home with their children, where they enjoyed the respect and veneration of the young. One ex-slave recalled: "Grandma lived in the same house with ma and us children and she worked in the loom house and made cloth all the time."[111] Another ex-slave recalled that he "used to follow mom and dad. In dat way we could help de other when dey got behind. All of us would pitch in and help momma who wasn't very strong." Noting that some overseers did not allow families to work together, he explained that his uncle was the foreman, and "he always looked out for his kinfolks."[112] The assistance of family and friends was important to the slave and provided the elderly with a deep sense of security in a system that posed a serious threat to obsolescent slaves. The slave community at large helped the elderly to cope with a precarious existence in a production-based system and helped to relieve the stresses and strains that accompany the aging process.

Genovese is instructive here: "The slaves themselves did everything possible to allow their old people to end their lives with dignity. If some responded to their parents and grandparents with indifference or hostility, others in the community would step in to assume responsibility. When freedom came, the old slaves faced the withdrawal of their masters serenely, confident that they would be taken care of by family, and the black community at large."[113] The young slaves' veneration of their elders provided a thread of dignity in an otherwise degrading institution. The consistency and firmness with which children were punished for violations of this particular code impressed upon them unequivocally that it was a grave mistake to "sass" the old folks. Frederick Douglass recalled about those who had attained the status of uncle that it was: "Not because they sustained that relationship to any, but according to plantation etiquette, as a mark of respect, due from the younger to the older slave. Strange and even ridiculous as it may seem among a people so uncultivated, and with so many stern trials to look in the face, there is not to be found among any people, a more rigid enforcement of the law of respect to elders, than they maintain. A young slave must approach the company of the older with hat in hand, and woe betide him, if he fails to acknowledge a favor, of any sort, with the accustomed 'tankee'."[114] Many of these fictive uncles were skilled slaves who were a part of an artisan class that was highly respected by the young who saw them as role models.[115] Perhaps it is a cruel irony that age earned the slave respect at the same time that his or her accompanying infirmities jeopardized existence in the slave system, perhaps contributing to the anxiety characteristic of the aging process.

If advancing age was a source of anxiety, elderly slaves drew strength and comfort from their strong and durable religious beliefs. With destiny outside their control, as master and overseer literally controlled life and limb, slaves focused away from the temporal to the spiritual. Unable to destroy slavery, they put their faith in a retributive God, who would destroy the evil institution, and focused their thoughts on a better life in heaven, which they proclaimed to the world through song as slaves merged their situation with the heroes and teachings of the old Testament Scriptures.[116] Old age might have brought them closer to death, but they had many times faced this adversary, and religion had sustained them in the thought of a better life. Molded from the crucible of African beliefs and African American exigencies, the slaves' worldview sustained them in a degrading institution that would soon be destroyed and replaced by a more just system that rewarded the suffering slaves.[117] In some sense, slave religion was escapist as the slave released emotions through singing the spirituals, shouting, antiphonal responses to the oratory of the preacher, and maintaining the unshakable belief in an after life. The slave, surrounded by the everpresent threat of death, was liberated from the fear of death. "As [the religion] helped him to live, so it helped him to die," concluded G. R. Wilson.[118]

Stanley Feldstein has argued that slavery was a dehumanizing process, an inexorable, self-perpetuating and relentless attempt to render a human being into a "thing," and that "elderly slaves, were in the most real sense, the end result of the dehumanization process."[119] Slavery was undoubtedly a cruel, degrading institution, but elderly slaves did not become "things," or sambos who internalized slave system values as Stanley Elkins has argued, stripped of their person by years of dehumanization. They remained individuals, human beings, with self-respect who enjoyed an exalted status in the community and the veneration of the young. In the crucible of slavery the slave community developed a supportive tradition that followed into freedom. A tradition of care for those who, because of age or infirmity, became incapable of productive labor, emphasizing their inclusion and belonging to a community that did not define its existence in terms of the larger society. This community, then, learned to cope with the senescent slave the same way as industrial societies are learning to provide for obsolescent corporate workers. No doubt the benefit was reciprocal as older slaves taught younger ones how to cope with life, the meaning of survival over destruction, and life over death. One must not romanticize the horrors of American slavery, but the story of the old slave is the final chapter in the triumph, not of the individual, but of the slave community over the impersonal forces of the plantation, indeed in a larger sense, the triumph of the human spirit over tyranny.

Slavery and Gerontological Theory

Since current gerontological theories were not developed for societal arrangement such as slavery, there is a need to apply these conceptual tools to that institution to add to one's understanding of elderly Blacks. Numerous sources cited throughout this chapter deal with many aspects of slavery and old age and provide information that make it possible to examine in broad outline slavery and gerontological theory. To date, the only systematic application of an aging theory to the institution of slavery is Janet Barber's study of slavery and the "life course theory." Her study demonstrated that on Mt. Airy, Virginia plantations old age constituted a distinct phase of life, especially for female slaves who "retired" to care for children and perform other tasks while men generally continued in the same occupation. Retirement, defined by Barber as "no longer given a job assignment," occurred 28 percent of the time for men and 78 percent of the time for women. Barber concluded that "from a strictly functional point of view, it can be argued that old age constituted a distinct life course for Mt. Airy slaves, particularly for women."[120]

Another theory of aging is "modernization," a theory that assumes the aged were well treated and venerated in traditional or preindustrial societies because of their control over families through patriarchal authority, control of family property, and knowledge of agricultural techniques, which led to strong respect patterns that were reinforced by a system of religious and cultural beliefs. On the other hand, the theory holds that the old in modernized societies, characterized by high technology, obsolescent skills, a high level of literacy, family nucleation, a diversified basis of authority, and widespread industrial-urban growth are relegated to a reduced social and economic state. Donald Cowgill, who has studied aging in societies in various stages of modernization, has hypothesized that "the role and status of the aged varies systematically with the degree of modernization of society and that modernization tends to decrease the relative status of the aged and to undermine their security within the social system."[121] There are twenty-two assumptions in Cowgill's cross-cultural theory that may be summarized as follows:

> Traditional Societies
>   Old age, a function of events, e.g., grandparenthood
>   Old are rare, but hold powerful, useful, valued positions
>   Society characterized by little or no mobility
>   Extended families typical
>   Economic dependency a family matter
>   Communal value system
>   Continued engagement, without retirement
>   Old respected, venerated, and enjoy high status
> Modern Societies
>   Old age, chronologically determined
>   Longer life spans, high proportion of older population-particularly women, widows, and grandparents
>   Rapid social change, residential instability, high rate of literacy
>   Nuclear families, neolocal residences typical
>   Economic dependency a state matter
>   Individual value system
>   Disengagement, retirement common
>   Old disesteemed, status ambiguous, youth respected[122]

If one applies the modernization theory to slavery, then slaves may be compared to industrial employees who were fixtures in a coercive, impersonal, and factory-like labor system that was run for profit and designed to extract as much labor as possible, as efficiently as possible from its labor force. The advancing age of workers decreased their productive value, lowered their worth in the marketplace, and led to their obsolescence. To the system, slaves were devalued in old age and could be disregarded much the same way as obsolescent corporate workers are pastured in modern societies.

Looked at from the perspective of the slave quarter community, slavery, in accordance with the modernization theory, resembled a traditional society with age-graded roles of importance, opportunities for leadership, and a belief system that reinforced age relationships. The slave society venerated the old because (1) the elderly were rare; (2) society was stable since slaves were actually denied mobility; (3) the oral tradition was immensely important to a people who were legally excluded from reading and writing skills; (4) the elderly performed functions of extrinsic and intrinsic value; (5) the structure of families was extended and generalized, which attached a high social significance to kinship; and (6) the slave quarter community was a communal society where attitudes and behavior superseded individualism with the good of the group. African Americans experienced in slavery the traditional society and the factory-like system simultaneously and did not move from one kind of system to another as part of a larger pattern of agricultural-industrial development.

One of the earliest theories in social gerontology was "disengagement," developed in 1961 by Cummings and Bennett, which posed the functional view that older individuals withdraw from a retreating society as part of a mutually beneficial process. Retirement, the focal point of the theory, allows the replacement of older with younger workers who are considered more efficient with a minimum amount of disruption. Thus, the old who relinquished their social roles are provided time for reflection on and preparation for death.[123] Slavery was an impersonal economic system that often accommodated old age by a reduction of work load, though there is little evidence that this took place through a systematic or planned process, but because the agricultural nature of slavery prevailed. Agriculturalists did not retire in the modern sense but "wore out." The theory of disengagement may apply to some aspects of society at large, but does not explain aging under slavery because disengagement from the slave system was neither the result of the old making room for a young worker nor the result of chronological age. Disengagement was not functional for the slave system that resisted "retirement" by either nonrecognition of aging or coercion. The withdrawal of the slave from work was for the slave system dysfunctional, though the slave no doubt welcomed the reprieve from work and did not experience a traumatic departure from some life "career." Withdrawal from the system provided commensurate engagement with or new social roles in the slave community, accompanied by respect from the young and an increase in social status, thereby contributing to the satisfactory adjustment to old age.

Viewed from this vantage point, that is, the replacement of social roles as a result of job loss with a new set of roles, the slave experience is more appropriately related to "activity theory." Activity theory assumes that even though some reduction in level of activity is expected in old age, those who age most successfully are those who are socially involved and active.[124] The elderly slave took on additional slave quarter responsibilities as mentors, advisors, counselors, protectors, that contributed to the social welfare of the group. Perhaps even additional time for gardening, hunting, fishing, and leisure contributed to the quality of life in old age—to the extent such an assertion is applicable to an inhumane system such as slavery. For his life satisfaction or psychological well-being, the slave turned to religion as well as a role in the family and community.

The "exchange theory" of aging attempts to explain the interaction of the elderly in terms of the relationship between support given and support received—reciprocity.[125] The process that explains the relationship between slave and slave master (slave system), and between slave and slave community, may be better understood under this theory that would view the system and the quarters as a series of exchanges in a power relationship. The relationship between master and slave, though coercive and unequal, took place in a context of maximizing reward and minimizing cost.

The master, who saw the relationship as strictly economic and made decisions on a strictly rational basis, demanded maximum labor, from women perhaps maximum reproduction as well, with minimal costs, that is, revolts, runaways, or day-to-day resistance (feigning illness, breaking tools, sabotaging, and so on). The slave, no wage earner whose performance was tied to promotion, pay, or status, sought to provide the least amount of work at the least amount of cost (punishment, withdrawal of rations, separation of family). Advanced age decreased interaction and contributed to stress, tension, insecurity, and ambiguity between slave and slave system. Since the relationship was nonreciprocal, that is, the slave master did not benefit from disengagement, and since the slave's old age threatened the system with the loss of labor and the female slave's loss of reproductive capacity, accompanied by increased medical expenses, the master (left with cost only) sought to discard the relationship (sell the slave, set the slave free, build a hut so the slave could fend independently, and so on). The slave, on the other hand, now elderly, wished the relationship maintained—that care be continued—but without power resources (labor) to bargain. For some slaves, for example, artisans, advanced age brought skill and experience valued in the exchange relationship, and disengagement was undesirable for the slave system. While the master expected to get the optimum reward from the slave, he was not immune to a paternalistic attitude toward some slaves, and it mediated the cold, impersonal relationship, particularly for a favorite slave or after long service to a single master. However, here there is a third-party interest—the state.

Indeed, state interest coincided with the interest of the slave system, which could not have existed without state support. But the state's latent interest diverged from the interest of the slave system in advanced age, and the state had to manifest its self-interest. The discarding of the relationship would mean that society must absorb the cost (via poor relief, building of asylums, bringing lawsuits against the master), so legislators sought to protect the state by passing laws to maintain the relationship, that is, prohibiting manumission, legally requiring care of old slaves, exempting slaveholders from taxes on elderly slaves, and requiring bonds or securities to free slaves. Thus, the state restored to slaves, though out of self-interest, what they considered their due after a long life of coercive labor, even though slave masters sometime freed their superannuated charges despite the laws.

Exchange within the slave community was based on relationships that were equal, reciprocal, and noneconomic—divested of coercion. Social interaction was not decreased because of old age, which brought acceptance, privilege, status, and friendships rather than disengagement. With the loss of productive capacity, senescent slaves needed increased security to provide psychological insurance, which was achieved through an age-stratified and age-graded community. Power in social affairs accompanied advanced age as the elderly took on social roles as advisors, healers, caretakers, caregivers, and guardians of tradition. Through a reduction of work in later years, the slave system often thrust the old and young together (caring for animals, polishing tools, totin' water, and so on), solidifying slave quarter relationships and unwittingly contributing to generational cohesion. The young had little reason to reduce interaction with these sages of their society. Moreover, the old who exercised power over the young as advisors, healers, and conjurors now assumed a psychic power as symbols of survival over the destructive forces of slavery, making interaction even more desirable.

Another aging theory that offers some insight when applied to slavery is the "identity crisis" theory, which contends that people derive their self-identity from their work and that withdrawal from their jobs causes workers to undergo a crisis, unless they can satisfactorily redefine their identities or reconstruct their self-images.[126] While working in the field had been the essential aspect of the slaves' daily round, the loss of this role seldom required personal redefinition, for that role in a coercive system was unsatisfying. It is more plausible that status was derived from the fact that old slaves *did not work,* standing them in complete defiance of the production-based system, particularly if it is true, as some historians contend, that status in the slave community was inversely related to status in the slave system.

However, removal from the field often signaled the loss of physical ability and marked a turning point in the slave's life. Perhaps, as Leslie Owens claims, "[T]he slave did, in fact, develop a part of his judgment of self from the vigor of his active existence."[127] That, of course, would not have been an unnatural assessment of one's self-worth, particularly in such a degrading society where threads of self-definition were so important. But it would not have been natural, as Coleman has suggested, for slaves to "have rated their social standing by their value in the market place."[128] To reach that conclusion requires the complete negation of the slave community. Even when a slave defined himself or herself by the "vigor of active existence," that self-definition was not contingent on nor defined by placing such vigor in the service of the master. Arnold Rose has written: "Complete and sudden retirement is almost unique to industrial society. In most societies there is gradual sloughing off of the primary occupation, and although the role and the group participations associated with it change, the individual's conception of himself does not change rapidly. In agrarian areas, many farmers are able to cut down on their work role gradually, thereby reducing the sense of loss which accompanies abrupt retirement."[129] While work was the slaves' primary occupation, it was not their primary environment. Even today, there is evidence that those in menial and low-paying positions look forward to retirement; therefore, there is little need to doubt that the no-income slave looked forward to withdrawal from coerced labor and did everything that could be done to hasten "retirement" from the master's field.

It is plausible perhaps that some plantation "elite" experienced identity crisis in old age since they sometimes derived their status and sense of self from their place in the plantation hierarchy. Certainly slaves who defined their worth and shaped their sense of being by their value to their masters would have found the onset of old age a critical period in their lives, but here perhaps the master's paternalism stepped in to provide comfort and solace.

Conclusion

Recent gerontological studies have found that the African American aged differ in significant ways from their White counterparts. Studies have shown that they have fewer anxieties about old age, maintain strong religious traditions, tend to remain a part of their family structures, and maintain useful and acceptable family functions; studies also show that they are well treated and respected, are rarely suicidal, are supported by bonds of mutual assistance, and are tolerated for behavior that others view as peculiar.[130] Because of these differences, those who seek to understand the aged African American need to realize that the theories that have been formulated for society at large may, though never perfect, need to be reformulated to include the duality of existence of Black people from slavery days to the present. Antonio Rey has suggested that the differences between old White and Black people may be explained by a new set of theories that are conceptually cognizant of the historical differences between the races.[131] The gerontological community would do well to bring the historical perspectives of old age and slavery to their analysis of contemporary problems.

2
"What charity more pure and sweet": The Development of African American Old-Age Homes with Special Emphasis on the Home for Aged and Infirm Colored Persons (HAICP)

> To shelter those who long have borne
> Life's chilling storms and searching heat
> In restful homes with love alight
> What charity more pure and sweet
> —Frances E.W. Harper, 1895

The conventional wisdom that holds that the structure and function of African American families obviated institutional care needs serious reexamination. In 1988 James H. Carter concluded in an article on African American attitudes toward health care that the Black family was the victim of a dangerous myth, namely: "The extended family, with its strong kinship ties, precludes out-of-home placement of elderly blacks." A myth, he maintained, that not only creates unnecessary guilt when placement is made, but also exacerbates community expectations and may even "deny the black elderly the opportunity for appropriate placement" when needed.[1] It is the contention here that Homes for the Black aged should be viewed as a traditional means of support rather than an alien practice; indeed, a transformation of a West African value—caring for the elderly—into an organized western form—old-age Homes. A form that does not preclude the family, but creates a mesh, a confluence of traditions that combined the family and institutional care into a useful framework for resolving gerontological problems today. A historical perspective can go a long way toward removing a dangerous myth and enhancing acceptability of institutional care by the African American elderly when no other alternative exists.

The first African American old folk's Home was founded during the antebellum period, but institutions increased precipitously during the late nineteenth century. Thus, Du Bois concluded in 1910 that they were the "most characteristic charity." This chapter examines the historical development of institutional facilities for the African American aged with particular attention devoted to the Home for Aged and Infirm Colored Persons (HAICP), which was founded in Philadelphia in 1864 by Blacks and Quakers. The history of the HAICP, which became the unrivaled leader in institutional care for the Black elderly, provides the background for later chapters that examine the lives of the Black elderly who live in the institution and for the career of Hobart Jackson, HAICP administrator from 1948 to 1978, who became the Father of Black Gerontology.

The first federal census in 1790 showed 757,000 Black people in the United States, 59,000 of whom were free (27,000 in the North, 32,000 in the South). By 1830 there were 319,000 free Blacks; thirty years later they numbered 488,070, while the slave population was nearly 4 million. At the time of the Civil War free Blacks were about evenly distributed between the northern and southern states but with heavy urban concentrations. Lured to cities in search of social and economic opportunity as well as the limited safety they found in numbers, Blacks were more than twice as urban as their White counterparts.[2] In 1860 there were 25,000 free Blacks in Baltimore, 22,000 in Philadelphia, 12,500 in New York City, 10,000 in New Orleans, and 3,200 in Charleston. The states of Maryland, Virginia, and Pennsylvania contained about 200,000 of the total free Black population in 1860. In 1870 five years after the Civil War and passage of the Thirteenth Amendment, outlawing slavery and involuntary servitude, there were 39.8 million Whites and 5.4 million Blacks who constituted 13.5 percent of the total population. By 1910 the Black population had reached 9.8 million (4,856,000 males and 4,942,000 females), which showed a decline to 10.7 percent of the total population of 102 million.

In 1870, 6.3 percent of the African American males and 5.7 percent of Black females were over fifty-five. By 1910 there was 7 percent of the Black population in this category. The percentage of the Black population sixty-five and over was 3.5 percent in 1910, but there were reportedly 2,675 Black centenarians of a total of 3,555.[3] From 1790 to 1910 the percentage of African Americans residing in the southern states remained almost constant (91 percent in 1790 and 89 percent in 1910). The decades following 1910 show the first significant regional shift in the Black population as Blacks moved to the northern, and after the 1940s, western cities, seeking better economic opportunities and fleeing racial persecution. By the 1970s only about half the Black population remained in the South, while 61 percent of the Black elderly, which had doubled from 3.5 percent in 1910 to over 7 percent in 1975, lived there, partly because of the outmigration of young adults.[4]

Despite urban concentrations, the majority of African Americans were rural, 80 percent in 1890 and 72.6 percent in 1910. In the South where most Blacks lived, they were even more rural, 85 percent in 1890 and 78.8 percent in 1910. Still a significant proportion of southern Blacks (21.2 percent in 1910) were urban, and their numbers were large enough to build viable communities by the beginning of the twentieth century. More to the point, nonsouthern Blacks were heavily concentrated in urban areas as four out of every five lived in cities by 1910.[5] At the same time, life expectancy was about 35 years for African Americans and 50 years for White Americans (women of both races outlived men by about 3.5 years). This vast discrepancy in Black-White life expectancy closed during the next few decades because of improvements in medical procedure, advancement in drug use, progress in sanitation, increased educational efforts in hygiene, and shifts in the African American population to areas with better health facilities. Nevertheless, estimates of life expectancy still favor Whites by 3 to 5 years.[6]

The antebellum slave population increased at a much faster rate than the free Black population whose rate of increase actually declined at each census from 1840 to 1860. Natural increase, that is, the excess of births over deaths, contributed to the growth of the free population, but it was often swelled by the addition of adults. Many slaveholding northern states, beginning with Pennsylvania in 1780, freed their slaves gradually after they achieved majority (twenty-eight in Pennsylvania). In the South, despite laws that generally disallowed manumission past age forty-five (see chapter 1), many slaveholders freed the elderly and infirm. An estimated 20,000 Blacks were manumitted by wills between 1850 and 1860, and many of these individuals were older adults. Mostly adult slaves escaped via the underground railroad; over 1,000 were said to have escaped in 1849 alone. The acquisition of new territory where some free Blacks lived and immigration (7,011 by 1860) also accounted for an older free Black population. The census report, *Negro Population, 1790–1915,* explains that the antebellum free population was older than the slave population "and on that account naturally subject to a higher mortality rate"; moreover, the report continues, the excess of females over males produced "a marital condition less favorable to natural increase."[7] Since about 20 percent of the free population was over forty in 1850 and only 15 percent of the slaves had reached that category, Ira Berlin concludes that the disproportionate number of old folks made the free population "a top-heavy group."[8] As a matter of fact the presence of Black centenarians in the antebellum population was a source of medical "controversy." In 1846 Dr. Charles Caldwell found more Black than White centenarians in North Carolina, which led him to conclude that the larger number of Blacks over age one hundred contradicted prevailing medical opinion that correlated a long life with an active intellect. In the same year Dr. James McCune Smith, an African American who had been trained at the University of Glasgow, attacked the physiological and anatomical "explanations" for Black inferiority in a *Hunts Magazine* article entitled "The Influence of Climate Upon Longevity."[9]

Urban areas provided free African Americans some opportunities, but from the American Revolution onward their social, economic, and political status declined, particularly after the 1830s and the Nat Turner Revolt. Although slavery was abolished in the northern states, race hatred remained, and African Americans faced increasing discrimination in almost all walks of life. In Pennsylvania, for example, where African Americans had voted freely, the new constitution in 1837 denied them the franchise, which was not restored until passage of the Fifteenth Amendment in 1870. Ohio passed a series of restrictive measures that were discriminatory and culminated in an attempt by Cincinnati to evict the Black population from the city. Some state constitutions such as Indiana prohibited the immigration of Blacks.[10] In Philadelphia riots in the 1830s and 1840s led to a decline in the African American population, and the influx of Irish immigrants forced many of them from their jobs as stevedores, hodcarriers, domestics, and other positions. Blacks in the Quaker City also faced segregation in public places and on streetcars.[11] The Supreme Court sanctioned these practices in the 1856 Dred Scott Decision that rendered Black people legal nonentities with no rights to be respected by White people.

In the South, the legal and extralegal restrictions African Americans faced rendered them an anomaly in a dyadic system built for Negro slaves and White slaveholders. Nowhere in the South could free Blacks own firearms, vote, or testify against Whites. Almost without exception they faced restrictions in employment and were denied an education and the right of mobility. Georgia and Florida required White guardians, and the right of assembly was everywhere denied. A particular psychological onus for free African Americans was the requirement that they carry freedom papers, which were to be produced on demand because slaveholding states presumed all Blacks to be slaves rather than free persons. Moreover, free African Americans could be enslaved for vagrancy or destitution and have their children taken from them. Like children, they could themselves be administered corporal punishment for infractions of the law, and adding insult to injury, they were required to pay poll and school taxes for privileges they were denied.[12]

One of the few rights free Blacks generally enjoyed was property ownership, and some managed to achieve some degree of economic independence. In the South, Cyprian Ricaud and Thomy Lafon of New Orleans, Macon, Georgia's Solomon Humphries, Savannah, Georgia's Andrew Marshall, William Johnson of Natchez, Mississippi, and Jehu Jones of Charleston, South Carolina, were among this group. In the northern states, James Forten and Stephen Smith of Philadelphia and New York's Joseph Cassy and William Platt are examples. The overwhelming majority of African Americans everywhere, however, were unable to overcome the legal and extralegal barriers to acquire significant real and personal property and essentially led a hand-to-mouth existence.[13]

As stated previously, the elderly did not retire in antebellum America but worked until they wore out or died. If they had no home of their own, then they lived with children, primarily without a source of income. For those who were indigent, the almshouse was pre–Civil War America's solution to their problem. By the antebellum period Americans had abandoned the colonial view that poverty was a natural component of a hierarchically constructed society and had come to believe that poverty, in a continent with the vast opportunity of America, was the consequence of one's own doing. In line with this belief, society was becoming more interested in providing indoor relief for the needy, and almshouses, poorhouses, or some similarly undesirable place with another designation, sprang up in every state. Although these institutions were not peculiar to this era, the stigma associated with them was derived from the belief that poverty was caused by improvidence, drunkenness, immorality or some other regulatory factor. Unwilling to accept responsibility for aberrant behavior, society sought to control the poor, to rehabilitate them through institutionalization, which became the hallmark of antebellum poor relief.[14] The family, ethnic beneficial societies, fraternal groups, and the churches partially relieved the burden but could not remove the necessity of the public almshouse.

> To the feeble, old, the weak and the sickly, the almshouse would offer care and attention, ministering to them with solitude and compassion. To the unemployed, the able-bodied victims of hard luck, it would, either in its own quarters, or in conjunction with a workhouse, provide the opportunity for labor, and thus dispense relief without enervating the recipient. To the vicious, the idle who wanted nothing else but a dole, it would teach the lesson of hard labor, insisting that everyone who received public funds spend his day at a task. The almshouse would serve all classes of poor.[15]

The undesirability of this catchall institution, housing orphans, the sick, old, insane, blind, and deaf and dumb, did not lead to an outright attack on the almshouse. There arose the public realization that the degraded almshouse was no place for certain classes of individuals. But this realization did not serve to motivate reformers to seek such alternatives to indoor relief as the colonial practice of placing the poor in respectable families.[16] Their social philosophy led instead to a drive toward specialized institutions.

In the 1820s Houses of Refuge were begun in New York, Boston, and Philadelphia, to remove impressionable children from exposure to hardened criminals in the public almshouse. The perpetuation of society itself, the argument ran, depended on the quality of the individuals fed into it; therefore, it was for the common good that these future adults be prepared to live socially responsible lives. These institutions did not always restrict admission to White children, but only a few Blacks were ever admitted during the period before 1860, and only in Philadelphia was there a separate section, built in 1850. Beginning with Ohio in 1861, county almshouses gradually discontinued the practice of accepting children.[17]

Before 1800 some hospitals, notably in Philadelphia and New York, accepted the insane, but the only institution exclusively for the mentally ill was the Williamsburg Asylum in Virginia, which opened in 1773, accepting African Americans from the beginning. Although there were efforts, it was not until the emergence of Dorothea Dix, "one feeble but militant woman," that public interest accelerated to the intensity of a movement to separately institutionalize the insane. Seeking better treatment for this group, Dix traveled all over the North and South, often with public institutions springing up behind her. When her crusade began in the 1840s, few saw the need to remove the insane from jails, locked rooms, cages, and the almshouses, and even fewer were willing to invest their money and energy on behalf of the insane.[18] In their admission practices, most of these institutions conformed to the exclusionary racial policies of the day, but myths relating to race and insanity became deeply ingrained in American culture, myths to which Dix and the leading theorists of her time were not immune. Many antebellum Americans subscribed to the view that insanity was the price of civilization and that slavery protected African Americans from stresses and strains that they were not constitutionally equipped to handle. Slavery, not insane asylums, was the best refuge for them.[19]

Other classes in the public almshouse were also singled out for special treatment. Leading the drive for separate institutions for the deaf and the blind, for example, were Thomas Gallaudet and Samuel Gridley Howe who were responsible for dozens of humanitarian institutions that opened during the antebellum period, especially in New England and the Northeast. Howe and Gallaudet studied in Europe and brought to the solution of these problems the most advanced knowledge of the day.[20]

The aged as a group did not constitute a social problem in antebellum America, that development was many years away, so there was no attempt to remove them from the almshouses. Albeit, the separation movement clearly had an impact on the elderly and spoke to the prevailing attitudes toward the old. By 1880 there were 66,203 inmates in the nation's almshouses with an average age of forty-five; in 1890 there were 73,045 with an average age of fifty-one. This was the result of several forces—the increasing number of destitute old people, the Charity Organization Society's stringent distinction between the "worthy" and "unworthy" poor that limited indoor and almost dried up outdoor relief, and as Amos Warner has pointed out, the "differentiation [that began in the antebellum period] which left old, infirm, and chronically ill in almshouses."[21] On 1 January 1910 there were 84,198 paupers in the nation's almshouses 6,281 of whom were Black (3,763 males and 2,518 females), which constituted only 7.5 percent of the total. Approximately 46,000 or 55 percent of the almshouses' population was over sixty-five years old. Some such places merely changed their names. For example, the New York City almshouse became the Home for the Aged and Infirm. Clearly, the public almshouses housed too many old people whose only problem was poverty.[22] Kutzik's remarks about the period from 1860 to 1900 are worth quoting here:

> Except for the relatively few private homes for the aged, the almshouses was the only life-sustaining resource of the severely incapacitated aged of limited means and mentally competent aged with no problem other than poverty.[23]

Black and White Americans sought to remedy public indifference by providing Homes for their aged as an alternative to the stigmatized almshouses. According to Fischer, the concept and practice of providing old-age Homes date back to the Roman Empire where, beginning with Constantinople, a system of old-age Homes, *Gerocomeia,* was established for the aged elite.[24] By the thirteenth century Homes were scattered throughout Europe, particularly Holland, Sweden, Norway, Denmark, Germany, and Yugoslavia. Homes in the United States began in the nineteenth century and multiplied rapidly during the prodigious wave of immigration of eastern Europeans at the turn of the twentieth century. In a new environment, faced with heightened nativism, first generation immigrants found the old folks Home the last ethnic reassurance in a foreign land.[25] Those whose cultural baggage contained the concept of Homes—Scandinavians and Germans, for example—outstripped other nationality groups in the number of Homes they provided, but according to Ethel McClure, "the most insistent [factor in the provision of old folks Homes] was the lengthening life span—the sheer increase in both the number and proportion of the aged among the American people."[26]

The first Protestant Home originated in New York in 1850 and was operated by the Methodist Church, which ran eight such institutions by the turn of the century. The Home for Aged and Infirm Israelites, the first Jewish Home, was founded in St. Louis in 1855; Jews operated eighteen such institutions by 1906. Also in 1855 a Catholic group founded the St. Francis Home in Buffalo, New York, but the most significant Catholic group to establish Homes was the Little Sisters of the Poor, a group organized in Saint-Sevran France by Jeane Jugan. Of course, their first institution was established in France in 1839, but they eventually operated Homes throughout the United States. In 1868 they founded their first American Home in Brooklyn, New York, and by 1874 they had thirteen in operation. Catholics operated 98 Homes in 1910, 142 in 1930, 314 in 1950, and 355 in 1962. Forty-two of the Catholic Homes in 1910, were under the auspices of the Little Sisters of the Poor.[27] Of all the Homes operated by White groups, those operated by the Little Sisters of the Poor were most accessible to indigent African Americans. About this society John Gillard wrote:

> In the care of the aged, credit must be given to the Little Sisters of the Poor who, while they have no home exclusively for aged Negroes, care for them whenever they present themselves. The Little Sisters of the Poor recognize no distinction of color.[28]

Although access to White homes relieved some of the burden of caring for the African American elderly, they did not rely on Whites to provide for their old. While Blacks were forced by racism to rely on themselves, their self-reliance was not a mere reaction to oppression but stemmed from deep cultural roots. As previously stated, their cultural baggage did not contain the concept of old-age Homes, but their West African reverence for the aged was extrapolated onto western forms to meet group needs. In this case the development of old-age Homes.

Black leaders insisted on respect for the elderly. Julia Foote, a nineteenth-century minister, recalled that the young had to respect the elderly. Boys had to "make a bow" and girls had "to drop a curtsy" to old people.[29] In the *Liberator* in 1831 Maria Stewart, dubbed America's first Black woman political writer, admonished mothers to teach their children to be responsible, to cultivate in them" a thirst for knowledge, the love of truth, the abhorrence of vice, and the cultivation of a pure heart . . . for a child left to himself bringeth his mother to shame . . . And you must be careful that you set an example worthy of following, for you they will imitate. There are many instances . . . where parents have discharged their duty faithfully and their children now reflect honor upon their gray hairs."[30] Fanny Jackson Coppin, a leading Black nineteenth-century educator and principal of the Institute for Colored Youth in Philadelphia, insisted that experience temper the thirst for education, which complemented formal studies. She instructed her students at commencement exercises in 1877 to respect their elders, "to defer to the opinions of worthy persons older than yourselves, whose knowledge, gained from observation and experience and ripened by age, will exceedingly supplant what you have learned from books."[31] In church leadership respect for old age was also shown. The ages of AME bishops at the time of their election between 1816 and 1910 ranged from thirty-six to sixty-six, averaging age fifty-one. CME bishops ranged in age from thirty-one to fifty-seven between 1873 and 1910 with an average age of forty-two. Because the CME denomination was not founded until 1870, it is quite possible that these numbers reflect the oldest members of the group. The Baptists, who were not divided over the question of a trained ministry, ordained ministers who were in their sixties in the period following slavery. African Americans then were not yet ready to discard the value of knowledge gained through long life.[32]

The earliest African American Home for the elderly for which there is a record was opened in 1848 in New Orleans by the Sisters of the Holy Family, a Black Catholic congregation founded in 1842. The Society was founded by Juliette Gaudin and Henriette Delille who "resolved to devote their lives, education, and wealth to the cause of religion and charity among their own people; to succor the helpless and old, to befriend friendless young colored girls, to teach the catechism to the young, and prepare young and old for the sacrament of communion."[33] The old folks' Home was named for Thomy Lafon, a wealthy mulatto businessman who gave one hundred thousand dollars to endow the institution and whose philanthropic efforts (including a protestant Home for the Black aged) were made without regard to denomination or race.[34] Also in the 1840s a private group in New York City, the Society for the Relief of Worthy Aged Paupers, operated a Home for elderly Blacks that received public support from the city.[35] Before the end of the Civil War other old-age Homes included in 1860 the Home for Aged Colored Women established in Boston, followed in 1862 by the Home for the Aged in New York City. The most significant development was the founding of The Home for Aged and Infirm Colored Persons (HAICP) in 1864 in Philadelphia, which is discussed later in this chapter.

With the end of the Civil War 4 million former slaves looked to the promise of freedom. About 200,000 freedmen were over sixty while a large number of those already free had attained that distinction. Although old slaves faced freedom with confidence in relatives and friends, they were deprived of the security as well as their roles in the slave quarter community, and with freedom came poverty, loneliness, and anomie.[36] The institutional infrastructure created before the Civil War could hardly accommodate the welfare needs of such great number. Private, religious, benevolent organizations such as the American Missionary Association, the American Tract Society, Freedmen's Aid Associations, and many others stepped in to provide for the needy, but thousands of ex-slaves died from exposure, hunger, and disease. In 1865 the Freedmen's Bureau (officially, the Bureau of Refugees, Freedmen, and Abandoned Lands) was set up to provide for the welfare of Blacks in their transition to freedom. Millions of rations were distributed, dozens of hospitals were set up, physicians treated hundreds of thousands of cases, and a network of educational facilities was provided. The Bureau also sought to provide for the security of Black labor, achieve recognition of Blacks in the court, and provide land to the freedmen. While the Bureau was successful in some of these objectives, particularly in supplying food and educational facilities, it failed to provide land and a firm legal standing for the freedmen, though the reasons for that failure undoubtedly ran much deeper than the short-lived Freedmen's Bureau.[37]

With the demise of Reconstruction and the failure of land reform, African Americans eventually faced a steep wall of segregation, a wall set in the constitutional foundation established in *Plessy v. Ferguson* (1896), which legalized separate but equal facilities. Blacks were driven from politics and deprived of their right to vote by grandfather clauses, understanding clauses, gerrymandering, poll taxes, and White primaries. Economically, African Americans were reduced to sharecropping, tenantry, and cheap farm labor that tied them inextricably to the White man's land. At the same time racial terrorism, Negrophobia, and anti-Negro thought reached their apogee. Accommodationist leadership in the age of Booker T. Washington emerged with its philosophy of self-help, self-reliance, and economic independence. It was during the era of racial segregation that today's elderly were born, socialized, and lived that defined patterns of behavior that continue to influence their lives. Ironically, in this context Black America experienced its most important institutional development, building on the time-tested concepts and practices of the African American past.[38]

The number of Homes for the African American elderly that had begun in the antebellum era continued to grow soon after the Civil War. In the South where Blacks were more rural, extended families militated against the development of Homes. But some Homes emerged in the immediate postwar era such as the Aged Men and Women's Home, founded in Baltimore, Maryland, in 1870 and a Home by the same name in Mobile, Alabama, in 1871. In New York in 1872 the Sisterhood of St. Phillip's opened a Home for the elderly members of the St. Phillip's Church, but it soon extended its charity to nonparish members who by 1906 constituted about half the Home's population of only fifteen. Floyd Appleton noted in his 1906 description of the inmates of the Home: "It is probable that most of those cared for would in time have become public charges for they

2: "What charity more pure and sweet" 69

belong to a long-lived race."[39] While the increasing proportion of the old in the population goes a long way toward explaining the development of old-age Homes for White and Black Americans, the latter's longer life expectancies at late ages must be considered a corollary contributing factor.

The high point in the development of old folks Homes for the Black aged was reached between 1880 and 1910 and coincided with the increased wave of immigration that led to the widespread establishment of old folks Homes among White Americans. In 1882 the Home for Aged and Infirmed Colored Women was founded in Pittsburgh, Pennsylvania (incorporated in 1884), established by "Christian colored women who were concerned about the welfare of indigent, infirmed elderly black women of the Pittsburgh community."[40] In 1896 the Alpha Home Association founded the Alpha Home in Indianapolis, Indiana; the Faith Home was founded in Henderson, Louisiana, in 1883; the Brooklyn Home for the Aged was founded in Brooklyn, New York, in 1890; and the Home for the Aged Colored Women was founded in Providence, Rhode Island, in 1890, as "a home for black women who, in their twilight years found themselves alone and afraid when they could no longer earn their 'board and room' in the service of others."[41] The Carter's Old Folk's Home in Atlanta, Georgia, was founded in 1906. In 1908 the Attucks Home was opened in St. Paul, Minnesota, "designed for the betterment of the Negro race, [and] to provide a home for the orphans, the aged, and the indigent of our race variety."[42]

A few Homes served only men such as the Home for Aged Men in Springfield, Massachusetts, and the Crawford Old Men's Home in Cincinatti, Ohio (1888). There were also Homes that sought to meet the Black community's needs on both ends of the life cycle, serving children and the elderly. These included the Home for Destitute Colored Women and Children in Washington, D.C. (1863), Colored Old Folk's and Orphan Home in Mobile, Alabama (1897), Old Folks and Orphan's Home, Kansas City, Missouri (1899) and the Colored Aged Home and Orphanage, Newark, New Jersey (1893). While this list could be multiplied, it illustrates that the alien practice of old-age Homes was becoming an African American tradition, one clearly established by the late nineteenth and early twentieth centuries. As W. E. B. Du Bois concluded in 1910:

> The most characteristic charity is the Home for old people. Nothing appealed from the earliest days more strongly to the freedmen than the care for old people.[43]

A most interesting development in the post–Civil War period was the recognition by erstwhile Black abolitionists that old freedmen faced particular hardships after emancipation. Sojourner Truth took up the cause of aged ex-slaves and campaigned in many parts of the nation advocating old folks Homes specifically designed for elderly freedmen. In 1888 South Carolina Congressman T. E. Miller, perhaps influenced by Sojourner Truth, introduced a bill in the House of Representatives to establish such a Home. Though nothing came of it, Miller's legislation called for $1 million to build a monument to Black Civil War veterans as well as a Home for elderly ex-slaves.[44]

Former abolitionist Harriet Tubman, a woman boundless in determination and resilient in spirit, also became concerned with the plight of elderly ex-slaves and campaigned for the development of institutional facilities for the African American aged. She urged members of the National Association of Colored Women (NACW), at its first annual meeting in 1896, to provide Homes for elderly members of their race. Never one to ask of others what she was unwilling to do herself, Tubman purchased land in Auburn, New York, for that purpose in the same year. In an appeal for the Tubman Home, Tuskegee Institute's financial secretary Robert Taylor explained that during each of his visits to the Tubman house over seven years, he had "found strangers under her roof—aged, maimed, blind, and orphaned. Nothing touches her heart more quickly than to see her race in distress. She has never been known to turn a deaf ear to the appeal of an unfortunate human being."[45] In 1903 Tubman deeded the land she had bought to the African Methodist Episcopal Zion (AMEZ) Church so that it could establish a Home that was to be named for John Brown, a man whom "she regarded above all others as a symbol of freedom."[46] In 1908 the institution opened its doors, an accomplishment of an eighty-nine-year-old ex-slave. But this Home was not to survive as a legacy to this daring and devoted woman. Administrators bickered over its operation, and financial problems caused them to eventually close the doors.[47] The Home's failure cannot help but seem an inadequate testimony to a woman whose sense of racial responsibility led her nineteen times into the slaveholding South to aid her fellow beings in acquiring freedom.

By any standard, the most significant event in the provision of institutional care for the African American aged and perhaps in Black gerontological history was the founding of the Home for Aged and Infirm Colored Persons (HAICP) in Philadelphia, Pennsylvania, in 1864.[48] This Home became the model for institutional care and played a significant role in the modern gerontology movement. It was at the HAICP that the career of Hobart Jackson was launched in 1948, and as a result of his efforts, the National Caucus on Black Aged (NCBA) was founded in 1970, which is now the leading advocacy organization for the African American elderly.

2: "What charity more pure and sweet" 71

A biracial effort, the HAICP, was founded by Quakers and Blacks who came together in early recognition of the peculiar problems that slavery and discrimination posed for Blacks in old age. African Americans, along with Native Americans, were always a concern for Quakers, though interest was often confined to individuals such as John Woolman, Anthony Benezet, Benjamin Lay, and William Southeby. Quakers, with rare exceptions, treated their slaves well and by the mid-1770s had abolished the institution among themselves. Even before the famous 1688 Philadelphia indictment of slavery, the founder of the sect, George Fox, had expressed concern for the spiritual well-being of slaves and had advocated equal treatment to other servants. Fox held that the "Inner Light" shone in all and believed all men to be equal. When Quakers freed their slaves they compensated them for their service, thereby setting a precedent future generations of slaveholders chose not to follow. In addition:

> There remained a close personal relationship between Quaker masters and their one-time slaves, an interest which carried over with Friends of later generations into Negro education, underground railroad activity and other projects on behalf of the colored race.[49]

By the 1830s the potential as well as the reality of violence had forced Quakers, except for a few like Lucretia Mott, from the forefront of abolitionism, though they supported the underground railroad, the free-produce movement, and legal action against slavery that did not jeopardize their pacifist beliefs.

A driving force behind Quaker charity was a sense of paternalism, especially toward erstwhile servants who had often lived with their families. Sarah Douglas, a Black educator who knew them well, believed that most Friends could only relate to African Americans in a master-servant, benefactor-recipient way, and only a "noble few" remained immune to the "foul stain of prejudice."

> I have heard it frequently remarked and have observed myself, that in proportion as we become intellectual and respectable, so in proportion does their disgust and prejudice increase.[50]

The prejudices of the larger society not only emerged in the attitudes of individual Quakers, but also in discriminatory policies toward memberships, seatings, burials, and meetings. These observations notwithstanding, the Quakers steadfastly supported the HAICP, and it stands as a monument to their attempt to help bridge the gap between preachment and practice. The Society of Friends could not be expected to be uninfluenced by the prevailing attitudes, that a few among them remained true to their faith is a tribute to them and its teaching.[51]

The Philadelphia Black community was the largest outside of the South with over 22,000 people in 1860 compared with 12,500 in New York City, the next largest community. By 1860 Black Philadelphians had undergone years of declining socioeconomic status characterized by foreign competition for even menial positions, violent race riots, political disfranchisement, and increasing segregation. Theodore Herschberg, using the Quaker censuses of 1837 and 1847, found that the individual worth of three-fifths of the African American households in Philadelphia did not exceed sixty dollars, and one-third of the mid-nineteenth-century Black families was female headed.[52] The poorest African Americans lived in particularly squalid buildings, crowded in narrow alleys, courtyards, and dark back-buildings with leaky roofs. There were slums in Southwark and Cedar Ward, but the worst was in Moyamensing, where 176 of 302 Black families occupied tenements and shanties and owned personal property with a combined worth of $603.50 or $4.43 per family.[53] Still, poor Philadelphians were not defeated in the face of poverty and racism and relied on families, friends, churches, and benevolent or beneficial societies that gave ethos to their communities.

Moreover, Philadelphia Blacks produced a middle-class community that stood in startling contrast to those who lived in abject poverty. The Quaker census of 1837 and 1847 gave evidence of this middle-class community with a few Philadelphia Blacks owning substantial wealth while others enjoyed a comfortable living. Examples of these individuals include sail maker James Forten, clothes dealer Peter Augustus, barber Robert Douglass, oysterman Cato Collins, and waiter George Johnson. There were also numerous beneficial associations, cemetery companies, churches, fraternal groups, literary societies, libraries, and so on. As we shall see later, in the year's following the Home's founding in 1864, there were many African Americans from many walks of life who had also gained substantial wealth and provided financial support as well as their energies and effort to the HAICP. These would include a large contingent of professional and business people of both sexes—doctors, dentist, lawyers, ministers, realtors, undertakers, caterers, and others—who would by the end of the nineteenth century give evidence of a viable African American community.[54]

It was middle-class Blacks and Quaker Whites, already accustomed to interracial cooperation, who came together to found the Home for Aged and Infirm Colored Persons. Although other social causes had coalesced this biracial group—temperance, women's rights, for example—most brought to the founding of the HAICP outstanding abolitionist credentials, having for many years been members and officeholders in the Pennsylvania Abolition Society that was founded in 1774. For example, Dillwyn Parrish, whose family belonged to the Abolition Society from its inception, served concurrently as the first president of the HAICP and president of the Abolition Society until his death in 1887. Joseph Truman, who had joined the Abolition Society in 1853, served as its secretary from 1861 until his death in 1902. Truman had been HAICP vice president from 1887 until that time. Others included Henry Laing, Lucretia Mott, and Israel Johnson, who were among the Whites who had worked for years in abolitionist activities around Philadelphia and devoted their energies, skills, and finances to the founding and managing of this Home. Among the Blacks with outstanding abolitionist credentials were William Still, vice president of the Abolition Society from 1887 to 1895, who had gained a comfortable living as a coal dealer, Jacob White, who owned real estate and held a partnership in a cemetery company, school teacher Sarah Douglas, poet and novelist Frances Ellen Watkins Harper, and William Whipper, who was a partner to lumber dealer Stephen Smith, who will be discussed later in this chapter.[55]

Although Blacks were worthy of charity because of racial oppression, Quakers still emphasized charity for the worthy and exemplary among them. According to the minutes of the first annual meeting, the Home was founded "for the relief of that worthy class of colored persons who have endeavored through life to maintain the charity of others."[56] Black beneficial societies denied benefits to the immoral and those who brought disaster upon themselves, but African Americans generally failed to separate the worthy from the unworthy, arguing instead that being Black in a racist society was ipso facto eligibility for charitable benevolence, thereby elevating victims of racial oppression to a category of their own. White America traditionally considered widows, children, and the elderly to be among the worthy, but worthiness, in the eyes of Blacks was not an issue, since that conception operated at the level of the individual. To them, sociological rather than psychological transformation was needed, and Blacks sought to restructure the society they lived in because they were products of an unjust system. In another context, William Jackson has made this point: "The issue, [was not individual worthiness, but] . . . the nonhuman status forced on Blacks by a society that accepted mistreatment of them and then converted social responsibility into individual moral fault."[57]

Particularly deserving of Quaker charity were elderly African Americans who had been deprived of the opportunity to prepare for their twilight years because of slavery and discrimination. Evidence indicates that Quakers felt a sense of guilt, a deep feeling of sorrow for the oppression of Black people, and a desire to remedy societal injustice. Lucretia Mott, speaking at the HAICP Association meeting 14 January 1869 reminded those in attendance that "we are 'verily guilty concerning our brother,' and efforts such as this are but a small return for the wrongs done to the colored people." Following Mott, another Quaker reiterated this theme and urged the supporters not to forget "the debt we owe this forgiving race."[58] Speaking in 1867 at the annual meeting of the Home, Edwin Coates, a former Quaker abolitionist, expressed this familiar theme. Slavery, he contended, had deprived old Blacks of their "natural support," their children, and "as we have permitted and encouraged this system, we owe it as a debt to them that they be provided for when unable to care for themselves."[59] Slavery and discrimination compounded by old age were doubly unjust to the Black American because the responsibility of the child to the parent was violated. "If their children had been enabled to go into business," Coates maintained, "as do our own, doubtless they would have been comfortable; as they were not, we actually necessitated their dependent condition and made ourselves liable for their maintenance."[60] Charity then was necessary for the Black elderly until their children were economically capable of reassuming this usurped social function.

Coates touched on one of the central themes in Quaker-Black relations: that Quakers were responsible for the injustices done to Black people, and the Quakers should make every effort to make amends. Blacks were then not a self-determining group and could not be blamed for their social and economic condition. Reasoning thus, Quakers found a philosophical justification for charity to Black people and were able to shift the blame to society, away from the usual explanations of vice, alcohol, or some other ill lodged in the moral fiber of the individual. This transition was a theoretical necessity, justifying special treatment by the Society of Friends. Although gerontological responsibility of the child to the parent remained inviolate, Coates posed the theory of double jeopardy of aged Black Americans—racism exaggerated by the burdens of old age—a century before it became a widely accepted model for explaining the plight of African American elderly.[61]

Perhaps the major motivating force behind Quaker support of the HAICP was their concern for their erstwhile domestics. Indeed the immediate reason for the Home's establishment was Quaker Mary Ann Shaw's discovery that a former domestic had been confined to the almshouse, which led her to seek supporters for an old folks Home. Since Quaker Mary Ann Shaw was herself in reduced circumstances, she understood former domestic Eliza Perry's situation clearer than most supporters.[62] A large percentage of Black Philadelphians, male and female, served as domestics, but the excess of women in the population was to some extent a function of opportunities in this area. Many of these workers shared their employers' households or lived in the same neighborhoods. During the antebellum period as many as one out of every five adults lived and worked in the home of White Philadelphians. The demand for domestics was not soon abated as 20 percent of the adult population were domestics in 1880, and 30 percent served in this occupation in 1896. In 1900 there were 26,646 Blacks (13,726 males, 12,920 females) out of a population of 62,613 engaged in domestic and personal service.[63] These domestics and their employers developed a mutual regard for one another, with a paternalistic bent, that endured long after the actual domestic-employer relationship was severed. The first annual report explained that the HAICP was founded for those who "have labored faithfully, and contributed largely to the comfort of many wealthy families, and while their sacrifices and self-denying exertions entitle them to respect, it was felt to be the only duty to provide them a comfortable home, where they could be sheltered from destitution and poverty."[64]

The most significant Black organizer of the Home for Aged and Infirm Colored Persons was Maurice Hall, who died during the Home's first year of operation. From the view of management, famous underground railroader William Still, vice president from 1873 to 1887 and president from 1887 to 1901, whose involvement spanned over thirty-five years, was the most influential member from the Black community until the Hobart Jackson era. However, it was Stephen Smith, Board member and vice president from 1864 to 1873, whose name the HAICP adopted in 1953 because of his outstanding financial contribution to the institution as well as the interest in the Home shown by him and his wife Harriett. Although a biography is well deserved, Stephen Smith has not been the subject of such extensive consideration. A few remarks are necessary here to understand how he came to endow a Home for the Black aged.

Slavery had been gradually abolished in Pennsylvania when Stephen Smith was born 13 October 1795, but he had to serve until age twenty-eight. Smith was purchased from a Harrisburg family by General Thomas Boude and moved to Columbia where his mother, Nancy, followed, unwilling to separate from her child. The owner's attempt to forcibly return young Smith's mother to Harrisburg led to the indignation of the Columbia citizens who joined Thomas Boude (who purchased Nancy Smith) in a solemn resolve to support the cause of the fugitive slave. This incident led to what has been called the "incorporation" of the underground railroad.[65] As Smith grew older he became an apprentice in his master's lumber business and at times supervised the entire lumber operation. Smith later purchased himself, married Harriett Lee, a mulatto domestic, and with fifty dollars started his own business. Although self-taught, Smith possessed an uncanny acumen for business and was adept at numbers. These qualities, combined with his "upright and patient labor," and Harriett's contribution from her oyster house, enabled him to produce an estate reputedly unequalled by any Black man in antebellum America. William Whipper, who became a well-known moral reformer, moved to

Columbia in 1835 and became associated with Smith in his lumber business. Martin Delany noted that they had the following inventory in 1849:

> Several thousand bushels of coal, two million, two hundred fifty thousand feet of lumber, twenty-two of the finest merchant men cars running on the railway from Philadelphia to Baltimore; nine thousand dollars worth of stock in the Columbia bridge; eighteen thousand dollars worth of stock in the Columbia Band; and besides this, Mr. Smith, was then reputed owner of 52 good brick houses of various dimensions in the city of Philadelphia, besides several in the city of Lancaster and the town of Columbia.[66]

It is one of those tragic paradoxes that Whites pointed to the poverty and ignorance of African Americans as justification for their anti-Black thought and behavior but reserved their greatest contempt for those who by arduous devotion to work and austere living managed to rise above the degraded mass. The resolve of Columbia's citizens at the time of the attempted return of Smith's mother had been long abandoned by the 1830s, and the pro-slavery ties of the borough were now manifest in the hostility toward Black Columbians. The poor slave boy who aroused public indignation over the return of fugitives was now a wealthy man whose accumulation of wealth "excited the envy and ill will of white people who claimed that his course was highly objectionable and must cease."[67] After a series of riots, Columbians called for the removal of all African Americans from the city, bringing them full circle from their earlier abolitionist position.

In 1842 Smith moved to Philadelphia, the "city of Brotherly Love," although it was not at the time living up to that designation. The city was plagued by racial violence throughout the 1830s and 1840s, particularly by Irish attacks on the Black community, and did not experience it's last riot until 1871, when Octavius V. Catto, a popular teacher and activist, was killed. But to Smith here was not only the safety of numbers, but also a growing class of Black people who were accumulating wealth and attaining upper-class status. Moreover, William Whipper was a trusted associate, enabling Smith to leave the business in his able hands. In Philadelphia Smith affiliated with the AME Church and became a minister, though he preached only on occasion and did not pastor. He often contributed funds to the *Christian Recorder,* the AME Church organ that always found itself in financial straits. Spreading his benevolence beyond Methodism, Smith built several churches, two of them for Baptist congregations.[68] He also maintained his activities in the Pennsylvania antislavery society and along with his partner William Whipper allowed the use of his lumber cars for underground railroad activity.[69] Smith embodied the consuming interests of African Americans—abolition of slavery and uplift of the free—and symbolized in his activities an acquisitive spirit tempered by Christian precept. Stephen Smith was interested in many humanitarian causes but none more than the Home for Aged and Infirm Colored Persons. One reason for his interest was his concern for elderly ministers and members of the AME Church, particularly Mother Bethel. As a matter of fact, Smith had made provisions (ten thousand dollars) in his will to provide for a retirement Home, and Maurice Hall and Mary Ann Shaw had to convince the Philadelphia community that the need to provide for elderly Black Philadelphians far surpassed Smith's intentions. Another obstacle facing the HAICP founders was the popular belief that the almshouse had been improved since the Guardians of the Poor had built a huge workshop and begun experimenting with token pay to inmates. This experiment grew out of the twin misconceptions that laziness was a key cause of poverty and that the work requirement would inure inmates to labor, coupled with the desire to make the almshouse self-sustaining. The poor physical and mental condition of the almshouse population militated against the success of this program, and the workshop cannot be said to have been much of an improvement. Moreover, close analysis showed that there were separate wards for the elderly, the young, and the insane for Whites of both sexes, but no such divisions existed for Blacks, males, or females.[70]

Racism operated to lump Blacks of all classes together in the already socially debased conditions of the public almshouse, and a Home for aged and infirmed Black Philadelphians could only prove a welcome improvement in institutional care. The timing was also unpropitious for the HAICP promoters because those interested in providing aid to Blacks in 1864 were already involved in that task through freedmen's aid associations and other relief efforts associated with the Civil War. Nevertheless, the Home for Aged and Infirm Colored Persons opened in 1865. To some extent the founding of the HAICP was part of a broader movement to care for indigent Philadelphia elderly that began with the establishment of the Indigent Widows and Single Women's Home in 1817 and culminated with the opening of twenty-two Homes for the aged between 1859 and 1890. This development, according to Carole Haber, was a clear demonstration that age segregation by the beginning of the twentieth century had become an acceptable feature of America's cultural landscape.[71]

The HAICP opened in a three and one-half story structure at 340 South Front Street, in a congested area of the city near Lombard and Pine Streets, which was the nucleus of the African American community. These quarters soon proved inadequate because of the tremendous housing needs among elderly Black Philadelphians, the Home's undesirable location (an 1869 fire nearby threatened to destroy the Home), and its architectural design for single-family dwelling. In 1869 Stephen Smith donated stone from his quarry and a lot for a new Home that was built in Olive Cemetery, away from the city, near Fairmount Park, across the Schuykill river, but accessible by streetcar. When the four-story structure, (at Girard and Belmont Streets), with a capacity for 130–40 residents was completed and residents moved to the new location on 7 August 1871, Smith had donated more than forty-thousand dollars toward the project. When he died two years later, Smith left the bulk of his fortune to the Home. The money was used to support residents and operate the institution.[72] The new structure was considered ideally located except for concern about the unavailability of gas for a structure located away from the city. At that time there was no concern expressed about the Home's location in the cemetery even though these old people literally spent their last days with one foot in the grave.

In 1894 a major addition was made with the Parker Annex, which increased the size of the Home, including space that was used for an infirmary, an area used by administrators, and a chapel. Edward Parker, an Episcopalian of Quaker background, had taught a Sunday school class at St. Andrews Church for elderly Black women and had left money to build a Home for his "scholars." His executor, former Pennsylvania Supreme Court Justice Edward Paxson, thought that the money was inadequate to build and support a separate institution. Through William Still's influence, who had known Judge Paxson from the antislavery days, Paxson provided for the Parker scholars by adding to the size of the HAICP and contributing to its operating expenses. By the time that the new addition was dedicated in June 1894 Still had located twenty-two of Parker's scholars, four of whom had already been admitted to the Home. Separate institutions might not have survived, and though the letter of Parker's will was not followed, the spirit of his bequest continues in the survival of the Stephen Smith Home.[73]

The HAICP grew rapidly as "residents" expanded from 21 in 1865 to 67 in 1875 to 112 in 1884 to 140 in 1910.[74] Although the first Home had served only women, the first male resident came 15 March 1872 probably because of Stephen Smith's interest in this population. In December 1875 the first couple was admitted. Living up to its designation, the Home also accepted the infirm, for example, Mary Derrickson, a thirty-six year old, was admitted in June 1874, Catherine Duncan, a fifty-three year old, was admitted in October 1883, and forty-year-old Mary Carson was entered July 1884, all crippled and two of them below age requirement at the time of admission.

Between 1865 and 1904 more than seven hundred residents (chiefly former domestics) were served, 21 percent men and 79 percent women.[75] Although there was an age requirement set at fifty in 1864, but later changed to sixty-five, residents averaged over eighty years of age between 1865 and 1872 and over seventy-five during the period 1865 to 1904. About

4 percent (thirty residents) were centenarians, half of whom achieved that status after admission. Mary McDonald was 118 when admitted 19 December 1887, Sarah Barnard was 110 when she entered 22 June 1870, and Mary A. Brown was 105 at the time of her entrance 5 September 1871. Female centenarians tended to be slightly more numerous than their proportion of the Home's population (83 percent). Although no male could boast of the entrance age of McDonald, John Gibson was said to be 115 when he came 14 November 1886. Residents came primarily from Philadelphia and other parts of Pennsylvania, but many had migrated there primarily from Maryland, Delaware, and Virginia. In the early years residents had been born in Africa and the West Indies, but they gradually disappeared. The HAICP also served boarders (fourteen between 1865 and 1900) who chose to pay a monthly rent rather than become life care residents, that is, for an admission fee and all property, the Home would provide all necessities of life and burial. The Home for Aged and Infirm Colored Persons, which served more than twenty-two hundred residents between 1864 and 1954, was a multipurpose institution with a residential program for Black boarders and life care individuals who were elderly or infirm who could not find a desirable home life in the community.[76]

To provide for the Home's operating expenses, the Board of Managers participated in all the money-raising activities of the day, including subscriptions, memberships (annual two dollars, life memberships twenty-five dollars), bazaars, concerts, lectures, and church solicitations. Residents, as part of the life care contract, were required to pay admission fees and relinquish all property to the Home, although most had little or no property. Some had memberships in beneficial associations (see chapter 4), and married couples sometimes turned over houses to the institution that had values well in excess of admission fees.[77] Those who came as boarders were generally better off than other residents, but they universally, it seems, converted to life care residents. Former domestic Lucy Taylor, for example, entered as a boarder in 1880 and lived there five months before her death, but "so deeply impressed was she with the excellence of the institution, and the desire to do her share towards benefitting her own race," she left the Home her savings of about four thousand dollars. The pattern of boarder conversion to life care contracts is roughly equivalent to the private-public conversion that is found in nursing Homes today.[78]

The Home was run on sound Quaker business principles. These included a system of checks and balances, avoidance of unneeded expense, obligation of funds for capital improvement only when they were all in hand, and the treatment of indebtedness like a sin. Among Black Philadelphians Quakers had a reputation for fair dealings, sound investing, and honesty and integrity in business. Indeed, when the Free African Society was founded in 1787, the choice for treasurer was a Quaker, and it was decided that "whenever another should succeed him, it is always understood that one of the people called Quakers . . . is to be chosen as a clerk and treasurer of this useful institution." [79] Early in the Home's history a decision was made to build up an endowment, which resulted in a portfolio reputedly valued at about $400,000 in 1920, by investing bequests, legacies, and large gifts. It was this decision, coupled with Quaker conservatism, that enabled the Home to survive the ravages of the nation's depression of the 1930s when many Black institutions and businesses had to close their doors.

Although Quakers provided the bulk of the Home's finances over the years, the Black community provided substantial support.[80] The largesse of Stephen Smith, though significant from a financial standpoint, was more important because it provided an inestimable and crucial symbolic value to Black Philadelphians. The Smith gift was a source of pride that provided the emotional attachment to as well as sense of identity with the HAICP that was necessary to extract widespread Black support over the years. Programs were held each year in recognition of Stephen Smith that perpetuated the Black community's sense of ownership in the HAICP.[81] Not many could match the munificence of Stephen Smith, but no small number left fortunes of $2,000 to $5,000 to the Home; such were Henry Gordon, Hettey Harvey, and Lucy Taylor. A few left substantial legacies to the HAICP. Catherine Teagle, a Black West Chester, Pennsylvania, woman left $98,000 to be divided equally among Lincoln University, Wilberforce College, and the HAICP. Edward Green, a junk dealer turned real estate broker, left his fortune of $40,000 to the Home. The *Christian Recorder,* without much, if any, exaggeration, estimated that the Black community's donations exceeded $150,000 between 1888 and 1890.[82] Nevertheless, the Home had tremendous needs that outstripped the support of the Black community, itself generally poor with many demands on its resources. The HAICP would not likely have survived without Quaker financial and managerial support, and their contribution to the modern gerontology movement must acknowledge this significant fact.

Black women's groups were particularly involved in the founding and operating of Homes for the aged, and their activities embraced a variety of welfare and self-help activities, including kindergartens, self-improvement programs, training schools, orphanages, and many forms of relief to the needy. The extent and diversity of their activities can be culled from a 1901 report of a Hampton, Virginia, club:

> Mother's meeting, 32; Public meetings addressed, 3; Girls's meetings, 2; sick visited 12; adults supplied with good and bedding, 15; clothes to children, 25;

children supplied with homes; 2; persons read to, 10; doctors sent to sick poor, 2.[83]

One group of about 250 women known as the Tent Sisters operated several Homes for the aged in North Carolina and Virginia. Their Homes were small (between seven and nine residents each), but their efforts were all the more remarkable when one considers that over one hundred of these women were over sixty years old. The Tent Sisters entered this kind of charity to care for their own old and disabled, but recognizing that such great need existed, they broadened their efforts to include others.[84]

The Women's Loyal Union operated a Home for the Aged in New Bedford, Massachusetts, founded in 1897; the Alpha Home Association of Indianapolis opened the Alpha Home in 1886 to a group of ex-slave women from age seventy-five to ninety-six. Women also operated the Phillis Wheatley Home in Detroit, Michigan, which provided a Home for twelve women in 1907; the Home for Aged Colored Women in Cleveland, Ohio, which was founded in 1903, and the Women's Twentieth-Century Club operated the Hannah Gray Home in New Haven, Connecticut. In addition to those under their auspices, women "adopted" Homes that they supported financially and through friendly visiting, and many Homes depended on them for handling their internal affairs, that is, preparing meals, decorating, cleaning, and generally seeing to the residents' welfare. Some of the efforts of women's groups met with such success that states assumed control of their operation.[85]

Black beneficial societies, secret orders, mutual aid associations, and fraternal associations provided relief to elderly members through sick benefits, pensions, foodstuffs, coal, and friendly visiting, as we shall see in the next chapter, but some operated old age Homes as well. The Masons at the turn of the century operated Homes in Pennsylvania, Illinois, Alabama, Tennessee, and Georgia. The Knights of Tabor had an old-age Home in Kansas. The Grand Order of True Reformers, founded in 1881 by the Reverend W. W. Browne, operated two old folks Homes at the turn of the century. The Reverend Browne envisioned an entire "system of old folks homes for the benefit of the poor of the Colored race." It was not profit that motivated him but benevolence, the sight of "old age mothers and fathers on the dump piles, scratching for cinders and something to keep warm." To achieve his purpose Browne bought a 634-acre farm in Westham, Virginia, which included a fourteen-thousand dollar building, and he appointed his son "General Superintendent of the Old Folks Department." Both the True Reformers' Homes remained very small (the Westham Home had three residents in 1894 and six in 1907), and the projected "system of old folks Homes" was never realized.[86] That the True Reformer's Homes remained very small is probably testimony to the tremendous cost of operating old-age Homes. But on the positive side, these developments show that Blacks embraced the idea of old-age care outside the family unit as part of their multifaceted vision of caring for their needy.

The late nineteenth century was a period of not only increased activity in the development of Black old-age Homes, but also establishment of many kinds of institutional facilities for the needy. Although segregation in the South emerged as the official policy in public welfare, Blacks were often altogether excluded from hospitals and health care agencies. Where separate facilities existed, they were always unequal despite the legal formulation to the contrary. Blacks who were not destitute often found that the only health care available to them was at the local almshouse, while those who were poor found that outdoor relief had almost dried up completely as the preoccupation with "science" invaded charitable organizations, and the stringent definitions of "worthiness" imposed narrowminded moral requirements.[87]

To solve their problems, Blacks founded hundreds of orphanages for parentless and neglected children and dozens of hospitals. Under the direction of Dr. N. F. Mossell the Frederick Douglass Memorial Hospital and Training School was opened in Philadelphia in 1895, which was soon followed by the Mercy Hospital in the same city. Black Chicagoans had earlier (1891) established the Provident Hospital while the Freedmans Hospital of Washington, D.C., the earliest of about forty hospitals, had been in operation for about three decades. Excluded, for the most part, from White medical schools, Blacks and northern missionaries founded twelve medical schools. Blacks, for example, established Louisville National Medical College (1888), Knoxville Medical College (1895), and University of West Tennessee (1900) while Northern missionaries founded Howard University Medical School (1868), Meharry (1876), Leonard Medical School (1882), and Flint Medical College (1900). These good developments were not all long lived, only Meharry and Howard medical schools survived the alleged inferior standards cited in the Flexner Report. Taken together, these efforts illustrate that the late nineteenth century was a period of heightened Black consciousness and self-help.[88]

The number of Homes for Black elderly that were founded since the Civil War cannot be accurately determined. Lenwood Davis claimed that between 1865 and the present there were two hundred to three hundred homes established, but this is an exaggeration. Davis lists seventy Homes, only one of which was founded after 1910, and that one was started in 1911.[89] In 1907 and 1910, W. E. B. Du Bois surveyed old-age Homes and listed twenty-seven and sixty-one Homes, respectively, although he claimed that there were probably many more.[90] Some Homes reported by Du Bois, which formed the basis for Davis's list, were still in the

2: "What charity more pure and sweet"

planning stage, or more accurately were merely the wishful thinking of a community leader. The overwhelming majority were small institutions with residents varying from 2 to 5, conforming to what one today considers personal care Homes. From the 1910 census report on benevolent institutions, Table 2 was constructed, showing that only nineteen of the Black Homes that responded to the survey had 10 or more residents.[91] There are some known omissions, or nonrespondents, however. For example, the Lafon Home in New Orleans was not included even though it had 71 residents in 1910, making it second in size to the HAICP, which had 140 residents. Also absent from the table are Homes exclusively for men, although two are known to have been in existence (the Home for Aged Men in Springfield, Massachusetts, and the Crawford's Old Men's Home in Cincinnati, Ohio). It is not known whether they had 10 or more residents, however. Nine of the nineteen Homes served women exclusively while in every instance where both sexes were accepted, females outnumbered males because they outlived men, married younger, and were more likely to be widowed or without family. Perhaps the most conspicuous thing, though no less understandable than it is conspicuous, was that the larger Homes were northern urban phenomena when Blacks were mostly southern and rural. The rural elderly usually remained with families and performed useful tasks throughout their lives, obviating the need for Homes.

About 75 percent of the Black old-age Homes were run by private groups with religious and fraternal organizations, respectively, falling behind. A one-hundred dollar to three-hundred dollar admission fee was generally required, but most Homes required that residents also relinquish other property. Although there was a trend toward increasing tax support for old-age institutions, there is no evidence that Black Homes received much support. In the North public Homes admitted African Americans and Whites, but in the South separate institutions were established for both races but without a semblance of equality. The HAICP received no public subsidies until its recent history even though Pennsylvania's allocations to Homes and related institutions increased from about $2.5 million in 1885 to $8 million in 1908.[92] A Missouri respondent in the 1910 Du Bois survey claimed that administrators of the Black-operated "old and invalid hospital home" convinced the county court to allow them to maintain aged Blacks with the understanding that the court would "give [them] what it would cost to keep [old Blacks] at the poor farm [while] we beg the rest of the money necessary." A Tennessee respondent in the same survey noted that the county "will appropriate a small sum for their [old age] maintenance if they are in some home." From Charleston, South Carolina, came the report that the city ran its own institution, the Ashley River Asylum, operated by a Black board of directors and

Table 2. African American Homes with Ten or More Residents, 1910

Name and Location	Fee	Founded	Men	Women
Home for Aged and Infirm Colored People, Mills College, CA	250	1892	3	8
Layton Homes, Wilmington, DE	100	1897	3	15
Sarah Ann White Home, Wilmington, DE	125	1886	4	10
+Home for Destitute Colored Women and Children, Wash., D.C.	none	1863	—	10
Home for Aged and Infirm Colored People, Chicago, IL	100	1898	7	16
Alpha Home, Indianapolis, IN	25	1886	—	13
Faith Home, Henderson, LA	none	1888	—	17
Aged Men and Women's Home, Baltimore, MD	100	1870	6	11
Shelter for Aged and Infirm Colored Persons, Baltimore, MD	150	1881	—	35
Home for Aged Colored Women, Boston, MA	none	1860	—	20
Phyllis Wheatley Home, Detroit, MI	300	1897	—	10
Colored Aged Home and Orphanage, Newark, NJ	150	1892	—	14
Brooklyn Home for Aged Colored People, Brooklyn, NY	150	1890	5	27
St. Phillip's Parish Home, Newark, NJ	150	1872	—	14
Cleveland Home for Aged Colored People, Cleveland, OH	200	1896	2	9
Home for Aged and Infirm Colored Persons, Philadelphia, PA	200	1864	31	109
Home for Aged and Infirm Colored Women, Pittsburgh, PA	150	1882	—	13
Home for Aged Colored Women, Providence, RI	150	1890	—	14
+Church Home for Aged and Disabled Colored, Lawrenceville, VA	none	1880	15	32

Compiled from "Benevolent Institutions," Department of Commerce and Labor, Bureau of the Census, Government Publications, Washington, D.C., 1910. (+There were 105 children in these two Homes, 86 in the former and 19 in the latter).

TABLE 3. PERCENTAGES OF HOMES FOUNDED
DURING SELECT PERIODS OF AMERICAN HISTORY

Period	Percentages
Before 1800	0.2
1800–1849	1.0
1850–1874	9.8
1875–1899	30.0
1900–1909	17.8
1910–1919	16.5
1920–1929	18.0
1930–1939	6.7

Compiled from "Care of the Aged in Old Peoples' Homes," *Monthly Labor Review* 50 (May 1940): 1047. (1,209 of 1,428 Homes reporting).

entirely for the Black elderly. In reality, the institution housed young as well as old and included a hospital and a farm and was no more than a segregated almshouse. However, the city of Charleston operated a White Home for the elderly where they provided better facilities, better medical care, and on that account had a much lower mortality rate.[93] The two Lafon Homes in New Orleans, Louisiana, received $150 ($30 and $120 a month) in public subsidy, and a Home in Baltimore, Maryland, and another in Alexandria, Virginia, received some minor tax assistance.[94] In the final analysis, caring for the African American old was primarily a private matter left to family and the community.

How long these Homes were in existence and how many have survived to now cannot be accurately determined. In 1929 the *Monthly Labor Review* reported 18 of its 33 Homes for African Americans were at least thirty-five years old, which was consistent with the view that the high point of the development of Black Old-Age Homes was between 1875 and 1910 (see Table 3). In 1940 the same source reported 50 Homes exclusively for elderly Blacks with almost 60 percent having been founded before 1909. It is clear that the Depression wiped out many Black old-age Homes and that many cities which had Homes earlier were without facilities in the 1940s. But the modern Civil Rights era was approaching, and it is worth noting that 325 of the 964 White Homes in 1940 reported no specific racial requirements. Of the 70 Homes Lenwood Davis listed in his bibliography in 1980, only 1, the HAICP of Philadelphia, was listed as presently in existence. In 1975 the Department of Health, Education, and Welfare (now Health and Human Services) published a four-volume directory of nursing Homes representing each area of the country. A comparison of the names and addresses of Homes in Table 2, reasoning that the larger Homes, that is, those with ten or more residents, would probably have a higher survival rate, showed that 6 of the 19 Homes in the table were still in existence in 1975. These were the Layton Home, Alpha Home, Stephen Smith Home (HAICP), Lemington Home (formerly Home for Aged and Infirmed Colored Women of Pittsburgh, Pennsylvania), and the Bannister House (formerly the Home for Aged Colored Women of Providence, Rhode Island). The Lafon Homes in Louisiana also still exists. Because many Homes moved or changed their names, undoubtedly a larger number than can be determined survived.[95]

Three factors contributed to the framework on which African Americans based methods for providing economic and social support for their impoverished elderly. The first of those factors was the Black family, which augmented and extended, reached out to aged relatives, whether close or distant, and sometimes to friends who faced poverty at the end of the life cycle. However, even the most adaptive family structures were not able to address the needs of all aged Blacks, particularly in the face of a growing population among that segment of society. So there was reason for the development of more formal methods to combat the vicissitudes of life for old people. The impetus for doing so came from the second factor shaping Black gerontological thought in the nineteenth century. That factor was a respect for the old, the roots of which was their West African heritage. This respect nurtured a commitment to care for the elderly that went beyond the family and called for a broad-based community effort. The many-faceted methods included churches, beneficial and mutual aid associations, burial societies, cemetery companies, and old-age Homes. That nineteenth-century Black Americans were flexible in their solutions and that they were inspired by their heritage to seek those solutions both inside and outside the family unit are salient facts to be remembered by those seeking solutions to the gerontological problems today in this country. In the face of growing institutionalization of the elderly, historical perspectives are needed to get beyond conventional wisdom so that institutions may be made more responsive to the needs of the African American elderly.

3
"Better off than poor white people": The Beneficial Society, the HAICP, and the Black Elderly

> The benevolent societies combined African heritage with American heritage to transform an amorphous free black population into a distinct free black community.
> —Robert L. Harris, Jr.[1]

Beneficial and benevolent associations formed a critical support for the African American elderly and helped to create an important infrastructure for the African American community. In three ways they provided social, economic, and psychological support to the Black aged and their families. First, members had the security of receiving temporary aid in times of sickness and burial expenses when deceased. Second, these organizations often provided friendly visiting ("sitting up") with ill members as well as regular meetings that broke the monotony for the isolated and lonely. Third, just as the old-age Home provided an alternative to the almshouse, the beneficial or benevolent society held out the possibility of independence in one's own home. This chapter traces the origin and development of these societies as their structure and function illuminate historical perspectives on the welfare of the African American elderly. It also examines their role in the Home For Aged and Infirm Colored Persons (HAICP), which provides in microcosm insights into the functioning as well as the demise of beneficial societies.

Unlike Homes for the aged that began as an alien practice that took on their own tradition, the beneficial association had African roots, growing out of the West African heritage, including a deep respect for elderly members of society. However, it is not of major concern here whether they represented an African carryover, a creolized form, or a parallel development that sprang full blown from the American environment.[2]

Since Black organizational life gave birth to numerous types of organizations, one needs to distinguish among the types of societies. While no definition of these organizations is completely satisfactory, it is necessary to try to distinguish the beneficial association from other organizations such as fraternal societies, mutual aid associations, friendly associations, literary societies, benevolent societies, secret societies, voluntary associations, fellowship societies, and moral societies. The beneficial society had the sole function of collecting dues from its members to provide temporary aid in times of crisis, pensions in old age or for widows, and burial for members and their families.[3] In contrast, the benevolent association or mutual aid society collected donations of materials or money from donors to provide for those in need without regard to membership and often stressed other objectives such as colonization, morality, or education. Secret orders and fraternal societies, such as the Masons and Odd Fellows, also provided for the infirm, elderly, orphaned, or widowed among their members, although protection and relief were not their sole reasons for being. This was also true of some of the temperance, moral, and literary societies that had special objectives reflected in their names. In other words, the beneficial function was subsumed by other organizations, but that was not their raison d'être.

By way of illustration, the African American Female Intelligence Society of Boston was founded in 1842, according to its records, "for the diffusion of knowledge, the suppression of vice and immorality, and for cherishing such virtues as will render us happy and useful to society."[4] The name as well as the description of its purpose indicates clearly that this was not purely a beneficial association, but Article Fifteen of its constitution provided a beneficial component. It read: "Any member of this society, of one year's standing, having regularly paid up her dues, who may be taken sick, shall receive one dollar per week out of the funds of the society as long as consistent with the means of the institution." Furthermore, Article Eighteen stated: "In case any unforeseen and afflictive event should happen to any of the members, it shall be the duty of the society to aid them as far as in their power."[5] The African American Female Intelligence Society was not a beneficial society, but it had a beneficial component to care for its members, and since the emphasis here is on function rather than structure, this kind of organization is considered important to the care of Black elderly.

While the beneficial function has been referred to as the "insurance" feature, neither the beneficial society nor the other organizations served as insurance companies. For one, mutual support rather than profit was the motive, though greed sometimes blurred the benevolent purpose in the minds of some founders and managers. For another, as distinguished in the case of *Commomwealth vs Equitable Beneficial Association* (1890), "indemnity or security against loss" was not the "dominant and characteristic feature" of the beneficial society which was founded out of benevolence and existed, unlike insurance companies, "to accumulate a fund from the contribution of its members . . . to be used in their own aid or relief in case of sickness, injury or death . . . or revert to the members at an advanced age." A third distinction from insurance companies was that beneficial societies were not operated on an actuarial basis, generally accepting members without regard to age or health.[6] Beneficial societies had a much broader purpose than strictly a business organization—they helped to relieve the needs of the poor and to structure the moral fiber of the community.

The abolition of slavery and uplifting of the free were antebellum Black Americans' two consuming interests. Free African Americans believed that only as they bettered themselves would their position augur well for abolition, and through exemplary conduct, they would force society to recognize them and their people as worthy of liberty. One way to accomplish this objective was to provide for the dependent by developing an organizational life to protect those who were not absorbed by families or who required temporary help in crisis situations so that they would not have to rely on public charity. Beneficial societies, therefore, symbolized the community's interest, structured its priorities, defined its cultural values and philosophical orientations as well as provided protection for individual members, young and old. While the old folks Home became a characteristic response to the needs of the Black elderly and a tradition in the community (chapter 2), most old people preferred, as they do today, to remain home with families or in independent households. For many of them the beneficial society provided the economic and psychological security that helped to make this option feasible.

In antebellum America old age posed a problem for many who were not wealthy, and the almshouse was a real possibility for those poor and childless. For African Americans who had the normal avenues of economic and social mobility closed to them by prejudice and discrimination, there was little chance of preparing for old age when their youth was best described as a hand-to-mouth existence. In urban areas where Blacks were concentrated such as New York, Philadelphia, Baltimore, Boston, and Cincinnati, they faced a hostile White world that forced them into the worst parts of town, into substandard housing in poor neighborhoods, restricted them to the most menial occupations as unskilled laborers and domestic servants, denied them access to or segregated them in schools and other public institutions, and except for New England, excluded them from the political process. Antebellum Black Americans, therefore, learned to rely on their own resources, and hundreds of beneficial societies in the North and South became the intermediary between dignity at home and the degradation of public charity. They stood between decent and dignified burial and the fear of the pauper's grave.

The Black citizens of Philadelphia tried to make the purpose of the beneficial society clear to the public through *Harvard's Register* in 1831:

> To these institutions, each member pays a sum varying from one to eight dollars as an initiation fee, and from twelve and a half to twenty five cents monthly. The funds are exclusively appropriated to the relief of such of its members as through sickness or misfortune, may be unable to work; to the interments of deceased members, and to the relief of their widows and orphans. . . most of the objects of these charities are pensions whose daily earnings are scarcely adequate to their daily wants; and many of them having large families, without some such aid they would necessarily become objects of public charity.[7]

Economically, these organizations were held together by a few "pennies which Negroes could scrape together," as E. Franklin Frazier had observed, "to aid each other in time of sickness but more especially to insure themselves decent Christian burial."[8]

The need for temporary relief and dignified burial, the fear of body snatching, and high medical costs all constituted major reasons for founding of beneficial associations. While a decent Christian burial was the objective of the beneficial society, it was not an easily obtained objective. For one, segregation was not confined to the living. Cemeteries, often associated with churches and among the earliest segregating institutions, were owned by Whites. In addition, public cemeteries generally excluded Blacks or relegated them to some remote corner of the lot.

To ensure decent burials, beneficial societies often had cemetery plots, (as did some churches), and in many places, Blacks organized burial companies to purchase plots for interment. Two of the best-known and wealthiest antebellum companies were Lebanon and Olive Cemetery companies of Philadelphia. By 1900, according to W. E. B. Du Bois, there were more than five hundred such enterprises nationally.[9]

Moreover, the funeral itself was too important to African American people to allow their last chance for dignity to pass without appropriate ceremony. Denigrated in life, families insisted that the dead were not to be degraded one more time in death. While Whites insisted that cemeteries "mirror the social order of the living," Blacks insisted that the funeral celebration transforms the dead into a person of worth and dignity.[10] Long services, large parades, and expensive dress often became necessary to accomplish the stated objective. In the mind of the Black American the dichotomy between spiritual and temporal existence was not cut and dried, and the likelihood of moving in both directions demanded an elaborate ceremony.

Another reason for the importance of beneficial societies was that medical students and doctors, needing cadavers for anatomical examinations, robbed paupers' graves and unwittingly contributed to the development of such organizations. Howard Rabinowitz's observation about the post–Civil War period also applied to the era before the War.

> Faced with the alternative of the involuntary donations of their bodies to the local medical school or paupers burial in an unkempt potter's field where body snatchers preyed, many Blacks not surprisingly contributed their pennies to beneficial societies.[11]

Medical costs also forced African Americans to pool their resources in beneficial associations. Living on the economic margins of society, they could hardly afford the costs of medical care and relied on home remedies, staying away from the medical establishment until sheer necessity drove them there.

There were few African American doctors during the antebellum period. Self-taught healers included New Jersey's James Still, Ohio's John P. Reynolds, and Boston Massachusetts's William Wells Brown, eclectic physicians, and David Ruggles, a well-known New England hydropath. There were a few Blacks such as Pittsburgh's Martin Delany and New Jersey's John Rock who had medical training. Most medical schools did not accept Blacks; both Rock and Delany were rejected by Philadelphia medical schools. The first Black to receive a medical degree from a school in the United States was David J. Peck in 1847, graduating from Rush Medical College of Chicago. Although nine northern medical schools had opened their doors to Blacks by 1860, some like the highly respected James McCune Smith had sought medical training in Europe, graduating from Glasgow in 1837.[12]

Needless to say, there were few doctors to meet the medical needs of free Blacks, North or South (See chapter 6 for further discussion). In Virginia Todd Savitt found that free Blacks were "at the bottom of the health care hierarchy," and domestic medicine was in extensive use. Nevertheless, he found that White doctors often treated Blacks knowing that they would not receive pay or receive pay in kind (labor) when more lucrative rewards were offered by more affluent patients.[13] He noted, however, that African American churches and beneficial societies typically connected with the church tried to meet their needs. The First African Baptist Church in Baltimore, for example, provided "nursing care and general assistance to diseased and aged Blacks."[14] The St. James church founded the St. James Male Beneficial Society in 1847, which cared for the sick, buried the dead, and provided a forum for the discussion of racial issues and instruction in parliamentary rules. The guiding force behind the organization was Harrison H. Webb, who became rector of the parish in 1856, where he served until 1872, having to resign because of old age. [15]

While the desire for decent burial was an important concern that spurred the development of beneficial associations, Savitt maintains that they grew out of the need to obviate the "excessive reliance upon the uncertain, inconsistent, and humbling benevolence of the white medical world" and to make "illness more comfortable to bear for those freedmen with the ties to such organizations."[16] Alfred Kutzik, who has examined the social provisions for the elderly in American history, has made the important point that elderly people of most ethnic groups benefitted directly and indirectly from beneficial society membership. "In addition to direct assistance to the [aged], mutual aid benefits to non-aged members of the family, of course, better enabled it to care for its aged members."[17]

Clearly, the beneficial society played an important role in the lives of Black Americans, particularly the Black elderly. Provisions were made for widows, pensions were provided for old age and sickness, and burial expenses were taken care of. The beneficial society stabilized families and communities. As Robert Harris has said: "The benevolent societies combined African heritage with American conditions to transform an amorphous free black population into a distinct free Black community."[18]

The oldest benevolent society, the Free African Union Society (FAUS), was founded in 1780 in Providence, Rhode Island. Although it clearly had a beneficial component—providing loans to members in sickness and for burial as well as providing pensions to widows—it was not purely a beneficial organization.[19] Since all the rules and regulations were never published with the proceedings, it is not clear whether it routinely paid sickness benefits or allowed a particular amount for funeral expenses. As far as can be determined, the Free African Union Society provided a fund from which money could be drawn for these purposes, but members expected repayment when the ailing individual was returned to health.[20] Its motives were decidedly benevolent, that is, broader than the beneficial component previously described, as it advocated colonization of Blacks and sought to provide a school for youth and older people as well as keep records of births, deaths, and marriages in the community.[21] Respect for the elderly, however, was an important feature of FAUS. William Thornton, evidently a White man seeking to interest Providence, Rhode Island, Blacks in colonization, wrote:

> It gave me much pleasure to be witness of the Respect that the young men paid to the Elders in the Meeting which I attended. It is a becoming Respect which redounds to the honor of both, and I hope that Reason will still continue to point out the propriety of a strict adherence to the Dictates of Experience.[22]

While there is no indication that respect for elderly members was built into the structure of the organization, Thornton's letter is to the "Elders and members of the Union."[23] More than likely the structure of the FAUS reflected its quasi-religious nature, and Elders were actually not only older men, but also officers in the association.[24]

Although there were earlier benevolent societies such as the FAUS just mentioned and the Perseverance Benevolence and Mutual Aid Association of New Orleans, founded in 1783, the most far-reaching benevolent society, not only from the standpoint of the present discussion, but also from the impetus it provided for the independent Black church movement, was the Free African Society (FAS) of Philadelphia. In 1787 when the prejudiced Whites of Philadelphia's St. George's Church sought to separate from their African American members, Richard Allen and Absalom Jones led Blacks from the church and formed the Free African Society, a name Charles Coleman has pointed out that expressed the desire for "Black identify, self-sufficiency, and self-determination."[25] Group members, who under Richard Allen later formed Bethel Church (1794) and under Absalom Jones formed the St. Thomas Episcopal Church (1791), pledged unity to one another and support to one another in sickness and death. Because of the prejudice against allowing Blacks to be buried in White or public cemeteries, a plot was purchased in Potter's Field to bury the dead. The relief offered to the needy members was to be dispensed in "Pennsylvania currency" on the condition that a "one year's subscription" was held and "provided the necessity was not brought on them by their own imprudence."[26]

When this function was taken over by the Friendly Society of St. Thomas in 1797, the first purely Black beneficial association came into being, that is, an organization designed strictly to collect monies from and provide aid to its members. For a $1.00 membership fee and $.25 a month dues, a sick member or an orphan or a widow of a deceased member, if she did not remarry, could receive up to $1.50 per week. In addition, an investment fund was to be established to make loans to members, and committees were established to visit the ailing. From this beginning in 1810, the African Insurance Company was founded, capitalized at $5,000 and located on Lombard Street, by St. Thomas officers.[27]

In philosophical orientation and organizational structure many beneficial societies followed the model of the Free African Society (FAS), collecting small sums to provide relief to the needy and expecting exemplary conduct from members. Generally, beneficial societies provided honest returns, paying between $10 and $20 as a death benefit and $1.00 to $3.00 for a sick benefit, which cost in premium about $.25. The Negro Convention Movement, which began in Philadelphia in 1830, where African Americans discussed mutual problems and defined strategies to improve their condition, was an important stimulus to the growth of beneficial and benevolent societies across the nation. By 1838 Philadelphia had well over a hundred of these organizations with memberships over seven thousand and funds amounting to over $10,000. Ten years later there were 106 societies with over eight thousand members, representing perhaps all of Philadelphia's Black community.[28]

Black New Yorkers' most important association was the New York African Society for Mutual Relief (NYASMR), which was founded in 1808 and chartered two years later.[29] The Society's purpose was to provide for its members in times of sickness, particularly when deprived of remuneration from work, and to relieve the distress of orphans and widows of deceased members. According to the preamble to its constitution, the association was formed "to improve our condition [by] . . . protecting ourselves from the extreme exigencies to which we are liable to be reduced."[30] For years, society members visited the sick and infirm and paid thousands of dollars to widows and relatives of members. The visitation requirement must have been very important to those who were isolated without family. In 1905 ninety-seven years after its founding, the NYASMR operated on a budget of $5,000, held a membership of forty-three (limited by its constitution to fifty), paid $15 a week for sick benefits, $600 to deceased members' heirs, and allowed members "the privilege of drawing $500 for permanent disability or old age."[31] The NYASMR was one of the most successful beneficial organizations that provided prestige and social status to the young, security in old age, a decent burial when dead, and comfort to the bereaved as well as stability to an uncertain community.

It was not long before other Black New Yorkers followed this example. In 1812 the Wilberforce Philanthropic Society was chartered; in 1829 the African Clarkson Society was founded; in 1831 the Brooklyn Woolman Benevolent Society came into being; and in 1845 the Brooklyn Tompkins Association was established. The Wilberforce Philanthropic Association was more social than the others, but all provided mutual aid for members, widows of members, and orphans. The African Clarkson Society, one of the few that operated on an actuarial basis, limited new members to those between the ages of twenty-one and forty. It charged monthly fees of $.25, and paid a $2 a week benefit for three months to those who held memberships for at least one year. Widows were dispensed a $20 annual pension and a $15 allotment for burial expenses.[32] African Americans in New York no doubt enjoyed a great deal of security from these organizations.

Although men operated the largest societies, women organizations were more numerous. The ratio of women to men in beneficial associations reflected the larger number of females at each national census from

3: "Better off than poor white people" 95

1820 to 1910 with more than 56,001 females to men in 1910, with the greatest disparity in 1870 when there were 962 males per 1,000 females. This was true in most cities North and South, although like the national trend, the direction was toward parity. In Philadelphia, for example, the ratio of women to men (females per 1,000 males) was 1,326 in 1838, 1,360 in 1870, and 1,127 in 1890.[33] Although the excess of females over males was primarily in the lower ages, the preponderance of females helps to explain why women probably outstripped men in the establishment of beneficial associations.

There is no way to be exact about the number or the nature of female or male organizations. Antebellum Black New York women organized the Female Benevolent Society of Troy, New York; the New York Benevolent Branch of Bethel; the Juvenile Daughters of Ruth; St. Cecilia Society; African Association; the Female Assistant Benefit Society; and the Abyssinian Benevolent Daughters of Esther Association. These were really a mixed bag of benevolent and beneficial associations. The Abyssinian Benevolent Daughters of Esther Association, which was definitely of the beneficial variety, restricted memberships to women between the ages of sixteen and sixty and excluded the drunken, polyandrous, and immoral. Since husbands were considered family breadwinners, benefits were provided "in case of the incapacity of the husband," but it "excluded any allowance for pregnancy."[34] In Philadelphia, for example, in 1831 there were sixteen male and twenty-seven female associations, reflecting the greater number among women.

Although women had more of them, the best-known, wealthiest, and most influential societies were undoubtedly controlled by men. Some accepted both sexes and in the early years were also interracial. The Free African Union Society (FAUS) of Providence, already mentioned, accepted Whites in its membership as well as on its Board of Directors, though its rule restricting Whites to four of eleven directors insured Black control. When the FAUS merged with the all-female African Benevolent Society in 1807, it called for two-thirds of the male members to be present to transact business, which insured male domination. This requirement was later changed to require only eleven members in good standing to achieve a quorum, removing the sexist requirement in the rules.[35]

In addition to the cities previously mentioned, the beneficial society was also prevalent in the northern cities of Boston, Albany, Cincinnati, Newport, Pittsburgh, and other places where sufficient numbers of Blacks were found. According to Leonard Curry, and this seems to be a conservative estimate, there were over two hundred beneficial societies nationally with about fourteen thousand members as early as 1840.[36] These societies were stifled somewhat in the South during the antebellum period because of the denial of Black people the right to assemble, municipal curfews, and restrictions on African American mobility. Even so, many organizations flourished in such cities as Baltimore, Richmond, Petersburg, Charleston, and New Orleans.

One of the best known and most written about benevolent societies in the South was Charleston's Brown Fellowship Society (BFS), founded in 1790.[37] According to the preamble to its constitution, the association was founded to relieve the same class of people to which other societies were targeted, singling out widows, orphans, and those in sickness and distress. Unlike others, however, the members of Brown Fellowship Society noted that its formation was made after "observing the method of many well-disposed persons of this state, by entering into particular societies for this purpose."[38] The Scots in 1730 had founded the St. Andrew's Society in Charleston; seven years later French Huguenots had established the South Carolina Society; and Jews in 1750 operated *Herbra Gemilot Hasidim* "specifically to care for the sick and bury the dead," which became the Hebrew Benevolent Society in 1799.[39] Perhaps it was these efforts that influenced Black Charlestonians.

The Brown Fellowship Society members, through the creation of the "Board of Burial Ground Trustees," made decent burial a pivotal part of its program. They also provided stewards to visit the sick, ascertain their circumstances, and report to the organization. Weekly benefits of $1.50 for sickness were provided, and funeral arrangements were made. Widows of deceased members were paid annual sums of $60 (dispensed quarterly), and orphaned children were to be educated up to age fourteen at society expense and thereafter apprenticed. As its motto "Charity and Benevolence" implied, the BFS extended its relief beyond its own members, providing assistance to "any poor colored orphan or adult" as long as their numbers did not exceed five, and for interment or burial, of "nonsubscribers and transient persons," though a $10 fee was charged. Daniel Alexander Payne, bishop of the African Methodist Episcopal Church and the leading Black theologian of the nineteenth century, was perhaps the best-known orphan educated by the BFS.[40] In 1843 the Brown Fellowship Society noted that some widows were too embarrassed to apply for relief, and they decided to accept applications from them in writing; if widows refused assistance, then they resolved to act as they deemed fitting. The members noted that "it often happens that at the death of a member of this society, his widow is placed under embarrassment, and she might from various motives, not wish to apply for the bounty of the society." Nevertheless, the practice of aiding widows was discontinued in 1873, evidently because of lack of funds, and one member's attempt to get members to agree to restore widows' stipends at a later date was defeated.[41] There were other societies founded in Charleston before the Civil War, notably the Humane Brotherhood, allegedly the darker skinned

Charlestonians' response to the BFS, the Ladies Union Benevolent Society, the Christian Benevolent Society, and the Unity and Friendship Society.[42]

Studies show that these societies were in existence in other parts of the South before the Civil War. Baltimore was a particularly fertile ground for beneficial associations, and as early as 1821, there were as many as thirty such organizations with memberships running from 35 to 150. The African Benevolent Society for Social Relief, the Daughters of Jerusalem, and the Star in the East Association are examples. There were several in Petersburg, Virginia; two of the best known were Consolation (1845) and the Beneficial Society of Freemen of Color. In Lexington, Kentucky, the Union Benevolent Society was organized in 1843; In Nashville, Tennessee, the Nashville Colored Benevolent Society was organized; and in Washington, D.C., in 1818 the Resolute Beneficial Society was established. These examples could be multiplied to include the cities of Richmond, Savannah, Augusta, Mobile, and other places where Blacks resided.

There is some indication that beneficial societies existed among urban slaves since they were often hired out and had the time to earn their own money. Forced to secrecy by laws against assembly, each member in a Virginia beneficial association was assigned a code number to facilitate communication and record keeping of payments. Members who obtained masters' permission to attend funerals were required to sit together and, where it was safe to do so, formed a processional to the cemetery.[43] Outside the United States, Blacks also formed beneficial societies. In Canada, for example, Blacks organized beneficial associations, referred to as True Bands, starting their first one in Mallden in 1859 and numbering fourteen two years later. These societies also flourished in Brazil, Cuba (cabildos), and other places, serving the same function as they did in the United States. Du Bois's observation in 1907 that "beneficial societies are thus seen to be universal among colored people," seems to be an accurate assessment.[44]

Needless to say, the emancipation of 4 million African Americans tremendously increased the number of beneficial societies in both northern but particularly southern cities. Thousands of Blacks flocked to the cities if for no other reason than the mere exercise of the right to leave the plantation. Most came, however, seeking the benefits of freedom, a job for a decent wage, or relief from the monotony of the plantation. Many came in search of family members or to sanction their marriages by civil authority. Whatever their reason, thousands of them died from disease, starvation, and exposure. The Freedmen's Bureau, dozens of Freedmen's aid associations, and religious groups tried to ease the difficult transition to independence. When these efforts were ended and Reconstruction closed, Blacks were left without a secure legal footing, primarily landless, with their political rights slipping away, and with not much hope for their future. Excluded from or segregated in social welfare organizations, Blacks relied on their own resources and looked to the infrastructure created by free Blacks during the antebellum period to guide them in their effort.[45] Beneficial societies played a key role in Black southerners' adjustment to freedom, their attempt to build stable families, to create a viable leadership class, and to develop stable communities.

Several examples will demonstrate their growth. Baltimore added seventeen beneficial societies between 1865 and 1870, and during the next fifteen years, twenty more were established. Beaufort, South Carolina, had ten societies in 1883 with about one thousand members; Nashville, Tennessee's Colored Benevolent Society had twenty-seven branches in 1873 and was joined by the Ladies Benevolent Society, which had hundreds of members in 1881. In a single Mississippi city, one mortician carried the account of twenty beneficial associations between 1888 and 1890. In Atlanta, Georgia, in 1883 there were fifteen societies with three thousand members, sporting such titles as Gospel Aid, Sisters of Charity, Sisters of Love, Mutual Aid, Daughters of Bethel, and Sisters of Jacob. A particularly important Atlanta group was an Old People's Society that was composed of sixty very old people who cared for their sick by taking turns at nursing care. This beneficial society embodied all the features of care for the old, combining economic independence with friendly visiting, nursing care, and social and emotional support.[46]

In 1897 Du Bois found that there were thirty-one beneficial associations in Philadelphia's seventh ward alone, though there were many more in the city. So important was the beneficial society to the old that those in Philadelphia who were too old for memberships in existing societies, had allowed memberships to lapse, or did not have the foresight to join an association when young, formed the Old Men's Association to meet their particular needs.[47]

In New Orleans some beneficial associations had unique features that were especially pertinent to caring for aged Blacks. Most aged and infirm were, as elsewhere, cared for by families and friends so that public dependency in New Orleans was low. The major reasons were the African American's abhorrence for public charity and the creation of several hundred beneficial associations, the oldest of which was the Perseverance Benevolent and Mutual Aid Association, founded in 1783.[48] Another society, La Concorde, founded in 1878, was purely beneficial and was organized specifically to help its aged and infirmed members. Except for medical costs, its pensions for aged members were its largest expense. Les Jeunes Amis, like La Concorde, organized by French-speaking Blacks, not only provided sick benefits, but also nursing care. Like most

3: "Better off than poor white people"

New Orleans societies, it had contracts with doctors, druggists, and undertakers, and like Black beneficial societies everywhere, it had a relief committee to visit sick members and make sure that they received benefits. In its attempt to guard the morals of members, mistresses and concubines were barred from memberships.[49] Another important aspect of the New Orleans societies, which Harry Walker estimated to number about six hundred as late as 1930, was the inclusion of "passive members," an important feature of male organizations. All dependents—wife, children, parents—when sharing the same household and "exceeding a minimum age" had passive membership status and were "eligible for medical treatment and drugs, and a death benefit for the same dues and fees paid by the member."[50] Although this feature must have posed a heavy financial burden on these organizations, it was a source of much security for a large household, particularly one with elderly members, since all were covered by a single membership. The relief committee, passive membership, extensive contracting with doctors, druggists, and undertakers, and their large numbers provided Black New Orleanians widespread security in old age.

Beneficial societies were not alone in offering aid to elderly members. A contingent of secret societies and fraternal orders offered aid to needy members and their families and pensions to the old. Some of these secret orders actually grew out of beneficial associations, and others maintained a beneficial component. According to Monroe Work, the Baltimore Mutual Aid Society gave birth to the Good Samaritans (1841), the Nazarites (1845), and the Galilean Fisherman (1856).[51] In terms of memberships, property holdings, and popularity, the two most important secret orders were the Masons, founded in 1784 by Prince Hall, and the Odd Fellows, established by Peter Ogden in 1843. Both organizations obtained legitimate English charters after being rebuffed by their White American brothers.[52] Others included the Knights of Pythias (1864), Knights of Tabor (1855), Mosaic Templars (1882), Elks (1889), Knights of Jericho, Independent Order of St. Luke, United Brothers of Friendships (1861), and the Grand Fountain of the United Order of True Reformers, founded in Richmond, Virginia, in 1873.[53]

After the Civil War, the fraternal and secret orders experienced astronomical growth, particularly after the 1880s. For example, the Odd Fellows had eighty-nine lodges in 1868, one thousand in 1886, and four times that number in 1904 with investments of over $3 million. In the same year, the True Reformers boasted of more than seventy thousand members with property valued at over $400,000. The Masons in 1904 had about two thousand members in over thirty states with an annual income of $500,000 and property assessed at $1 million.[54] It is no small wonder that these organizations gradually replaced the smaller beneficial societies after the

1890s. Some, like the True Reformers, began the transition to legitimate insurance companies by using an actuarial basis for membership. No doubt these organizations provided significant support for elderly Black people, but the level of such help cannot be accurately determined. Extant information allows for some conclusions.

The protection the beneficial association offered from the vicissitudes of unskilled labor was responsible for the small percentage of institutionalized paupers as well as the low incidence of outdoor or home relief among Black people. About African Americans in Philadelphia and Baltimore, Alfred Kutzik concluded that "rather than racial discrimination, it is the extent and effectiveness of Black mutual aid that primarily accounts for the relatively small number of Black public assistance recipients."[55] By the middle of the nineteenth century, almost every family in these two cities belonged to at least one beneficial society. For this reason, they shared no more than their proportion of the almshouse population even though they were the poorest segment of society and denied the normal avenues of economic and social mobility. For example, the percentage of Blacks in the Philadelphia almshouse between 1837 and 1847 was reduced from 14 percent to about 5 percent (from 235 to 78 according to Kutzik). Beneficial societies deserve partial credit for this reduction because "nearly all of the city's approximately 30,000 Blacks—including the aged—were covered by the [Black] mutual aid welfare system," says Kutzik.[56]

In reality, the pattern of outdoor relief also helps to explain the drop in the almshouse population among Black Philadelphians. In 1847 there were 442 Black families on "outdoor" assistance, representing about 10 percent of all Black families. As far as can be determined, there were no Black families on outdoor relief in 1837 because the Blockley Almshouse, completed in 1834, was designed to obviate that form of relief. In 1835, the Guardians of the Poor, to whom the needy were entrusted for care, outlawed home relief, and it was not allowed again until 1839, and then on a six-month renewable basis. In 1859 Blacks constituted about 4 percent of the population and numbered 179 (95 women and 84 men) of the 2,911 inmates of the Philadelphia almshouse.[57] In Baltimore County, Maryland, for example, between 1850 and 1860, free Blacks constituted an average of about 12 percent of the population but averaged less than 10 percent of the almshouse population, despite "the practice of setting free superannuated slaves aided to swell the ranks of the destitute."[58]

In later years increased racial discrimination, immigrant competition for jobs, the influx of large numbers of unskilled Blacks into the nations cities, and the denial of outdoor public relief operated to increase Blacks' share of the public dole. Nevertheless, a strong tradition of self-help and mutual assistance among African Americans continued to militate against public dependency. John Daniels noted of Boston that despite "special adversities" African Americans did not share disproportionately in public charity because of their beneficial and fraternal associations. He concluded:

> It is a fact that seldom does one find a Negro begging on the streets. The members of this race possess in high degree the quality of human kindness and are ever ready to help their fellows in time of need.[59]

Statistical information, besides that already mentioned, would help to show the effectiveness of these societies, but extant statistics are skimpy. Between 1830 and 1831, 43 (16 male and 27 female) beneficial societies paid out almost $6,000 in benefits to needy Black Philadelphians. In 1848, 76 of Philadelphia's 106 societies provided relief to 681 families. The Female Benevolent Society of Troy in 1838 paid a total of only $9.00 in sick benefits and $8.00 for funerals. Although this seems to be a small pittance, it probably provided substantial help to those in need. In 1884, 40 of the beneficial associations of Baltimore had buried, since their beginning, over 1,400 members at a cost of over $45,000 and had provided sick benefits that amounted to $125,000. Also 30 societies had paid $27,000 to widows.[60] In 1889, the Mutual Beneficial Association buried 9, provided for 203 sick, and between 1885 and 1890 spent $10,000 performing these kinds of services.[61] In Nashville in 1881 one branch of the Ladies Benevolent Society paid over $1,500 for sick benefits, $330 for funerals, and over $30 for charity to nonmembers.[62] In New Orleans, *La Concorde,* between 1878 and 1884, paid $1,848 for burials of 55 members, $2,453 for doctors and druggist bills, and $1,083 in pensions for the aged and infirm.[63]

The larger fraternal and secret orders outstripped the beneficial associations. For example, between 1882 and 1894, 50 of the Odd Fellows' lodges buried 83 members, aided 76 widows, and provided for 70 orphans. In 1884 alone the Good Samaritans spent $5,000 providing relief, while the Seven Wise Men buried 24 members and provided aid to 201 at a cost of $4,300. The True Reformers, during the twenty years from 1881 to 1901 paid $600,000 in death claims and $1,500,000 in benefits to the sick.[64] These examples could be multiplied, but there is no need to belabor the point. It is clear that those who had membership in beneficial societies, fraternal, or secret orders, enjoyed some degree of social security in old age.

It is important to remember that undergirding these numbers were provisions for nursing care, friendly exchange, and visits that broke the isolation of a sick room. Typical was the Colored Men's and Ladies Protective Association of Columbus, Georgia, organized in 1890, which required within twenty-four hours of learning of a members illness the appointment of a sick committee of twelve members, two of whom were to sit up with the ailing member "each night, commencing alphabetically and continuing until the roll is completed if necessary."[65] The effectiveness of the beneficial society, therefore, went beyond economic support, though that was substantial, and provided tremendous social and psychological support to the old and infirm in the African American community. When one considers that African Americans were not likely to participate in any pension program, that few companies had retirement packages, and how the forces of racism conspired against Black economic mobility, beneficial associations, which were often the only source of support in crisis and old age, certainly helped to provide economic stability to the Black family and community. A former slave, who organized the first beneficial society in his hometown of Bay St. Louis, Mississippi, in 1878 remembered:

> The benefits pay for a doctor and medicine in sickness, small weekly pensions in distress, and bury the dead. In my Association the dues are $.50 a month with $2.00 additional per year for doctor bills. In this way, we are *better off than the poor white people* [emphasis mine] who often have no way to meet these expenses. Nearly all our people in some way or the other manage to keep up their dues.[66]

Joshua Brown wrote to his beneficial society:

> Allow me to thank you kindly for the prompt attention I received from your company, the People's Relief Association during my illness. Sir, I must confess your company is strictly a reliable one and I hope that your membership may continue to increase.[67]

Although many beneficial societies paid old-age pensions, some did not. Therefore, it was possible to maintain membership for thirty or forty years without collecting from the association. One ex-slave complained:

> I payin' more and more . . . and I nebber could git sick, so I git a nickel of dat money back. I ain't hab no ailment 'cep'n my feet jis swol up and I can't get nuffin' fur dat.[68]

Although this ex-slave enjoyed good health and received no financial return on his investment, he had the emotional and psychological security of beneficial society membership, an intangible of inestimable value. Beneficial associations most often provided direct relief to families, since they were designed to help keep members out of institutions, but sometimes they aided institutionalized elderly.

The relationship between the Home for Aged and Infirm Colored Persons (HAICP) and the beneficial associations to which residents belonged provides a microcosmic view of how these societies protected old Black people and provides some rare insights into how beneficial associations functioned, practically and philosophically. This analysis is also important because it discusses an attempt to combine institutional and non-institutional care for the Black elderly, the confluence of two African American traditions.[69] While many people probably came down on one side or the other of indoor or outdoor relief for the needy, those who provided Homes for the Black aged were not doctrinaire in their benevolence. For example, because the HAICP was always filled to capacity, there was a waiting list, and the Board of Managers occasionally provided outdoor help to these individuals, more often, however, when they felt that such relief would keep applicants out of the almshouse. Faced with the same problem, the Home for Aged Colored Women (HACW) of Boston took a systematic interest in caring for those waiting to gain admission. In 1907, when the Home had reached its capacity of twenty residents, it provided outdoor relief to more than twice that number, ranging from two dollars to six dollars a month based on individual need.[70]

Beneficial associations were expected to play a key role in caring for the elderly of the HAICP. When the Board of Managers convened at its first annual meeting in 1865, one of the rules adopted read: "Those that are pensioners of any benevolent institution or society it is expected will have their pensions continued to assist in their support and that their funeral expenses will be paid." (See appendix for all the rules and regulations and bylaws).[71] Although it is not known whether Susan Silvey, the first resident, belonged to a beneficial society, Amelia Webster, an eighty-nine-year-old Delaware native, the second admittee, arrived with full-fledged membership in the Morris Brown Society. As far as can be determined over the years residents belonged to the following societies:[72]

Daughters of Cornish
John Cornish Society
Sons of St. Thomas Society
Alfa Society
Keystone Beneficial Society
Rev. R. Moore Society
Rev. Henry Davis Society
Sons and Daughters of John Wesley
Benevolent Daughters of John Wesley

The Joshua Woodland Society
Joseph Parrish Society
Knights of Pythias
Rev. Jabez Campbell Society
Rev. William Moore Society
Rev R. Robinson Society
Daughters of St. Paul
Elijah Society

Such memberships were more than a source of resident support: they served as confirmation that the institution was meeting the needs of the "worthy" class for whom it was intended. The HAICP was not unique in its receipt of beneficial association funds. For example, the Colored Aged Home of Irvington, New Jersey, which had fifteen inmates, received forty dollars from beneficial associations in 1908, but it is not known whether the payments covered sickness or death claims.[73]

The amount the HAICP paid to beneficial societies before 1877 cannot be determined, for this expense was not listed separately in the treasurer's reports; nor is it possible to determine exactly how much the Home received from these organizations. The 1870 annual report, for example, shows collections from two societies for two residents. The 1871 report shows that the Joshua Woodland Society and The Morris Brown Society paid $15.00 and $18.00 respectively for M. Tillotson and Amelia Webster, but there are no payments to beneficial societies reported in the treasurer's report. The Home paid $58.44 in 1877, the first year there was a listing, but the amount declined from $82.09 in 1878 to $4.26 in 1891, the last year there was separate reporting.[74] Applications to the Home requested that applicants list their properties or assets, and they are available from 1898 to 1918. An examination of this source shows that less than 10 percent of applicants listed property or a benefit of any kind. Sarah Fummel claimed to have had "insurance full paid up," Harriet Miles had an "Alfa Society sick benefit," William Knight "Prudential $75 at death," and Joshua Bowers had a benefit from the "Knights of Pythias." One applicant responded to the question by inserting the words "a slave" in the appropriate space.[75]

The pattern of beneficial association memberships in the HAICP followed developments in the larger society. That is, the records showed a decline in beneficial society participation by the 1890s, which conforms to their historical displacement by larger fraternal organizations and bona fide insurance companies. While their discontinuation in the HAICP illuminates problems in society at large, the committee on management, a standing committee of female board members entrusted with the "internal arrangements" of the Home, had concluded as early as 1872 that the "disadvantages [of maintaining membership] outweighed the advantages."[76]

It was the management committee's responsibility, delegated to long-time Board member Mary Campbell, wife of African Methodist Episcopal Bishop Jabez F. Campbell, to collect the sick and death benefits from beneficial associations. She collected an estimated $445.00 between 1877 and 1891 while the Home paid $423.00 in premiums, a profit of only $21.65 over fifteen years. Board members Henry Laing, Sarah Sleeper, Dillwyn Parrish, and William Still as well as the matrons on occasion received money from these associations, but the amounts are not separately reported; they, therefore, cannot be accurately included in the above computation.[77] Since residents came to the Home enfeebled after maintaining "insurance" policies for years, it is likely the HAICP received a larger amount than can be accurately determined.

The HAICP had a variety of problems dealing with these associations. These included difficulty collecting payments, disputes over the HAICP burial practices, and legal problems that might also have contributed to the Home's relaxation of the early policy. In January 1871 Phillis Smith was denied her sick benefit by the St. Paul Beneficial Society, and the managers discussed legal action. As far as can be determined, sick benefits were never paid; but when Smith died in 1875, the Home received $40.00 for burial, evidently from two societies.[78] Bedridden as she was from 1871 to 1875, it was probably unrealistic to expect these societies, designed to provide temporary rather than long-term aid and with such small amounts of capital, to pay weekly benefits for such an extended period. Indeed, organizations varied in the number of weeks they provided assistance. The Free African Society simply provided "three shillings and nine pence per week" for an unspecified period. Some societies made three allowances on a decreasing scale. For example, the Jabez P. Campbell Society paid $3.00 a week for the first allowance, $2.00 a week for the second, and $1.00 a week for the third, but did not specify the duration of a particular allowance. The African Friendly Society paid a maximum of $1.50 a week for four weeks and then assessed the amount upward or downward as each situation deemed necessary. The African Clarkson Society paid $2.00 a week for a maximum of three months.[79]

In April 1880 the Sons of St. Thomas Society was singled out by the HAICP Board for its unwillingness to pay the death benefit of B. Calloway, and in May the matter was turned over to the solicitor for collection. In December 1889 the Board thought that the Mutual Union Aid and Beneficial Association was responsible in Emily William's death but they evidently did not want to pay. Since these associations were not classified as insurance companies, as previously discussed, and therefore not subject to the laws as such, how the solicitor handled these problems is unknown.[80]

The Sons of St. Thomas, founded in 1823, had by 1880 diminished in membership and stature and probably maintained a large percentage of elderly members. However, the difficulty with St. Thomas was not financial but philosophical in that it held that it was relieved of its obligation to pay benefits by the HAICP's life care contract system, that is, the agreement between the resident and the Home that for an admission fee and all possessions, the Home would provide residents with all life's necessities and a decent burial. As a matter of fact, when old-age assistance payments were introduced with the Social Security Act in 1935, some states, including Pennsylvania, did not allow payments to life care residents of old-age Homes.[81] The point of contention between the

HAICP and St. Thomas was, therefore, theoretical, even foreshadowing problems that emerged with the first national attempt to deal with the problems of aged Americans generally. Community pressure militated against nonpayment, but beneficial societies that were founded during the antebellum period were by the late nineteenth century overcome by the sheer aging of members. Perhaps managerial inexperience exacerbated the problem as well, but there is little reason in the St. Thomas case to resort to explanations of fraudulence, chicanery, or abdication of responsibility.

In some ways the HAICP's burial policy sheds some light on the functioning of beneficial societies. Contending that the Home's policy did not provide the accustomed services, relatives who could afford the expense, and some who could not, buried their kin personally. One woman in February 1873 buried her mother because the HAICP used the coarse and inexpensive muslin for shrouding while she preferred the finer merino.[82] The daughter also requested a return of the twenty dollar funeral benefit paid to the Home by the beneficial society to which her mother belonged. The Board refused at first but in 1880 formalized the practice of contributing to burials away from the institution by a resolution of the Board that provided for a "sum of not more than $20.00." Persistent problems forced the Board to agree to a fixed sum of twenty dollars in 1902.[83] Some families claimed their relatives for burial because the Home practiced the commercialistic and impersonal policy of burying more than one in a grave, "after burying the ground over commencing at first grave." Certainly this practice stood in contradiction to the "African Negro's penchant for burial pomp" that historian Carter Woodson claims provided the "nucleus" for the development of beneficial societies.[84] In other words, the Home's burial policies struck at the heart of the purpose of beneficial associations.

The HAICP never repealed its 1865 rule but adopted a policy of individual assessment, maintaining some premiums and rejecting others, perhaps based on the track record of each beneficial association. Several times between 1884 and 1895 residents requested that dues in the societies they belonged to should be kept up as an advantage to the HAICP, and the Board concurred. What had been a blanket policy in 1865 was changed, for various reasons, to an individual one.

As one can see then, the reasons for the demise of the beneficial society are numerous, complex, and interrelated. First, as previously stated, by the 1890s the larger fraternal organizations outgrew the purely beneficial associations and in many cases replaced them. Second, overlapping this development was the beginning of the legitimate Black insurance company, that is, an organization actuarially based and run for profit. White insurance companies either refused insurance to Blacks or, like Metropolitan Life, charged exorbitant premiums because of alleged high-mortality rates. This practice became particularly widespread after the Prudential Insurance Company's 1881 study and the 1896 publication of Frederick Hoffman's *Race Traits and Tendencies of the American Negro* that "corroborated" society's racist notions about Black living conditions, social habits, and attitudes.[85]

In addition the decline of the beneficial association cannot be blamed entirely on external developments because there were some serious internal problems that foresaged their ultimate collapse. For one, while most of these organizations were run by honest men, the fraudulent embezzled funds or turned monies to their private use, contributing to public distrust. For another, payments were not timely distributed by some organizations, while others used technicalities as excuses for nonpayment. Third, favoritism, poor record keeping, and inefficiency prevailed because officers lacked managerial experience and education. There were also difficulties in collecting dues from these poor people, and some members, despite rules against it, "took sick" to collect benefits. Finally, the organizations contained the seeds of their own demise, accepting members regardless of health and often without regard to age. Founded during the first half of the nineteenth century, most of these societies by the 1890s were simply overcome by the sheer old age of members who were not being replaced by new ones to offset operating costs.[86]

Some of these problems can be illustrated by an examination of the minutes of the Brown Fellowship Society (BFS) of Charleston. Throughout the late nineteenth century the BFS struggled along with a few faithful souls, and with each member's death, quorums became harder to achieve. As early as 1850 the average age of members was forty-seven, a clear indication that new members were needed as the society incurred expenses as individuals claimed their pensions, demanded sick benefits, or died and widows needed help. The BFS was evidently not able to attract members, and the existence of twenty beneficial societies in Charleston after the Civil War indicate that younger Blacks started their own, making it difficult for the BFS to attract new blood. Thus, the organization became confined to a small group of old men. In 1890 only ten members attended the Centennial meeting of the association, and the next year the president was residing in an old folks Home. Moreover, his elderly successor was forced by illness to be absent from meetings for six months in 1891. Recognizing the myriad of problems they faced, BFS members in 1893 reorganized the society into the Century Fellowship Society but experienced little success in its attempt to revitalize the association with new members.[87]

The Free African Union Society (FAUS), founded in 1780 in Providence and ten years older than the BFS, faced similar problems as early as the

1840s as it struggled to replace elderly members with new recruits from a much smaller African American community. The failure of these efforts predicted inevitable demise for these important organizations. Some societies had problems peculiar to their unique history. The Humane Brotherhood, according to James Browning, "committed race suicide" because it was composed of dark-skinned individuals. He claims that "as they [members] accumulated property they almost invariably married fairer women and frequently the offspring dropped the name of their Black progenitors."[88] The Free African Union Society was forced to dissolve in 1794 because of the "bad name" being given to it by the widow of a deceased member, although they reorganized the group under the same rules and regulations.[89] While this might seem to be an extreme response to any charges it might have faced, it must be remembered that these were quasi-religious organizations designed to be exemplary of the high moral standards of the African American community.

These private efforts constituted the backdrop for the public pension movement that began around the turn of the twentieth century when over 50 percent of the almshouse's inmates were sixty-five and over. Although the federal government maintained a program of veterans' pensions after the War of 1812, and significantly increased pensions after the Civil War, the first manifestation of the state's concern for elderly citizens began with Massachusetts in 1907 when the state set up a commission to study the pension problem. The drive for pensions slowly accelerated into mid-1910 but did not grow rapidly until hastened by the effects of the stock market crash in the fall of 1929. There were six states with pension laws in 1928, viz., Colorado, Kentucky, Maryland, Montana, Nevada, and Wisconsin.[90] By 1935 there were twenty-eight states with such laws with an average allotment of sixteen dollars a month. Nevertheless, most of America's 6.5 million elderly people still relied on charity, institutional care, or their children. Although industrial insurance had made inroads into the beneficial society system by the 1930s, Blacks in some places like New Orleans still relied heavily on beneficial association membership.[91] In 1935 the Social Security Act was passed, which ignored the peculiar problems of the Black elderly by excluding domestics and agricultural workers, where most African Americans were employed. This inequity was corrected in the 1950s. However the omission, combined with the cost of living increases in 1972 that were indexed to inflation on a percentage basis and that African Americans more often than Whites opt for Social Security benefits at age sixty-two, has the present effect of providing smaller Social Security checks to the Black elderly than the ones their White counterparts receive.

The beneficial society over and above its aid to the elderly had the salutary effect of providing African American men and women with man-

3: "Better off than poor white people"

agerial experience unavailable elsewhere in the community, and it served as a symbol of what might be accomplished by group action and cooperation. Moreover, these organizations "served as cocoons from which emerged several of the black insurance companies."[92] The True Reformers in particular marked the transition to the practice of using life contingency tables or estimates of mortality. This change was a major step toward the establishment of legal reserve companies. Seven of the existing thirty-four insurance companies founded, owned, and operated by Blacks were set up around the turn of the twentieth century.[93]

The beneficial or benevolent society never quite disappeared from many rural areas of the South, where it remains associated with the church. Its major benefit is burial, though there are still friendly visits to the sick and shut-in and monthly or quarterly meetings that help to remove the loneliness and isolation of the older, rural, Black resident. In the Georgia countryside Arthur Raper concluded in 1936 that "hardly a single rural Negro church, regardless of how small its membership, is without an organization of some description which pays death claims and sick benefits."[94] A survey of the rural area around Augusta, Georgia, found this still to be the case. For example, Second Mt. Carmel Baptist Church had a Young Folks Society and An Old Folks Society that paid respectively $150 and $200 for burial. The Rosemont Association, a consortium of eight churches, founded in 1902, no longer paid for burials and used its funds for college scholarships.[95] Although some other societies were still in existence, they had changed their focus, and interest seemed confined to a few elderly people.

The beneficial association provided direct and indirect economic and psychological security to African American families. From a few pennies scraped together by an impoverished people, they sought to ease the hardship of widowhood, to allay the financial burden of sickness, to secure families in times of adversity or misfortune, to provide security in old age, and to relieve the anxiety of the pauper's grave. Additional benefits were derived from the camaraderie of meetings, visitation of fellow members—in times of sickness or distress—nursing care, and heightened group consciousness. These were valuable ingredients, combining West African heritage of respect and veneration of the old with American heritage to create a vital and dynamic tradition of a multifaceted approach to caring for those in the words of Frances Harper, "around the verge of parting life."

4

"But she was white": Race, Gender, and Residency in the HAICP

> Whose hands, enriched with golden store,
> Gave of their wealth to build this Home,
> And changed a narrow domicile,
> Into a grand and stately dome.
> —Frances E. W. Harper, 1894

Previous chapters have described the multidimensional tradition in which African Americans sought to resolve gerontological problems. This tradition of mutual care, derived from West Africa, nurtured in slavery, was materially represented in the development of old-age facilities and the establishment of beneficial associations. The focus shifts in the remaining chapters from the external occurrences that shaped the larger perspective of gerontological problems to an analysis of solutions to those problems in a particular setting, not any setting, but the Home for Aged and Infirm Colored Persons (HAICP), described in chapter 2. Here we discuss the Home's organizational structure, examine the residents, employees, and administrators, analyze management policies, and evaluate the impact of these policies on residents, all through the backdrop of forces operating within the institution and the larger environment outside the Home. The chapters that follow analyze the institution's social structure, examine health care, and discuss the career of Hobart Jackson, administrator of the HAICP from 1948-78, who became the Father of Black Gerontology. A concluding chapter recapitulates the major themes of the study and reiterates the value of gerontological history for gerontologists and practitioners. Through the microcosm of the HAICP the ideas of the previous chapters inform the case study and enhance the overall understanding of the history of the Black aged.

The biracial beginning of The Home for Aged and Infirm Colored Persons, founded by Blacks and Whites (Quakers), extended into its operation. Although the resident population of the Home was limited to African

Americans from its founding in 1864 up to 1953 (when the first White residents arrived), the Board of Managers was always composed of Blacks and Whites, males and females. Indeed, the racial and gender responsibilities of the administrators, employment patterns, and the governance process (administrative hierarchy, committee structure, and decision making) often mirrored the racial, sexual, and philosophical assumptions of the day.[1] Therefore, problems endemic to the operation of the institution manifested themselves in racist or sexist terms, influencing the quality of care of the residents, (referred to as "inmates" up to about 1938)[2] and sometimes affecting the philosophy that undergirded the Home's operation, threatening the existence of the institution. The handling of these difficulties tested the managers' commitment to equality, reflected the growing consciousness of women, and provided a context for Quakers, both Hicksite and Orthodox, to measure their religious teachings against their behavior. Quakers were also confronted with their historic commitment to racial and sexual equality vis-à-vis toleration of behavior they considered outside acceptable boundaries. In some ways, then, the HAICP presaged modern times and offers important lessons for those who study or work with racially diverse old people and who must come to grips not only with their own attitudes toward aging but also with outside influences on their institutions.

There were always more applicants to the HAICP than there was available space even after the move in 1871 from the first Home on South Front Street to a new building on Girard and Belmont Avenues. The new facility was a commodious structure of two thousand square feet, designed specifically to house elderly residents.[3] The building was four stories in height with a cellar and mansard attic. The exterior of the building was of stone with protective casing of brick inside. On the first floor were the general dining room, laundry, two parlors, kitchen, and four rooms that would later be used by couples, though that was not the original intention. The other three stories duplicated each other; all had a wide corridor that ran east to west the length of the building, nine rooms, bathrooms, and wash rooms. Four of the nine rooms were furnished with four beds, four with six beds, and one with two beds. Private rooms were uncommon. After 1872 men lived on the fourth floor while the lower three floors were reserved for women. Twenty residents were moved from the old Home on South Front Street to the new Home, which was formally occupied 7 August 1871. Because of infirmity, a few had to be moved "in beds and large chairs." The new building had been dedicated 29 June 1871 with a ceremony that included singing by the famous Elizabeth Greenfield, the "Black Swan," a moving speech by Lucretia Mott, and a "few feeling remarks" by Stephen Smith.[4]

The Parker Annex, built in 1894, added additional space, including a chapel, conference room, and administrative headquarters. The resident capacity of the Home was brought to 110 women, 30 men, and 4 married couples.[5] To accommodate the sick more efficiently and to isolate them from other residents, steam-heated infirmaries or hospital wings were added in 1884 and 1901. In 1883 an elevator was added that enabled residents to gain access to most of the house and provided the opportunity for a few infirm residents to come downstairs or to go outside for the first time in several years.[6] The stairways, the infirmary, and other parts of the building were fireproofed in 1891, but managers were rightly concerned about so many old people handling dangerous lights. Therefore, gas jets in corridors were installed in 1891 to provide light that inmates could not control. In the same year, the floors were connected through "speaking tubes," thereby easing the labors of the matron.[7] In summary, the residents of the HAICP had the good fortune, at a time when few could boast of such a Home, to occupy an institution built specifically for the old and to have managers who attempted to stay informed of technological progress to use it to make the physical features of the Home responsive to residents' changing needs.

The HAICP was always filled to capacity. The first resident was an eighty-year-old New Jerseyite, Susan Silvey, who arrived on 7 March 1865. Four days later, Amelia Webster joined her. There were 21 residents at the end of 1865, but Susan Silvey was not among them. Because she died after eleven weeks, the managers believed the Home had been sanctified by the death of the first entrant. Although there were no formal restrictions against male residents and Stephen Smith and others were particularly interested in this group, the Board was forced to limit the initial Home to women because of inadequate facilities. The first male resident, William Butler, came 15 March 1872, and the number of male and female residents continued to increase over the years. There were 20 residents in 1871, 67 in 1875, 112 in 1884, and 138 in 1910, the number fluctuating between 130 and 140 from the 1890s to the 1930s. The hardships of the depression significantly reduced the number of residents in the 1940s and threatened to close the institution.[8]

Residents' places of birth reflected the slave experience and the migratory patterns of the Philadelphia population. The primary donor areas were the nearby states of Virginia, Delaware, and New Jersey. Because some early residents were former slaves, such areas as Africa and the West Indies were also represented. Over time, the provenance of residents' birth broadened to include areas as far north as Nova Scotia and as far south as Florida. Because of the eroding vestiges of slavery, none of the residents after 1919 came from Africa or the West Indies.[9]

It should be remembered that at the time of admission, the residents had been longtime residents of Philadelphia or nearby areas. The Home, a prototypical institution, came to be held in such widespread high esteem that visitors came from Cleveland, Chicago, Baltimore, St. Louis, Wilmington, and even Kansas City with the expressed intention of modeling a Home after it.[10] It is doubtful, however, that its widespread reputation was sufficient to motivate old people to trek across country to find refuge within its walls, even though on occasion there was such an occurrence. Indeed, it was designed to meet the needs of the Philadelphia community. Though an occasional resident came from afar, the Home was not a place of refuge for those who might be unworthy venturers from far-off places. The HAICP was founded during the Civil War, but its establishment was not in anticipation of migrant elderly slaves, as some supporters later claimed. Adequate safeguards imposed by the entrance requirements insured that residents had a history of hard work and previous independence, substantiated by adequate testimonials and respectable references. By 1953 residents were required to have lived at least one year in Delaware, Montgomery, or Philadelphia counties.[11] In all, about twenty-two hundred residents were accommodated by the HAICP between 1864 and 1953, 78 percent female, 22 percent male.[12]

There was an age requirement for admission that changed from fifty in 1864 to sixty-five by 1910, but the residents' average age between these years was over seventy-five, well above the minimum age requirement. Over time the average age of entrants actually declined. In the early years the old remained at home or with relatives longer, but changes in occupational patterns and family nucleation due to modernization eventually brought residents to the Home at an earlier age. The blind and crippled (whose condition presented no threat to other residents) were accepted regardless of age, though the HAICP generally conformed to the standard practice of accepting well or healthy persons; those who developed incurable diseases or mental illnesses were removed to the almshouse, the Home for Incurables in Philadelphia, or Norristown State Hospital (see chapter 6). The great majority of residents were under life care contracts, an agreement between the resident and the Home that the HAICP would provide basic necessities and burial in exchange for an admission fee and all personal property (see copy of agreement in appendix). The Home accepted boarders, and a few chose this status, which they considered offered them more independence.

There were only fourteen boarders between 1865 and 1900, twenty-one between 1865 and 1935. After Social Security legislation was enacted, boarders became more numerous because they could pay with old-age assistance checks, but before this time the life care contract offered a great deal more security. It was significant that the Home made this allowances even if few took advantage of it, perhaps because the rules placed boarders in a precarious position. According to one regulation: "No boarder shall be received or continued in the Home to the exclusion of those entirely dependent. Two weeks notice, however must be given for removal of any boarder."[13] Since the published reports seldom gave separate listing, probably to avoid invidious distinctions, there were probably more boarders than have been identified. Three of the fourteen located before 1900 died within the first six months of their stay, another lived about two years, two left, and one has been lost to history. Two others, Margaret Cuff and Isaiah Cropper, lived in the Home eight and four years respectively. The remaining five before 1900, and four of the seven afterward, converted to life care residents. Most likely, Cuff and Cropper also changed over, even though nothing has been found in the records showing that they did.

The pattern was to change from boarder to inmate during the first six months of residency rather than exhaust funds that could be used to purchase life care.[14] Board money, at a rate of $2.50 a month in 1865, $35.00 in 1930, and $85.00 in 1950, could not be applied retroactively toward the required admission fee. However, those who entered as permanent residents and decided to leave during the six-month probation period were returned the admission fee minus board during their stay. Entering as a boarder, then, served no ostensible advantage and was financially prohibitive.

Since private patients today often are required to exhaust their resources before seeking public assistance, the conversion from boarder to inmate has its counterpart in modern nursing Homes.[15] Sometimes those who lacked the foresight to seek approval of their conversion to life care residents exhausted funds that could have paid for their permanent stay. For one, sickness unexpectedly exhausted funds, and the Board of Managers found themselves with a boarder without money. Treated the same way as suspensions, these residents were placed in private homes with a month's rent paid by the HAICP. Unless, of course, a benefactor stepped forward to pay for a life care contract.[16]

After the passage of the Social Security Act, a resident could enter by agreeing to pay old-age assistance money to the Home while he or she received an allowance. Life care contracts were ended with the Hobart Jackson administration in 1949, although he inherited primarily life care residents. Essentially all residents were boarders with the abolition of life care. Of course, as mentioned in chapter 3, some states refused assistance to life care residents. Jackson believed that the requirement that residents relinquish all their property was "manifestly unfair," but by Jackson's time, the concept of life care had outlived its usefulness because total indigence was removed with Social Security.[17] In other words, the assumption of public responsibility for the care of elderly citizens rendered life care contracts outmoded. In the earlier era, however, without it many would have been deprived of institutional care because a monthly payment was beyond their means. Boarder-to-"inmate" conversion testified to that fact as strongly as private-to-public conversions today serve as testimony to the need to reform the present health care system to provide reasonable long-term care to nursing Home patients.

The HAICP was not stigmatized as the poorhouse or almshouse, even though indigence was an important factor in the decision to move into the Home. Where relatives existed, they did not view moving into a Home as a severance of family ties or affection, and thus they did not experience the guilt normally attached to institutionalization; for them, the move was merely a change of residence. The managers did not share this view; their social philosophy dictated that children must be responsible for the care of elderly parents and grandparents at home if at all possible. Managers felt compelled in 1902,

> to emphasize . . . the sacredness of the obligation which children owe their parents and they should not too readily shift this obligation, when age and infirmity overtake them, upon an institution, however wide its doors might be open. Those who have children comparatively well-to-do, are not we think, legitimately beneficiaries of its bounty. Friendlessness should be implied when an application for admission to the Home is made.[18]

Records seldom depicted the family structure of residents or provided information on relatives that could be used to generalize about the family support system before entrance into the Home. Applications for sixteen males and fifty-seven females from 1898 to 1918 indicated that 66 percent were widowed, 22 percent were single, and 12 percent were married, though only 4 percent listed a spouse by name. Probably, some of those who claimed to be married were without a mate, not having undergone the formalities of divorce or having experienced desertion. Although useful conclusions may be questioned from such small numbers, males were more than four times as likely to be married as females, over 31 percent compared with 7 percent and almost 72 percent of the women were widowed compared with about 44 percent of the men. The percentages of unmarried, either single or widowed, approached 88 percent, the overwhelming majority. As for residents with relatives other than a spouse, 23 percent listed a son or daughter, 5 percent a brother or sister, 11 percent a niece or nephew, and 8 percent a cousin or in-law. Forty-nine percent of the applicants were without relatives.[19] A breakdown in the family support system and its attendant consequences were probably the most insistent reasons, then, that residents came to the HAICP.

Although there were a handful of former slaves and a few distinguished personalities (among the latter were Madame Selika Williams and William

Forten), most of the "legitimate beneficiaries" of the HAICP were former domestics who had worked in the homes of wealthy White Philadelphia families. The records are clear on this point. For example, the annual report for 1897 noted that the inmates "long and faithful services in the homes where they were once indispensable entitle them to the ease and comfort which they find here."[20] References and sponsors also bear out this fact. One rule read: "No person will be admitted in the Home but such as bring satisfactory testimonial of the propriety of their [sic] conduct and the respectability of their [sic] character."[21] Preserved in the Home's records from 1865 to 1904 are the names of the 418 references or sponsors that constitute references for over 61 percent of the residents.[22] Fewer than 3 percent were referred to the HAICP by a son or daughter and fewer than 2 percent were referred by other relatives. Since 47 percent had at least one living relative, it is fair to say that relatives were evidently not in a position to attest to applicants' conduct or character. Seventy-one percent or 297 of the references were individuals of unknown relationship, but indications are that they were often former employees. Some held life memberships in the Association; others were annual members or contributors. Wealthy Quakers—Mary Jeanes, Anna Jeanes, Sarah Marshall, and Mary Johnson—were among this group. Ninety, or 22 percent, of these referees were individuals who were or had served on the Board. About half this group were Black managers, especially William Still, the Campbells (Jabez and Mary), Margaret Jones, and Henrietta Duterte. Twelve, or 3 percent, were referred by a minister, and the two remaining were referred by a "Friend."[23]

These individuals were not mere referees but sponsors. Their interests were strong and long lasting, as attachments between domestics and their wealthy benefactors remained after the formal relationship had severed. Sponsors were often responsible for admission fees and maintained an active interest in these old people, visiting them, bringing them items such as food or medicine (both against the rules), listening to their problems, and in general looking out for their welfare. These individuals were particularly visible when problems arose and they sought to determine why residents were dissatisfied or dismissed. Sponsors sometimes negotiated separate graves or buried erstwhile domestics at their expense.[24] To some extent, they acted as ombudsmen do today, investigating complaints, reporting them to the Board of Managers, and in general looking out for the welfare of residents. Unlike ombudsman these individuals were paternalistically expected to control the residents whom they sponsored, that is, to encourage residents to comply with the rules. Overall, the sponsors looked out for residents' interests outside the Home and must have been a tremendous source of psychological comfort to those who had entrusted their lives to other people and were otherwise without family in a potentially despotic environment.

The administrative structure also reflected the biracial beginning of the Home. As previously stated, the residents were Black, the Board of Managers, with traditional officers, was composed of Blacks and Whites, males and females. The Board was chosen at an annual Association meeting composed of life members who paid a minimum twenty-five dollar fee and annual contributors who paid at least two dollars.[25] In the early years interested groups of Quakers, Orthodox and Hicksite, Black leaders, and important Philadelphians from all walks of life attended these affairs, inspecting the Home, visiting with erstwhile domestics, and chatting with old friends. This was perhaps the only institution where Hicksite and Orthodox Quakers, who had split in 1828, set aside their ideological differences, placing the welfare of aged Black Philadelphians above personal religious preferences. As we shall see, this unselfish behavior was characteristic of Quaker participation in the HAICP.

The Board acted in its administrative capacity through committees chosen from among its members (see organizational structure in appendix). There were three standing committees created in 1864, an all-male committee on property and finance, an all-female committee on management, and a supply committee composed of both sexes.[26] According to the constitution, the men and women were given separate responsibilities, "the twelve men constituting a committee to have charge of real estate and finances of the Home and the women shall be a committee on its internal arrangements."[27] While men and women served on the Board of Managers, the committee structure divided responsibilities to conform to societal divisions of labor based on gender.

Although the constitution provided for an equal number of males and females, it did not require any particular racial distribution. Nevertheless, the twenty-four member Board was initially composed of an equal number of Whites and Blacks. Stephen Smith, who was elected vice president in 1864, was the first Black officer. William Still succeeded to the vice presidency after Smith's death in 1873 and went on to become president after the death of the Quaker Dillwyn Parrish in 1887. Still held the post until he died in 1901 and was undoubtedly the most influential African American in the early years of the HAICP's administration. In 1894 the *Christian Recorder* noted that "the name of William Still will perpetuate itself no less in the efficient management of this Home than in his admirable conductorship of the underground railroad."[28] Real estate broker S. J. M. Brock served as vice president from 1908 to 1915, but Still was the only Black to become president. With the decrease in Quaker influence in the Home and the diminution of their population at large, the Board became increasingly dominated by Blacks. In 1938, for example, there were nine Whites and twenty-one Blacks on the Board.[29]

At no time was there a female president, vice president, or treasurer. The officers were all male until 1908 when Sarah Chambers became secretary. In 1923 this same dedicated Quaker spinster invaded the all-male domain of the finance committee. No African American was treasurer or secretary, and White men dominated the important committees, particularly property and finance. Blacks dominated such committees as religious affairs and interments. At the same time, the management committee, which oversaw the internal affairs of the HAICP, was exclusively female. In summary, despite Quaker egalitarianism and the interracial makeup of the Board, the organizational structure reflected in some ways the racist and sexist characteristics of the environment in which it was created.[30]

The Board made all major decisions, but the management committee, subdivided into a house, a visiting, and a clothing committee, actually ran the Home through a live-in matron. A few male Board members were always in and out of the HAICP, but except for the women who made weekly, sometimes daily visits, the Board frequently made decisions based on impression or secondhand information. The quality of care to be provided to residents, for example, divided the Board, which yielded to demands to increase the size of the resident population. The number of old people went from 20 in 1871 to 67 in 1875. After reaching 112 in 1884, the management committee expressed the enlightened opinion . . .

> that the Board [should] decide upon the *number* of inmates which constitute the family—and let it be *positive*—for we are fully satisfied a larger *family* than the present one would not be only unmanageable—but would take away the *feature* that makes it a *Home* in the true sense of the *word* for in a Home each member should be the *special care of our* head [,] otherwise it soon degenerates into *machinery*" [their emphasis].[31]

Clearly, women managers, from the vantage point of the management committee, were in a better position than the men were to understand problems, and they sought to provide care beyond the old people's physical needs, or they sought to provide in Ethel McClure's words "more than a roof." Nevertheless, the number of residents continued to increase, reaching 111 in 1894 and 138 by the turn of the century, where it remained until the hardships of the depression reduced the number of residents to about a third of the normal capacity.

In spite of the Home's division of responsibilities by gender, the number of women volunteers continued to increase. In 1875 a cooperative committee was created to help relieve the management committee of its many duties and to accommodate the large number of supporters.[32] At first, it was composed of six members, including two men, but by 1877 it had become all female. The cooperative committee grew rapidly but bore no constitutional relationship to the Board. It was a cadre of women who, in addition to doing much of the actual work in the Home, formed a training ground for female Board members, since the practice developed of replacing vacancies on the Board based on seniority on the cooperative committee. The result was an important screening process that sent capable and experienced women to the Board of Managers while filtering out the unsatisfactory before they gained any influence in the decision-making process. Although the committee was important in that it attracted women from the community who worked with the Home on a trial basis before making a full commitment to Board participation, those who remained became discontented with their second-class status. They did the work while they exercised no authority at Board meetings. In January 1907 their discontent reached Board level, and the solicitor was instructed to determine the steps necessary to give them full standing. The secretary noted that these women were "regular in their attendance to Board meetings, as faithful in their duties as are Board members, but without authority."[33] The next year the Constitution was amended to accommodate forty Board members (thirty-one women and nine men at the time) with no mention of male-female distribution or representation.[34] Significantly, these women refused to accept their exploitation, and though men continued to hold key positions despite the large number of women, the absorption of the cooperative committee reflects Black and Quaker women's historic role outside "the cult of true womanhood" as well as women's growing consciousness in the late nineteenth and early twentieth centuries.

Employees were generally African American, though the first matron was White, coming to the HAICP from Pennsylvania Hospital, where she was assistant matron, and on occasions other Whites were hired. The live-in matron was the chief employee in whose hands the residents' welfare was entrusted. Even though she exercised little administrative authority, the matron had the power to make residents' lives meaningful or miserable. The essential attributes of a good matron were described in 1884 after controversy forced the appointment of the new matron. The Board asked for cooperation from employees and described a successful operation in the following manner: "The requisite qualifications for a successful administration in an institution of this kind, are system combined with forethought, a firm, kind and gentle spirit, manifest in the matrons intercourse with these old people, thus winning their affection, confidence and respect."[35] The job, however, required patience, tact, understanding, and a deep concern for the well-being of old people. Otherwise, only the visiting committee served formally as the countervailing force to the potential despotism of the matron. It was its duty to steer an even course between matron and residents, which required the ability to extract fact from fancy without insulting the matron and without leaving legitimate grievances unadjusted.

The matron's position experienced frequent turnover, but the attrition rate was especially high for some jobs and seemed to have been related to the degree of contact with the residents. Between 1865, when the first matron was hired, up to 1938, when the institution employed its first superintendent, there were about a dozen matrons. Those with the longest tenure in this arduous position were Ann Laws (1868–79), Charlotte Riker (1889–98), Mary Dixon (1913–29), and Alma Briscoe (1929–38). After a restructuring in 1938, a superintendent was hired, but it is unclear whether the matron's position was discontinued or merely stripped of its authority. Both Riker and Laws became inmates in the HAICP after their "retirement," but Laws went full circle from Board member to matron to resident. Her forced resignation in 1879 was a sad occasion:

> Should any of you spend the same length of time feeling a warm heart and live in your work and your habits fixed by years of labor in a single direction you may feel as I do that there is nothing earthly more distressing than to be compelled to resign at the age of [80 inserted in the record in pencil] years which I do.[36]

Laws was forced to leave her post because of her poor health. A year earlier the Board had hired a housekeeper to "lighten the labor" of their "worthy matron," but when the housekeeper died, Laws was replaced.[37] In 1883 the management committee again requested a housekeeper or assistant matron because, as they put it, "the labors of the matron are too onerous for one person."[38] The committee hardly overstated the case, and there is some indication that Law's health was adversely affected by her work. That seems also to have been true of Belinda Jackson, who died in 1884 of a nervous condition at age fifty-seven, and Charlotte Riker, who later suffered from a mental illness that made her violent, forcing her to be sent to Norristown State Hospital. At the doctor's recommendation, the matrons during the 1890s and 1900s took frequent and extended leaves (two to three weeks) from their arduous duties to protect their health, but the Board only partially bore the financial responsibility for these long reprieves.[39]

After the matron and assistant matron, the major employees may be divided into two categories, viz., those who had little or no interaction with the residents and those who constantly interacted with them. The former category included the cooks and baker who prepared the food, the laundry worker who cleaned residents' clothes, and the engineer who was responsible for the smooth operation of the physical plant. The seamstress interacted with residents more often than others did in this group, and she often succeeded to the matron's position. The latter category was composed of nurses, porters, orderlies, aides, and chambermaids, who were responsible for caring for the sick, including carrying meals, cleaning rooms, making beds, and bathing and dressing residents as well as a wide range of other activities that helped the aged and infirmed and maintained the sanitary aspects of the Home. The jobs in the former category did not experience rapid turnover. For example, there was only one baker between 1901 and 1938, and there were only four engineers during the period from 1886 to 1940. Although there were exceptions (Caroline Woody was nurse from 1874 to 1898 and Charles Hammond served as a nurse's aide from 1891 to 1905), those who worked closely with the elderly inmates came and went like birds of passage. Managers were in an incessant search for suitable employees, and residents' self-esteem must have suffered from the never-ending adjustment to new faces and different personalities posed by constant employee turnover.

These jobs were burdensome and depressing, requiring the aforementioned qualities of patience, understanding, and human compassion. These traits were rare among the employees the Board recruited because there was little opportunity for employee training. Thus, there was a constant cry for good help, but the matter was essentially out of the Board's control. Problems of insubordination to authority, quarreling with matron or residents, inattention to duties, and inefficiency or unsatisfactory work were commonplace. Occasionally a nurse or orderly had to be dismissed for striking a resident as was the case of the nurse Addie for striking "Aunt Cassie" after "getting out of patience."[40] The Board sought to determine the character of potential employees before hiring them and to retain workers on a probationary period. Even the matron after 1885 had to be approved each month until she had proven herself capable of handling her "onerous position." Another solution offered was to hire "older people" who "would be more likely to have an interest in the aged members of the family."[41] There is no evidence that the Board ever systematically applied any of these proposed solutions.

The absence of a fixed salary schedule for each position and a systematic method of promotion contributed to the turnover problem. Salary and mobility were left to the discretion of the visiting committee, or more accurately the management committee, a practice that sometimes undermined the authority of the matron. In 1874 the matron earned $20.00 a month, but by 1910 the matron at the time earned $50.00 a month, and by 1930 she earned $100.00 a month. Typically, nurses in the HAICP at the turn of the century earned $4.00 a week or $20.00 a month while orderlies and aides in the infirmary were paid $4.00 a week or $18.00 a month. The nurses' salaries were raised to at least $7.00 a week in 1909 because the matron felt they "needed more pay to get good help."[42] The cook in 1910 earned $32.00 a week, an amount he received only after he threatened to quit. At the lowest rung of the financial ladder were the seamstress at about $3.00 a week in 1910, the chambermaids at an average of $3.25 a week, and laundry workers who were paid from $2.50 to $3.00 a week.[43] Although salaries were low across the board, those who worked closest with the relatives tended to earn slightly higher salaries, but these small discrepancies failed to raise morale and could hardly stem the massive turnover in the HAICP. Being at the beck and call of the sick and infirm therefore had few pecuniary rewards, and the personnel problems that constantly plagued the HAICP beset the operation of nursing Homes today.

Comparative data are hard to find, but it does seem that the HAICP was efficiently operated. The St. Luke's Home for Aged Women of New York had 86 residents that they maintained at an annual cost of $14,653 between 1893 and 1904. The cost of maintaining 116 residents in the HAICP in 1890 was $16,391 while it cost $24,484 to care for 138 residents in 1910. Perhaps more meaningful is the per resident cost, which was $190 in 1890, $274 in 1903, and $284 in 1904 in the St. Luke's Home. Per resident cost in the HAICP was $78 in 1880 but virtually doubled to $141 in 1890. By 1910 it had increased to $177 per person, which was still substantially less than the per capita cost of operating St. Luke's Home.[44] The correlation between cost and quality of care is not perfect, but these numbers do indicate that the HAICP's operation was cost effective.

The consciousness of women that had led to the inclusion of cooperative committee members as full-fledged Board members carried over into the operation of the HAICP. While women accepted gender demarcations in the responsibilities of the Board, they were determined not to allow sex discrimination in the treatment of residents. The issue of tobacco use illustrates the demand for equal treatment of male and female inmates. Although both sexes considered the use of tobacco evil and filthy, managers allowed male residents to use tobacco in specific areas of the Home (at least as early as 1890 men were using tobacco freely), accepted it among its donations, and bought it along with other supplies. Even though women managers faced the added problem of having tobacco juice spat all over the sitting rooms and would rather have had its use prohibited altogether, they vehemently objected to the Board's discriminatory policy and repeatedly pointed out the sexism of this practice. In July 1896 the Board relinquished to female managers, giving women residents the same privilege as men regarding the use of tobacco, but added the admonition that they should not smoke in bed.[45] It is significant that women put their

4: "But she was white" 123

philosophical belief in the equality of the sexes above their consideration of tobacco use as an evil and unhealthy habit.

The division of responsibilities by sex, however, inevitably led to conflict. When the mode of communicating problems to the Board broke down, tension between men and women occasionally flared because of the structure of the administration. In 1885 matron Esther Barnes resigned under pressure, charged with neglect of duties and maltreatment of residents. An investigation of the charges led to some damaging criticisms of Barnes and dictated a change in administration.[46] Nevertheless, the women felt part of the problem was the attitude of the Board itself, especially the male members who were "too ready to believe reports" without substantiating "them to be true." In their report women managers noted:

> That there should be dissension in the Board is not only unfortunate but sad and seemingly unnecessary. It is not to be expected that we would view all matters in just the same light, but surely the one subject at heart viz., the comfort of those under our care, we should be able to discuss the situation without personal prejudice.[47]

The gender division of responsibilities within the administration of the Home led to the manifestation of functional problems in sexual terms, all of which could have been avoided by the minimal requirement that men serve on the committee on management. Of course, that would have required an attack on the traditional spheres of what constituted men's work and women's work. Nevertheless, the friction within the administration would have been simply between the management committee and the Board, not between women and men. But here was a male-dominated Board that made policy while the committee on management, composed of women, was entrusted to carry out its decisions. When men like William Still, H. M. Laing, and Israel Johnson demonstrated their vigorous interest, they were thrust into the position of looking over the women's shoulders. At annual meetings, religious gatherings, holiday celebrations, Board day, or just ordinary visits, male managers listened to old peoples' complaints—just and unjust. When the allegations were discussed with employees or brought up at Board meetings, women felt the men had not only overstepped their authority but also solicited negative complaints. They stated their position in 1890.

> All right-minded members of this Board must feel that it is out of the province of this Board to go to the inmates of this Home and under-employees, and question them as to the actions of the superior officers, and then and there make charges upon them, within the hearing of the inmates, [it] is an insult to

which our matron and housekeeper should not be subjected. Yet this they have had to bear.[48]

According to the investigation, Esther Barnes was inattentive to the sick and undignified in her actions, and she held the residents in low esteem. According to the minutes: "There seems to be an unfortunate impression among them that the matron thinks them of but little account, and that whenever any are sick the sooner they die the better."[49] There was no mention that Barnes was White, even though there is reason to believe her color was part of the problem. There seemed to have been an organized silence, almost a conspiracy of silence, about race in the management of the HAICP, in spite of, or perhaps because of its interracial character. The only direct reference to race in the internal records preceded Barnes's dismissal by a year, as one female inmate expressed to the visiting committee that "she had no fault to find with the matron, that she was kind and careful of them, *but she was white*" (emphasis in original).[50] No doubt this rare remark was the tip of the racial iceberg in the HAICP. Particularly in light of increasing anti-Black thought in the United States and systematic segregation in the southern states. The records clearly showed need for greater vigilance by women managers, and Barnes's criticisms were never seriously contested. As a matter of fact, women admitted "some trifling failings," after having at one time visited the matron at a "most unpropitious time." Perhaps here is the clue to the problem. The unannounced visits of the male managers were more effective in uncovering problems than the planned visits of the management committee. (Perhaps a point that should not be lost on present-day ombudsmen). The concern to the women, however, was not the charges per se, but the improper channels by which complaints reached the Board.

In 1889 William Still, who had brought the residents' accusations against Barnes, brought charges against Mary Jordan, the housekeeper, accusing her of neglect and mistrust. An investigation by the committee on management found that there "was no sufficient ground to censure Mary Jordan, but believe her to be industrious and efficient, and that her character for honesty as far as we know is unexceptional."[51] Complaints continued to find their way to the Board, skirting the visiting committee and embroiling the Board in acrid discussions. In 1890 the matron, Malinda Brown, who had succeeded Esther Barnes, and Mary Jordan each resigned. At their April meeting, which always preceded that of the full Board, the women, now disgusted, requested a statement of feeling to be presented to the Board of Managers. Written by Sarah Pennock, a towering figure in the Home's management, the paper reflected, to some extent, the growing consciousness of women engendered by the club and suffrage movements. Taking the position that men "were doing what they know nothing about" the paper explained clearly the dissension within the Board:

> The women managers after a cool deliberation in body assembled, feel that the Home has suffered for the want of a cool, clear unprejudiced judgement on the part of some of our officers. The Board meetings have been so undignified, disorderly and unChristian, and the character of the women for good judgment so compromised, that we feel the Home has sustained a serious loss. The matron and housekeeper are placed there by the *Board* and by the Board should be supported and strengthened in the performance of their arduous duties, and if they do not fill their places in a becoming and proper manner, and the said Board should quickly investigate, free from prejudice, and if the trouble cannot be removed then should the Board take means to supply their places . . . It is supposed that a company of intelligent, thoughtful women and good housekeepers, who have charge of the Home, and who faithfully, attend to the comfort of its inmates, visiting it always weekly, and sometimes daily, going into every part of the House, *Should be as capable of judging what is right as for men who know but little of the difficulties, and only gain what they know from a few old people who take the cue of their answers from the manner in which the questions are put.* [my emphasis][52]

The Board rejected the paper as "too strong," but the problem had been aired and the extent of the female managers' discontent was now out in the open.

To some extent, these comments were aimed at William Still, who evidently was used for channeling complaints between the residents and the Board, bypassing the accepted mode of communication through the visiting committee. Race was probably one reason residents chose Still to communicate their problems, but this was not the entire explanation because the Quaker Israel Johnson and others were sometimes used for this purpose. Moreover, Black women composed a large part of the membership of the management committee. Perhaps it was racial identity and the traditional leadership and authority roles attributed to males. Then too, some residents complained to anybody who would listen, and Still, Johnson, Laing, and others afforded them plenty of opportunity.

In a more recent study, Comilda Weinstock and Ruth Bennett found that the lines of communication in a racially mixed nursing Home tended to reflect the positions held by residents' counterparts on the outside. In their study Blacks complained to Black nurses while Whites sought out the White administrator and secretary. Although the proper mode of communication was to nurses, these positions of authority held by Blacks were bypassed by Whites because they would not have held such positions over Whites on the outside. For the most part, the study confirmed the assumption "that it is easier to adapt to a new milieu and the communication processes within it when it parallels the larger society."[53] If this is so, Whites who held power inside and outside the HAICP should not have been sidetracked.

Undoubtedly, residents bypassed the management committee because it was composed of females, even going around its Black members. Since women did not hold positions of power on the Board, it is possible that the visiting committee was not perceived as a reliable method of seeking redress and was bypassed in favor of those in authority, preferably males. The communication patterns in the HAICP, therefore, reflected the racist and sexist structure of the institution. If organizations naturally tend to reflect the realities of the larger society, it is necessary that nursing Homes and other institutions develop means of resolving residents' problems in ways that reject prevailing racist and sexist assumptions; they must develop processes that demonstrate effectiveness in a racially and sexually diverse group while resisting conformance to historical patterns of discrimination.

In 1892 the Board acknowledged that the women had a special relationship with the residents: "The minutes of the Household committee show a relationship existing between them and the old people, that secures with but few exceptions, a feeling of contentment and mutual confidence. Wants are looked into, and as far as practicable supplied; complaints are heard and considered."[54] Nevertheless, the management committee remained exclusively female until 1948 when Hobart Jackson, the Home's new administrator, eliminated it altogether. He retained its subcommittee on House that took on an ad hoc status with membership chosen without regard to gender or race.[55]

The HAICP was administered by an interracial group of Blacks and Whites, males and females, in a society becoming increasingly anti-Black and anti-old. Its organizational structure in some ways reflected the prejudices of the larger society, and these attitudes occasionally crept into its operation, manifesting themselves in the Home's grievance process, administrative network, communication process, and employment patterns. However, it was the good fortune of the residents of the HAICP that administrators willingly put personal philosophies and prejudices aside in the interest of their elderly charge. It is to their credit, particularly the women who rejected their own exploitation and demanded equal treatment for female residents, that these outside forces were resisted. The historical perspectives provided by the management of the HAICP should help all those who operate or work in institutions today, administrators and ombudsmen in particular, better able to care for their charge. How these factors and others affected the daily lives and health care of the residents constitute the topics of the next two chapters.

Profile of Residents

There were more than twenty-two hundred residents served by the HAICP between 1864 and 1953. They were overwhelmingly female, 78 percent, unmarried, 88 percent, but probably had a living relative, 51 percent. The typical resident was about seventy-five years old, lived somewhere in Philadelphia, but migrated there, more than likely from Virginia or Maryland. Although she was uneducated, she brought a history of hard work and industry, often testified to by a former employer who chose to sponsor her. She came in robust condition but sometimes suffered from chronic ailments or blindness. Upon arrival, she was given a room that she shared with at least one other person, but most often with several individuals. No formal induction procedure or orientation program was used to introduce her to congregate life; she was left on her own to adjust to her social situation. Here she remained until her death before the fifth year, often within the first year, but she outlived her male counterpart, who occupied the fourth floor. She came to the Home under a life care arrangement, but on occasion she chose to be a boarder, in which case she often converted to a life care resident, making her decision within the first six months. Deaths and admissions in the HAICP averaged about nineteen per year, maintaining a resident population around 135.

The following vignettes were chosen to reflect the types of residents that were served by the HAICP. The quotes in the descriptions are taken from the annual reports.

Ester Becket (1781–1873)

At age eighty-four when she entered the Home, Ester Becket was a strong and able-bodied woman. She was evidently as strong in character as she was in body. The matron writes: "She knew no rule but her own will, which she said she brought with her." For four months preceding her death in July 1873, she suffered greatly, confining herself to her room. Her death, however, was peaceful and happy. Again the matron noted: "She expressed regret at having said many unkind things to those about her; she now loved every one and was glad to hear that I have nothing in my heart against her." Ester Becket died 25 July 1873 at the age of ninety-two.

Emmareta Murphy (1798-1870)

This resident, a native of New Jersey, came to the Home in May 1865 at age sixty-seven. Mrs. Murphy, a former slave, suffered constantly from a blow to the head that she received from her master. As a result the matron explained that "she very frequently felt giddiness and dimness of sight." Except for God's will, Emmareta Murphy felt that she would be driven mad by the pain, which she bore with patience and quiet. Her speech was "so thick" that she communicated more often by her motions. Mrs. Murphy often requested an end to her head pain so that she may enter the Father's house. She died 17 January 1870.

Mary Edwards (1770–1874)

One of several native Africans who spent their last days in the Home, Mary Edwards was said to have arrived in Philadelphia from Santo Domingo "about the time of the insurrection." Although she came as a slave and worked as a domestic, she spent over half a century as a vendor of ground-nut cakes at Third and Market and Second and Pine Streets. A deeply religious woman and a devoted Catholic, reputedly over 100 years old at the time of her death, Mary Edwards was one of dozens of centenarians who lived in the Home. She died 2 October 1874 at age 104.

Phyllis Hogwood (1777–1882)

"Aunt Phyllis," had a clear mind and good sight throughout her life, sewing and reading without spectacles. The care she received in the Home was a great source of happiness and cheer to her, expressing "eternal gratitude for the providential situation she occupied in the Home." She entered 5 August 1875. "Grandmother Hogwood" was a constant Bible reader and hymn singer who performed these duties as a sacred obligation to her fellow residents. Blessed with a remarkable memory, she would reminisce about the incidents in her eventful life to the delight of visitors. They often noted the ease with which she seemed to recall incidents from a vast storehouse of experiences. Such recollections seemed to energize the fragile body of a woman who found great comfort in the expectation of an everlasting life. Her demeanor was exemplary:

> It is not too much to assume that the influence of her orderly life and strong faith had a very potent effect in strengthening and encouraging many others in their advanced years. Unmistakably it had the effect of increasing the pleasure and interest of the managers, as they observed her thankful spirit and were assured that they had her gratitude. In this gentle and Christlike spirit she entered the Home and in this self-same spirit she constantly lived and let her light shine, until her final change arrived.

Phyllis Hogwood died on 16 July 1882 at age 105.

Lucy Taylor (1800–1880)

Mrs. Taylor was one of the few boarders who lived in the Home, entering 18 September 1879. These individuals could pay their own way rather than enter on a life care basis. After fifty-five years as a domestic in a wealthy Philadelphia family, she was able to accumulate more than four thousand dollars, paying her board with the interest from this money. She came to the Home to enjoy "the pure air of the country and the beautiful scenery." After a stay of less than six months, Mrs. Taylor became ill and died, leaving her fortune to the Home—"so deeply impressed was she with the excellence of the Institution, and the desire to do her share towards benefitting her own race." In her death she exemplified faith, joy, and resignation to her Heavenly father's will, and left a memory of kindness to all around her. Her will was contested, but the Home won in court.

Hannah Todd (1786–1890)

Hannah Todd was born a slave in Missouri and came to Philadelphia in 1854 via the underground railroad, having been taken from her mistress while traveling in the North. She was eternally grateful, expressing appreciation "to her kind friends for their intercession in her behalf." Hannah Todd had seven masters, one of which she said, "traded me for a wagon," because she had rheumatism and was unable to work. Her first master, "a very poor man," was the cruelest. She recalled: "I was treated by this man more [like a dog] than a human being, fed like a dog from a wooden trough, and slept alone in an outhouse some distance from one occupied by the family."

For many years after her freedom, Hannah Todd worked for the Gillingham family of Philadelphia, faithfully discharging her duties. A member of Bethel African Methodist Episcopal Church, she was a deeply religious person who remained steadfast in her faith through many bitter and varied experiences. Hannah Todd entered the Home on 13 November 1882 and died at age 104, 10 December 1890.

Annie G. Stout (18__–1909)

Mrs. Stout was born in Chester County, Pennsylvania, and was said to have been educated in the public schools. In 1866 she and her husband, married in 1843, moved to Philadelphia and found employment in the dental offices of Dr. Edwin T. Darby. In 1878 Mrs. Stout was engaged by Dr. James Truman in the supervision and distribution of materials to dental students at the University of Pennsylvania. Along with other duties it was her responsibility to provide each student with all materials and medicines in the operative clinic, receiving the costs when sheets of gold were involved. For twenty-seven years she performed these duties, earning her the nickname "Golden Annie." The kindness, honesty, and ability of this devoutly religious woman endeared her to all the students.

> Her days of toil were not those calling for brilliant deeds, but one to enforce the beauty of simple life and its power to compel admiration in all classes of men; such was exemplified in the fulfillment of the daily duties by Annie G. Stout. . . . who always had a cheery words for the disturbed student.

When age stripped Mrs. Stout of her strength, faculty and students raised money for her admission to the HAICP. She died 26 September 1909.

Mary McDonald (1770–1900)

At the ripe age of 118 Mary McDonald entered the Home in December 1887. She was in good health, having all her faculties, and spent her time sewing carpet rags. She was born a slave near Valley Forge and claimed to recall the years 1777 and 1778 when the Revolutionary forces were camped at Valley Forge. On one occasion, the soldiers came to the home where she was a slave girl, and she directed them to find food and received a word of praise from George Washington—"God bless you, little one, you have done well for me and my men, may you live long and do well."

This account raised some questions about her age. Representatives from the Daughters of the American Revolution (DAR) visited Mary McDonald and found her account to be substantially correct. She died on 29 April 1900 at age 130.

William Forten (1823–1909)

William Forten was grandson of the famous African American sail maker James Forten of Philadelphia. He entered the Home 6 April 1898, promising to end his interest in political affairs because managers felt these activities would require his staying out late at night. Forten immediately took up his old ways, staying three days away from the institution without permission. Managers were upset that he continued his old habits after assuring them that he would "come under rules for the benefit of the aged and infirm." His family background notwithstanding, they felt no partiality should be shown Mr. Forten.

These were short-lived misgivings because Forten turned his attention to the welfare of those in the Home. He read and talked to the old men individually and in groups, turning their thoughts away from themselves to other matters such as politics, even teaching them the importance of the franchise and to reject the political machines that were buying votes. His adjustment so pleased the matron and managers that they felt the Home had lost one of it's most positive influences when he died on 8 March 1909.

Stephen Smith Home for the Aged, Philadelphia, Pa. Photo courtesy of the Home.

Parker Memorial Chapel, built in 1894 by Edward Parker, Stephen Smith Home for the Aged, Philadelphia. Photo courtesy of the Home.

Kitchen, Stephen Smith Home for the Aged, Philadelphia, Pa. Photo courtesy of the Home.

Bedroom, Stephen Smith Home for the Aged, Philadelphia, Pa. Photo courtesy of the Home.

Lavatory and bathroom at Stephen Smith Home for the Aged, Philadelphia, Pa. Photo courtesy of the Home.

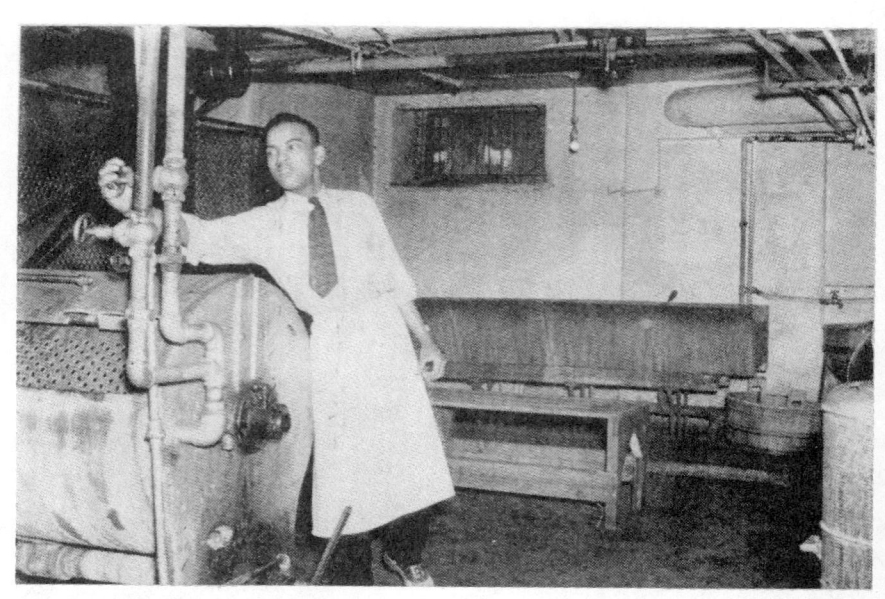

Laundry room, Stephen Smith Home for the Aged, Philadelphia, Pa. Photo courtesy of the Home.

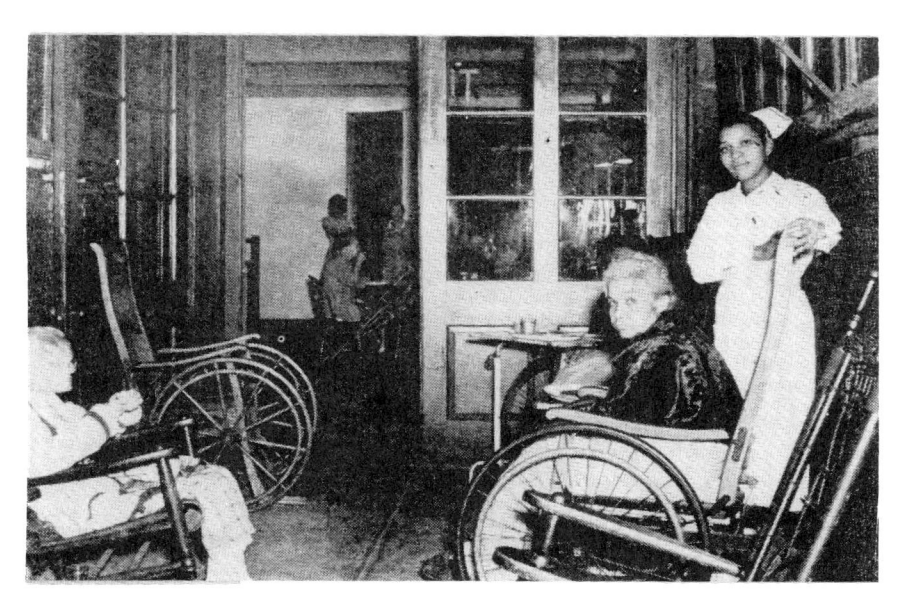

Sun porch, Stephen Smith Home for the Aged, Philadelphia, Pa. Photo courtesy of the Home.

Dining room, Stephen Smith Home for the Aged, Philadelphia, Pa. Photo courtesy of the Home.

Stephen Smith (1795–1783) was a founder of the Home for Aged and Infirm Colored Persons who left his estate to the Home, which adopted his name in 1953. Photo courtesy of the Home.

Edward Parker (1821–1887) left his estate to build an old age home for his aged Black "scholars." The money was used to enlarge the Home for Aged and Infirm Colored Persons and to construct a chapel, rather than a separate Home which his executor thought would not survive. Photo courtesy of the Home.

William Still, of Underground Railroad fame, was the only African American to become president of the Home for Aged and Infirm Colored Persons, serving from 1881 to 1901. Photo courtesy of Charles L. Blockson, Temple University.

Juliette Gaudin was a founder of the Sisters of the Holy Family, which established the first Black old age home. Photo courtesy of Sister Boniface and the Sisters of the Holy Family.

Henriette Delille was another founder of the Sisters of the Holy Family. Photo courtesy of Sister Boniface and the Sisters of the Holy Family.

Hobart Jackson became administrator of the Home for Aged and Infirm Colored Persons in 1949 and was known as the chief advocate for the Black elderly. He was the founder of the National caucus on Black Aged and is considered the "Father of Black Gerontology." Photo courtesy of the Home.

5

"Complaint to the Lord": Social Structure in the HAICP

> Where homeless ones shall never weep,
> Nor weary aged wanderers roam,
> But walk amid the golden streets,
> Secure within our Father's home.
> —Frances E. W. Harper, 1894

The philosophy undergirding the social structure of the HAICP was essentially custodial and consisted of several major tenets. First, and perhaps foremost, was the stereotypical view as well as its attendant consequences, that old people were like children. This view, though not peculiar to the HAICP, was exacerbated by a sense of paternalism characteristic of Quaker-Black relationships. Second, managers thought the old were limited by age in their capacities and aspirations, and also in the case of older African Americans, by previous social condition. Third, events and entertainments that were provided to relieve the daily routine were to be chiefly religious to satisfy a particular religious craving of African American people. The result of this philosophy was a narrowing of the social world in which the residents lived, limiting their potential and failing to appreciate the exigencies of congregate life. Children, for example, cannot make decisions for themselves. Residents reacted to imposed restrictions in a variety of ways, particularly by disobeying rules or rebelling against them, though most inmates adjusted to the realities of institutional life. An examination of the social structure in the HAICP, in a time less enlightened than our own, provides insights and perspectives for today's gerontological theorists and practitioners who must strip away stereotypical views and come to see old age as a time of opportunity, bounded only by physical capacity.

Daily life in the Home was well ordered, and rules (see appendix) were familiar to most residents because they were read to them at mealtime. Oversight for the orderliness of the HAICP was the responsibility of the matron, whose actions were subject to the authority of the management committee, whose members were almost daily in and out of the Home performing their duties. In addition Board members enjoyed an open-door policy, and managers of both sexes and races were frequent visitors to the HAICP.

Residents arose early each morning for breakfast, and those who were capable of doing so made their beds, swept their floors, and straightened out their rooms before mealtime. A bell was rung ten minutes before meals were served so that residents could repair to the table. Grace or a moment of silence preceded the eating of meals. Those who were sick or infirm remained in their rooms and were served by orderlies or aides with the matron or visiting committee members sometimes pitching in to help. Three meals a day were typical except during winter months when residents slept later and two meals were common. A typical day's meals consisted of, perhaps, a breakfast of scrapple, eggs, potatoes, bread, and tea or coffee. For dinner, perhaps, a soup served with beef, potatoes, beets, lettuce, and bread. Also for dinner, fish was a popular dish as well as roast pork, turkey, and vegetables (greens). Food was not to be removed from the table or to be taken to rooms because the practice invited roaches or infestation. Uncooked fruit was allowed in rooms and provided for those who wanted it. Crackers were also placed in the dining room for between-meal snacks.

Generally, residents spent their day in idleness, conversing with one another or observing visitors, who were allowed after 10:00 A.M. and before 5:00 P.M. There were often children's groups visiting from such schools as the Institute for Colored Youth, Catto School, or Home for Destitute Colored Children. Some residents preferred to knit, sew, and help with chores around the house, including comforting individuals more infirm than themselves, while others preferred raising vegetables in the Home's garden. Those who wished to leave the HAICP to shop or visit friends obtained permission to do so and rode the streetcars into the city if necessary. Overnight stay away from the Home was disallowed except under extreme circumstances.

There were frequent religious activities in the Home, and speakers were always there to perform related duties. Formal services were held in the HAICP three times on Sunday, at 10:00 A.M., 3:00 P.M., and 7:00 P.M., rotating among the various religious denominations in the city. Friends' Day was every fifth Sunday, which was perhaps the only occasion that brought Hicksite and Orthodox Quakers together. Residents who were members of churches in the city attended these institutions, and travel arrangements were generally worked out for them. There were also classes and services during the week with Wednesday a popular day for prayer service. Nonreligious activities included lectures, occasional picnics, concerts, and recitations, all designed to break the monotony of the Home. Residents were expected to retire each night by 10:00 P.M., when the matron went through the house to extinguish "unnecessary fires and lights."[1]

According to the rules, grievances were to be made directly to the visiting committee, bypassing the matron because the Board decided that residents should not directly interfere or find fault with her. It was up to the visiting committee to investigate *all* complaints, separating the real from the fancied. Problems that could not be solved or required administrative decision were then taken to the Board with the committee's recommendations. When rules were violated, the matron was empowered to "admonish" offenders for first and second offenses. A third infraction was to be handled by the visiting committee after formal complaint by the matron. Although a fourth offense was taken to the full Board and constituted grounds for dismissal, the Board reserved expulsion as a last resort. Generally, punishments prescribed, depending on the infraction, went through several stages. At first managers, through an ad hoc committee, investigated the problem and tried to persuade refractory residents to mend their ways, or as they put it, they "labored" with the rule breakers. Second, the rules were read to those who violated them either in a group or in private. When these tactics failed, the privilege of leaving the institution was withdrawn, or residents were asked to remain in their rooms. The most extreme punishments, consistent with managerial view that the elderly were like children, restricted the unruly to a diet of bread and water or locked them in their rooms until they mended their ways.[2] The routine of the Home was imposed for the good of the group, but rules governing human behavior were much more easily made than enforced.

On 26 June 1885 Catherine Phillips and Rebecca Conard, members of the visiting committee, arrived at the Home in time for breakfast. This practice was not unusual. Observing meals, sometimes from preparation to consumption, was one way of being assured that food was properly prepared, residents had plenty to eat, and the nonambulatory or bedridden were properly nourished. On this occasion the committee, not uncharacteristically, chose to join "the family" for breakfast. John Johnson, a seventy-four-year-old Virginia-born resident, consented to give Grace, and asked those present to bow their heads in prayer. Perhaps because of the presence of the committee, Johnson's prayer unexpectedly strayed from the usual thankfulness at meal-time. He used this opportunity to make an earnest and fervent plea for better care in the Home. Johnson, believing in a God of retribution, informed the Lord that his provisions had not been given to them and evidently requested his divine intervention on behalf of the residents.

Not surprisingly, Rebecca Conard and Catherine Phillips were greatly disturbed over Johnson's "Complaint to the Lord"; to them, his prayer was "most sacrilegious." The breakfast table was decidedly not the proper place for airing personal grievances, nor the Lord the proper person to whom they should be directed. Johnson, the committee noted rather uncharacteristically, was an ingrate and suggested that if he did not like the Home, then he "should find such living as he can outside the walls." Furthermore, they contended, as for future blessings, "he is quite unfit to conduct religious exercises in the Home—of any kind," and was never to be called on again.[3]

Johnson's prayer was made about three months before the matron Esther Barnes resigned, charged with neglect of duty among other things (see chapter 4). Yet few residents managed to draw such heated comments from the usually coolheaded and business-like committee. On occasions members were irked by those whom they labeled "chronic complainers" and "constant grumblers," noting at one time, for example, that "all are not inclined to adopt the rules or accept the restraints necessary for the government of so large a family. While many are grateful and happy in their surroundings there are but a few turbulent spirits ever ready to stir up discord."[4] It was the sacrilegiousness of Johnson's complaint that angered the visitors. Conard and Phillips, like all the managers, were deeply religious and God-fearing individuals, who believed their presence in the Home to be motivated by Christian precept. Johnson's complaint was thus singularly unfair.

Problems in the HAICP seemed to have come in clusters: 1877–78, 1885–86, 1889–91, and 1906–07, 1935–36 were particularly turbulent years. Problems grew to such an extent in 1885 that the committee on management asked the Board as a "body" to visit the Home "to impress the old people with the importance of a willing acquiescence in the rules of the Home."[5] A note from the secretary respectfully declined the invitation. However, by 1892 the Board had come to realize that its ad hoc way of dealing with problems was inadequate. A standing committee on discipline was thus created to institute "speedy and vigorous action."[6] The powers of the newly created disciplinary committee were the same as the appointed body it supplanted. It handled problems brought to it by the management committee at the monthly Board meetings, and though its action was sometimes vigorous, it was understandably rarely speedy.

Johnson's complaint to the Lord was not about only meals, but food was a major problem. It was impossible always to please the taste of such a large number. If the choice of meat happened to be satisfactory—and how could 140 people be satisfied with a concoction called "scrapple"— the vegetables were unsuitable. Criticism was endemic: Meals were too spicy or perhaps underseasoned or too rare or overcooked. Most residents enjoyed their meals. But two meals in winter hardly nourished an old body, and wouldn't it have been more pleasant, some thought, if they could be served earlier or later? And that ungodly bell that rang at ten-minute intervals before mealtime hardly gave one time to repair to the general table, especially on those days when the rheumatism was acting up. Some therefore chose to remain in their rooms to be accommodated with the sick, even though they were quite capable of coming to the dining room.[7]

The meals were varied as much as the managers thought reasonable and economical. On some days, several different meats and types of vegetables were served to offer residents a choice. Sometimes women managers expressed the opinion that the number of meats was extravagant and that the meals, described earlier, were better than those served on their own tables.[8] Although there was plenty of pork, chicken, and vegetables (greens) as well as some watermelon, there was no discernible attempt to serve what is commonly referred to today as soul food, or foods that were thought particularly well suited to Blacks or the elderly.[9]

Special diets were not infrequent, but they required a doctor's recommendation. One elderly woman claimed that she needed oysters three times a week and was angered when the doctor informed the visiting committee that he could not determine why she needed them.[10] Few went as far as Ezekiel Henderson, who threatened to beg on the streets if necessary, to get his special menu and to inform the public of his ill treatment in the Home.[11] One man in 1888 felt that the cook should always be female and that Calvin, the cook then, did not cook well enough for a dog.[12] Problems did not end with complaints, as some residents took matters into their own hands, hoarding favorite items from the dinner table, taking them to their rooms, there to breed roaches and vermin. Others had goods sent to them by former employers, bought their own, went to neighbors for food, or begged relatives, friends, and visitors—all of which displeased managers to no end. A few desperate souls attempted to cook in their rooms or built fires around the Home for that purpose, endangering the lives of all residents.[13]

Another source of complaints was about clothing, not just the type of garment, but who owned it, how it was ironed, or how it was washed. Technically, all clothes belonged to the HAICP, and after a resident died, clothes that were not sent to relatives were reused as the house committee redistributed them,[14] adding perhaps another psychological burden to these old people. Although there was a full-time seamstress, residents and managers held sewing day once a month to provide clothing, and on occasion a male or two would join in the sewing, knitting, or quilting.[15] Complaints usually followed changes in temperature or seasons as residents clamored for heavier or lighter clothing, but there were also requests for a variety of clothing for Sundays and special occasions, and sometimes clothes were hoarded like food. Denied use of the laundry, residents also washed clothing in their rooms and hung it in closets to dry.[16] Male outer garments included overcoats and pantaloons, but some preferred not to wear red flannel underwear, though it is not clear whether the material or color met with dissatisfaction. Instead of flannel underwear, "merino drawers [were] bought for the women."[17] Women could also be seen in colorful ribbons, shawls, bonnets, and some Quaker attire.

Particularly unsettling to residents were cleaning days, when they felt administrators held "raids on their rooms."[18] The residents considered this practice an invasion of privacy that deprived them of items they had owned for some time and from which they derived a sense of rootedness, though managers viewed them as rubbish. A sense of support and attachment was derived not only from clothing, but also from a piece of furniture or a place at the dining table, providing psychological anchorage for residents. At one time managers decided to number the bags for each inmate, and later clothes were numbered. They also used laundry slips so that items would not be confused. Managers recognized the dehumanizing effects of these practices, but all too often "efficiency" won out.[19] In addition the clothes of boarders were at one time initialed in red so that their items would not be confused with those of the other residents whose clothing technically belonged to the institution. Although boarders were not to be treated differently from other residents, their status sometimes called for ways that differentiated them from the rest and must have been a source of invidious distinction to the others.[20]

"Spiritous liquors" presented another problem that taxed managers' patience. This problem had its moral as well as its managerial side, since managers tended to be activists in the temperance movement.[21] Alcohol was not absolutely barred from the institution, but it was not "to be used in the Home unless ordered by the physician, and then to be administered by the matron."[22] Even then, the managers kept a watchful eye out for those who might influence the good doctor. In 1897 they thought Louise Ervin had become dependent on her "whiskey toddy" prescribed by the doctor. They became thoroughly convinced, however, after learning that it was being administered "twice a day."[23] The managers requested the doctor take her off it, and he acceded to their wishes, though it cannot be determined if his decision was contrary to his professional judgment.[24] Those unsuccessful with the doctor were forced to visit the local saloons, often returning intoxicated or reeking of alcohol.[25] In 1897 Charles Ross was amazed when the visiting committee singled him out for admonishment for going to the saloon. Many others, he explained, did the same thing and returned with their packages. After investigation, the committee noted that Ross was telling the truth, thereby confessing their ignorance of the extent of the problem.[26] The Board sought to control the problem externally and over the years complained to the mayor about the sale of alcohol to residents, opposed the issuance of licenses to saloons in the area, and urged dealers and bartenders to refrain from the sale alcohol to the old people.[27] None of these efforts met with much success, and old men continued to satisfy their desire for alcohol. Although women sometimes visited bars, they tended to be more inventive and made their own alcohol. In 1890 Jane Stausburg made a large batch of wine and celebrated her accomplishment by sharing it with her friends.[28] Nannie Carrie was another of these resourceful individuals who several times over the years was found "fermenting grape juice," only to have the managers or matron take it away."[29] Alcohol posed a problem for managers because of their temperance beliefs and because its acquisition required breaking the rules. Perhaps most of the Home's residents were opposed to drinking on religious grounds, and it cannot be said that addiction was a problem in the HAICP.

While problems associated with food, clothing, and alcohol were easily classified, there was a multitude of miscellaneous problems to be coped with over the years. Some seemed to have happened only once or twice and involved only one individual. One man who was never seen without his cane developed the dangerous habit of using it on his fellow inmates, though he always claimed self-defense. Another potentially dangerous individual threatened the nurse and other employees with his knife, only to have it taken away from him, though it is not clear who accomplished this dangerous task.[30] Some residents could not get along with roommates and quarreled constantly over room temperatures, beds, or other items.[31] Mary Smith claimed that the doctor had released her from taking a bath, but he failed to corroborate her story. Hannah Jackson and Grace Williams were also in a "Panic" over their being forced to take weekly baths.[32] There were at least two cases of public nudity that disturbed administrators, but they were clearly due to insanity.[33] While there were other minor problems (for example, using profanity and throwing trash from upstairs windows), three more tenacious problems deserve attention because they shed light on the philosophy of managers and provide insight into residential life in the HAICP. These were fraternizing between the sexes, leaving without permission, and "hiring out," which are discussed separately in the following pages.[34]

Married couples and marriage itself presented both a practical and ethical question for the Board, and it was not until 1913 that there was a clear statement of policy. The Board decided at that time that "where the applicant has a husband or wife living, such an applicant will not be admitted unless the husband or wife is also admitted."[35] Yet, the first couple to enter the Home had been Robert and Elizabeth Beatty, way back in December 1878.[36] Why then, the implementation of a rule as late as 1913? Perhaps the Board faced an unusual situation; for example, one spouse desired to enter the Home and the other refused admission. In any event, the policy was not without irony, for the Home admitted couples but refused to allow marriages among the residents. As early as 1873, the Board decided: "That on the marriage of any of the inmates of the Home, they are to be immediately deprived of and debarred from any of the benefits of the Home."[37] Although the HAICP policy posed a paradox, it was not alone in its position. The Hollenbeck Home of Los Angeles, which had been opened in 1896, also accepted couples but denied marriage among its residents. Their reasoning? "A temporary infatuation, a relief from loneliness, might be taken for love."[38] A malady one supposes afflicting only those in old age. Although this position was borne out in some cases, the historian of that institution observed that some simply "continued lovers" as "the embargo on marriage" failed to dampen their affection.[39] This was no less true in the HAICP, and fraternization between the sexes was a constant source of administrative concern. Men were barred from visiting women in their rooms and from using their toilets, but sexual contact continued as there was always present a sprightly and gallant old gentleman who was unremitting in his attention to the ladies. Perhaps because of the scarcity of men in the Home, women often took the initiative, inviting men to their rooms, planning prayer meetings on the fourth floor where males resided, or generally gathering outside the men's quarters to chat and indulge in the use of tobacco.[40] It seems that little could be done about such things, and there is not much evidence that administrators adopted a prudish attitude about this.

The rule that required the matron's permission to leave weighed most heavily on the residents because it was considered a denial of a right that one attained as an adult. Former slaves must have considered the requirement reminiscent of slavery. At any rate, residents violated it with impunity. William Striker in 1902 spoke for most when he informed the visiting committee that he had long attained the age of twenty-one, and if he remained in the house, regardless of the rules, it would be simply because he so chose.[41] The rule was enforced, it was argued, mainly to protect individuals from injury to themselves or the family. The senile or the forgetful might wander away without returning and cause the administrators to worry. How this rule would deter this from happening one cannot determine. However, injury from the introduction of contagion was a real possibility, especially during epidemics in the city, and over the years the Home had to be quarantined because of epidemics of smallpox, diphtheria, influenza, and measles. Although germ theory was not widely accepted until the 1880s, managers were always particularly careful of vermin and filth in the Home. In 1876 Henry Braddick was summarily expelled "on account of his intemperate and filthy habits."[42] Francis Morris was noted absent on 13 November 1889, and managers observed that this was the fifth time that he had absented himself without permission. They also pointed out that "three times it was necessary to burn his clothing."[43] In 1890 William Hurt was also disciplined for "bringing in vermin."[44] The rule against leaving without permission remained until Hobart Jackson instituted an "open door policy" in 1949, but by that time the risk of epidemics in the Home had been substantially reduced.[45] Anyway, the rule never deterred those who desired to leave from doing so despite the risk of disease to residents.

The most trying test of managers of the HAICP was combatting idleness among the approximately 140 residents, and "hiring out" or working outside the institution was made illegal for three reasons. First, jobs away from the Home would have required residents to be mobile, going and coming as they pleased. Second, working outside the Home would have increased the danger of contaminating the family. Finally, residents would have had to relinquish their earnings to the Home because the rules required the transfer of all property to receive life care in the HAICP. This was a complex problem. On one hand, boredom and an idle existence resulted in the residents' constant self-consciousness and endless focus on their old age and impending death. On the other hand, there was a desire for discipline, the need to regulate activities of individual residents for the sake of all. Administrators were caught between the proverbial rock and a hard place.

The Board recognized the need for useful activities, but they failed in light of such recognition to provide adequately for them. The work allowed (cleaning rooms, sewing, knitting, and cultivating vegetables in the Home's garden), were all for the benefit of the institution.[46] Yet the annual reports emphasized the least diversion as a positive influence on the residents. In 1875 they noted that the passing of streetcars "prevents their minds being too much absorbed in their own physical condition."[47] The next year it was working in the garden that broke the monotony: "Thus, by having their minds profitably occupied, withdraw their thoughts from their own ailments."[48] In 1877 the annual visit to the zoological garden "could not fail to exert an enlivening influence, by diverting their minds from their real or imagined ailments."[49] In 1901 after describing the work in the Home—preparing vegetables, assisting in the laundry, sewing carpet rags, and cleaning knives—the Board noted: "Anyone who has ever known the torture of enforced idleness will appreciate what a blessing in their monotonous lives this little diversion proves to be."[50] Recognition of the problem, however, did not provide a solution, and generally the Board adhered to a custodial philosophy that reflected the popular belief that old age was a time of leisure and preparation for the spiritual world beyond.

The management committee, constantly in touch with the problem and the psychological affects of the caretaker philosophy, continuously asked the Board for guidance and to work out programs designed to stimulate residents or to provide useful activities. Steadfastly emphasizing its policy against hiring out and earning personal income, the Board never seemed to understand why old people wanted to work, particularly since there was plenty to be done in and around the Home. Silk culture was proposed in 1881 and was thought particularly well suited to the residents of the HAICP but never tried.[51] Perhaps the Board learned of the failure of such an attempt in the 1830s by the Guardians of the Poor in the Philadelphia almshouse.[52] Also in 1881 there were those who felt more sewing could be done in the Home, but the Board did not concur. It explained that "washing, ironing, scrubbing, hoeing, digging up roots, and 'grubbing' are not the occupations that leave hands fitted for the nimble and delicate needle. But they do what they can and who shall require more."[53] Nevertheless, the private money-earning enterprise of inmates and the omnipresent occupation was sewing carpetbags that could be made at the Home and marketed elsewhere. Over the years, residents were found husking corn, selling peanuts or other items, barbering, janitoring, and doing various kinds of domestic work.[54]

The desire to solve this problem led the Board in 1893 to ask the discipline committee to devise means to stimulate residents.[55] Assigning this responsibility to the discipline committee made it clear that managers perceived the problem to be isolated from the total institutional program, involve only a few residents, and an aberration in the normal run of things. By narrowing the problem in this way, the Board prevented the development of an undergirding management philosophy that sought to stimulate the entire resident population. In 1894 the Board, in an effort to placate women managers, promote activity, and help to solve the problem of hiring out, reached what can—from our vantage point be regarded as the incredibly unrealistic decision—to give recognition to those who earned money for the institution by mentioning them "creditably" in the monthly meetings.[56] When Ed Preston was reprimanded for selling peanuts, he explained that he needed spending change, not creditable mention, and that his partial blindness prevented him from concealing his actions as others did.[57] Throughout the 1890s and the first decade of the 1900s, the idea of a workshop for the men who had "some talent" permeated the thinking of the Board of Managers, both male and female. The workshop, it was thought, would give "satisfaction to the inmates and compensation to the Home."[58] This was clearly not a solution to this complex problem because the majority of the residents were neither male nor talented. The workshop was never built, and the managers seemed to have forgotten the idea.

In 1901 women managers, determined to find a suitable solution to this problem, formed a committee, consisting of Edith Abbott, Lydia Pennock, and Emily Campbell, to investigate other institutions that had to deal with this difficult situation. No committee report has survived, but Emily Campbell, a Black manager who served on the Board from 1894 to 1936, left her findings in a letter to the committee in 1901. She reported visiting six institutions, four of which were as "vexed" as they over the problem. Of the other two, a Home for blind women allowed the sale of goods made after 5 P.M., and the other had a display case where goods were sold that were made by the residents. The money, except for 10 percent, belonged to those who made the items. Campbell concluded that the subject required delicate and sensitive treatment because residents were accustomed to years of independence and self-reliance. The Home followed Campbell's advice and developed a display case for sale of items that residents made, but from all indications, it did not seem much of a stimulus, probably because there was little interest in them and no market. In 1922 about forty persons were involved in an "experiment" sewing carpet rags for the blind men's institution. The residents had long sewed carpet rags, the significance of this experiment was that the money went to the residents instead of the Home, a major shift from the earlier policy. It is hardly surprising that there was a large participation in the 1922 project, but it was short-lived, and the problem of finding useful employment for the residents continued beyond the depression years. Whatever the project, success was limited; in none was there sustained participation.[59]

It has been suggested by gerontologists that the loss of work roles in old age does not carry the same impact for African Americans as it does for Whites. The African American's high unemployment rate and sporadic work history have meant that leisure and idleness had to be coped with throughout life and not just during old age. Therefore, careers or jobs have not been for them the only source of self-definition and self-identity. African Americans, it is said, bring to old age a realistic attitude toward leisure, fostered by a broken work history, and do not experience the identity crisis associated with the loss of work role.[60] This suggestion is reasonable for those who conformed to the assumptions in the theory, but it does not hold for those who brought past lives of independence to the Home for Aged and Infirm Colored Persons. Lack of work was the most critical aspect of residents' adjustment to the Home. If the theory holds that a broken work history fosters adjustment to leisure and idleness, it was paradoxical that those who conformed more closely to the requirements of admission to the Home were the very individuals whose histories precluded easy adjustment to congregate living.

The nexus between useful activity and psychological well-being was not entirely lost on the managers. The management committee always noticed the cheerfulness and happiness of those who found some usefulness for their time, whether this was working in the Home's garden, laundering their clothes, reading to fellow residents, or helping the less capable to get around the house. For one, they stood out like a mirage in a desert of resignation. Nancy Graham, who entered in 1892, explained that she had been in the Home for eight years and had never been confined to bed and never been sick. To the visiting committee she suggested "using exercise about the house," but that enlightened offer was many years ahead of its time and evidently not seen as a viable solution to the problem.[61] By 1911 the women managers had decided that the failure to provide "occupation and entertainment" was the cause of mental deterioration. In their words, it was "distressing to see so many of them losing their minds, certainly in some cases for want of something to do."[62] These were not easily solved problems, but the caretaker philosophy hardly helped to find a solution, certainly precluding such a far-fetched idea as exercise. Old age was viewed as a time of waiting and preparation for death, not a time of activity, renewed interest, and experimentation. The managers' attitudes toward teaching blind and other residents to read also indicates the limiting nature of the caretaker philosophy. As early as 1864 a reading committee was created to read to residents. It was composed of women who were "to be appointed monthly to visit the Home frequently and read to the inmates from the Scriptures, or other suitable books."[63] By 1878 the committee had been eliminated because volunteers from the Board and community at large made it unnecessary. It never occurred to managers that reading for themselves was an option open to these old people. The management committee noted in 1882:

> A blind man called during the day, sent by the Bible Society to inquire if we would be willing to have our old people taught to read by means of his new letters. We consented, as it was a free will offering, no charge to be made, but could not give him much hope of success, *presuming our inmates would think it rather late in life to become a reading people.* [My emphasis].[64]

The reports, however, showed that many of the old people were anxious to learn to read and were elated at almost any progress made toward the acquisition of the new skill. Some pondered over the Bible or other books for hours like eight- or nine-year-old children, and though it was the result of "a labored and difficult effort," they demonstrated to the visiting committee their newly acquired skills.[65] In 1897 the committee noted: "Abram

Strand who has been in the Home for about two years has by great effort and perseverance learned to read the Bible which seems a great comfort and delight to him."[66] Several years later they observed: "Samuel Williams, the blind man, has been taking lessons in reading raised print and has a Bible and hymn book he much enjoys."[67] The major point to be drawn from this discussion is that administrators' philosophy limited the range of activities of these old people even in areas that did not require physical strength. Old people were to be cared for and not to care for themselves after years of hard work and self-reliance. Unlike the almshouse where the goal was to "inure" the residents to work, the HAICP only accepted those so habituated. Ironically, they made a history of hard work a precondition of admission to a leisure-ridden institution.

The Board never seems to have grasped the full significance of the discipline problems in the HAICP, perhaps one reason was its understanding was obscured by a Quaker fondness for silence and solitude. The problems were seldom perceived by the Board as coping with institutional restraints or adjusting to a structured social environment. Most often problems were viewed as the result of a breakdown in the screening process. The "worthy," the Board believed, would be proud of this Home and would understand that deference was the only proper demeanor toward one's benefactors. Samuel Emlen, soon to be treasurer and later vice president, spoke for most in 1885 when he asked that residents "manifest their gratitude by being obedient to the wise and wholesome rules of the institution."[68] The next year Samuel Godwin "expressed a desire that the old people would daily live so as to cause as little trouble as possible to those having charge of them."[69]

In an age more authoritarian than our own, the Board was unable to recognize aberrant behavior as an attempt to cope with the problems of congregate living. It could only see the residents as ingrates whose disobedience was an indication of previous lives of impropriety. The problem suggested the answer: revamp the screening process to insure the admission of only those who could demonstrate their worthiness with a documented history of austere living. The admissions committee, it argued, should be more vigilant in filtering out the unworthy who endangered the purity of the family. In 1876 the Board decided on six-month's probation for all entrants "so that their dispositions and character may become better known to us, and thus guard to some extent against the admission of improper inmates."[70] This approach failed to solve the problem, and infractions of the rules continued. But the Board failed to alter the contention that the refractory were those who escaped proper screening and polluted an otherwise pure family. In 1893 it urged that those interested in candidacy for admission use "wise and discriminating judgement as to their moral character and to endeavor to contribute to [rather than detract from] the respectability of the family," for only in this way could the Board succeed in "keeping the family select." Therefore, close attention should be paid "to the past life and present habits of those they propose to benefit by placing them [in the Home]." The report continued:

> Homes are provided for the intemperate and those with no self-control, more suitable for them than this one. While caring for the bodily comforts and health of those committed to our charge, the social and religious element is likewise fostered, and we find that those who are unaccustomed to self-discipline, yield grudgingly to the discipline of the house, though it is kindly administered, and these are a menace to the peace of the household.[71]

The Board's view of human nature circumscribed residents' lives, and at no time did administrators agree on the need for a specific orientation program or a formal procedure for induction into the routine of the Home.

Another explanation for discipline problems was that the aged were like children, a widely held if dubious belief. Many antebellum Whites considered African Americans inferior and thus like children because they were incapable of intellectual development. During the slave period as one slavery apologist claimed "the Negro, who in his true nature, is always a boy, let him be ever so old . . . childhood was a perpetual state of mind." When Blacks in some states gained their freedom, then they were required to have White guardians. The attitude in the HAICP was reminiscent of slavery but attributable to old age as a state of second childhood rather than racial theory. The residents were hardly children infantilized by the exigencies of a "total institution,"[72] but because of senescence, which naturally brought on childlike behavior. In 1883 the Board urged employees to "ever remember that these old people are many of them but children of mature growth, with strong desires natural to their years."[73] Two years later the point was reiterated, picking up an earlier theme of slavery and poverty, as the Board claimed that the old people's "faults may be attributed mostly to the disadvantages of their former social condition, and their present childishness of age." Again in 1898 the Board reiterated that the old, referred to in the report as "oldsters" like "youngsters," were in a "state of second childhood, needing the watchful care such a condition demands."[74] The second-childhood view was agreed to by the management committee, but they believed that residents, "like disorderly children, need restraints."[75] In 1888 the house committee noted that the residents, "have been petted and indulged too much like spoiled children, the more you give way to them, the more they demand."[76] Yet they recognized that these old people presented different discipline problems, explaining that "so many old people cannot be managed entirely by rule as children can."⁷⁷ These stereotypes often formed the basis for interaction in the HAICP.

Just as slaves lived in a dual system—the slave system and the slave community—residents of the HAICP experienced a bipartite existence, and paternalism in the Home resembled the way it operated during slavery. As discussed in chapter 1, it was directed toward house servants or favorite slaves. In the HAICP, it led to a system of favoritism that was designed to influence behavior by rewarding the obedient and punishing the refractory. Although paternalism was characteristic of such institutions, its presence in the HAICP was the result of long-held practices and beliefs outside the Home. It also included the nomenclature derived from slavery, as these old people were referred to as "aunt," "auntie," "uncle," and "grandmother," which runs like a refrain through the records. These old people were also referred to as "pets" and "favorites," which also reduced them on the scale of humanity.⁷⁸ Children cannot make wise decisions and had to be cared for in the tradition of a kind father, and these attitudes reinforced the custodial philosophy.

An informal pattern of social stratification among the residents resembled practices in the slave community as well. Centenarians were placed at the top of the Home's social ladder by the administrators and were often the subject of favorable sketches in the reports. Respected for their rarity and age, they were held in high esteem by both managers and residents. Like slavery, however, those most venerated by the residents were individuals who turned their talents to use by the group. Among these were the educated who read to or wrote letters for the residents or those who sacrificed their own needs to help the sick or weak much the same way that artisans and servants turned their positions to benefit the quarters. Mary Ann Scott, a seventy-eight-year-old Pennsylvania native, helped employees, waited on the sick, read to the blind, wrote letters for those who asked, and taught a reading and writing class. She was endeared to all the residents. The visiting committee observed: "Her whole life in the Home was that of a thoroughly conscientious and consistent Christian."⁷⁹ Another example was William Forten, the grandson of the famous Black Philadelphia sail maker James Forten, who had been active in the political affairs of Philadelphia through the Equals Rights League. Forten's entry on 6 April 1898 was a source of concern:

> Much to our surprise he before one night had passed, signified his desire, to occasionally attend political meetings, which meetings would necessitate his remaining out late at night and has already spent three days from Home without permission from matron. After the assurance of himself and friends that he was willing to give up his old life and come under rules made for the benefit of the Aged and Infirm. We do not think this augurs well for the future—as

other inmates cannot be allowed such liberty, we cannot show partiality in his case without making trouble.[80]

Partiality was unnecessary, but Forten did not jettison his old ways. Instead, he turned his political interests toward the old men of the Home and sought to teach them about the political process and the advantage of the franchise. The matron informed the managers in 1898 that "Forten's influence in the House was felt for good. He reads and talks to the old men, interesting them and turning their thoughts away from themselves, and a better feeling is apparent in consequence."[81] During the next ten years, Forten earned the respect of all by reading to residents, writing letters for them, discussing the ins and outs of politics, and it seems, keeping them from falling prey to the Philadelphia political machine. He died in 1909, and managers and residents alike felt a great sense of loss.[82] Perhaps Forten's death left the old men without political direction, and they came under the influence of the Philadelphia machine. In 1911, according to the visiting committee, the "organization wagon" came to the Home and "took off our old men to vote them and that the Boss was seen to hand them something which they put in their pockets." The committee on discipline was asked "to take up the matter with [the] men [and] to teach them to use their franchise for good government rather than sell them."[83] Once more a resident had broadened the horizons of other residents in a way considered unfeasible by managers whose philosophy was confined to custodialism.

In addition to those who could read or write, residents who sang or spoke well, told stories well, or otherwise entertained the group were highly respected. Men, never more than one-fifth of the HAICP population, seemed to have enjoyed a high status because of their rarity. Former slaves were prized because of their experiences, particularly if they had come to freedom via the underground railroad or had firsthand information about Africa. Among the residents was at least one conjuror whose power over the inmates elevated his status. In 1896 the management committee discovered that some residents thought that they were "under a spell of some kind owing to the supposed power of others to conjur them and in many way to disturb their rest and peace." The committee members thought that the trouble was "rather serious as it may spread and cause the weak to come under the influence of the more designing and we would suggest that some of those who are in the habit of talking with the 'old people' on First Days [Sundays] might take pains to try and disabuse their minds of all such dreadful superstitions."[84] Since churches generally provided for the retirement of superannuated ministers, particularly the methodist groups, there is no evidence of ministers living in the Home. There is no way to determine where they would have ranked in the social hierarchy, though one might surmise that they would have enjoyed respect.

Those who enjoyed the respect of managers were subjects of favoritism that emerged most blatantly in the HAICP in requests for carfare, spending change, and the privilege of bequeathing some sentimental item to a relative or friend. The matron requested guidance in 1885 because she was caught in the middle of such requests, but she was told that these matters were "left to her own discretion."[85] In practice, however, the matron was not the source of favorite treatment because she exercised only meager administrative responsibility. The house committee denied Elizabeth Anderson's request to leave her featherbed to her son because it would set a bad precedent. But since Ann Childs, six months earlier, had bequeathed two shawls and a gold ring to a friend and grandchild, the precedent clearly already existed.[86] Harriett Henderson's request for carfare to New York was peremptorily denied as "against the rules" in October 1897, but Maria Staat's request to visit the same city in May 1898 was granted "as she is a satisfactory inmate."[87] Sarah Miles's request to visit a friend away from the city was at first granted but later withdrawn because "she failed to follow instructions." The instructions were not determined, but the residents, in one of their instances of group consciousness, protested to the house committee, pointing out that its decision had not been impartial.[88] Why the residents chose to protest this particular case is unknown, but it points out that they were not ignorant of favoritism in the Home, and, more important, they were capable of group action. In 1878 residents banded together to petition the Board for more heat in the Home. In 1911 when the Seventh Day Adventists were denied the privilege of holding services, residents protested, though none was Adventist, and services were allowed.[89] Perhaps such a partisan system developed because of the managers' attempt to treat residents as individuals with unique problems, rather than imposing a uniform set of restrictions without regard for individual needs. If so, managers should be credited for emphasizing the residents' humanity above the rules, but the reality of the situation was that obedient residents enjoyed the paternalistic indulgence of the system while the refractory were denied the same privileges, and most residents recognized the system for what it was.[90]

Although unruly residents were occasionally locked in rooms or put on diets of bread and water, physical coercion was not used to make residents obey, and removal to the dreaded almshouse constituted the ultimate punishment and disgrace. It was not unusual for managers to employ the paternalistic technique of requesting former employees or sponsors to discipline a violator much the same way as parents today are summoned to schools to discipline unruly children. Because sponsors took an active interest in residents' welfare, this was understandable, and former employers tried to persuade them to obey the rules or suffer the consequences of the almshouse, where they could expect no further support.[91]

Managers were remarkably tolerant of those who violated the rules, and one might trace troublesome individuals through the records for months or even years before final action was taken, that is, removal to the almshouse. It was only after months of misbehaving that the visiting committee decided in October 1886, that Elmira Burr and Sarah Morris were "to be made examples of because of their long and continued disregard of the rules."[92] They were to be removed to the almshouse. When Burr was to be taken:

> She pleaded so earnestly not to be taken away, and promised so faithfully to obey the rules and to be a good example to the others that the Committee concluded to let the matter rest and give one more opportunity to prove [by] her conduct that her promises were sincere.[93]

The Board's compassion was not rewarded with model behavior as they noted at the same time that they were "much mortified to find that her conduct is still unruly and her temper ungovernable."[94] She was therefore dismissed and removed to the public almshouse. An interesting aside is that Jabez Pitt Campbell, African Methodist Episcopal Bishop and Board member from 1871 to 1891, was elected to the thankless position of removing residents to the almshouse. According to the records of October 1886, Campbell had been elected "some time ago," but "in his absence, someone needs to remove Elmira Burr to the almshouse."[95] Perhaps because of his great influence but possibly because managers felt that a Black person could best perform this service, Campbell was chosen.

The case of Patrick Harmon best illustrates that the Board did not act impulsively and tolerated misbehavior for long periods. Although Harmon entered in 1888, apparently it was two years later before he became troublesome. In 1890 the house committee requested that one of the employees ask Harmon to refrain from throwing trash from the window, but Harmon warned him that "he would tread upon him and crush his breath out."[96] Every month thereafter, Harmon's name was mentioned as a cause of disturbance, and in March 1891 his case first came before the Board, but no action was taken. Harmon continued his antisocial ways, and his case was again brought before the Board in July 1892, only to have the charges dismissed because his behavior was thought to be due to his old age. In the meantime, Harmon continued to disregard regulations. He took meals away from the Home, worked or hired out, "brought in vermin," left (always without permission), used candlelight after hours to "blacken his shoes," drank, quarreled with his roommates, and struck the laundry man. "Disturbing Element," though he was, his "ugly temper" was continually tolerated.[97] In 1896 a fight between Harmon and Richard Taylor, another resident, occurred that proved Harmon's undoing. The incident evidently caused some friction between the matron and the housekeeper because the records noted that they were "in trouble over the matter." The management committee concluded that "the time has come for some decided action in Patrick's case," and his eight-year sojourn came to an abrupt end.[98] Patrick Harmon's case cannot be said to have been typical since few residents were tolerated as long as he, but the managers recognized the need to be sensitive toward those whose behavior deviated from the rules of the House. Their rhetoric and their actions did not always demonstrate an acute grasp of social problems, but impulsive action was not the Quaker way.

According to the rules, those who were unmanageable were to be removed, but the records are unclear about what is meant by those who left, withdrew, or were dismissed.[99] For example, in 1878 June Thompson was said to have "left," but five others had preceded her, including Ann Davis Smith, the first departure.[100] In 1886 ten residents "withdrew from the Home," including those who were listed as "left" in the earlier reports.[101] From 1886 to 1892, all those who departed were referred to as "withdrawals," but in 1893 Elizabeth Boltwick, Thomas Thompson, and his spouse, Anna, were said to have "left," when they were all but formally dismissed.[102] The distinctions among these categories were clear, even though they were used interchangeably in the published reports. Those who "left" usually did so unceremoniously and were later discovered missing. Sometimes their whereabouts were unknown until they requested their clothing or applied for a partial refund of their admission fees. For example, the visiting committee went "to remonstrate" with Hannah Benson, but discovered that the "bird had flown."[103] Withdrawals were usually more formal and were accomplished after dissatisfaction was expressed and intention to leave made known. Those who chose this method usually had family outside or had some place else to go, perhaps a friend's house, or had some source of income. Since there was no ill feeling in such cases, refunds from entrance fees were generally made if room and board had not absorbed the entire amount. This category of departures was preferred, as it was less damaging to the image of the Home, and the one managers wished to project to the community. Finally, those who were dismissed or discharged were evicted almost invariably because of unacceptable behavior. For example, between 1873 and 1910, twenty-four residents, seven men and seventeen women, were dismissed from or left the HAICP, which represented a very small percentage (less than 4 percent) of the residents served. Residents usually left or were dismissed within the first year. Of thirty-five of these residents for which data were found between 1873 and 1925, 60 percent left the first year, 80 percent by the end of the second year. It is significant to point out that the first year was crucial to an adjustment to congregate life, but the HAICP had no formal induction procedure beyond the reading of the rules.[104]

The rules allowed for unconditional removal, but it would have been inhumane simply to evict these people. Therefore, managers developed the practice of placing the unwanted in boarding houses with one or two weeks expenses paid, giving them a "gratuity," or placing them in the poorhouse. Occasionally, the Quaker policy of placing them with a family was followed if a suitable one could be found."[105] Sometimes these actions were tantamount to suspensions as residents pleaded to return after several months trying to make it on their own or in the almshouse. The records seem to indicate that their spirits had been broken. Temperance Saulsbury returned from her outside interlude "reformed" because she had a hard time.[106] Frances Davis left "for no cause" but was allowed to return in 1891, where she remained without a single reference to her behavior until 1920 when she died.[107] Obviously, most of those who left the Home, for whatever reasons, did not return, but those who did had learned that unobtrusive behavior was the key to permanent residence at the HAICP.

To break the routine of the Home and perhaps to ease inmate adjustment, many entertainments were held that were said to "go far towards relieving the tedious monotony of the lives of those whose little world is compassed by four walls."[108] Holidays, particularly Christmas, Halloween, and Thanksgiving, were festive occasions with dinners and entertainments as were special days such as Friends, founders, decoration, donation, and sewing days. A major shortcoming was that these entertainments and events were almost always of a spectator nature: lectures, recitations, concerts, magic lantern exhibitions, prayer meetings, Bible readings, preachings, stereoscopic exhibitions, and musicals that included dozens of local groups, but occasionally residents enjoyed the Fisk Jubilee and Jubilee singers of Hampton. Except for the annual picnics sponsored by several churches each year and the visits to the Zoological Garden down Girard Avenue, none of the activities required active resident participation. Participatory programs were the most enjoyable, stimulating, and needed, but the most infrequent, coming most often at the initiative of the residents.

Since managers recognized the need for occupation and entertainment, denial of the former necessitated an emphasis on the latter, particularly religious activities, which were thought well suited for African American people. Managers thought religion was the key to a well-ordered life, but in the case of Blacks, it was assumed to satisfy a craving peculiar to their race. For the African American resident, religion proffered comfort, afforded an outlet for his frustrations, and sustained him by focusing on a hereafter.[109] Religious services were considered "a delight to join" because they were "very satisfying to their nature."[110] They were said to be well attended, not for want of something to do, but because they gave "great satisfaction to the aged inmates, whose craving for religious fellowship is a strong characteristic of their race, and which has been through many a weary day, a drop of nectar in the cup of life."[111] The Reverend Dr. McCook at the 1888 annual meeting expressed the belief that all Blacks were Christians and that never in all his years had he encountered a "disbeliever."[112] This stereotype was repeated continuously by the managers and supporters, who believed that African Americans were naturally creatures of religion, in a way the more favored Whites could never be.[113]

When the chapel was added in 1894, former Judge Edward Paxson explained that Black "people are by nature devotional and their faith reveals to them many things which are hidden from others who claim higher wisdom."[114] This stereotype gave way to religious indulgences of these old people who claimed to have seen their spouses or visited heaven during the night. In 1914 when Mary Lee received a spiritual call to go to Asbury Park because the Almighty had called her to preach the gospel, the visiting committee granted her permission to carry out her revelation.[115] Religion was thought to be the life blood of Black folk whose "lives would be incomplete without the revivifying influence of the Holy Spirit."[116] It was religion that allowed the residents to cope with death—a release from the suffering, trials, and tribulations of this earthy world. Sustained through "an unwavering faith in a blessed hereafter,"[117] residents waited for their call in "patient endurance," "childlike faith," and "loving submission."[118] "On the watch tower and ready for the summons," to go to a "better and everlasting home," confident in an "all-wise and loving Father [who] banishes all fear," residents concurred.[119]

The Home maintained a tradition of nondenominationalism by accepting residents of various religious backgrounds. By 1885 the following pattern of worship had evolved: first Sunday, Presbyterians, second and fourth Sundays, Episcopalian, and third Sunday, meetings by Methodist. Fifth Sundays, when they occurred, were considered Friends' days at the Home and were largely attended until about 1920.[120] There were also afternoon and night services that were rotated among the churches with the local preachers association coordinating the activities. Services and classes were held about three times during the week, and Wednesdays were reserved for prayer meeting.[121] In addition one rule provided that:

After rising in the morning, and again before retiring at night, all who are able shall be assembled in a suitable room and a chapter from the Bible read to them, after which an opportunity shall be afforded for silent or vocal worship.[122]

In 1899 the matron took a census of the religious denominations in the Home for the Sunday School Association. Including employees, there were eighty-six members of the African Methodist Episcopal Church, twenty-eight Baptists, twelve Episcopalians, two Friends, eleven Presbyterians, and two Roman Catholics. There were nineteen who were listed as "not belonging to any religious body."[123] Although not necessarily an indication of disbelief, this revealing statistic might have come as a shock to the Reverend Dr. McCook.

Although only two expressed membership in the Society of Friends, evidence indicated that many more (including those listed above as unaffiliated) were fellow travelers, having adopted many traits of Quaker culture after forty to fifty years of work in their homes.[124] Henry Cadbury who has studied Black membership in the Society of Friends has demonstrated that a combination of factors militated against a large Black membership, including record-keeping procedures, mode of accepting members, and prejudice. He added that "quietness of worship" was not necessarily a hindrance, and "religious temperaments vary without regard to difference in color: Therefore, "we no doubt generalize too easily along that line."[125] Certainly, students of religion have stressed the emotionalism and activism in Black religion, but Quakers who were involved in the administration of the HAICP adhered tenaciously to this stereotype. Their definition of African American religious needs undoubtedly contributed to a belief that Quakerdom was unsuited to the Black American's naturally emotional and devotional nature. Religion no doubt helped old people to cope with impending death, but some must have felt that they were not dead yet, and a few programs with a little earthly enjoyment might have added to their will to stay on this side of Jordan a while longer.

One of the most festive nonreligious occasions was the Association meeting, which attracted large gatherings of Blacks and Whites from the Philadelphia area. Throughout the nineteenth century and into the twentieth century, numerous speakers were engaged for these annual occasions, the central theme of which was the former antislavery movement with a strong emphasis on Quaker participation. This emphasis was understandable because many supporters had been actively engaged in the abolitionist movement. But the residents must have tired of listening to these escapades that ran ad infinitum in the annual reports. A majority of the speeches were prideful reminiscences that recaptured the Quaker role in the drama of the underground railroad but relegated Black participation to the back of the underground train. Matron Cordelia Attwell noted in 1899 a reciprocal theme in these remarks: "the speeches," she noted, "were reminiscences of the anti-slavery struggle and several [Quakers] expressed their conviction that the patience and humility of the Negro race had helped to mold their own characters satisfactory [sic]."[126] Moreover, to history-conscious Quakers this theme provided a link to an important past.

Often Black supporters such as Stephen Smith, Fanny Coppin, William Still, Frances E. W. Harper, and Jabez Campbell spoke on these occasions. Over the years, many well-known Blacks accepted invitations to address the annual meetings, including W. E. B. Du Bois, Ida B. Wells, R. R. Wright, George H. White, James Weldon Johnson, Leslie P. Hill, Ira De A. Reid, and Horace Mann Bond. One of the most striking facts about these activities was the high level of race consciousness and pan-Africanism that characterized them over the years. The lectures rarely concerned topics other than race, and the struggles of Blacks everywhere were reiterated. Lectures on Africa were frequent up to the turn of the twentieth century, but no longer in vogue, lost their popularity. In 1903, for example, Bishop Coppin gave a talk on Africa and "four African natives" helped him to explain the facts about that vast continent. One of the misgivings about this African theme was that many references to the topic came from missionaries whose attitudes conformed to the misconceptions and stereotypes of the day. Typically, they referred to African barbarism and heathenism, which they contrasted to civilization and Christianity, explaining that the latter produced such institutions as the HAICP, and one should be proud that he or she no longer inhabited that dark and backward continent.[127]

One Robert Hasan explained in 1891 that only civilized countries cared for the sick and elderly while barbarians practiced gericide, leaving their old to be devoured by wild beasts or to be drowned in mighty rivers.[128] Those who were in the Home in 1885 were told about aging in India by Rev. H. L. Wayland, who informed them that if they lived in that backward land, they would have been marched to the banks of the Ganges and suffocated in the "Sacred mud," truly a reason to be thankful for such a fine institution as this Home.[129] Until the 1890s, the Home celebrated both West Indian Independence on 1 August and American Independence on 4 July, but while it lasted, the former remained the most gala of the two.[130]

One of the most interesting lectures was provided in 1899 by Dr. H. J. Brown, brother of one of the residents. Dr. Brown lectured on Phrenology and Physiology and excited many of the White people in the audience with his learned remarks, "several of whom were so much interested in the phrenological examination and delineation of the character of Richard Parker, one of our family, that they engaged Dr. Brown to visit them and examine the heads of their children and thus assist in delineating which pursuits were best for them."[131] This was a decided shift from the perennial lectures and speeches on abolition, race progress, and African civilization.

Gerontologically, managers seemed to have grasped the peculiar need for intergenerational contact, emphasizing programs that brought together those on both ends of the life cycle. Children were an omnipresent element in the Home. Lucretia Miller and Fanny Coppin brought young people to the Home from their schools, the Catto School on Lombard Street and the Institute of Colored Youth, for a period of over sixty years. Children also came from the Home for Destitute Colored Children, the Shelter for Colored Orphans, the House of the Holy Children, and a host of other places.[132] During holidays, many groups of children brought gifts, participated in the annual tree shaking at Christmas, sang or held concerts, and put on skits in which old people were delighted to participate. The House of Refuge and the Allen Chapel Bands provided favorite entertainments for the old people. In 1898 a young lady referred to as "Miss Maxwell" from the King's Daughters of Emanuel Presbyterian Church was upset by so much sadness in the Home: "She came to me [the matron] flushed and tearful because she found so many unhappy old women there—I promptly explained the situation to her."[133] Perhaps it was such innocent sympathy from those not yet inured to the ways of the world that lent itself to the joyous relationships between these young people and those in Frances Harper's words "around the verge of parting life."

The philosophy undergirding the HAICP's operation emphasized the physical aspects of care and restricted the old people's lives to the administrators' worldview. This philosophy stressed that the old were to be cared for by their benefactors, rather than make decisions for themselves and to exemplify their gratefulness by unobtrusive behavior. Stereotypically viewing the refractory as children, the managers were unable to recognize the problems of adjustment to a structured social environment. The Home was operated, therefore, on a system of social control that rewarded model behavior and denied privileges to those who broke the rules. Some residents sought an involved existence and made periodic group protests of their treatment while some others constantly rebelled against the administration and were placed in the public almshouse or elsewhere. Most succumbed to the routine of the House, but a few chose independence above security and withdrew to live with relatives or to eke out whatever existence they could outside. Since the managers viewed old age as a time for leisure and preparation for death, they provided entertainments with a religious orientation, believing that religion comforted residents in the thought of death and satisfied a peculiar craving of Black people.

An important lesson to remember from this study of a more authoritarian era than our own is that old people must make their own decisions and that old age may be seen as a time of expanding horizons, developing potential to its fullest and experimenting with life, rather than a time for restrictive philosophies and narrow views of life's choices imposed on them by others. It was not until the modern gerontological movement that self-determination for the old was formalized by Hobart Jackson, whose administration of the HAICP led him to the broader arena of advocacy for the black aged. Before turning to that important story, let us examine health care in the HAICP.

6
"The rugged path of faltering age": Health Care in the HAICP

> And from the annals of the poor,
> We would unfold a shining page,
> And tell of kindly hands that smoothed,
> The rugged path of faltering age.
> —Frances E. W. Harper, 1894

If social activities in the HAICP were restricted by managers' philosophy of old age, it was overseeing health care that was their most significant and challenging function. Several factors influenced the delivery of health care in the Home. First, the staff consisted of individuals lacking in medical skills, sometimes in inadequate numbers and unsuited in temperament, who experienced a high rate of turnover. Moreover, as we have seen, there was no system of employee promotion or remuneration. Second, prevailing attitudes toward the old and insane influenced health care practices in the Home. Third, medical practices outside the HAICP, including variant medical procedures within the medical field, determined the type of treatment in the Home, especially when it came to the Board's choice of physicians. Finally, just as we have seen that management philosophy influenced the treatment of residents, the philosophy that guided health care, essentially custodial beliefs that emphasized the barest necessities of care, also shaped medical practices in the Home. These variables singularly and dynamically influenced medical practices in the Home, but health of residents was generally well maintained, considering the elderly residents' susceptibility to disease at a time when much of the medical knowledge and practices that we take for granted today were unknown. Understandably, death was an omnipresent visitor to the HAICP and to some a welcomed release from "the rugged path of faltering age."[1]

The Board's policy was to accept applicants who were in good physical and mental health. For example, extant applications from 1898 to 1918 revealed that 81 percent of the potential residents were in good health while the remaining 19 percent suffered from various degrees of blindness or chronic ailments that were not serious obstacles to admission. After the admissions committee ruled on applicants' character, the Home's appointed physician certified to their physical and mental condition before the Board made its final determination. Sometimes the doctor accepted certification from another "physician of good standing," but this was seldom the case without at least a cursory examination.[2] Although the Board did not generally accept applicants of unsound body, The Home for Aged and Infirm Colored Persons was not a misnomer, for a few, even with acute and chronic conditions, were accepted as special cases, sometime well below the minimum age requirement.[3]

Incurables and the mentally weak were rejected outright, but the Board was most understandably concerned about admittees who might introduce contagion into the Home, endangering the health of the entire family. As stated elsewhere, managers were particularly chagrined by those who failed to obtain permission before leaving the institution and returned with "vermin." The house committee or matron burned these residents' clothes or brought the individuals before the disciplinary committee, but if they persisted, then the Board dismissed them rather than continue to jeopardize the family's health.[4] Thus, the managers understood the connection between disease and filth and sought to maintain an antiseptic environment to prevent the transmission of disease.

The risk of epidemics was real, and the precautions taken were often at the instructions of the City Board of Health or the State Board of Charities, which usually inspected the Home after 1874.[5] Several times during the Home's long history, it had to be quarantined to prevent the spread of disease. An epidemic of smallpox in the city led to the suspension of visiting rights and delay of admissions to the Home from December 1871 to March 1872, when the quarantine was rescinded.[6] Although no deaths occurred, three were hospitalized in 1895 because of diphtheria. A quarantine was imposed for three weeks, and residents on visits were not allowed to return to the institution.[7] One hundred and sixteen residents and employees were vaccinated during the quarantine from December 1901 to March 1902 because of another epidemic of smallpox in the city, the longest quarantine in the Home's history.[8] Brief periods of isolation occurred in 1906 because of cases of the measles and typhoid in the Home.[9] The most common disease affecting large numbers of residents was the grippe or influenza, but it was rarely serious enough for managers to impose restrictions.[10] In 1917 the Home was put under strict quarantine because of influenza and the visiting committee was unable to inspect it for a week. The nation was hard hit with the flu epidemic in 1918, but it does not seem to have resulted in an unusual number of deaths in the HAICP. In 1932 a full-scale quarantine was imposed by the doctor "when practically every one in the house was affected" by the flu.[11] Generally, residents and employees understood the need for periods of isolation and accepted their confinement patiently and sympathetically. It was a tribute to doctors, nurses, matrons, and managers that none of these incidents led to widespread occurrence of death among such a susceptible population.

The policy of accepting applicants who were well by no means obviated medical attention. The number of infirm residents increased with time and as the family grew in size. As early as 1876 the managers noted: "One of the most pressing wants is the need of apartments entirely separated from the main building, to be used as an infirmary, to which the seriously sick, especially those afflicted with contagious diseases could be removed; and in a family like ours there are almost always some needing such a provision."[12] The call for an infirmary was echoed annually after 1876 as the residents increased in size from 67 in 1876 to 104 in 1881. In the latter year a sick ward was once again called for to house the sick for economical and health reasons. "A sick ward could be heated and ventilated far more thoroughly and at the same time, at less expense than the large rooms in different parts of the building." In addition "the work of attendance would be greatly lessened."[13]

Although the partial introduction of steam in 1879 had helped to achieve a uniform temperature throughout the House, the call for an infirmary was particularly important since it was maintained that "old people are naturally chilly and being sick are more so." Moreover, managers concluded that "it is neither healthy nor convenient to have sick and well in rooms together. It is a restraint upon the well ones, and not pleasant for the others."[14] In 1883, the Laing Building was opened, which was not designed as an infirmary, but made some space available to house those who suffered from sickness and incurable disease. While this addition soon proved inadequate to accommodate all the sick population, the Home's new elevator was a boon to residents and employees. It eased the nurses' burden of carrying meals upstairs to the sick and concomitantly enabled the feeble to come downstairs for the first time in months, perhaps years, since it removed the risk of accident while descending the stairs with an infirm grip on the balustrade.[15]

The Laing building was never used exclusively as an infirmary, and the doctor by 1892 was again requesting space for that purpose.[16] The "Parker Annex" two years later provided a chapel and increased rooms for a larger number of residents, but not an area specifically for infirmary purposes, though the situation was relieved somewhat by the additional space. On 21 March 1901 a three-story infirmary or hospital wing was opened, a separate stone building connected by concrete landings at the second and third floors, built with funds from the estate of Edward Parker for the expressed purpose of separating the invalid from the well.[17] The capacity of this structure was twenty residents and was quite ample for the time because no more than an estimated 10 percent to 15 percent of the resident population were in need of medical facilities and nursing attention. A room on the first floor served as a morgue.[18] As life expectancy increased accompanied by chronic disease, the Home experienced the need for additional medical and professional services to meet its residents' needs. This development led in 1960 to the construction of a fifty-unit modern medical and nursing facility to accommodate the chronically ill, handicapped, and disabled. It was this addition that brought the newest medical technologies to the residents and more than anything else marked the HAICP's transition to a nursing Home.

The health of the residents depended to some extent on the Home's ability to recruit and maintain good physicians. The bylaws required in 1865 (see appendix) that two physicians be appointed annually by the Board, "to look after the health of the inmates," but was changed in 1868 to "one or more."[19] The Home's physician was responsible for all aspects of the HAICP's welfare, from the sanitary condition of the kitchen, the infirmary, and other areas, to administering to the real and fancied needs of the residents. Since the doctor visited once a week, the matron, as early as 1872, expressed the need for a doctor "nearby" in case of "sudden illness," but none was appointed specifically for this purpose until 1880 when one Dr. Mueller offered, and the Board accepted his services "gratuitously" in case of emergency. Although there were several on-call physicians, the Home was fortunate to have had several physicians who served for long periods, viz., David Roselle, 1866–67, 1872–77, James Collins, 1866–77, Jessie Thatcher, 1877–85, Samuel C. Henszey, 1885–1901, William Evans, 1901–27, who had served as Henszey's assistant for five years before his appointment, and Frances Eaton, 1927–36. Several Black doctors, besides David Roselle, just mentioned, provided services to the HAICP, including James Wilson, who was appointed in 1865, but died soon after his appointment, Caroline Anderson, daughter of William Still, T. Creiah Imes, and C. T. Shafer. The last three individuals were involved in the Home as members of the Board as well as physicians.[20]

On his weekly visits, the doctor attended patients in their rooms until 1896 when a room on the second floor was provided for his purpose, making it necessary only to visit the bedridden.[21] The doctor was able to interview patients more conveniently and consult with matron and nurses on health-related matters of the institution. He could also leave instructions to those who ministered to the care of the residents and leave prescriptions for patients. Doctors served without charge from 1865 to 1877, but from 1878–88 they were paid "$100 per annum." After 1888 the doctor's salary was $200 and raised to $300 in 1903.[22]

Dr. Mueller, the on-call physician, was also druggist from 1880 to 1887, providing prescriptions at "actual cost value."[23] Since neither the state nor federal laws controlled drug distribution, the HAICP, through the supply committee, purchased prescriptions for the doctor. In 1896 the managers decided to allow the doctor the privilege of purchasing his own prescriptions because he was "embarrassed in that his prescriptions [were] purchased for him."[24] Drug costs roughly coincided with the salaries of the doctors, ranging in annual cost from around $100 from the 1870s to about $350 by 1910. This expense was low considering that the HAICP cared for such a large number of feeble old people. One reason for the low cost was that throughout the 1870s, 1880s, and into the 1890s individuals and drug companies, without drug regulations, donated large quantities of medicines to the Home. Generally, after the 1890s, drugs were donated by dispensaries or drug companies such as Rosengarten Sons, Charles Crittenton and Company, Johnson, Power and Weighman, Baker and Company, Warner and Company, and a host of others. Donations of medicines, which had been consistent throughout the late nineteenth century, virtually disappeared by the beginning of the twentieth century because of increasing public awareness of the need to control such substances that resulted from the progressive movement. The publication of Upton Sinclair's *The Jungle,* an exposé on the Chicago meat packing industry, led in 1906 to the passage of the Food and Drug Act that instituted controls on drugs for the first time.[25]

The HAICP neither invested in nor maintained medical equipment except such things as wheelchairs, spectacles (glasses), bed pans, and crutches; it did buy a galvanic battery in 1873 to treat residents with rheumatic and paralytic problems. The HAICP attempted to bring the latest medical technologies and procedures to the residents via its own physicians and the use of outside agencies and practitioners while keeping cost low. Quaker conservatism as well as fiscal accountability militated against purchase of such equipment as static electric machines, multi-nebulizers, and radiant heat cabinets, even if such items had been deemed of value to the residents. These items were probably not available in private Homes but could be found in some veterans Homes to treat aged victims with rheumatism and respiratory diseases. After a complete study of the HAICP in 1938, social worker Emma Irwin recommended that the HAICP buy blood pressure apparatus, portable X-ray machines, a fluoroscope, physiotherapy equipment, and an electrocardiograph, but there is no evidence that the Home, undergoing serious financial hardship at the time, ever seriously considered such investments.[26]

Drugs were another matter. The Home after 1892 provided a room on the third floor (later moved to the same floor of the infirmary) where it kept an extensive supply of drugs and medical supplies in lockers around the wall. The following list was compiled from drug donations, supply records, Board minutes, and so on:

Belladonna plasters	Soap plasters
Powdered rhubarb	Sweet marjoram
Paregoric (or elixir of)	Saltpeter
Sulphur	Soluble pheneyle
Powdered borax	Quinine
Chloralum	Bromide potassium
Laudanum (Brown's mixture)	Epsom salt
Powdered alycine	Castor oil
Turlington's balsam	Tar drops
Iodoform	Cream of tartar
Flax seed	Plantain salve
Glauber salt	Sweet oil
Calcined magnesia	Wild cherry bark
Magnetic salve	Sassafras bark
Yarrow life everlasting	Soap liniment
Carbolic acid	Bone dust
Chamomile flowers	Rose water
Asafetida	Powdered charcoal
Calomel	Burnt sienna
Yellow ochre	Spirits of camphor
Essence of peppermint	Camphor
Prunes	

In later years the drug room carried an even greater variety of drugs, and residents kept in their rooms such items as aspirins, alcohols, cough syrups, castor oil, milk of magnesia, vaselines, and so on. Records are not available about how doctors, nurses, or other personnel applied specific drugs to specific ills, but evidently, drugs were used to treat a variety of ailments: constipation (asafetida, castor oil, prunes); cancer (belladonna, iodoform, chloride, opium); burns-cuts-bruises (calcined magnesia, iodoform, camphor, soap liniment, opium, life everlasting, laudanum); colds (belladonna, opium, asafetida, morphine); bronchitis (Brown's mixture); diarrhea (charcoal, camphor, rhubarb); fevers (opium, rhubarb, sienna, calomel); headaches (camphor, opium); hysteria (asafetida, laudanum, paregoric, camphor, potassium bromide); influenza (opium); pain (belladonna, laudanum, paregoric); rheumatism (belladonna, soap liniment, camphor, opium); ulcers (opium, belladonna); dysentery (calomel, iodoform, opium, rhubarb); asthma (belladonna); heart disease (belladonna plasters); chapped hands (rose water); and nausea (opium, peppermint). This inventory, unlike the stockpile in later years, seems to reflect the homeopathic procedures of the HAICP.[27]

Some of these drugs had even wider use than shown here, particularly belladonna and opium and derivatives paregoric and laudanum. The above uses were available to the HAICP, and while it is clear that these remedies were a part of the drug-room inventory, it is not altogether clear that they were used in these ways.[28] Expectantly absent from this list were nineteenth-century patent medicines such as Dr. Raphael's Cordial Invigorant, Mormon Elders' Damiana Wafers, or a glandular extract such as Orchis Extract, or Bakers Glandol, which all claimed in some way or another "to restore sexual vitality to aging, to cure sexual debility or impotence, or to improve sexual performance."[29] Despite administrators' grief over the fraternization of the sexes, one might surmise that saltpeter was not in liberal supply.

There was a need for more medical personnel than a visiting physician. Residents were generally treated by doctors, but those who became "excited" or posed danger to themselves or others were administered sedatives by the nurse or matron on the advice of the doctor. For example, in 1888 when Hannah Benson tried to leave the HAICP, the matron convinced her to stay and administered "medicine from the doctor to sedate her—committee found her in bed."[30] In 1938 Irwin found a lax use of sedatives, sodium bromide, and phenol-barbitol because there were no records showing how they were used or amounts given, and she suggested that some patients were overdrugged. By necessity the nurse, and perhaps even the matron, must have exercised considerable latitude in the treatment of residents in an environment where there were many sick people, and the doctor came once or twice a week.

The bylaws did not require a nurse, but two were hired by 1872, one for each department, male and female. The Board employed additional nurses during times of epidemic or other emergencies and eventually hired a nurse for each of the four floors.[31] There was also a contingent of orderlies and aides that performed health-related tasks about the Home. The nurses' duties were not always distinguished from the aides and orderlies and might include dressing patients, preparing them for the doctor's visit, dressing sores, bathing the sick, carrying meals, feeding the helpless, monitoring special diets, overseeing the sanitary conditions of the infirmary, or even fanning flies. A nurse's exclusive province, it seems, was holding clinics, administering medicines, making the rounds with the doctor, preparing drugs, and filling prescriptions. The reason for the lack of clarity could well have been that the nurses lacked training. As early as 1883, Dr. Caroline Anderson had requested a trained nurse to help take care of the sick because the doctor visited only once a week, but the Board, perhaps in part because of their unavailability, did not adopt the policy of hiring only trained nurses until the twentieth century. The first trained nurse was Mary Conway, who was hired in August 1902 but left in February 1903.[32]

When nurses were replaced, which was often, the managers hired untrained individuals or rotated existing employees; for example, in 1886 Henry, the nurse in the male department, left and was "replaced by Joe from the Kitchen," who was fired 9 September 1897 for quarreling with the matron.[33] When it was discovered that Caroline enjoyed working with ailing residents, she was released from sweeping, scrubbing, and other custodial duties to care for the sick—evidently an excellent decision since she served from 1874 to 1898.[34] Some simply could not work with the sick and elderly; others were dismissed for inattention to their duties, improper behavior, mistreatment of patients, disagreement with matron or managers, and even striking the residents.[35] Nurses, therefore, were not only lacking in training, but also generally lacking in the essential qualifications of patience, understanding, and an interest in elderly people, a problem the committee on management thought might be corrected "by employing of older persons who would be more likely to have interest in the aged members of the family."[36] The turnover rate of nurses was higher than all other occupations, and their attrition probably had a negative psychological impact on the residents of the HAICP, but there is no evidence that the turnover was abated by the hiring of trained nurses. During the HAICP's decline in the late 1930s and 1940s, the Home cut back its medical staff to a practical nurse and an infirmary maid, but the physician came biweekly, visiting Mondays and Thursdays. A resident who became ill on Thursday, after the doctor had made his rounds, had still to await the doctor's Monday visit. In 1938 the doctor left a signed death certificate for a resident on her deathbed on Thursday and instructed the nurse to fill in the particulars when the inmate died. On his Monday visit the doctor found that it was unnecessary for the nurse to use the affidavit, although the records are not clear whether the patient wished to see the good doctor again. When Hobart Jackson became administrator in February 1949, he inherited two nurses and a biweekly physician. The next year he initiated a twenty-four-hour nursing program supervised by a registered nurse and three practical nurses, working continuous eight-hour shifts.[37]

What was not provided directly in the Home was made available through external medical assistance. The need for medical attention from outside practitioners was arranged on a call basis by the matron with approval of the visiting committee. For example, Dr. William Zimmerman was the optician used by the Home during the 1890s. Eye examinations were done free by Pennsylvania University and Pennsylvania Hospital when the Board decided not to use Dr. Zimmerman any longer. Wills Eye

Clinic was used during the 1930s and 1940s, but residents were still required to obtain proper authorization.[38] The "house Dentist" was appointed in 1905 and had served eight years before the Board voted him seventy-five dollars a year in 1913, requiring him to be on call when needed. Nevertheless, the dentist's services were dropped the next year as the Board felt he "had too little work."[39] Opticians, chiropodists, podiatrists, and other specialists were made available when the residents needed them and when they followed the correct procedure to obtain these services. The Home refused to pay for services not contracted by an authorized representative of the HAICP, although residents occasionally obtained medical attention and had the Home billed anyway. This was particularly true when residents were on visits away from the city.[40] One woman refused to accept the doctor's decision to withhold knee bands and insisted on visiting Pennsylvania Hospital for advice.[41] Another woman frequently left the Home to attend the clinic at the University of Pennsylvania as a subject of the lectures there for compensation. In the words of the visiting committee," she has a peculiar heart and some chronic condition of one limb which makes her case interesting."[42] The Board expressly forbade these practices, and there is no evidence that the residents were ever used for any experimental purposes. This is not a point to be skirted readily. African Americans were aware of the widespread reputation of hospitals for using them for medical experimentation.

The HAICP did not affiliate with outside organizations and several times over the years rejected benevolent offers. For example, in 1898 the Nightingale Association, "a company of Colored persons wishing to act as ancillary to assist in caring for special sick ones in the Home," was informed that bylaws did not permit connections with outside associations.[43] Of course, individual help was welcomed, and residents who had relatives were fortunate enough to have them frequently in and out of the HAICP. This way residents were assured of proper treatment and comforted by having kin outside interested in their welfare, although administrators sometimes complained of interference from relatives who brought their own doctors, made their own diagnosis, and administered their own medicines.[44] Many did not have relatives, but there is little indication that those residents who had them were ever abandoned. As a matter of fact those with relatives in the HAICP seemed to defy the prevailing notion that institutionalization and abandonment went hand and hand.

Perhaps the most important complement to the Homes' health program was peer care, or mutual assistance, residents offered to one another, which grew out of the African American supportive tradition. Some took care of their roommates or others like "dutiful daughters" and worked tirelessly to nurse the sick back to health. In typical fashion the annual report in 1881 observed that: "The stronger ones show a cheerful alacrity in waiting upon the sick and it is often deeply touching to see one of these companions in age and infirmity helping along another who is blind or more feeble than himself."[45]

The same could be found in 1900 as the managers noted that "many of the younger and stronger of our inmates cheerfully lend such aid as they can to their helpless companions."[46] Rebecca Reason, Mary Ann Scott, Nellie Ford, and Martha Howard were residents who stood out over the years as caring and comforting the sick and less vigorous than themselves. For example, in 1897 one woman went about the House informing people of how Nellie Ford had cared for her during her illness. "Let it be known," she repeated constantly and emphatically.[47] Sometimes friendships led to or resulted from such care, and the death of one was quite distressing and heartbreaking to the other. So widespread was the practice of peer care that the Home attempted to institutionalize it in the 1930s by informing residents that they were expected to care for one another and even assigned stronger individuals to care for feebler ones. But stripped of its natural qualities, the program appears not to have enjoyed much success. In summary, the attitudes of caring for each other that had been acquired by Black people from experiences outside the Home carried over into mutual care, comfort, and companionship inside the institution.

The Board's appointed doctors did not always satisfy the residents, but they were not allowed to choose their physicians because such exercise of free choice did not coincide with the financial exigencies of the life care contract. Nevertheless, the rule that denied such freedom of choice was changed in 1878. The change allowed residents to use their own physician or another of their choosing as long as two conditions were met: (1) consent of the Home physician was obtained, and (2) the Home was under no obligation for such an arrangement, financial or otherwise.[48] Obviously few took the liberty of exercising this right because of prohibitive cost, no family physician, or satisfaction with the physician appointed by the Board. Those who did take advantage of the privilege usually had relatives outside; others chose doctors and had the Home billed in violation of the rule.[49] It was not ideal to have residents choose their physicians because these doctors were obligated only to their own patients. Someone had to be responsible for the sanitary conditions of the entire household, including dining room, kitchen, infirmary, and other parts of the Home where disease might be transmitted; otherwise, neglect of important sanitary precautions could lead to sickness throughout the HAICP community.[50]

The choice of a physician in 1865 ran more deeply than the simple exercise of medical preference. The medical profession at the time was just emerging from what has been called "the age of heroic medicine," characterized by "excessive blood letting" for almost every condition, and the use of "huge doses of calomel and other dangerous mineral drugs, as well as purgatives and emetics to cleanse the system of irritants."[51] Besides, there were many schools of medicine competing with the regular or allopathic model, which included Thomsonianism, hydropathy, eclecticism, and homeopathy. Based on the theory *Similia Similbus Curantur,* "like is cured by like," homeopathy prescribed in tiny doses the kinds of medicines that were known to cause symptoms similar to the patients' diseases if given large amounts. In other words, the ability of a drug to cure diseases lies in its ability to mimic the symptoms of the disease—a concept akin to the purpose of immunizations. According to the distinctions made by homeopathy's founder, the German physician Dr. Samuel Hahnemann (1755–1843), traditional medicine, from which his school had defected, was allopathic; that is, allopaths used large or heroic doses to produce effects contrary to the patient's disease.

Homeopathy was brought to America in 1825 by a German doctor, Hans Gram, who moved to New York City, which was to become the center for the practice. By the late nineteenth century the homeopathic school was threatening to overshadow allopathy.[52] At its founding meeting in 1847, the American Medical Association (AMA) passed a resolution known as the consultation clause, which prevented allopaths from conferring with homeopaths or administering to their patients' needs (unless the homeopath was dismissed from the case) thereby elevating the allopathic position above the welfare of human beings they were morally and professionally obligated to serve. Having repudiated the homeopaths, the AMA in the 1860s further narrowed its membership by denying participation to African Americans and women. Thus, the AMA appeared intolerant at the theoretical and personal level.[53]

The managers of the HAICP very early had to deal with bigotry within the medical profession, and there is some reason to believe that amending the bylaws to require two physicians was done to satisfy the allopathic and homeopathic followers on the Board of Managers. While the services were gratis, doctors were accepted without regard to which school of medicine they belonged, but after the Board agreed to pay the physician "$100 per annum," some concern emerged about medical and professional beliefs. The Home's physician for many years (1866, 1867, 1872–77) had been the allopath, Dr. David Roselle. In January 1877 he was not reappointed "owing to the desire of some of the Board of managers of adopting homeopathy."[54] The dissidents prevailed, and the Board appointed a homeopath, Dr. Jessie Thatcher.

On 12 July 1877 Dr. Thatcher recommended that Alexander Maxfield, a ninety-year-old native of Delaware with tendencies to violence, be taken to the insane ward of Blockley Almshouse. To effect his removal, Dr. Thatcher obtained the required second signature from a Dr. Banks, another homeopath, to the completed affidavit. The Home's secretary, George W. Hancock, presented the papers to the almshouse authorities on 14 August 1877 only to learn that the Guardians of the Poor, county officials who oversaw the needs of the indigent, required the signature of their "outdoor" physician, one Dr. Mullen, who was visiting physician for the twenty-fourth ward, where the Home was located. Dr. Mullen refused to sign, expressing his opinion that he could not associate with homeopaths and remain in good standing in the profession. He offered to examine Maxfied and issue a new certificate, however.

On 15 August 1877 Alexander Maxfield jumped from the fourth story window of the Home to his death, and the controversy was now waged in the open.[55] The press followed the investigation of the incident closely, siding with the homeopaths. An inquiry was called by the coroner, but the press accused the Guardians of trying to exonerate their doctor. State law required "two or more reputable physicians" to attest to the sanity of individuals and that their commission to an insane asylum be made by legal guardians or relatives and friends. The Guardians rather than the state legislature required an "outdoor" physician's signature.[56] The requirement was aimed at quacks, but the Guardians placed homeopaths within this group. The newspaper ceaselessly reminded the Guardians that homeopaths graduated from universities chartered by the Commonwealth of Pennsylvania and their degrees therefore were as valid as other physicians', and nonrecognition was violation of the law. *The Sunday Dispatch* called Maxfield's death a "pathy" homicide and argued that such practice "furnished the fraternity of undertakers with lots of business." The *Dispatch* also accused the Guardians of running a public institution in the interest of a particular school of medicine.[57]

During the inquiry, the schools of medicine became polarized with the allopaths clearly on the defensive. One, Dr. Dwight, called in on behalf of the allopaths, declared that he had examined Maxfield before he entered the HAICP and that Maxfield suffered from dotage or somnabulism and not from mental illness. Dr. Dwight, therefore, implied that homeopaths could not properly distinguish between the sane and insane. He also took the opportunity to implicate the HAICP, accusing it of inadequate supervision and a singular desire to rid itself of Maxfield. He evaded the question of his association with homeopaths by declaring that "homeopathy and allopathy are as separate as oil and water."[58]

The final report cleared Dr. Mullen of wrongdoing. It declared that Maxfield was never presented to the almshouse and that Mullen was not guilty of dereliction of duty. *The Sunday Dispatch* cried "whitewash,"

6: "The rugged path of faltering age" 175

"evasion," and that the findings were "insulting to the community."[59] For his part, Dr. Mullen revealed in a letter to *The Sunday Dispatch* that he was busy until ten o'clock the evening of 14 August and therefore could not examine Maxfield. When he arrived at the Home the following day, he contended, the matron informed him of Maxfield's death. Yet the day after the first article appeared in the *Dispatch,* Mullen had come to the newspaper office and had displayed the certificate he had completed after his examination, explaining at that time that Maxfield died before obtaining the required second signature. Mullen, the editor claimed, "must be afflicted with a treacherous memory."[60] Nevertheless, the Guardians' requirement went unchanged.

The death of Alexander Maxfield brought medical controversy to public attention but did not solve the problem. The press and the managers of the HAICP generally favored the homeopaths. Homeopath Thatcher remained the Home's physician but offered to resign the next March because he could no longer render free services. It was evidently the gratuitous offer from Dr. Thatcher in January of 1877 that enabled those interested in adopting homeopathy to prevail when the Board was deadlocked over the issue. In April 1878 the Board retained Dr. Thatcher for eighty dollars a year.[61] In September 1878 S. Mason McCollin was appointed to render service to those who desired allopathic treatment, a position that he obviously had to reconcile with the provisions of the consultation clause. In 1880 McCollin was replaced by allopath Caroline Anderson, who was perhaps spared the need for such reconciliation because she was Black, female, and on both accounts excluded from membership in the AMA.[62] The allopathic Philadelphia City Medical Society expelled its homeopaths in 1843 and adopted a resolution in 1867 stating that they "cannot offer any encouragement to women becoming practitioners of medicine, nor on these grounds, can we consent to meet in consultation with such practitioners."[63]

Homeopathic treatment seems compatible to African Americans on two accounts. First, their antipathy for heroic medicine coincided with Hahnemann's abdication from allopathy. Second, African Americans had a tradition of using herbal prescriptions to cure disease. Robert B. Leach in 1852 became the first Black homeopathic practitioner, graduating from the Homeopathic College of Cleveland. Thomas Creigh Imes, who graduated from Philadelphia's Hahnemann Medical College in 1884, was a respected Black homeopath and chairman of the HAICP Board in 1903 when he died. The first African American to get a medical degree was James McCune Smith, who was denied admission by U.S. medical schools and graduated from the University of Glasgow in 1837. In an 1847 letter to the *Annalist,* a medical journal, Smith showed that he shared the prejudices of fellow allopaths: "May the regular practitioner of medicine battle against the most deadly quackery that curses the nineteenth century, in the form of homeopathy."[64] Quakers generally supported women in medicine but argued especially hard for equal acceptance in institutions where women were treated. The hiring of Dr. Anderson, who served until July 1884 was clearly in line with their belief about women, and probably their belief, along with those of Black Board members, that African American doctors should serve African Americans, though that position did not prevail in 1877. The annual report noted in 1882 that "our physicians both Homeopathic and Allopathic have been attentive and efficient in their departments; and the health of the family, for so large a number of aged people, has been, we think remarkably good."[65]

There was tension among the Board members that was broader than the choice of medical procedures. In August 1885 growing dissatisfaction in the Home came to a head when William Still, then vice president and chairman of the Board, read a paper showing the unsatisfactory condition of the Home and a letter complaining of improper treatment from one of the residents, J. C. Jones, which was written to Mrs. Ryers, a large contributor and perhaps Jones's former employer (sponsor or ombudsman).[66] The women managers on the committee on management were instructed to investigate and report at the next Board meeting. Since so many members were out of town, the management committee left the investigation to the house committee previously assigned to visit the Home. The committee's report was made to the Board on 9 September 1885. They agreed that dissatisfaction existed and Jones's allegations were justified. Heavy blame was then laid on the matron. Finally, the charge that the sick received no special menus was valid. More specifically, the committee reported that William Stokes believed he would have starved to death if it had not been for his daughter, and Hannah Todd had a carbuncle that the matron had never seen. Another, it was said, fell out of bed and remained there overnight. The committee concluded that there was the "unfortunate impression among them [the residents] that the matron thinks them of but little account, and that when any are sick, the sooner they die the better."[67]

In defense of the matron, the committee found no reason for censure in Johnson's death, that the residents in some cases were disrespectful toward her, that she was "industrious," "energetic," and a good manager and that part of the problem was dissension within the Board itself[68] (see chapter 5). The next month a committee chaired by Israel Johnson, the treasurer, and composed of Dillwyn Parrish, William Still, Sarah Smith, Elizabeth Coates, and Thomas McCollin made a different report. Though acknowledging that the charges were not in the main substantiated, five very damaging criticisms of the matron were made that:

6: "The rugged path of faltering age" 177

(1) She is wanting in dignity, (2) does not exercise necessary control over her subordinates. (3) Not sufficiently attentive in caring for the sick. (4) Used indiscreet and unwise expression to and concerning the inmates. (5) She does not seem to possess those qualities which are requisite for the harmonious and efficient government of so large a family when the characteristics of gentleness, sympathy, dignity and firmness should be united and without which there can only be confusion and consequent infelicity.[69]

The report concluded that in the best interest of the Home, a new administration was necessary to restore order in the Home and unity within the Board. The matron, Ester Barnes, resigned October 1885 "without a dissenting" voice, and at a special meeting the next week, Malinda Brown was chosen as matron.[70] These events pointed up how a matron in overseeing the health of the residents without adequate supervision from the visiting committee could easily lapse into dictatorial rule over a helpless and powerless group. The doctor was not directly implicated in these charges, but the report included the statement that: "While there was not much outspoken opposition to the doctor, we think the majority would prefer the old School [allopathy]. Edward, the nurse, says those under his care would much prefer the old treatment."[71]

His reputation tarnished, Dr. Thatcher resigned. He was replaced by allopath Dr. Samuel Henszey December 1885 at a salary of one hundred dollars per year.[72] In January 1886 the women managers decided "to look into the possibility of hiring Dr. Giles for the old people who prefer homeopathic medicine," but there is no evidence that an agreement of any kind was ever consummated. The appointment of Dr. Henszey marked the end of a major role for homeopathic medicine in The Home for Aged and Infirm Colored Persons.[73] Ironically, the Home began its relationship with homeopathy when the AMA had adopted an adamant posture against it and ended its use in 1885, when the field was becoming respectable, and orthodox physicians and their societies were beginning to adopt toward it increasingly liberal attitudes. Due to its attraction to the wealthy and influential, homeopathy grew steadily in the United States until about the end of the first decade of the twentieth century and virtually disappeared until recently when homeopathic treatment was revived from its "vestigial state," due in part to the natural health movement. The battle waged in the HAICP between these two schools of medical thought was repeated in other institutions. The contest has been portrayed as one in which homeopaths won a few skirmishes, but allopaths won the war. In reality, according to Rothstein, homeopaths merged with regular physicians by abandoning the infinitesimal use of drugs for their application as regular physicians, by adopting clinical specialties, and by opening their practices to medical advancement. In other words, Rothstein maintains, it was not so much that one sect won over another as the triumph of science over sectarianism.[74]

The death of Alexander Maxfield raised public questions about the mental health of residents of the HAICP, but the real issues were confronted within the institution. Mental illness presented a constant problem to management and a source of frustration to the employees and matron, often from the standpoint of discipline rather than of medicine. In point of fact, psychological ailments symptomatic of depression probably went unremarked, if not unnoticed, in an atmosphere chiefly characterized by resignation. The policy of the Home was to send the insane to other institutions where they could be properly restrained and treated, particularly Norristown State Hospital as well as the wards for the insane at Blockley Almshouse and the Pennsylvania Hospital.[75] Since the HAICP was equipped neither to render proper treatment nor to provide adequate restraint for the insane, their removal to an institution so equipped was perhaps in the best interest of all concerned. Between 1877 and 1910, twenty-seven cases of mental illness were clearly identified.[76] Nineteen of these individuals were females (71 percent) and eight (29 percent) were males. Since the ratio of women to men in the HAICP was 79 percent to 21 percent, there was a slightly greater tendency for men than for women to become afflicted with mental disease. While about one-fourth of the cases were contracted during the first year, about two-thirds became mentally ill within the first three years. Nathan Mugler was in the Home for twenty-three years before his removal, but few managed to live for such a long time after admission to the Home.

While about half the mental cases were taken to Norristown State Hospital, those with relatives demonstrated a marked unwillingness to allow them to be taken to the insane asylum. This reflects Black people's distrust of public institutions as well as the strength of Black families. Indeed, one is led to believe that those who were taken to the insane asylums were always those who had no relatives outside the HAICP. When relatives were informed of the Board's intention to commit their kin to a public asylum, they took them under their own roofs or made arrangements for them elsewhere. For example, in 1886 Esther Quann was "taken away by her family who was unwilling to allow her to go to the insane asylum."[77] In 1889 Margaret Hagen was taken away by her daughter who subsequently could not live with her or had some particular antipathy for the Norristown Asylum. Perhaps also her mother was placed in the New Jersey asylum because she was closer to her there than in Norristown.[78] In 1905 when Mary Willets became insane, her sister took her into her home rather than send her to Norristown.[79] Nathan Mugler, mentioned earlier, had not lost contact with his daughter after twenty-three years, and when she learned of his intended removal, she took him away rather than allow him to go to the insane asylum.[80] There was no way to determine the full extent to which relatives manifested their reluctance to allow their kin to be removed to institutions for the insane, but suffice it to say, there is not a single instance in the records where kin was informed of the home's intention to commit a resident to an insane asylum and removal subsequently authorized. Relatives had not ended their caring for their loved ones nor abdicated their responsibility to them despite their institutionalization.

Early removal was the HAICP's objective, but it sometimes took several months. The doctor's recommendation had to be made to a once-a-month Board to set the procedure in motion, and that was followed by certification procedures, further examinations, guardian approval, and so on. With so much potential for abuse these remarks are not meant as criticisms, but to point out that the HAICP had to provide for the insane within its walls until removal could be achieved. At first, the matron or engineer, depending on the particular problem, that is, whether the afflicted person was violent, simply locked the door to the insane person's room. But this proved inadequate and the managers provided "cage" rooms. The request was made to the Board in 1886 when the committee on management asked that "bars of strong wire be placed over the windows of a room which is to be set aside for the use of those whose minds have become feebled to such an extent that their safety is not secure without this kind of protection." The request was granted and reported completed by the property committee at the next Board meeting.[81] Because of increased need, several rooms were later grated off at the eastern end of two floors of the infirmary where iron gratings were used inside to create cells that the managers referred to as the "mental department."[82]

Generally, the insane received no special medical attention in the Home, nor was there particular effort to prevent mental deterioration through comprehensive activities or to stimulate this group through occupation or other activities, even though they subscribed to the belief that mental illness was treatable. Informed Philadelphians were aware of Benjamin Rush's pioneer work in psychiatry and that later carried on in the city by Dr. Thomas Kirkbride. In 1865 Kirkbride informed the readers of the Quaker *Friends' Intelligencer* that the key to successfully working with the insane was early detection followed by "perseverance of treatment."[83] In 1872 he reiterated these remarks, claiming that the insane should not be "simply cared for but cured." The Pennsylvania Hospital was said to have cured "80 percent of recent cases" and to have a "50 percent overall cure rate." In 1871 fifty-four males and fifty-nine females were discharged from Pennsylvania Hospital "cured."[84] One of the fundamental reasons for this success besides early detection and constant treatment, argued Kirkbride, was a program of useful occupations,[85] an argument the managers would have done well to take to heart as a preventive to mental degeneration in The Home for Aged and Infirm Colored Persons. In 1911 the managers noted a correlation between useful work and mental health. The management committee observed that it was "distressing to see so many of [the residents] losing their minds, certainly in some cases for want of something to do."[86] It was not that managers believed mental illness to be incurable, though there seems to have been more emphasis on care in the early years of the HAICP's existence than the period following the turn of the twentieth century. As stated in chapter 1, senility was not a term only applied to the old during the antebellum period, but in the late nineteenth century it became a natural condition of old age, which helps to explain the lack of emphasis on treatment in later years of the HAICP's history. Moreover, the field of psychiatry by the twentieth century had lost some of its faith in the ability of therapy to cure mental illness and had abandoned what has been called the "cult of curability."[87]

The administrators seemed overly concerned that the mentally ill would disturb the routine of the Home because there were times when infractions of the rules were improperly associated with insanity. Aberrant behavior, the cause notwithstanding, did not conform to the rules of the House, so mental cases were handled by the disciplinary committee. In addition the doctor was asked to examine a fractious resident sometimes with the prejudicial comment, "looking toward his [or her] placement in Norristown."[88] For example, Elijah Davis was thought by the managers to be deranged, but the doctor diagnosed his case as "unsettled" because of a "change of surroundings."[89] Sarah Morgan, whose thoroughly unbecoming behavior earned her the reputation of a perennial troublemaker, was referred to Dr. William Evans, the Home's physician, to determine her mental condition. Dr. Evans concluded that her behavior was a result of "old age and a naturally peculiar disposition," therefore, not a candidate for the insane asylum. Nevertheless, she was sent to the asylum at Norristown four months later, where she died 11 September 1908.[90] Sometime between March, when Sarah Morgan was first examined, and July, when she was taken to Norristown, her "naturally peculiar disposition" evidently degenerated into mental illness. The doctor also thought that some residents were disoriented as a result of "severing of old ties" that seem symptomatic of mental illness. Such was the case of one woman who would not relinquish her possessions, some of which she claimed to have had since she was a bride.[91] In summary, managers drew a thin line between mental illness and refractory behavior, and some residents likely ended up in insane asylums simply because they could not subordinate years of independence to congregate living.

Worthy or "sane" individuals, managers thought, simply did not go

6: "The rugged path of faltering age" 181

around breaking rules and annoying those who provided them such an excellent place of refuge from the vicissitudes of old age. Therefore, early removal was not always for proper care, but administrative expediency. Otherwise, the policy would have applied to all those with mental disease and not simply the refractory. Aberrant behavior was not seen as a temporary problem of adjustment to congregate living or uprootedness from accustomed environments. In cases where mental illness occurred immediately after entrance, managers emphasized preexisting conditions. Catharine Robinson entered 15 October 1884 and was removed to Norristown five days later because "she became crazy soon after entering the Home."[92] Consequently, those who contracted mental disease and were allowed to remain in the HAICP fell into the category, as an 1888 report put it, "quiet but . . . evidently . . . not at home."[93]

Removal from the HAICP did not constitute abandonment but placement in a more adequately equipped institution. The management committee periodically requested reports from mental institutions, and the managers also occasionally visited Norristown or Blockley to check on former residents. Sometimes managers like Marie Warrick and Alice Pennock journeyed to Norristown merely out of personal interest.[94] In January 1913 Elmira Short, after five years at Norristown, was adjudged sufficiently recovered to be returned to the Home for a thirty-day trial period. Her "parole" began the following month and lasted for over sixty days, but she "regrettably" had to be returned April 1913.[95] Quaker and Black managers maintained a continued sense of responsibility toward those they placed in insane asylums because of a moral obligation to residents, relatives, and "sponsors" who had entrusted them to their charge. Neglect or abuse of these people, they felt, carried the weight of a violation of a moral trust.

Barred windows, locked doors, and cage rooms was the temporary policy of the Home, a policy that was probably necessary to maintain the safety of patients and residents. Removing the mentally ill for treatment was achieved as soon as possible, followed by periodic reports on patients progress. With the general increase in life expectancy because of improvements in the field of medicine, with public health programs that controlled epidemics of infectious diseases and with the development of antibiotics, there emerged an increased number of aged who lived long enough to become mentally ill. In 1945 the National Mental Health Act was passed to help meet this increasing need, and the introduction and widespread use of tranquilizers in the 1950s opened a new chapter in the treatment and care of the insane.[96] Hearing loss, decline in learning ability, visual problems, memory lapses, and a general decline of cognitive functioning that accompanies old age have always made the old prime targets for mental hospitals, especially when coupled with reduced economic status, or in the case of African American, continued poverty.[97]

As one would expect, death was a constant visitor to the HAICP—a scream during the night, a cough in the adjoining room, a roommate's groan, an empty chair at the breakfast table, a locked door, a funeral in the Home's chapel, an inadvertent glance into the dead room, and the shrouder or undertaker's presence. If all else failed, then one needed only to look out a window or to take a noon stroll, and there on the same grounds of the Home one could see Olive Cemetery, a vast wasteland of tombstones that served as an ever-present reminder of the reality of death. When the bodies were removed in 1923, the Managers noted that the cemetery had not just "tended to depreciate property, but must not have been a cheerful sight to those whose fate it was to live here in their declining years."[98] Such hardly overstated the obvious, for too often an old folks Home symbolized a place to wait for death, but the presence of the cemetery inescapably represented an earthly end. One cannot help but ponder the favorable reputation enjoyed by the Home, since those who lived there literally resided a step away from the grave.

Here was a ripe harvest waiting submissively and patiently for death, characteristically described as waiting with "childlike faith," "patient endurance," and in "loving submission." These were the attributes the managers found exemplary because they sprang from deep religious beliefs. Death was the will of God, and like life, it was to be borne patiently and unquestionably. His will be done. Yet so little effort was made to lighten the heavy load of resignation that permeated the Home that even the most unbelieving could not escape the influence of the Grim Reaper hovering constantly over their heads.

Between 1865 and 1905 about 19 percent of all residents died within the first year (17 percent females, 21 percent males).[99] The number of deaths from all causes averaged about seventeen per year. The causes were not always identified in the records because doctors' reports were often mere acknowledgments of gifts of medicine. The Board in 1877 required that annual reports from physicians be included in their report to the Association, but there was no record of such until Dr. Caroline Anderson's 1883 report was published in the annual report for 1884.[100] Her report was a recollection of each resident's death, but her precedent was seldom followed. For example, Phyllis Anderson and Margaret Cuff, respectively aged 105 and 103, were reported to be "apparently free from disease, and simply slept away"; Phillis George, Elizabeth Beven, Marie Lee, and former Matron Ann W. Laws "having attained the age usually allotted to man" also "quietly passed away." Three others, Julia Fountain, Mary Jackson, and Mary Ann Laws, entered the Home "all suffering," two from heart disease and one from nervous trouble, "their speedy close was inevitable." Chronic disease took the lives of Martha Simpson, Elizabeth Beatly, Ruth Hill, and Lousie Smothers. The lives of Mary Derrickson, Maria Wallace, and Rachel Brown were filled with "intense suffering," caused in each case by an "abnormal growth" that allowed them "no rest save the grave."[101]

The leading killer diseases were heart and brain diseases. Diseases that manifested themselves externally or were otherwise "offensive," such as tuberculosis, the leading cause of African American deaths outside the Home, were not usually tolerated, and the individuals who contracted them were removed to the Home for Incurables or some other place. Although cases sometimes escaped admission's screening process, they seldom got past the required physical exam. Since the Home operated on a life care basis, sometimes a previous condition was handled by special agreement as in the case of Patience Johnson:

> In view of the fact that I have been a sufferer from cancer, which is now pronounced cured, I do most faithfully promise, that if at any future time, there shall be a return of the symptoms of cancer, or other sores, for which I have received treatment, I will at once notify the managers of such symptoms; and will be willing to forfeit all my rights as an inmate, and to leave the Home.[102]

This agreement was signed with her X, witnessed, and filed among the Home's records 15 October 1903. The inhumanity of this arrangement was mitigated by an agreement signed by Eliza Bucknell, probably a former employer or sponsor:

> If at any time, it becomes necessary for Patience Johnson to leave the "Home for Aged and Infirm Colored Persons," I promise to provide a home for her.[103]

Patience Johnson died a resident of the Home on 27 November 1906, her disease as stated having been cured.[104] A case with a different outcome was that of Louisa Mastion, who was removed because she had "an incurable, malignant disease which makes her very undesirable as an inmate."[105] Mastion was a boarder rather than a life care resident and probably for that reason escaped the HAICP's intense screening process. This policy of removal was consistent throughout the Home's history, and several others over the years were removed because they contracted incurable diseases.

Not many deaths occurred as a result, but accidents were common occurrences inside and outside the Home and a source of great suffering. Several accidents were caused by an impatient streetcar or trolley driver who carelessly pulled off before the elderly person was firmly seated. In 1903 the trolley company, or its insurance company, paid a resident ten dollars because of a premature start that resulted in her injury. The Board then decided that further settlements would be handled by the solicitor.[106] The most common source of accidents was due to the introduction of steam heat in 1884 because the hot pipes were exposed. Residents sometimes died after much suffering, and the doctor continually requested insulation to cover them. Other accidents resulted from rising from bed without aid, trying to avoid inconsiderate drivers, wandering off, and falls out of windows or down the stairs.[107]

The source notwithstanding, when death occurred, burial took place in the Home's cemetery, the final requirement of the life care contract between the HAICP and the resident. In 1867 a committee on interment was created to "make all needful arrangements for the funeral of our inmates, and at least one of [the committee] shall be present on such occasions."[108] The first residents were buried in Lebanon Cemetery in lots purchased through Jacob White, Sr., Board member who was manager of the Lebanon Cemetery Company, but after the new Home was built in Olive Cemetery by Stephen Smith, it became the official burial site.[109] When the residents owned private burial plots, the Home buried them in these places, but the policy was to bury the dead in the burial ground provided by the HAICP. If there were family members buried elsewhere, residents sometimes negotiated their burial near them before entrance, and if family were alive, they were allowed to claim the body for burial, as long as the funeral was of no expense to the HAICP. This policy was a source of dissatisfaction to relatives who wanted to bury their kin where they wished, and the Board was forced to adopt the practice of contributing to the funeral expenses.[110] Some families claimed their relatives because the Home practiced the commercialistic and impersonal policy of burying more than one in a grave—sometimes as many as three—starting at first grave and burying the ground over, that is, using all available burial plots then returning to the first grave (see chapter 3 for difficulties raised by this practice). Olive Cemetery was filled by the turn of the century, so the Home purchased lots in Eden Cemetery near Darby, Pennsylvania, in 1903.[111] Since the Board felt that it purchased enough lots "to bury at present rate of deaths per annum for one or two hundred years," the policy of burying three in a grave was changed to two in 1908.[112]

Sometimes residents negotiated separate graves, and at other times "sponsors" paid an extra amount above the admission fee for a resident's separate burial.[113] The Society of Friends, like most Whites, generally did not allow outsiders to be buried in their cemeteries. Some residents of the HAICP were Quaker in everything except official membership in the Yearly Meeting, having lived in some of the Quaker homes for forty or fifty years. These domestics dressed like Quakers, sounded like them, and adhered to their austere life style. Perhaps for this reason, records reveal the burial of three residents in Friends' cemeteries: one in 1886, another in 1907, and the last in 1910. Julia Needs, whose body was removed from Eden Cemetery in 1907 at the request of one Mr. Peabody, was buried in Friends' Cemetery in Frankford where her husband was interred; the other two were buried respectively in Friends' Cemetery in Bristol and Abington.[114] Since it is not known how many residents wished to be buried in Friends' cemeteries, HAICP burial is probably not a good index to Quaker liberalism.

All things considered, residents of the HAICP received good health care in an institution designed specifically for the aged. Consistent with the time, administrators hired a once-a-week physician, placed a doctor on call, and recruited untrained nurses. Fortunately, some of these individuals—physicians, nurses, matrons—were dedicated to their charge, though the high attrition of health personnel probably had a negative psychological impact on the old people. The sanitary conditions of the Home were always of some concern because of the ever-present possibility of contagious diseases, but no epidemic caused widespread death among the family, and quarantines were understandably accepted and successfully supervised. Relatives were an important complement to the health care program, nursing the sick, sometimes employing their own doctors, removing the insane, and sometimes burying the dead. They were a psychological lift to residents who had them and demonstrated that institutionalization did not mean abandonment by loved ones. Peer care also supplemented the health care provided by the Home, since the old people who had learned outside to care for one another, turned to one another for comfort and solace. Medical bigotry, reflected in the clash between allopathy and homeopathy, which was a microcosm of the larger battle outside the Home, had no long-range adverse impact on the Home's health care program, although the choice of physicians determined the type of medical procedure the residents received.

Residents constituted a large vulnerable group, but to the credit of Quaker and African American managers, medical experimentation was forbidden, and few racist notions invaded the medical records. In addition there was no discernible effort to seize the opportunity to learn about health care of old people and the aged's reactions to various diseases or to develop a system of treatment to be shared or handed down to future generations. Geriatric medicine was a thing of the future, and perhaps, opportunity lost was the old residents' gain. During the depression years all aspects of the Home declined, including the quality of health care, and the Home almost closed its doors. How the institution was revitalized and formed the nucleus for broader activities in the field of aging is the subject of the next chapter.

7
Hobart Jackson: The Father of Black Gerontology

> May the memory of the giver,
> In this home where age may rest,
> Float like fragrance through the ages,
> Ever blessing, ever blest.
> —Frances E. W. Harper, 1894

The philosophy that undergirded the administration of the HAICP remained essentially unchanged from its founding in 1864 up to the 1940s. During the nation's worst depression the Home nearly collapsed because of a variety of reasons. They were: (1) declining community support, (2) an aging physical plant with constant need for repairs, (3) soaring costs of residential care that led to the depletion of the permanent fund, (4) indifferent and poorly trained personnel, (4) lax enforcement of and undefined rules and responsibilities, (5) absence of standards of care, and (6) unimaginative administrative leadership. Largely, the terrible state of the institution could be attributed to the old philosophy, tenaciously maintained despite a society transformed by political changes such as the passage of Social Security legislation, advances in medicine and medical technology, and a growing geriatric and gerontology movement.

In 1949 Hobart Jackson became the chief administrator of the HAICP. It was through his innovative leadership and arduous work that the Home was revitalized and brought into modern times. Sometimes a theorist, but first and foremost a practitioner, Hobart Jackson worked to provide a caring context for those people entrusted to his care in the Home. Several themes emerge from an examination of the recrudescence of the HAICP. First, the limited view of old age—that the elderly were like children who needed guardians and that old age was a time for reflection and inactivity—gave way to the view that old age was an expansive time of life unrelated to chronological age and limited only by physical condition. Second, the Home became integrated into the community at large as a vital program of care for the elderly. Third, the Home was racially integrated by accepting White residents, extending its biracial history to the resident population. Fourth, in response to changing needs the HAICP broadened its service to embrace nursing care as a major component rather than a peripheral aspect of care. Fifth, residents were seen as self-determining individuals, partners in their own welfare. Finally, a holistic approach was taken that coalesced all various parts of the HAICP program into a single mission, an ethos, a sense of purpose. In all of these things the catalyst and architect was Hobart Jackson, who revitalized the HAICP and recaptured the community spirit that brought Quakers and Blacks together almost a century earlier. In addition he broadened his activities beyond the Home to become the leading Black personality in the new and burgeoning field of gerontology, founding the National Caucus on Black Aged (NCBA) in 1970, which gave structure to his ideas and a means to implement them. Taken together Jackson earned the title, in my opinion, "Father of Black Gerontology."[1]

Throughout its long, rich history the Home for Aged and Infirm Colored Persons was the unrivaled national leader in institutional care for the Black aged and served as a model for other such facilities.[2] As we have seen, there were 21 residents in 1865, 67 in 1875, 112 in 1885, and 138 in 1910; it remained around this level until the 1940s, when the Home experienced the effects of the depression. For example, there were 131 residents in 1931 but only 49 in 1941. The most precipitous decline was between 1938 and 1941, when the Board evidently stopped accepting residents. By this time the HAICP had undergone a period of gradual decline, the reasons for which are not difficult to discern. First, there was a decrease in Quaker support for at least two reasons, viz., the Quaker population had declined substantially, and fewer members of the Society of Friends shared the same motivations as their parents and grandparents for supporting programs to help African American people.[3] Second, to the disappointment of many supporters, Blacks themselves failed to fill the void left by the loss of help from the Society of Friends. Therefore, life memberships in the association virtually disappeared. Between 1898 and 1925 there were only six new life members, and only one afterward, the artist Harry T. Burleigh in 1933 joined the Association.[4] Third, individual donations declined while costs increased, particularly medical costs and the cost of upkeep on an aging physical plant. Fourth, the HAICP had a substantial endowment that exceeded $300,000 by the 1920s, but managers dug deeply into it to pay operating costs. Therefore, income from the permanent fund declined from about $15,000 in 1930 to about $2,500 in 1942.[5] The consequences of these unfortunate occurrences were a reduction in residents and staff, a decrease in services, a neglect of the physical plant, and a divided Board, the combination of which put the HAICP on the brink of collapse. Significantly, there was the real possibility of losing the substantial gift of Stephen Smith and the interracial legacy of caring for the African American elderly that had no counterpart elsewhere in American gerontological history. It is somewhat ironic that its decline occurred simultaneously with African American control, making its survival and success all the more important.

Apparently aware of the institution's precarious state, the Board of Directors contracted Emma Mae Irwin, a trained social worker, to evaluate the Home's services and make recommendations for improving them. Presented to the Board on 17 February 1938, the study, perhaps the earliest survey of a Home for the aged and a comprehensive evaluation of all aspects of the Home, described some grim aspects of the institution. Irwin cited inadequate food-handling precautions, poor selection of menus, inadequate fire protection, an unsuitable location, low standards of housekeeping and maintenance, lack of adequate medical attention, meager hygienic facilities, and a lack of social life among the residents. Compounding the problems, Irwin argued, was a Board of Managers divided by lethargy, dissension, and lack of leadership when faced with a host of problems. Moreover, the small staff of nineteen had little training and little interest in their work, and the residents were resigned to their fate while management did nothing to change their outlook and offered little in the way of diversion.[6]

Irwin's report notwithstanding, there was little change made. No doubt cost was prohibitive, but the failure to upgrade the institution was more likely due to the disagreement of the Board over whether to renovate or move the Home. According to Board member Dorothy Warrick, who in 1946 as a "fitting tribute" replaced her mother, Marie Warrick, after thirty-eight years of service, the Board was paralyzed by inaction while dissolution of the HAICP emerged as a real possibility: "There was talk of closing the Home; of moving to smaller quarters; of shutting off the fourth floor (a fire hazard); of moving to one of our houses on Belmont Avenue; of going to the Douglass Hospital on Lombard Street."[7] Consideration was also given to turning the Home over to the state.[8] Some Board members, including Board chairman Shippen Lewis, favored building a new Home on the site the Home owned on Conshohocken Road, away from the city and its network of social problems.[9] Warrick, who had often accompanied her mother on visits, described what the Home was like when she joined the Board in 1946: "I began my membership during a very low period of the Home's existence. There was an air of dejection and poor repair. People found it too depressing to go see their friends and stayed away."[10]

In September 1948 Ann Caution, the superintendent of the Home died (this position had been one of the recommendations made by Irwin), and the matron, Catherine Johnson, filled the position until the Board could find a replacement. Several months earlier (March 1948) Philadelphia's two Black hospitals, Mercy and Douglass, had merged after several years of financial difficulties and problems meeting required hospital standards.[11] When Hobart Jackson, public relations director at Mercy-Douglass Hospital, learned that the HAICP was accepting applications for a new administrator, he applied for and received the position.[12]

Hobart Jackson was born in the small town of Lyerly, Georgia, in 1916, but grew up in Chattanooga, Tennessee. He graduated from Morehouse College, Atlanta, Georgia, with honors with a B.S. degree in science and taught in the public schools of Chattanooga for one year (1936–37). He returned to Atlanta to manage the Atlanta University Bookshop and serve as the school's purchasing agent, a position he held from 1937 to 1945. In the meantime Jackson completed all the work for a masters degree in business and economics (except the thesis) at Atlanta University, which enabled him to work part-time as an accountant for J. B. Blayton and Company and teach part-time at Reid's Business College, both in Atlanta. In 1945 Jackson took a job as field representative for Interstate Department Stores in Philadelphia, Pennsylvania, where he worked one year before going over to Carroll House Department Stores as manager for another year. In 1947 he became business manager of Frederick Douglass Memorial Hospital, a position he lost to seniority in the merger between Mercy and Douglass Hospitals in 1948, becoming public relations director in the new arrangement. It was at this point that Jackson became chief administrator of the HAICP. He still taught part-time until 1955 at William Penn Business Institute and completed a masters degree in social work at Bryn Mawr college in 1960, where he later lectured in gerontology. Other aspects of Jackson's career are interspersed throughout this discussion.[13]

Therefore, Hobart Jackson did not join a bandwagon of gerontologists; nor did he enter the field with the zeal of a religious convert. In fact, he brought no formal training to the field and had no particular interest in old folks except for that borne from a deep sensitivity to and compassion for the human condition of the poor and downtrodden. He also expressed concern that the significant gift of Stephen Smith and the traditions of the HAICP would be lost. In a career he sought only an opportunity for intellectual stimulation and growth in a challenging administrative environment. Aging, a new and developing field that demographic trends indicated major growth in decades to come, provided a career framework for Jackson's ideas and aspirations. A new field, not yet guided by a major paradigmatic view, gerontology was an area in which Jackson believed he could make his contribution.[14]

When Hobart Jackson became administrator of the Home on 15 February 1949, he inherited an institution well into its second decade of stagnation and decay. The Home, he claimed, was like "a chamber of horrors."[15] The assertion was no exaggeration, Irwin had observed in 1938 that roaches were everywhere, falling from doors when one entered rooms and opened closets, and there was little evidence that things had changed much over the past decade. As a matter of fact, the city had condemned the Home, the fourth floor closed as a fire hazard, and the Board ordered to move the residents.[16] Jackson's training in business and economics led him to negotiate a new position that made him sole administrator, responsible to the Board, but with all other employees under him. Although the Board had been moving in this direction since 1938, when the first superintendent was hired, it had continued to act as both policy maker and administrator, a practice that contributed to delay and neglect in the management process. With Jackson as administrator, the Board became solely a policy-making body, entrusting the implementation of its decisions to the administration. Moreover, the management committee was eliminated and with it the division of responsibilities between the sexes. Retained was the subcommittee on house that was appointed on an ad hoc basis from among all Board members without regard to gender, a decision that removed the friction that had occurred historically between men and women in the operation of the Home. Although the members of the Board of Directors were not unanimous in their acceptance of these changes, improved administrative efficiency was soon apparent as Jackson demonstrated his diverse skills in business, social work, and public relations.[17] Dorothy Warrick described Jackson's impact:

> His views were quite modern and forward looking. Things began immediately to take on a new conception. All the world loves a winner so the general attitude of the community changed. Clubs began to be interested in bringing cheerful programs to the Home for the enjoyment of residents.[18]

Jackson was determined to revitalize the HAICP, and he had the energy, talent, and forbearance not to succumb to the challenging problems he faced.

As previously stated, the philosophy guiding the Home's operation was much as it had been at its founding in 1864. The HAICP was viewed as a worthy charity designed to provide sheltered care for those Blacks whose only recourse was public relief. This view contributed in large measure to the Home's poor condition and had by the 1950s become myopic and outmoded due to longer life expectancies, passage of Social Security legislation, society's growing interest in the welfare of its older members, and the professionalization of gerontology and geriatrics. Jackson's philosophy was shaped by the tremendous community response and wider developments in society, particularly in the field of institutional care. As a result, he sought to transform the HAICP from its custodial emphasis to caring within a philosophical context, that is, operating the Home based on advanced thinking in gerontology, health care, and institutional management.

While addressing the many maintenance problems and improving the living conditions within the Home, Jackson worked to develop closer relationships with churches, schools, civic groups, and other organizations, for he believed that the way the community viewed the Home was necessary not only for financial success, but also for residents' adjustment to their new environment.[19] Outside affiliations were also sought to meet the myriad and varied medical needs of the residents, as such institutions as Mercy-Douglass Hospital, the Arthritis and Rheumatism Foundation, and the Philadelphia Society for Better Hearing made available their services to residents. Moreover, the residents created their own groups, including the Hobby Club, Golden Age Clubs, and Current Events Club. As might be expected, the Board was somewhat reluctant to affiliate with outside organizations, but Jackson informed Board members that the Home must be integrated into the community, and living arrangements must be made as much like home as possible. Furthermore, Jackson argued, community ties were the heartbeat of the HAICP, and the Board's most significant contribution might be made in the area of public relations.[20] The administrator had his way, and the Board created a publicity committee to act as liaison between the HAICP and the community. In addition a Council of Auxiliaries was formed in 1951 to coordinate the many programs of the churches, schools, and clubs involved in planning the social activities of the residents.[21] The Council of Auxiliaries became a source of encouragement during crucial times, and Jackson often depended on it for mustering support for his efforts. The HAICP had joined the Community Chest in 1942, and its annual allotment of fifteen thousand dollars to twenty thousand dollars, along with the residents receipt of old-age assistance payments provided crucial support. Jackson's success in developing new community ties was reflected in renewed community interest and increased finances. Before Jackson implemented his new philosophy, annual contributions totaled only about two thousand dollars. Between February 1949 and December 1950, they reached fifteen thousand dollars, excluding special gifts and donations of goods and articles.[22] Not since the days of Maurice Hall, Stephen Smith, Dillwyn Parrish, William Still, Lucretia Mott, Israel Johnson, and others way back in the nineteenth century had the community responded with such significant support.

Not only the Home must be integrated into the community, but also its mission and operation, Jackson contended, must be guided by the most advanced knowledge in institutional care. Encouraged by Dr. Ira De A. Reid, Haverford sociologist and active Board member, Hobart Jackson was one of eight Blacks to attend the first National Conference on Aging held in Washington, D.C., in 1950 under auspices of the Social Security Administration. The conference exposed Jackson to advanced thinking on aging, helped to shape his ideas on the subject, and afforded him the opportunity to meet with many important persons in the field. Two years later his administration of the Home and broader activities in the field earned him the invitation to become the first Black Fellow of the Washington-based Gerontological Society.[23]

When the National Committee on Aging was organized in January 1950 under the direction of the National Social Welfare Assembly, Hobart Jackson was among the members, representing individuals concerned with problems of aging in such fields as education, institutional management, social work, and industry. In 1953 a committee on standards for sheltered care, of which Jackson was a member, published the first national standards of care for old people in *Homes for the Aged and Nursing Homes*. The guidelines developed in this document covered a wide range of areas of institutional concern that included administration, physical environment, finances, and personnel as well as the recognition and definition of needs and delivery of services to older people in institutions. This document, which Hobart Jackson helped to produce, formed the basis for Jackson's administration in the HAICP.[24]

These experiences kept Jackson attuned to the changing times, and his philosophy of aging began to crystallize. By providing encouragement to the staff and revitalizing the Board, he sought to create for the first time a stimulating social and physical environment for the residents. To achieve the proper corrective atmosphere, Jackson felt a change in attitudes was essential, rejecting simultaneously the stereotypical assumptions that prevailed inside and outside the HAICP that old age was a time of waiting as well as the "lady bountiful" attitude that poor folks should be cared for as they await the Grim Reaper:[25]

> Both of these attitudes are harmful and must go—must be pulled up by the roots and discarded if we are to properly integrate older people into our society. In their stead we must adopt and make our own the attitude that the aged are not just a category, but "people"—individuals with varied backgrounds and hence varied needs and aspirations. Basically, they have the same rights, requirements, and needs which people in other age brackets have. Some of these rights are the rights to maximum self-determination, privacy of person and thought, and personal dignity. Some of these needs are the need for work, play, love, and worship.[26]

Jackson emphasized that old people were not fragmented personalities with a divisible set of problems, but whole individuals with rights and responsibilities like other human beings and should be so treated. The problems, he urged, were inextricably intertwined with the social, cultural, and medical aspects of care. As he put it, "seventy-five percent of the problems of the old are social, cultural, and political rather than medical."[27] Recognizing that the Home's resident population was becoming increasingly infirm and needed medical service, Jackson maintained that the Home was primarily a living arrangement, and though it stressed health, it was not a hospital:

> In implementing its purpose the Home emphasized that despite its health service it was a living arrangement first. Its program was designed to enable its residents to move toward a goal of dynamic and purposeful reactivation of life; to enable them to participate in planning in their own behalf up to their maximum capacity to do so; and finally to give and seek protection and appropriate care for those unable to engage themselves in their own behalf.[28]

In transforming the Home for the Aged and Infirm Colored Persons from one of shelter to one of care, Jackson was bringing the Home abreast of the times.[29] More important, he was rejecting the old philosophy of custodialism and replacing it with an ideology and vision for the future.

To bring the old era to an end, a new name was also needed to bring the Home up to date as the present one seemed outmoded. Thus, in 1953 the Stephen Smith Home for the Aged (SSHA) was adopted, which symbolized the new philosophy while remaining loyal to the best of the past traditions. The title was initially rejected because it was said to smack of "racialism." It was Dorothy Warrick's recommendation that this name be adopted, though it took three years before it became a reality. Hobart Jackson supported the name because one reason for his taking the job was to help preserve the Smith gift. In early years there were annual programs honoring Stephen and Harriet Smith, so it made little sense to reject the title that was in keeping with the spirit of the founders. Besides, changing the name from the Home for Aged and Infirm Colored Persons to the Stephen Smith Home for the Aged was designed to remove the designation of exclusion.[30] Consequently, the Board adopted the policy of admitting applicants regardless of race, color, class, or creed to be consistent with the policy of openness and integration. It was also said to close the perceived gap between preachment and policy and to put the Board members, as assistant treasurer I. Maximillian Martin said, "in a position as citizens of the Community to call on other institutions for the aged to open their doors [to all] without discrimination."[31] On 7 November 1954 the first White residents arrived. Three in number, the newcomers were welcomed by Jackson at the Founders Day Program on the Home's ninetieth anniversary:

> This we believe has far reaching Christian implications—embodying those tenets and teachings which we all must follow. We believe too that here we have assumed the mantel of leadership which must spread up and down the ladder of institutions similar to our own.[32]

The biracial effort, began in 1864, when Quakers and Blacks came together to found the HAICP, was now extended to the residents. Perhaps no single occurrence more clearly marked the end of the old era than the racial heterogeneity of the new resident population.

At the practical level, Jackson sought changes inside the institution that were congruent with his philosophy, with current knowledge in gerontology, and with providing self-determination to the elderly. Although the nature of the institution dictated some monitoring of visitors' and residents' whereabouts, the strict observance of visiting hours and the requirement of permission to leave the Home were removed. Instead, the policy was instituted of allowing mentally and physically capable residents to leave without permission from administrators. When a resident was found dead in the snow in 1952, Jackson came under attack for his "open door" policy, but the policy of allowing human beings the right to go and come as they pleased was the only humane alternative to an antiquarian and totalitarian policy.[33] In 1951 the House Council was created to give residents a voice in their affairs through a formal system of self-government. The executive committee of the Council, the House Adjustment Committee, handled all complaints and grievances and made recommendations for changes to administration. The next year the "Home Recorder" was established to allow residents to express their views to the administration and the general community.[34]

Perhaps the earliest of Jackson's decisions was to abolish the life care system that required residents to relinquish all their possessions to the Home in exchange for life care and decent burial. In Jackson's opinion that requirement was "manifestly unfair."[35] In reality the system had by Jackson's time outlived its usefulness because total indigency was removed with the enactment of Social Security legislation, specifically, old-age assistance. In an earlier era, many would have been deprived of institutional care without it since a monthly fee was beyond their means. Also early on, Jackson sought to rehabilitate residents through clubs, arts and crafts, movies, excursions, vacations, and other activities that dramatically raised the level of social participation.[36] All these changes were designed to foster among the residents a sense of identification with the Home and to enhance their self-respect. A cardinal tenet of the Jackson philosophy was the right to self-determination. Later Jackson wrote:

> Older people have certain characteristics which arise in the aging process. At the same time they have the same essential rights and requirements that all people possess—the right to maximum self-determination, privacy of person and thought, and personal dignity. Infringement of these rights, or failure to provide services for properly exercising them, violates the older person's prerogatives as a human being.[37]

Jackson's emphasis on the "wholeness" of the individual led him to stress the interrelatedness of all aspects of care and institutional management. Not only was the individual a "whole," but the institution had to be managed organically as well. Those employed at the SSHA, regardless of rank or position, must not only have defined duties and levels of responsibility but also enjoy dignity and self-respect as well as those who are served. Jackson advocated training, especially in-service education, for those who worked with the old and called for removal of the perception that these were "philanthropic" positions. "We will never achieve wholeness for our residents until we achieve social justice, equity and dignity for these employees," he claimed.[38]

The environment also must contribute to the well-being of the residents. The physical surroundings must not only be pleasant and attractive, but also be designed to meet the varied needs of individuals throughout the continuum from well and independent to sick and dependent. Therefore, services and facilities for the elderly had to be modernized to be corrective and to provide the milieu appropriate for optimizing individual potential and for solving the individual's problems. Some Board members wanted to move the Home to the country to achieve the appropriate setting, away from what they considered a myriad of urban problems such as traffic, noise, and crime. Hobart Jackson was vehemently opposed to such a move, arguing that the serenity of the countryside was no desirable alternative to the availability of services in the city. Again the administrator had his way. In 1953 the Board voted fifty-three thousand dollars for renovations, and after a successful financial campaign that raised another fifty thousand dollars, the Home was renovated, restoring to use the fourth floor, adding a new elevator, making needed repairs to kitchen and laundry, rehabilitating the heating and electrical systems, and installing hygienic facilities.[39]

The needs of the residents were changing as well. By the end of 1953, it was apparent that the number of residents who needed medical attention was increasing, and the SSHA had to reassess the role of nursing care.[40] With Social Security legislation, total indigency was removed as a major factor that brought residents to old-age Homes. They now came for the medical and social services that could be attained in an institutional arrangement. Since Blacks who came to the Home rarely held the kinds of jobs that provided retirement plans or annuities for employees, the majority of Stephen Smith's residents received old-age assistance. A steady income gave the old a "new freedom" that allowed them to remain in their own homes or to choose the kind of living arrangement best suited to them.[41] By the 1950s, medical advances had eliminated many of the deadly diseases "so people are left to wear out with slowly increasing disabilities caused by the so called chronic diseases."[42]

Jackson, inheriting two partially trained nurses and a bi-weekly physician, instituted an around-the-clock nursing program for the first time in 1950 with three practical nurses working continuous eight-hour shifts, directed by a registered nurse, but he continued the twice-a-week arrangement with the doctor.[43] Jackson insisted, however, that the Home must not model itself after a hospital, living arrangements must be as much like home as possible. Applicants still had to be in good health when they came to the Home, but those coming after 1953 were provided with a wide range of health care and rehabilative services: casework, psychiatric treatment, and physical and occupational therapy as well as standard medical care.

To examine the main developments since 1953 is really to recount the Home's growing response toward meeting a variety of needs of aged Philadelphians. In doing so, one sees the Home striving to realize its goal of becoming a total gerontological and geriatric community. By 1956 the Board realized that expanded accommodations for the sick were needed to replace the structure built back in 1901, and in 1961 a new infirmary with modern medical facilities was completed.[44] The new unit was capable of accommodating fifty handicapped, disabled, and chronically ill individuals and was built at a cost of $500,000. A grant of $150,000 from the federal government's Hill-Burton program, which was originally designed to aid hospital construction, and a successful financial campaign in 1960 helped to pay for the new structure. In that year there were 190 residents in the Home, and four out of every five applicants were in need of some form of nursing care.[45]

Since the HAICP had accepted boarders as well as life care residents from it inception and occasionally provided assistance to those in their own homes awaiting admission, it was traditionally a multifaceted institution. While the SSHA was moving toward a nursing facility, there was still a need to provide for those who were independent. In 1967 a $1.5 million apartment complex was built with 120 efficiency and 20 single-bedroom apartments. This structure, The Stephen Smith Towers, was designed for the ambulatory or independent resident. Though idealistic, one of the Home's goals was rehabilitation so that residents might be returned to the community. The Towers, therefore, provided the placement facility for those who successfully completed a program of reactivation and could be discharged from the Home.[46] The Home thus provided for those who managed independently and for those who needed intensive nursing care. Those individuals classified as intermediate or semi–independent lived in the buildings constructed long ago by Stephen Smith and Edward Parker. Actually, The Stephen Smith Towers provided for the elderly who in earlier years would have constituted the Home's residents, and its completion marked the transition of the old Home for the aged to a nursing facility.[47]

A separate Board of Directors, whose members were chosen from the parent Board, operated The Stephen Smith Towers as a subsidiary corporation. In the fall of 1970, without changing the administrative structure, the Home's Board chose a new name, "The Stephen Smith Geriatric Center," a name designed to subsume the many and varied services of the institution.[48] Between 1970 and 1971, a day care center was established for those in the community who needed services without institutionalization. Two new centers, the Smith-Pinn and Smith-Shepherd Centers, were operated for the benefit of the community's aged. Both centers provided a nutrition program, social activities, and ancillary medical services. Many participants in these nonresidential programs actually had made applications to the Home; thus, the Home continued a tradition that began in the nineteenth century by providing for individuals who must await admission. These services were aimed, however, at those individuals who could use them during the day and return to their homes at night.[49] By the mid-1970s the centers were providing institutional and non-institutional services for over six hundred elderly persons, some of whom lived in their own homes.

In 1978 the Home was rebuilt, preserving the historic Smith building for social and cultural use, and services expanded to include casework, psychiatric treatment, physical and occupational therapy as well as those previously mentioned. By providing a variety of different services the Home broadened its scope and now spanned the gamut of care from independence to intermediate to skilled care. In doing so, the Jackson administration strove to realize its goal of becoming a total gerontological and geriatric community by implementing the philosophical and practical changes that transformed the Home from custodial to holistic care.

Since its acquisition in 1985 by the Mercy-Douglass's Center, the Stephen Smith Geriatric Center has been renamed The Stephen Smith Multi-Service Center (SSMSC). The center operates The Stephen Smith Home as a 180-bed facility that provides for intermediate care; the nursing facility built in 1961, the Smith-Cunningham Personal Care Facility, provides for fifty-two elderly individuals who need help with such daily routines as dressing, eating, and bathing. Service programs also include case management, which provides for assessments and coordinates services to the elderly in their own homes. The Smith-Pinn and Smith-Shepard Centers continue to operate programs for well elderly, including recreation, meals, seminars, and referrals. A home meals program provides daily meals to community elderly. Rounding out the many services are an adult day care center for those who are able to remain with family at night, a respite care program to provide relief to caregivers of the frail elderly, and a shared housing project designed to rehabilitate the personal homes of area elderly. In summary, the center has continued the HAICP tradition of providing a continuum of services to meet the needs of the Black Philadelphia elderly.[50]

Hobart Jackson broadened his activities beyond the Stephen Smith Home, and by the 1960s his efforts had made him a well-known figure in institutional care. He had become not only the first African American Fellow in the Gerontological Society, but also had served on its executive board and had chaired its social research, planning, and practice section. He had also become vice president of the National Council on Aging by the mid-1960s and from 1960 to 1965 chaired Pennsylvania's Governor's Advisory Committee on Aging. At the national level he served on the Presidential Task Force on Aging in 1967–68 and was intimately involved in the White House Conferences on Aging in 1960 and 1970, serving on the executive committee. His experiences in the Home, continued training in the field, and activities around the nation afforded Jackson the knowledge to become an important advocate for all aged as well as the leading advocate for the Black elderly. In 1963 the Urban League established a subcommittee on aging that produced the study *Double Jeopardy* the following year, a study that laid bare many of the inequities Blacks faced in preparing for old age. This work took the unequivocal position that African Americans because of race and age constituted a distinct group among the aged population.[51] Hobart Jackson chaired the committee that produced the report, and it reflected his contention that the problems of elderly Black people were but a microcosm of the problems that all African Americans faced in the larger society—poverty and racism—compounded by old age. There had been earlier attempts to analyze the peculiar problems Blacks experienced in old age and to bring public attention to their specific needs, but it was *Double Jeopardy* that provided a conceptual framework and proved most successful in accomplishing this noteworthy objective.[52]

As an advocate and student of Black aging, Jackson's single most significant contribution, and arguably the most significant occurrence in Black gerontology, was the founding of the National Caucus on Black

Aged (NCBA) in Philadelphia in 1970. The caucus brought together a contingent of sociologists, gerontologists, social workers, and educators who were concerned about giving visibility to the plight of the Black elderly and who worked to mobilize existing resources to resolve their problems. Established in anticipation of the 1971 White House Conferences on Aging, the caucus was designed to insure a representative input from the African American community. Jacquelyne Jackson and Inabel Lindsay, retired dean of the School of Social Work at Howard University, prepared the working paper for the conference. Published in November 1971, it was titled "The Multiple Hazards of Age and Race: The Situation of Aged Blacks in the United States." As a result, included in the 1971 White House Conference was a "Special Concerns Session on Aged Blacks."[53]

The NCBA, based in Washington, D.C., gave structure to Jackson's belief that African Americans had unique problems that were urgent, critical, and deserving of national attention. It also provided the framework for his belief that organized action in the social and political arena is the only way to achieve equity in American society. The NCBA was organized on the grounds of the Stephen Smith Home for the Aged, founded by a biracial group that appears to have recaptured the enthusiasm that motivated Quakers and Blacks who came together in 1864 to make provisions for neglected elderly Black Philadelphians. While separated by more than a century, both groups, in their own way, sought to remedy the injustice they saw in a society where Black people, "around the verge of parting life," could not find dignity and self-respect. The NCBA has become the leading advocacy group for providing training programs on and improving services to the African American elderly.[54]

In October 1973 with funds from the Administration on Aging (AOA) the National Center on Black Aged, the brainchild of Jacquelyne Jackson, was founded, and Hobart Jackson became director until 1975. According to him the center was designed to serve as a base where researchers will "be collecting data, supporting and promoting beginning and existing services, disseminating information, and developing liaison relationships with other organizations in the field at the national, state and local level."[55] The next year, Jacquelyne Jackson issued a challenge to gerontologists to "support and respect" the center. Specifically, she called for gerontologists to meet the challenge by joining the NCBA, increasing the involvement of Blacks in planning for the elderly, providing for Black participation in training programs, electing politicians sensitive to the needs of elderly Blacks, overcoming the emphasis on homogeneity among the aged, carrying out recommendations made by the 1971 Special Concerns Session, and working for increased life expectancies of Black people, among other things.[56]

Institutionalization, however, remained the focal point of Hobart Jackson's concern for the Black elderly, and their denial of access to White-run housing facilities was a source of despair. Gerontologists, Jackson felt, obscured the problem by their emphasis on deinstitutionalization or alternatives to institutional care at a time when the Black elderly needed to devise strategies to get them into institutions. Confronting the paradox in 1971, Jackson claimed:

> The problem essentially is not how to keep the older Black person out of an institution, it is rather how to get him or her into a good one. Older Blacks are already in their own homes or other places or residence but, of course, without necessary and essential services, many times without visibility and without access to or even knowledge of existing resources or services.[57]

The nursing Home system, Jackson argued, was "one of the real atrocities of our time," and he called for "a strong and viable system of nursing home care" in the Black communities, "strategically located" and, if necessary, government financed to remove the Black elderly's second-rate citizenship.[58] Jackson would undoubtedly agree, that what was once alien to African American culture should be viewed as traditional, and the nursing Home should be seen as one facet of a multifaceted approach to solving gerontological problems for African American people.

Up to the time of his death in 1978, Hobart Jackson was an active participant in gerontological conferences, a much sought after consultant, and an indefatigable lecturer.[59] He presented dozens of papers at workshops and seminars all across the country, including twenty colleges, held memberships in numerous organizations related to aging, advised dozens, perhaps hundreds, of students interested in gerontology, served on countless task forces at the national, state, and local levels for presidents, governors, and mayors, received more than fifty awards, and testified before both houses of Congress. Primarily a practitioner, Jackson's published works grew largely from his experiences rather than from original scholarly research. Jackson felt that too often research was isolated from the "activities of the real world" and failed to combine "an activist component," which was necessary to resolve the "myriad of current problems" that the elderly encountered.[60] His experiences over almost three decades made him an expert in Black gerontology, particularly institutional care. Jackson was truly an advocate of the Black aged, and his ideas were given structure with the birth of the National Caucus on Black Aged, while his understanding of the need for scholarly activity and for the compilation of data in order to change attitudes toward the aged is reflected in his work at the National Center on Black Aging.

An assessment of Jackson's achievements in gerontology cannot be done justice simply by recounting individual successes. One, for example, cannot begin to gauge the significance of the preservation of the Stephen Smith Home by listing successful programs instituted or changes brought about under his administration. Nor can one gauge the full impact of his contribution to the NCBA, in which he was the prime mover, or National Center, which he directed through its early years. Their full meaning in public policy, education, and other areas remains to be seen. The significance of Jackson's contributions cannot be separated from the context in which they were made and the quality of life he struggled to insure for the future aged. When Hobart Jackson died in 1978, the Black aged had lost a good friend, and all of America's elderly were a little poorer. Indeed, more than anyone else, Jackson had come to symbolize the drive for dignity and individual worth for old Black folk. If the Black aged are a little better off today, it would be hard to deny that Hobart Jackson deserves some of the credit. It was altogether fitting that the leader among advocates of humane treatment of the African American elderly should be associated with the nation's oldest Black Home for the aged, and it is most fitting as well to consider Hobart Jackson the Father of Black Gerontology.

8
Epilogue: A Word to Gerontologists

> Ah nothing is too late
> Till the tired heart shall cease
> to palpitate . . .
> For age is opportunity no less
> Than youth itself, though in
> another dress . . .
>
> —Henry Wadsworth Longfellow

Much of what is known about the African American elderly lacks historical context. Therefore, three overriding but interrelated assumptions have governed *Complaint to the Lord*. First and foremost was the assumption that Black aging history would bring about a better understanding of the African American elderly and help to refine old-age policies, leading to better service delivery. Another assumption was that a study of the Stephen Smith Home would illuminate the importance of history to gerontology, providing a historical context for those who face aging issues daily. Finally, it was theorized that the study would foster a better understanding of the Black experience in America, though focusing on elderly African Americans. In all these, the goal was to respond to Achenbaum's admonition "to create a reliable historical perspective with which to assess the elderly's current conditions and expectations about the situation for older Americans in the years ahead."

In the crucible of slavery African Americans developed a supportive or mutual aid tradition that transformed African heritage into practices that sustained them in slavery and were extended into freedom. Major components of this tradition were a deep respect for the old, a strong kinship system, and a communal network that extended beyond family boundaries. It was this supportive tradition that slaves depended on in old age as they performed valuable functions that provided them dignity and respect. The mutual aid tradition became so pervasive that it entered the knowledge base as conventional wisdom, at the root of which was the unidimensional notion that the African American family took care of

8: Epilogue

all needs and obviated agencies outside the extended family unit. History points out, however, that the supportive tradition was multifaceted, carrying over into freedom in such organized forms as beneficial societies and old-age Homes. The former provided assistance to widows, allotments for temporary illnesses, and burial expenses. In general, beneficial societies helped the old remain at home in independence. Another aspect of the many-sided support for the Black elderly that also challenges conventional wisdom was the development of Homes for the Black aged, the first of which was founded over 150 years ago. Through increased usage and changing conditions, Homes took on their own tradition. Today, there is a greater possibility of African Americans going to nursing Homes, and conventional wisdom exacerbates the guilt usually associated with placement. It should be discarded for the frame of reference that Homes are a traditional means of resolving gerontological problems in the African American community. This is the necessary first step toward making these better places to live and more responsive to the cultural and social needs of the African American elderly.

The state of gerontological knowledge today has moved far beyond the working understanding of those who managed the Home for Aged and Infirm Colored Persons, but its operation provides historical perspectives in microcosm that contribute to our understanding of aging in an integrated society, particularly as race, age, and gender stereotypes played out in the context of the HAICP administration. We learned that what exists has not always been that way and that future changes may be more far reaching, and in doing so we recognize pitfalls to be avoided and lessons to be followed.

At the root of meeting the needs of residents of nursing Homes, an industry that will continue to expand in the years to come, is the need to provide personnel (social workers, nurses, administrators, orderlies, aides, and anyone who comes into contact with aged people) who are trained in gerontology and geriatrics. Physicians should be employed on a regular basis and should bring the requisite attributes of sensitivity to and compassion for the elderly as well as appropriate credentials in geriatric medicine. Hobart Jackson's caveat that there will not be dignity for residents until there is dignity for those who care for them should be heeded.

It is also essential that those who make policy for the old understand the cultural traditions and distinct histories of the elderly populations they seek to serve. They must take into account family structure, helping patterns, mutual aid and respect patterns, attitudes toward health, dietary patterns, and coping mechanisms. For Black Americans, born during the segregation era and living through decades of exclusion from American political and social institutions, interracial contact was uneasy, even the visit to the doctor was an indignity—greeted by an impolite nurse or a stay in a dingy waiting room. How reasonable is it today to expect these people to seek out services outside their community? Ways to promote cultural diversity and encourage religious traditions that validate residents of institutions must be constantly sought. Preliminary research shows that African American elderly prefer Black-owned institutions because they believe that cultural and religious traditions will be respected and enhanced. Hobart Jackson's call for a viable system of community-based long-term care is still much needed as well as is the promotion of curricula about African American and minority elderly in the preparation of health professionals.

Stereotypes of all kinds must be recognized and rejected for their destructive nature. Attitudes of paternalism and noblesse oblige as well as stereotypes of the old as children and old age as a period of reflection must not be allowed to intrude policy formulation, influence administrative decisions, or limit self-determination. How might the life satisfaction of the residents of HAICP have changed if managers had put aside their conception of old age as a time for reflection and implemented, for example, the observation of Nancy Graham in 1892 that they employ "exercise about the house." Administrators' stereotypes and negative attitudes limited the old peoples' lives while residents themselves sought to expand opportunity and maximize potential.

In the HAICP, families were not abandoned and current institutions must find creative ways to involve them in all aspects of care. Relatives inquired about treatments, visited their kin, withdrew the mentally ill, and maintained ties that were not severed by institutionalization. They were important support mechanisms for the residents. That families must be integrated into all aspects of institutional care is represented in the Nursing Home Bill of Rights, but it cannot be overemphasized, lest practitioners lapse into the view that they, as trained professionals, know best and come to view family members as meddlers, who, if they could do better, should have kept the aged person home. Family members must be vigilant in seeing to it that their relatives are adequately attended to throughout their stay in institutions.

There is evidence that those with "sponsors" received better attention to their needs. In cases where there are elderly people without families, the potential for abuse is increased. Thus, the need for a strong, vital, and viable ombudsman program (combined with enforcement of standards imposed by medicaid or state human resource programs) is essential. While licensing and certification procedures may impose guidelines, one should not assume that quality inevitably follows, and ombudsmen must be empowered to visit institutions without notice as well as play a vital role in relicensing and recertification processes. Communication patterns must be reviewed, analyzed, and updated, and the ombudsmen program must be seen as useful and effective by those who need and use it. Otherwise, there is no control in a potentially despotic environment. Notwithstanding the enlightened times, there is still widespread abuse in Homes, particularly neglect, overuse of restraints, overreliance on tranquilizers, and inadequate medical attention.

In the last analysis, we must examine our own attitudes toward the elderly, support training in gerontology, work for better facilities of care, advocate a strong national health care system for all Americans, and plan for our own aging. That way, perhaps our prayers will not be in the form of complaints.

Appendix 1
Bylaws: 1864

ARTICLE I.

The Managers shall meet on the second Fourth-day evening in every month, at 8 o'clock.

ARTICLE II.

Special Meetings may be called by the Chairman, or at the request of any three members.

ARTICLE III.

All Reports of Committees shall be made to the Board in writing.

ARTICLE IV.

The meetings of the Board shall be conducted according to the Rules of Order usual in similar bodies.

ARTICLE V.

Standing Committees on the following subjects shall be appointed by the Chairman at the first meetings in each current year:

   1st   A Committee of Management
   2nd A Committee on Property and Finance
   3rd   A Committee on Supplies

ARTICLE VI.

The Committee of Management shall consist of the female members of the Board. They shall have a general supervision of the internal arrangements of the Home,

Appendix 1

and shall propose to the Board any regulations or measures which may be needed for its government. They may draw on the Treasury for sums not exceeding fifty dollars per month. They shall divide themselves into the following subcommittees:

1st. A Visiting Committee of four, to be appointed monthly in rotation; any two of whom shall visit the Home twice in each week, and endeavor to be present once during meals. They shall make themselves acquainted with the situation and wants of the inmates, generally direct the concerns of the family, and report their observations in a book provided for this purpose. They shall receive and enter applications for admissions, and make the necessary inquiry in regard to the applicant, previous to the action of the Board thereon.
2nd. A reading Committee of four, to be appointed monthly, to visit the Home frequently, and read to the inmates from the Scriptures, or other suitable book, and also furnish reading matter for the Institution and supervise any arrangements of an educational character.
3rd. A Committee of four, who shall superintend the making and distribution of clothing, give directions in regard to any industrial employments for the inmates.

Article VII.

The Committee on Property and Finance shall consist of the male members of the Board, and shall have charge of the real estate and financial affairs of the Home.

Article VIII.

The Committee on supplies to consist of three persons, who, in conjunction with the Matron, shall make all necessary purchases for the Home.

Article IX.

The Board shall appoint annually two physicians, to look after the health of the inmates.

Article X.

Order of Business:

1. Calling the Roll.
2. Reading the Minutes.
3. Report of the Treasurer.
4. Unfinished Business.
5. Reports of Standing Committees.

6. Reports of Special Committees.
7. New Business.

Life Care Contract

For the more effectual enforcement of Rules 4 and 8, the Managers of "The Home for Aged and Infirm Colored Persons" have adopted (Sixth month 14th, 1871) the following Agreement, to be signed by all inmates upon their entrance into the Home:

Form of a Bond

In consideration of being admitted into "The Home for Aged and Infirm Colored Persons," I, the undersigned, do hereby assign, transfer, set over, and forever relinquish to the said Home (for the use of said Home) all money, rights, credits, goods, chattels, and effects, now belonging to me, or to which I am in anyway entitled. And I do further Agree with, and promise to the Managers of said Home that, if I shall hereafter receive or become entitled to any money, or other property of any kind, real or personal, I will immediately give information thereof to the Managers of said Home, and will, if requested by them so to do, assign and transfer the same to said Managers for the benefit of said home, if I continue therein. And I do also engage and promise that I will comply with the Rules of the Institution.

Witness my hand this _____ day of 18 ____

_____

_____

Will

_____19

First—I declare this to be my last will, hereby revoking all former wills and codicils at ant time heretofore made.

Second—I give, devise and bequeath all real and personal property which I may own at the time of my death to The Home for Aged and Infirm Colored Persons, its successors and assigns.

Third—I nominate and appoint as executor of this my last will and testament the treasurers of The Home for Aged and Infirm Colored, who shall be in office at my death, and his successors in office.

Signed, sealed published and declared
by the above named testator as and for
a last will and testament in the presence
of us who, at the testator's request,
in the testator's presence, and in the
presence of each other, have hereunto
subscribed our names as witnesses: _____ SEAL

_____

Appendix 2
Rules and Regulations: 1864

RULE 1.

The Matron shall have the entire charge of the Home, and keep it in neat order under the direction of the Committee of Management. She is to enforce the Rules, be present at the meals, see that they are properly served up, that everything is on the table before the family is seated, that suitable nourishment is provided for the sick, and proper order observed at the table. She must be respectful and kind to every one in the Home, and attentive (without partiality) as their circumstances require. She shall promptly check any quarreling or other improper conduct in the inmates, and, if necessary, report the name to the Visiting Committee. She shall keep a record of all expenditures, and furnish the Committee with a monthly account thereof. She shall be expected to go through the house about 9 o'clock, A.M., and see that all unnecessary fires and lights are extinguished.

RULE 2.

No person will be admitted into the Home but such as bring satisfactory testimonials of the propriety of their conduct and the respectability of their character.

RULE 3.

Those received into the Home must be at least fifty years of age, and shall pay to the Treasurer the sum of 30 dollars, and furnish a good bedstead, bedding, and furniture for room; or shall pay 40 dollars without furniture. This Rule may be varied from if so directed by the Managers.

RULE 4.

Any colored persons being life members of this Association who shall become so far reduced in their circumstances and physically disabled as to be fit subject for admission into the Home, shall have the preference over all others; and the sum which they may have paid into the Treasury shall be credited to them and deducted from the full charge for admission.

RULE 5.

Any property or personal effects which an applicant may be possessed of must be made over for the benefit of the Home prior to their admission therein; and if any inherit property while in the Home, and prefer remaining, the said property must likewise be transferred to the Managers for the use of the Institution: all such transfers being recorded in a book kept for this purpose.

RULE 6.

Colored persons over the age of 50, of respectable character and furnishing satisfactory references, may be boarded in the Institution, upon such terms as the Managers may decide; but shall be subject to the same rules, and have no privileges different from the other inmates. Satisfactory security must be given for the regular payment of the board previous to their admission.

RULE 7.

No boarder shall be received or continued in the Home to the exclusion of those entirely dependent. Two weeks' notice however, must be given for the removal of any boarder.

RULE 8.

A register shall be kept of the names of all applicants, the persons by whom they are recommended, their place of residence, and the report of the Visiting Committee thereon, and any other information that may be deemed important.

RULE 9.

Those that are pensioners on any benevolent Institution or Society, it is expected will have their pensions continued to assist in their support, and that their funeral expenses shall be paid.

RULE 10.

Those received into the Home will be cared for without other expense during their lives, provided the Managers have the funds.

Rule 11.

The inmates are prohibited from soliciting aid from outside of the Institution.

Rule 12.

After rising in the morning, and again before retiring at night all who are of ability shall be assembled in a suitable room, and a chapter from the Bible read to them, after which an opportunity shall be afforded for silent or vocal worship.

Rule 13.

Religious meetings shall be held in the Home on the first day of the week, at 10 1/2 o'clock, A.M., and 4 o'clock, P.M., for those unable or not desirous of attending elsewhere.

Rule 14.

Any one of the inmates may be visited (with their consent) for religious purposes at any suitable time, but if a religious opportunity is desired with all the family, it must be first approved by at least two of the Managers.

Rule 15.

A bell will be rung ten minutes before each meal, when all who are able will repair to the dining room. When seated, a suitable pause shall be observed before eating.

Rule 16.

The sick or infirm will be accommodated with meals in their rooms, but all others will be expected to take them at the general table.

Rule 17.

It will be expected that all who are capable will make their own beds, and sweep their rooms early every morning; such as are not, will have it done for them.

Rule 18.

The inmates are expected to sew, knit or do any other service for the benefit of the Home in which they are capable.

Rule 19.

Any of the inmates desiring to visit their friends, must give information to the Matron as to the length of their stay, and where they may be found, so as to prevent any uneasiness on their account.

Rule 20.

If any of the friends of the inmates present articles for individual use or for general distribution, the same must be placed in charge of the Matron and furnished at her discretion.

Rule 21.

No stimulants or liquors to be used in the Home unless ordered by a physician, and then to be administered only by the matron.

Rule 22.

No person will be permitted to interfere or find fault with the Matron. Any complaint should be made to the managers for their action.

Rule 23.

All visitors shall be properly treated and shown through the Home, especially those visiting for religious purposes. Visitors will not be admitted before 10, A.M., or after 5, P.M., except in special cases.

Rule 24.

The strictest attention must be paid by each one of the family to these Rules. For the first and second offence the Matron will admonish the offender; for a third, she will complain to the Visiting Committee; and a fourth, removal from the Home, if so directed by the Board.

Appendix 3
Organizational Structure

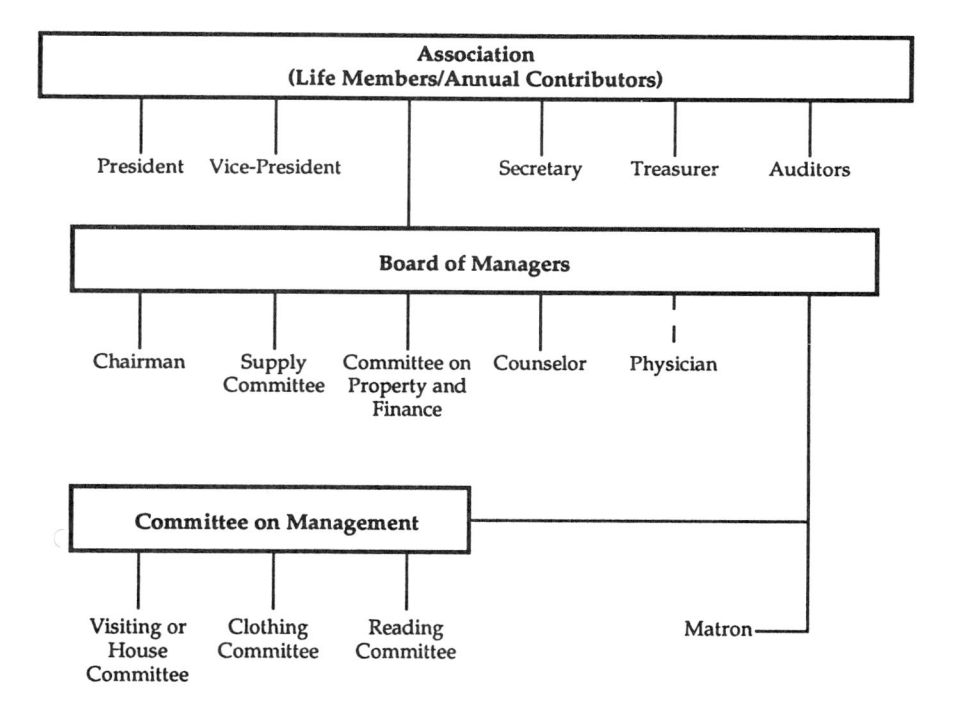

```
┌─────────────────────────────────────────────────┐
│                   Association                    │
│        (Life Members/Annual Contributors)         │
└─────────────────────────────────────────────────┘
    │        │              │         │        │
President Vice-President  Secretary Treasurer Auditors

┌─────────────────────────────────────────────────┐
│                 Board of Managers                 │
└─────────────────────────────────────────────────┘
    │         │           │           │          │
Chairman   Supply    Committee on   Counselor  Physician
          Committee  Property and
                      Finance

┌─────────────────────────────┐
│   Committee on Management    │
└─────────────────────────────┘
    │          │          │
Visiting or  Clothing   Reading                  Matron
  House     Committee  Committee
Committee
```

Notes

Introduction

1. A stanza from two poems by Frances E. W. Harper open many of the chapters. She was an African American poet and novelist who supported the Home for Aged and Infirm Colored Persons (HAICP). The poems were written for the Home's twenty-fifth anniversary and for the dedication of the Parker Annex in 1894. The original poems can be found in Leslie J. Pollard, "Frances Harper and the Old Poeple: Two Recently Discovered Poems," *The Griot* 4 (winter/summer 1985): 52–56. Historically, Homes for the aged were institutions that cared for the physically independent at the time of admission, though they invariably added infirmaries. The term is used here to refer to its historical use as well as the modern meaning that includes nursing Homes and other long-term care facilities, but should be understood in the context in which it is used. In addition the word *Home* is capitalized throughout this study to distinguish these institutions from private homes. The elderly referred to throughout the text are those chronologically old, that is, sixty-five and older. Where the old do not conform to this definition, the chapter on slavery for example, a separate definition is provided. For various roles of the Home for the aged see Murray Wax, "The Changing Role of the Home for the Aged," *The Gerontologist* 2 (September 1962): 128–33. Julius Weil, "Changing Trends in the Care of the Aged," *Journal of Gerontology* 2 (1947): 145–55. Blanche Coggan, "Gerontologic Reviews: A Review of Facilities Available for Older People," *Journal of Gerontology* 6 (1951): 394–97.

2. W. Andrew Achenbaum, *Old Age in the New Land: The American Experience Since 1790* (Baltimore: The Johns Hopkins University Press, 1978), 168. See also David Fischer, *Growing Old in America* (Oxford: Oxford University Press, 1978), 151. At the turn of the century gerontology existed as a discipline, and geriatrics has been a term applied to medical problems of the old since 1914, but gerontology did not reach full-fledged academic status until the 1950s.

3. James S. Jackson, "Growing Old in Black America: Research on Aging Black Populations," in *The Black Elderly: Research on Physical and Psychological Health* (New York: Springer Pulishing Company, 1988), 4.

4. Walter Beattie, "The Aging Negro: Some Implications for Social Welfare Services," *Phylon* 21 (summer 1960): 135. See also T. A. Tally and Jerome Kaplan, "The Negro Aged," *Newsletter of the Gerontological Society* 111 (December 1956): 6. For an early demographic view of elderly Blacks see T. L. Smith, "The Changing Number and Distribution of the Aged Negro Population of the United States," *Phylon* 28 (1957): 339–54.

5. National Urban League, *Double Jeopardy: The Older Negro in America Today* (New York: The National Urban League, 1964), frontispiece. The National Caucus on the Black Aged (NCBA) was founded in 1970 and is discussed in

chapter 7. Native Americans, Asians, and Spanish groups have in recent years organized to meet their particular needs.

6. Jacquelyne Jackson, *Minorities and Aging* (Belmont, Calif.: Wadsworth Publishing Company, 1980), 63. Since her review of the literature that appeared in the *Gerontologist* in 1967, Jackie Jackson has demonstrated her expertise in gerontology. Jacquelyne Jackson, "Social Gerontology and the Negro: A Review," *The Gerontologist* (September 1967): 168-78. This review was followed by two others; "Negro Aged: Toward Needed Research in Social Gerontology," *The Gerontologist* (spring 1970): 52-57; "The Blacklands of Gerontology," *Aging and the Human Development* 2 (1971): 156-71. Some of her works include: Jacquelyne Jackson, "Negro Aged and Social Gerontology: A Critical Evaluation," *Journal of Social and Behavioral Sciences* 13 (1968): 42-47; "Aged Negroes: A Potpourri Towards the Reduction of Racial Inequities," *Phylon* 32 (1971): 260-80; "Compensatory Care of the Black Aged," *Minority Aged in America, Occasional Papers in Gerontology 10* (Ann Arbor: Institute of Gerontology, University of Michigan—Wayne State University, 1972); "The Plight of Older Black Women in the United States," *The Black Scholar* 7 (1976): 47-55; "Myths and Realities About Aged Blacks," in *Readings in Gerontology,* ed. Mollie Brown (St. Louis: C. V. Mosby, 1978), 95-113. Jackson is also the editor of *The Journal of Minority Aging* (originally *Black Aging*) designed to disseminate information on elderly African Americans to influence policy, research, and services. It was founded as the mouthpiece for Black Aging Inc., which Jacquelyne Jackson founded in 1975. See Jacquelyne Jackson, "About Black Aging," *Black Aging* 1 (October 1975): 1.

7. E. P. Stanford, "Diverse Black Aged," in *Black Aged: Understanding Diversity and Service Needs,* ed. Zev Harel et al. (Newbury Park: Sage Publications, 1990), 35. This is not meant as a criticism of Jackson but to point out the need for historical analysis.

8. Leo Simmons, *The Role of the Aged in Primitive Societies* (New Haven: Yale University Press, 1945), 177. For a discussion of some of these questions in a practical context see Joseph Dancy, Jr., *The Black Elderly: A Guide to Practitioners, with Comprehensive Bibliography* (Ann Arbor: University of Michigan—Wayne State University, 1977).

9. There is now a substantial number of studies of ethnic groups in West Africa that demonstrate their veneration of the elderly in traditional societies. These will be cited in chapter 1. See D. Shimkin et al., "The Black Extended Family: A Basic Rural Institution and a Mechanism of Urban Adaptation," in *The Extended Family in Black Societies,* ed. D. Shimkin et al. (Chicago: Mouton Publishers, 1978), 25-47; Herbert Gutman, *The Black Family in Slavery and Freedom* (New York: Pantheon Books, 1976), passim; Herbert Foster, "African Patterns in the Afro-American Family," *Journal of Black Studies* 14 (December 1983), 201-32; Hamilton Bims, "The Black Family: A Proud Reappraisal," *Ebony* 20 (March 1974), passim.

10. Robert Wylie, "Attitudes Toward Aging and the Aged Among Black Americans: Some Historical Perspectives," *Aging and Human Development* 2 (1971): 69. See also Robert B. Hill, *The Strengths of Black Families* (New York: Emerson Hall Publishers, (1971), 5-6; "A Profile of the Black Aged," *Minority Aged in America Occasional Papers in Gerontology,* no. 10., ed. Elias S. Cohen et al. (Detroit: Institute of Gerontology, University of Michigan—Wayne State University, 1971), 37-38; "A Demographic Profile of the Black Elderly," *Aging* (November 1978), passim.

11. E. Franklin Frazier, *The Negro Family in the United States* (Chicago:

University of Chicago Press, 1939), 114–24; William Huling, "Evolving Family Roles for the Black Elderly," *Aging* (September–October 1978), 21–27; Andrew Billingsley, *Black Families in White America* (Englewood Cliffs, N.J.: Prentice Hall, 1968), passim; Hans Von Hentig, "The Sociological Function of the Grandmother," *Social Forces:* 389–92. See also Bonnie Gillespie, "Black Grandparents: Childhood Socialization," *Journal of Afro-American Issues* (summer 1976): 432–47.

12. Joyce Ladner, *Tomorrow's Tomorrow: The Black Woman* (Garden City, N.J.: Anchor Books, 1972), 70–72.

13. Lee Rainwater, "Crucible of Identity: The Negro Lower Class Family," in *The Making of Black America,* vol. 2, ed. August Meier and Elliott Rudwick (New York: Atheneum Publishers, 1969), 472. See also Daniel S. Smith, et al., "The Family Structure of the Older Black Population in the American South in 1880 and 1890," *Sociology and Social Research* 63 (April 1979): 549–63.

14. Jacquelyne Jackson, "Compensatory Care of the Black Aged," in *Minority Aged in America Occasional Papers in Gerontology,* no. 10, ed. Elias S. Cohen et al. (Detroit: Institute of Gerontology, University of Michigan—Wayne State University, 1971), 15.

15. W. F. Dickerson, "Problems of the High Risk Elderly," *Journal of the Black Studies* 14 (December 1983): 257. See also Monroe Anderson, "The Pains and Pleasures of Old Black Folks," *Ebony* 28 (March 1973), passim; Dean W. Morse, "Aging in the Ghetto: Themes Expressed by Older Men and Women in a Northern Industrial City," *Industrial Gerontology* 3 (winter 1976): 1–10.

16. Elmer Martin and Joanne Martin, *The Black Extended Family* (Chicago: University of Chicago Press, 1978), 21.

17. Ibid., 91; Willamae A. Kilkenny, "Toward Empowering the Black Elderly: An Institution of Alternatives/Solutions," in *Aging and Old Age in Diverse Populations* (Washington, D.C.: Minority Affairs Institute, AARP, 1990), 122. See also Dorothy B. Lee, "A Study of the Development of the Happy Haven Home for the Negro Aged in Atlanta, Georgia, from March 1947 to May 1950," (masters thesis, School of Social Work, Atlanta University, Atlanta, Georgia, 1951), 1–3; Charles Whitcomb, "Programming in Long-Term Health Care Facilities and the Extended Black Family Concept, pt. 3," in *The Black Elderly in Long-Term Care Settings, Proceedings of Workshops,* 14–15 February 1975 (Oakland: University of South California—Ethel Percy Andrus Gerontology Center and Advisory Committee for Continuing Education: Services to the Elderly, 1974), 21.

18. Josephine Yelder, "Social Climate in the Long-Term Setting: An Overview," in *The Black Elderly in Long-Term Care Settings,* 1.

19. Lillian Stokes, "Growing Old in the Black Community," in *Current Practice in Gerontological Nursing,* ed. A. D. Reinhardt and Mildred Quinn (St. Louis: C. B. Mosby, 1979), 111. Racial differences in utilization patterns notwithstanding, 50 percent of those sixty-five and older today will be institutionalized at some point in their lives. See Stephen Stahlman, "Nursing Homes," in *Gerontological Social Work: Knowledge, Service Settings, and Special Populations,* ed. Robert L. Schneider and Nancy P. Kropf (Chicago: Nelson—Hall Publishers, 1992), 240; John Weeks, *Aging: Concepts and Social Issues* (Belmont: Wadsworth Publishing Company, 1984), 270.

20. Linda M. Chatters and Robert Taylor, "Social Integration," in Harel et al., *Black Aged,* 237.

21. Donald L. Davis, "Growing Old Black," in *Multiple Hazards of Old Age: The Situation of Aged Blacks in the U.S.:* A Report by the Special Committee on

Aging, U.S. Senate 2 November 1971 (Washington, D.C.: U.S. Government Printing Office, 1971), 47.

22. Hobart Jackson, "Housing and Geriatric Centers for Aging and Aged Blacks," in *Proceedings of Black Aged in the Future,* comp. Jacquelyne Jackson (Durham: Duke University Press, 1973), 28. The late Hobart Jackson, former administrator of the HAICP, is the subject of chapter 7.

23. Freida Butler, *A Resource Guide on Black Aging* (Washington, D.C.: Institute on Urban Affairs, Howard University, 1981), passim.

24. National Caucus and Center on the Black Aged (NCBA), "The Status of the Black Elderly in the United States," Select Committee on Aging, House of Representatives (Washington, D.C.: U.S. Government Printing Office, 1987), 29. The nursing Home has been the subject of widespread concern for some time now. See, for example, Subcommittee on Long-Term Care of the Special Committee on Aging, United States Senate, "Nursing Home Care in the United States: Failure in Public Policy: Introductory Report" (Washington, D.C.: U.S. Government Printing Office, 1974); Subcommittee on Long-Term Care of the Special Committee on Aging, United States Senate, Supporting Paper No. 6, "Nursing Home Care in the United States: Failure in Public Policy" (Washington, D.C.: U.S. Governing Printing Office, 1975).

25. Huling, "Evolving Family Roles," 27.

26. Ibid.

27. Jacquelyne Jackson, "Family Organization and Ideology," in *Comparative Studies of Blacks and White in the United States, Quantitative Studies in Social Relations,* ed. Kent Miller and Ralph Dreger (New York: Seminar Press, 1973), 436. See also, "Help Me Somebody I's an Old Black Standing in the Need of Institutionalizing," *Psychiatric Opinion* 10 (December 1973): 6–16. Hobart Jackson, "Housing and Geriatric Centers . . . ," 28.

28. NCBA, "The Status of the Black Elderly in the U.S.," 129. The decrease in the number of Black community hospitals, from 144 to 10 over the past fifty years is a related issue since Homes are now connected to these facilities. Vanessa N. Gamble, *The Black Community Hospital: Contemporary Dilemmas in Historical Perspectives* (New York: Garland Publishing, 1989), 59; James H. Carter, "Health Attitudes/ Promotions/ Preventions: The Black Elderly," in James Jackson, *The Black Elderly,* 292.

29. Life expectancy is defined by Manuel as "a measure of the average number of years of life remaining at a given age as determined from death rates observed at a specific time." Roy C. Manuel, "The Demography of Older Blacks in the United States," 140; Andrew Billingsley, "Understanding African American Family Diversity," in *The State of Black America,* ed. Janet Dewart (New York: National Urban League, 1990), 85–108; Mary S. Harper and Camille Alexander, "Profile of the Black Elderly," in *Minority Aging: Essential Curricula Content for Selected Health and Allied Health Professions,* in Health Resources and Services Administration, Department of Health and Human Services, DHHS Publication No. HRS(P-DV-90-4), ed. M. S. Harper (Washington, D.C.: U.S. Government Printing Office, 1990), 193–222.

30. James D. Manney, Jr., *Aging in American Society: An Examination of Concepts and Issues* (Ann Arbor: The Institute of Gerontology, University of Michigan—Wayne State University, 1975), 104–5.

31. Nathaniel Calloway, "Medical Aspects of the Aging American Black," in *Proceedings of Black Aged in the Future,* comp. Jacqueline Jackson (Durham: Duke University Press, 1973), 53. See also Kenneth Manton, "Differential Life

Expectancy: Possible Explanations during the Later Ages," in *Minority Aging: Sociological and Social Psychological Issues,* ed. Roy C. Manuel (Westport, Conn.: Greenwood Press, 1982), 63–68. The racial crossover phenomenon is not a sudden occurrence, for the difference in life expectancy between Blacks and Whites at age sixty is only two years. According to Chatters and Taylor, "selective pressures" weeded out the weak and produced "current cohorts of hardy old Black adults," Chatters and Taylor, "Social Integration," 94.

32. Wilber Watson, "Black Aging," in *Aging and Social Behavior,* ed. Wilber Watson (Belmont: Calif.: Wadsworth Health Sciences Division, A Division of Wadsworth Inc., 1982), 145.

Chapter 1: "Massa . . . you can't make me work no more": Old Age and Slavery

1. William Cheeks, *Black Resistance before the Civil War* (Beverly Hills: Glencoe Press, 1970), 15.

2. Frederick Douglass to John Dancy, 17 December 1894, *Journal of Negro History* 66 (summer 1981): 141–43. The opinions and thoughts of ex-slaves are interspersed throughout this discussion. It should be pointed out to the critics of the use of slave narratives that gerontologists generally agree that the importance of an event in the life of an individual is a more important index to the reliability of memory than chronological distance to or from it. This is Douglass's point here.

3. Richard Steckel, "Slave Mortality: Analysis of Evidence from Plantation Records: *Social Science History* 3 (1979): 91–94; James Oakes, *The Ruling Race: A History of the American Slaveholder* (New York: Vintage Books, 1982), 195–96.

4. Kenneth M. Stampp, *The Peculiar Institution: Slavery in the Antebellum South* (New York: Alfred Knopf, 1956), 318.

5. Janet Barber, "Old Age and the Life Course of Slaves: A Case Study of a Nineteenth-Century Virginia Plantation" (Ph.D. diss., University of Kansas, 1983), 318.

6. Charles Sydnor, "Life Span of Mississippi Slaves," *American Historical Review* 35 (April 1930): 566.

7. Barber, "Old Age and the Life Course of Slaves," 313.

8. Jessie W. Parkhurst, "The Role of the Black Mammy in the Plantation Household," *The Journal of Negro History* 23 (July 1938): 349–69. See also Deborah White, *Arn't I A Woman? Female Slaves in the Plantation South* (New York: W. W. Norton and Company, 1985), 47–61.

9. Emily Burke, *Pleasure and Pain: Reminiscences of Georgia in the 1840s,* (Savannah: The Beehive Press, 1978), 33.

10. Frank Owsley, *Plain Folk of the Old South* (Baton Rouge: Louisiana State University Press, 1949), 95.

11. The old were exalted in early America. Fischer, *Growing Old in America,* 26–76.

12. Andrew Achenbaum, *Old Age in The New Land: The American Experience Since 1790* (Baltimore: The Johns Hopkins Press, 1978).

13. George R. Woolfolk, "Taxes and Slavery in the Antebellum South," *Journal of Southern History* 26 (May 1960): 122. The 1843 Alabama taxes, for example, were $.25 for a slave child under five, but $1.10 for a slave between fifteen and thirty, thereafter declining to $.20 for those under sixty with no tax obligation on those older. The age consciousness of slaveholders also emerged in the machin-

ery to control the institution. Alabama, for example, required slaveholders to perform patrol duty up to age sixty, while nonslaveholders were relieved of this obligation at age forty-five.

14. Charles Perdue et al., *Weevils in the Wheat: Interviews with Virginia Ex-Slaves* (Charlottesville: University Virginia Press, 1976), 151.

15. John Stealey, "Slavery and the Western Virginia Salt Industry," *Journal of Negro History* 49 (April 1974): 105–31.

16. Todd Savitt, "Slave Life Insurance in Virginia and North Carolina," *The Journal of Southern History* 43 (November 1977): 583–600. See also Robert Starobin, *Industrial Slavery in the Old South* (New York: Oxford University Press, 1970), 72; Eugene Genovese, "The Medical Insurance Costs of Slaveholding in the Black Belt," *The Journal of Negro History* 45 (July 1960): 146–47. Insurance companies rejected free Blacks as unnecessary risks. Beneficial societies often met their needs; see chapter 4.

17. William and Ellen Craft, *Running a Thousand Miles to Freedom* (New York: Arno Press and *The New York Times*, 1969), 10.

18. Perdue, et al., *Weevils in the Wheat*, 7.

19. Ibid.

20. Norman R. Yetman, *Life under the "Peculiar Institution": Selections from the Slave Narrative Collection* (New York: Holt, Rinehart, and Winston, 1970), 130.

21. Perdue et al., *Weevils in the Wheat*, 205.

22. Helen T. Catterall, ed., *Judicial Cases Concerning American Slavery and the Negro* (Washington, D.C.: Carnegie Institution of Washington, 1926), 77, 618; *Murphy v Insurance Company* 6 LA An 518 (May 1851); *Spruill v Insurance Company*, I Jones, NC 126 (December 1853). Future references to judicial cases will be cited "Catterall" with cases, state, and date.

23. Catteral, 111, *Peers v Davis* 29 Mo. 184, (October 1859), Missouri, vol. 3: 208; vol. 3, Georgia Cases: *Davis v Murray*, 2 Mill 143 (May 1818), SC; Soundness included mind and body according to prevailing judicial opinion. In *Stinson v Piper*, 3 McCord, 251, SC (April 1925), it was held that a "warranty of soundness embraces soundness of mind as well as body"; in *Major v Howard* 6 GA 213 (January 1849), a case involving an imbecile, the court held that the warranty only applied to the slave's body since the word "sound" had been replaced in the bill of sale by the word "healthy"; a buyer who was dissatisfied with the moral condition of a slave hauled the seller into court. However, the judge ruled in *Davis v Murray, I McCord* 220, SC (May 1821), that the required warranty of soundness "was never extended to the moral qualities of a slave."

24. John Brown, *Slave Life in Georgia: A Narrative of the Life Sufferings, and Escape of John Brown, a Fugitive Slave* (Savannah: The Beehive Press, 1972), 96–98.

25. William Wells Brown, *Narrative of the Life of William Wells Brown: A Fugitive Slave* (Boston: 1847; Johnson Reprint Corporation, 1970), 43.

26. Burke, *Pleasure and Pain*, 33.

27. Kenneth M. Stampp, "The Daily Life of a Southern Slave," in *Key Issues in Afro-American History*, ed. Nathan Huggins et al. (New York: Harcourt Brace, Jovanovitch, 1971), 118–19.

28. Eugene Genovese, *Roll, Jordan, Roll: The World the Slaves Made* (New York: Pantheon Books, 1974), passim; Gutman doubts slave's mutual obligation toward his or her master. See Herbert Gutman, *The Black Family in Slavery and Freedom* (New York: Pantheon Books, 1976), 315–20. For earlier comments see

James B. Sellars, *Slavery in Alabama* (Birmingham: University of Alabama Press, 1950), 127.

29. W. E. B. Dubois, *Efforts of Social Betterment among Negro Americans* (Atlanta: Atlanta University Publications, no. 10, 1898), 65.

30. Oakes, *The Ruling Race,* 114.

31. Edward A. Pollard, *Black Diamonds Gathered in the Darkey Homes of the South* (New York: Pudney and Russell Publishers, 1860), 32.

32. Quoted in James O. Breeden, *Advice among Masters: The Ideal in Slave Management in the South* (Westport, Conn.: Greenwood Press, 1980), 207.

33. Breeden, *Advice Among Masters,* 2; Proslavery writer William J. Grayson put this theme to poetry: "Guarded from want, from beggary secure, he never feels what hireling grounds endure." For entire poem see William J. Grayson, *The Hireling and the Slave* (Charleston: 1856), 434–35.

34. Yetman, *Life Under the "Peculiar Institution,"* 275.

35. Harriet Jacobs, *Incidents in the Life of a Slave Girl* (Boston: 1861), 142.

36. Frederick Douglass, *Narrative of the Life of Frederick Douglass: An American Slave* (New York: Signet Books, 1968, first published in 1845), 61–62; For some examples of extremely cruel treatment of elderly slaves, see John Blassingame, ed., *Slave Testimony: Two Centuries of Letters, Speeches, Interviews, and Autobiographies* (Baton Rogue: Louisiana State University, 1977), 162–63, 400–1. For conflicting views on the treatment of elderly slaves in other societies see, for example, Carl Degler, *Neither Black nor White: Slavery and Race Relations in Brazil and the United States* (New York: The Macmillian Company); Horace Orlando Patterson, *The Sociology of Slavery: An Analysis of the Origins, Development, and Structure of Negro Society in Jamaica* (Rutherford: Fairleigh Dickinson University Press, 1967).

37. Ulrich B. Phillips, *Life and Labor in the South* (Boston: Little, Brown and Company, 1927), 175–76, passim.

38. Ibid.

39. Breeden, *Advice Among Masters,* 289. See also Gerald Mullins, *Flight and Rebellion: Slave Resistance in 18th Century Virginia* (Oxford: Oxford University Press, 1972), passim.

40. Bertram W. Doyle, *The Etiquette of Race Relations in the South: A Study in Social Control* (Chicago: The University of Chicago Press, 1939), 29.

41. William Scarborough, *The Overseer: Plantation Management in the Old South* (Baton Rouge: Louisiana State University Press, 1966), 67–101. Slave children generally went to the field around age nine or a little older. Some slaves like Jermain Loguen claimed they did not know that they were slaves until they were old enough to do field work. The protected childhood theory of slave childhood is being rejected by scholars of slavery. Scott Howlett, "'My Child' Him is Mine': Slave Children in the Old South," paper delivered at the Southern Historical Association Meeting, Atlanta, Georgia, 4–7 November 1992.

42. Quoted in Phillips, *Life and Labor in the South,* 312.

43. Norman R. Yetman, *Life under the "Peculiar Institution": Selections from the Slave Narrative Collection* (New York: Holt, Rinehart, and Winston, 1970), 218.

44. Catterall, vol. 3, Georgia Cases, *Fooke v Hardeman,* 7 GA (20 June 1849), 23.

45. Charles Sydnor, *Slavery in Mississippi* (Gloucester, Miss.: Peter Smith, first published in 1933, American Historical Association; reprinted by permission

of Appleton-Century-Crofts), 66. Sydnor argues that the old and infirm were well treated by Mississippi slave owners.

46. Catteral, *Brunson v King*, 2 Hill Eq. 483. Ed. (1836), SC, 362.

47. Ibid., *Paup v Mingo*, 4 Leigh 163, (January 1833); "It is my particular interest . . . that my old faithful Negro man, Landon, who has labored hard with me for forty years and upwards, be kindly, carefully, and well treated as long as he lives," *Sheftall v Roberts*, 30 GA 53 (January 1860), 74; Robert Snodgrass provided that his executors hire his "old woman Magg" and "money for her hire was to be used for her support if she were unable to work; *Handy v Snodgrass*, 9 Leigh, 484 (July 1838), 38.

48. Yetman, *Life under the "Peculiar Institution,"* 35.

49. Ibid., 119. Owners of rice plantations chose youth over experience because drivers were ordinarily chosen under age thirty in the hope of providing long service. See James Clifton, "The Rice Driver: His Role In Slave Management," *South Carolina Historical Magazine* 82 (October 1981): 332.

50. Robert Fogel and Stanley Engerman, *Time on the Cross: The Economics of American Negro Slavery* (Boston: Little, Brown, and Company, 1978), 74–75.

51. Charles Joyner, *Down by the Riverside: A South Carolina Slave Community* (Chicago: University of Illinois Press, 1984), 63–65.

52. John B. Cade, "Out of the Mouths of Ex-Slaves," *Journal of Negro History* 22 (July 1935): 309.

53. Ronald Killion and Charles Walker, eds., *Slavery Time When I Was Chillun Down on Marster's Plantation* (Savannah: The Beehive Press, 1973), 8.

54. Sydnor, *Slavery in Mississippi*, 204.

55. Burke, *Pain and Pleasure*, 88.

56. Deborah White maintains that female slaves performed tasks based on physical capacity as "full female hands worked as hard as men with no strict differentiation of field work." This assured women a kind of equality with men. The same was true of tasks assigned to boys and girls. See White, *Arn't I A Woman*, passim.

57. Judith Hushbeck, *Old and Obsolete: Age Discrimination and the American Worker, 1860–1920* (New York: Garland Publishing, 1989), 20.

58. Todd Savitt, *Medicine and Slavery: The Disease and Health Care of Blacks in Antebellum Virginia* (Urbana: University of Illinois Press, 1978), 204.

59. Stampp, *Peculiar Institution*, 103–5.

60. Perdue, *Weevils in the Wheat*, 127.

61. Yetman, *Life under the "Peculiar Institution"* 14.

62. James Mcpherson, *The Negro's Civil War* (New York: Random House, 1956), 122; Paul Escott, *Slavery Remembered: A Record of Twentieth Century Slave Narratives* (Chapel Hill: The University of North Carolina Press, 1979), passim. The average age of retirement of ex-slaves in Escott's study was 80.7. At the time of interview (873 reporting) 48.5 percent of the ex-slaves received primary support from the family, 38.1 percent from the government, 3.4 percent from other Blacks, and 8.4 percent from White charities. One-fifth of the interviewees lived with children or other relatives.

63. Quoted in Genovese, *Roll, Jordan, Roll*, 521.

64. National Caucus and Center on Black Aged, Inc., *The Status of the Black Elderly in the United States*. Report for the Select Committee on Aging, House of Representatives (Washington, D.C.: U.S. Government Printing Office, 1987), 21.

65. Savitt, *Medicine and Slavery*, 202.

66. Weymouth T. Jordan, "Plantation Medicine in the Old South," *Alabama*

Review 101 (April 1950): 85. For an overview of medical practices in the south before the Civil War, see John Duffy, "Medical Practices in the Antebellum South," *Journal of Southern History* 25 (February 1959): 53–72; Kenneth and Virginia Kiple, "The African Connection: Slavery, Disease and Racism," *Phylon* 41 (fall 1980): 215.

67. Lawrence Levine, *Black Culture and Black Consciousness* (Oxford: Oxford University Press, 1977), 64–65; Richard Shyrock, "Medical Practice in the Old South," South Atlantic Quarterly 29 (April 1930): 172; Savitt, *Medicine and Slavery,* 175; William Cheeks claims that the use of mammies as "doctors" was for the expressed purpose of saving money, and slaveholders couldn't care less about the health of superannuated slaves. See William Cheeks, *Black Resistance Before the Civil War* (Beverly Hills: Glencoe Press, 1970), 6; for the health care of slaves on a particular plantation see Bennett H. Wall, "Medical Care of Ebenezer Pettigrew's Slaves," *Journal of Southern History* 38 (December 1950): 451–70. For comments on separate treatments see Jordan, "Plantation Medicine in the Old South," 90; Phillips, *Life and Labor in the South,* 266.

68. Yetman, *Life under the "Peculiar Institution,"* 91.

69. Perdue, *Weevils in the Wheat,* 91.

70. Yetman, *Life under the "Peculiar Institution,"* 200.

71. Walter Fisher, "Physicians and Slavery in the Antebellum Southern Medical Journal," *Journal of the History of Medicine and Allied Science* 22 (1978): 36.

72. Wilbert Jordan, *"Black American Folk Medicine,"* 269–74.

73. Todd Savitt, "The Use of Blacks for Medical Experimentation and Demonstration in the Old South," *Journal of Southern History* 48 (August 1982): 330–36.

74. Shyrock, "Medical Practice in the Old South," 174–75; Fischer, *Growing Old in America* 164;

75. Achenbaum, *Old Age in the New Land,* 31.

76. Charles Prudhomme and David F. Musto, "Historical Perspectives on Mental Health and Racism in the United States," Charles Willie et al., eds., *Racism and Mental Health,* (Pittsburgh: University of Pittsburgh Press, 1973), 25–55; see also Thomas Szasz, ed., *The Age of Madness* (New York: Anchor Books, 1975), 43–49.

77. William D. Postell, "Mental Health among the Slave Population on Southern Plantations," *American Journal of Psychology* 110 (July 1953), 52–54; See also Barbara Bellows "Insanity is the Disease of Civilization. The Founding of South Carolina Lunatic Asylum," *South Carolina Historical Magazine* 82 (July 1981): 269.

78. Arthur Zilversmit, *The First Emancipation: The Abolition of Slavery in the North* (Chicago: The University of Chicago Press, 1967), passim; Also Edgar Mcmanus, *Black Bondage in the North* (Syracuse: Syracuse University Press, 1973), passim.

79. Benjamin Klebaner, "American Manumission Laws and the Responsibility for Supporting Slaves," *Virginia Magazine of History and Biography* 43 (1955): 443–53; Sumner E. Matison, "Manumission by Purchase," *The Journal of Negro History* 33 (April 1948): 146.

80. Klebaner, "Manumission Laws," 148; Catterall, *Judicial Cases,* 268; Ivan NcDougle, "Slavery in Kentucky," *Journal of Negro History* 3 (July 1918): 311–29. McDougle argues that laws protected the old and infirm from becoming a burden on the community, and slaveholders willingly cared for the old and invalid. Richard Younger claims that southern grand juries "took it upon themselves to enforce laws relating to slavery." While he cites examples of indictments

for cruelty and neglect, he does not cite a case in which a slave master is indicted for freeing an old or infirm slave. See Richard Younger, "Southern Grand Juries and Slavery," *Journal of Negro History* 40 (April 1955): 174.

81. Matison, "Manumission by Purchase," 145–50; Klebaner, "Manumission Laws," 145–67; passim. One result of this legislation was increased Black slave ownership. See also Luther P. Jackson, "Manumission in Certain Virginia Cities," *The Journal of Negro History* 15 (July 1930): 298; John Russell, "Colored Freemen as Slave Owners in Virginia," *Journal of Negro History* 1 (July 1916): 233–42; Carter Woodson, *Free Negro Owners of Slaves in U.S. in 1830, Together with Absentee Ownership in U.S. in 1836* (New York: Negro University Press, 1968).

82. Bell Wiley, ed., *Slaves No More: Letters from Nigeria 1833–1869* (Lexington: University of Kentucky, 1980), introduction.

83. Tom Shick, "A Quantitative Analysis of Liberian Colonization, 1830 to 1843 with Special Reference to Mortality," *Journal of African History* 12 (1971), 47. See also Charles Foster, ""The Colonization of Free Negroes in Liberia, 1816–1835," *The Journal of Negro History* 38 (January 1985): 41.

84. Klebaner, "Manumission Laws," 452; for some examples in a Mississippi County see W. A. Evans, "Free Negroes in Monroe County During Slavery," *Journal of Mississippi History 3* (January 1945): 37–42.

85. Leslie Owens, *This Species of Property: Slave Life and Culture in the Old South* (New York: Oxford University Press, 1976), 49.

86. Ira Berlin, *Slaves without Masters: The Free Negro in the Antebellum South* (New York: Pantheon Books, 1874), 152–53, 176–77. See also James M. Wright, *The Free Negro in Maryland, 1534–1860* (New York: Columbia University Press, 1921), 256.

87. Klebaner, "Manumission Laws," 452. See also William Goodell, *The American Slave Code: In Theory and Practice* (New York: John Gray, Printer, 1853), 153–54.

88. Burke, *Pain and Pleasure*, 25.

89. Owens, *This Species of Property*, 50.

90. Edward Magdol, *A Right to the Land: Essays on the Freedmen's Community* (Westport, Conn.: Greenwood Press, 1977), 16. The terms *slave quarter community* and *slave community* are referred to regularly in this chapter and are used here in the same sense as historians Blassingame, Webber, Genovese, and others use them. Webber, for example, held that a community was formed whenever slaves constituted a group of fifteen or twenty or more, and "related to a slave quarter as the center of their social activities and relationships, who shared a common set of values and attitudes, were organized in a familiar social structure, and displayed an awareness of their uniqueness and separate identity as a group." Thomas L. Webber, *Deep Like the River: Education in the Slave Quarter Community, 1831–1865* (New York: W. W. Norton and Company, 1978), 10; Blassingame, *Slave Community*, 1–40.

91. Nana Araba Apt, "Aging in Africa," in *Aging in Cross-Cultural Perspective: Africa and the Americas*, ed. Enid Gort (New York: Phelps—Stokes Publication, 1988), 26. See also Michele Teitelbaum, "Singing for Their Supper and Other Productive Work of the African Elderly," in Gort, *Aging in Cross Cultural Perspective,* 61–68. Other studies that establish African attitudes toward the elderly are Austin J. Shelton, "Ibo Aging and Eldership: Notes for Gerontologist and Others," *The Gerontologist* 5 (March 1965): 20–23, 48; Malcolm Arth, "Ideals and Behavior: A Comment on Ibo Respect Patterns," *The Gerontologist* 8 (1958):

242-44; "Aging: A Cross Cultural Perspective," in *Research Planning and Action for the Elderly: The Power and Potential of Social Science* ed. Donald Kent, Robert Kastenbaum, and Sylvia Sherwood (New York: Behavior Publications, 1972), 352-65. In 1969 Robert Wylie visited a Hausa Village in Nigeria and found strong veneration for elderly family members who performed important roles in the family and community. See Robert Wylie, "Attitudes toward Aging and the Aged among Black Americans: Some Historical Perspectives," *Aging and Human Development* 2 (1971): 68. See also Catherine Coles, "The Older Woman in Hausa Society: Power and Authority in Urban Nigeria," in Sokolovsky, *The Cultural Context of Aging,* 57-81; Leopold Rosenmayr, "More Than Wisdom: A Field Study of the Old in an African Village," *Journal of Cross-Cultural Gerontology* 3 (1988): 21-40. The impact of modernization (demographic changes as well as industrialization and urbanization) on the extended family and the status of the elderly is a major concern of African nations. See *Report of United Nations Center for Social Development and Humanitarian Affairs, Technical Meeting on Aging for the African Region,* hosted by the federal government of Nigeria 24-27 February 1981, Lagos, Nigeria. Report obtained from Tarek M. Shuman, Executive Secretary, World Assembly on Aging, Vienna, Australia. Portions of this discussion were published previously: Leslie J. Pollard, "Age and Paternalism in a Slave Society," *Perspective on Aging* 6 (November-December, 1978): 4-8; "Aging and Slavery: A Gerontological Perspective," *The Journal of Negro History* 67 (fall 1981): 228-34.

92. A. O. Stafford, "The Mind of the African Negro as Reflected in his Proverbs," *Journal of Negro History* 1 (January 1916): 42-48; Apt, "Aging in Africa," 25-26.

93. George Rawick, *The American Slave: A Composite Autobiography* (Westport, Conn.: Greenwood Publishing, 1972), 48-50; Levine, *Black Culture and Black Consciousness,* 30.

94. Melville Herskovits, *The Myth of the Negro Past* (Boston: Beacon Press, 1941), 41; Eliott J. Gorn, "Black Spirits: The Ghostlore of Afro-American Slaves," *American Quarterly* 36 (fall 1981): 594-95; Lerone Bennett, *Before the Mayflower: A History of Black Americans* (New York: Penguin Books, 1982), 98.

95. Sterling Stuckey, *Slave Culture: Nationalist Theory and the Foundations of Black America* (New York: Oxford University Press 1987), 43.

96. Blassingame, *Slave Community,* 41.

97. Webber, *Deep Like the River,* 65; Escott, *Slavery Remembered,* 67-68; Blassingame, *Slave Community,* 1-40; Jacquelyne Jones, *Labor of Love, Labor of Sorrow: Black Women Work and the Family from Slavery to the Present* (New York: Basic Books, 1984), 40-41.

98. John Blassingame, "Status and Social Structure in the Slave Communityy: Evidence from New Sources," in *Perspectives and Irony in American History,* ed. Harry P. Owens (Jackson: University Press, 1976), 139.

99. Achenbaum, *Old Age in the New Land,* 86. Carole Haber rejects this notion and contends that respect for the elderly was inextricably tied to patriarchal control over family property. See Carole Haber, *Beyond Sixty-Five: The Dilemma of Old Age in America's Past* (Cambridge: Cambridge University Press, 1983), 12. It should be noted that task system slaves were said to own substantial property in horses, hogs, cattle, wagons, and so on. "By the middle of the nineteenth century, if not before," Philip Morgan claims, "slave property was not only being produced and exchanged but also inherited." See Philip D. Morgan, "Work

and Culture: The Task System and the World of Low Country Blacks, 1700 to 1800," *William and Mary Quarterly* 39 (October 1982): 592.

100. John Boles, *Black Southerners, 1619–1869* (Lexington: University of Kentucky Press, 1983), 91.

101. Perdue, *Weevils in the Wheat*, 246.

102. Blassingame, *Slave Community,* passim; Genovese, *Roll, Jordan, Roll,* passim; Stampp, *Peculiar Institution,* 336.

103. Joanne Rhone, "Social Service Delivery System among Slaves (1619–1790)," Section 1, *Social Service Delivery System in the Black Community during the Antebellum Period* (1619–1860), ed. William S. Jackson et al. (Atlanta: Atlanta University School of Social Work, 1973), 7–8.

104. Herbert Gutman, *Black Family in Slavery and Freedom,* passim.

105. Niara Sudarkasa, "Interpreting the African Heritage in African American Family Organization," in Harriette P. McAdoo, *Black Families* (Newbury Park, Calif.: Sage Publications, 1989), 35. The kinship system in African societies provided a mutual aid system that protected the elderly from abuse and guaranteed appropriate care and respect. Frank Sisya, "Kinship Patterns and the Caring of the Elderly in Traditional Africa," paper presented at the Seventh Annual Meeting of the Association for Afro-American Life and History, 7 November 1987, Durham, N.C.

106. Gutman, *Black Family in Slavery and Freedom,* 220–22.

107. Ibid.

108. Chatters and Robert Taylor, "Social Integration," in Zev Harel, *Black Aged,* 91; Colleen Johnson and Barbara Barer, "Families and Networks among Older Inner City Blacks," *The Gerontologist* 30 (December 1990): 726–33; Cheryl Stewart Grace and Linda S. Noelker, "Clinical Social Work Practice with Black Elderly and Their Family Caregivers," in Zev Harel, *Black Aged,* 239.

109. Andrew Billingsley, *Black Families in White America* (Englewood Cliffs, N.J.: Prentice Hall, 1968), 47.

110. Gutman, *Black Family in Slavery and Freedom,* 175; Herbert J. Foster, "African Patterns in the Afro-American Family," *Journal of Black Studies* 14 (December 1983): 218–20. Lerone Bennett claims that there was a "circle of elders" who were "roughly equivalent to the position the elders in West African society." Bennett, *Before the Mayflower,* 98.

111. Killion and Walker, *Slavery Time,* 110.

112. Perdue et al., *Weevils in the Wheat,* 26.

113. Genovese, *Roll, Jordan Roll,* 522.

114. Douglass, *Narrative of the Life of Frederick Douglass,* 60; Hundreds of references to respect for the elderly during slavery can be found in the slave narratives. Most of the ex-slaves lamented the loss of respect. One woman remembered that when old folks were in conversation "you didn't no more come in there than you would stick you head in the fire." Another recalled: "In dem days chillun were chillun, now ev'ybody is grown. Chillun den was seen an' you better not heard. When ole persons came 'round, moma sent us out an' not be seen. Now e'ybody grown." It is perhaps characteristic of all elderly to complain about a loss of respect among the young, but these recollections vividly reminded me of growing up in a rural Georgia where it was still a cardinal mistake not to become adept at timing one's entry into old folks' conversation—a skill we learned at an early age, though we often paid a prime price; Fisk University, *The Unwritten History of Slavery* (Nashville: Social Sciences Institute, 1954), passim; Perdue, et. al., *Weevils in the Wheat,* 120; Jacobs index to the American slave

narratives contains 450 separate entries (509 page numbers) under the section titled, "Black Attitudes toward the Younger Generation." They run the entire gamut from praise to bitterness toward the young. Two are rather insightful and are worth quoting. The first was from a former school teacher. "In some respects the modern frankness is an improvement over the old suppression and repression in the presence of their elders. At the same time, I think the young people of today lack the proper reverence and respect for age and experience it brings as a guide for them." The other was from one who was just plain smart. "Honey, Pa always say dat you couldn't expect no more from a child dan what you put in de raisin' . . . Pa says Sylvia, raise up you chillun in de right way and dey'll smile on you in your old age," see Donald M. Jacobs, ed., *Index to the American Slave* (Westport, Conn.: Greenwood Press, 1981; Contributions in Afro-American and African Studies No. 65); The above quotes are taken from the South Carolina Narratives, pt. 1, 347; Arkansas Narratives, vol. 9, pt. 4, 231. There was at least one instance of friction between old and young slaves, but that is not entirely clear. It seems that Charles Ball's grandfather had some harsh words for the young, referring to them as a "mean and vulgar race," allegedly because he was replaced by a younger slave. See Charles Ball, *Fifty Years in Chains, or the Life of an American Slave* (New York: 1859; reprinted by Negro History Press).

115. Magdol, *A Right to the Land*, 116.

116. E. F. Frazier, *Negro Church in America*, 1–9; H. H. Proctor, "The Theology of the Songs of the Southern Slave," *Southern Workman* 36 (November 1907): 584–92. See also the December 1987 issue, 652–56; Howard Thurman, *The Negro Spiritual Speaks of Life and Death* (New York: Harper and Row, 1969; First Published, 1947), 113–14.

117. Frazier, *Negro Church in America*, 24.

118. G. R. Wilson, "The Religion of the American Negro Slave: His Attitude toward Life and Death," *Journal of Negro History* 8 (January 1923): 41–71; Clarence Walker, *A Rock in a Weary Land: The A.M.E. Church during the Civil War and Reconstruction* (Baton Rouge: Louisiana State University Press, 1982), 61–63, 71; See also Boles, *Black Southerners*, 153; See Allen C. Carter, "Religion and the Black Elderly: The Historical Basis of Social and Psychological Concerns," in *Minority Aging: Sociological and Social Psychological Issue*, ed. Roy C. Manuel (Westport, Conn.: Greenwood Press, 1982), 103–7.

119. Stanley Feldstein, *Once a Slave: The Slave's View of Slavery* (New York: William Morrow and Company, 1970), 127.

120. Barber, "Old Age and Life Course of Slaves," 346. See also John R. Weeks, *Aging Concepts and Issues* (Belmont: Calif.: Wadsworth Publishing Company), 29.

121. Donald Cowgill and Lowell Holmes, eds., *Aging and Modernization* (New York: Appleton Century Crofts, 1972), 1–2, 305–23; Margaret Huyck, *Growing Older: What You Need to Know* (New York: Basic Books, 1961), passim; Antonio Rey, "Activity and Disengagement: Theoretical Orientations in Social Gerontology and Minority Aging," in Manuel, *Minority Aging,* 192.

122. Ibid.

123. Elaine Cummings and William Henry, *Growing Old: The Process of Disengagement* (New York: Basic Books, 1961).

124. Robert Atchley, *Social Forces and Aging: An Introduction to Gerontology* (Belmont: Wadsworth Publishing Company, 1991); Harold Cox, *Later Life: The Realities of Aging,* 2d ed. (Englewood Cliffs, N.J.: Prentice Hall, 1988), 30–31.

125. James Dowd, "Aging as Exchange: A Preface to Theory," *Journal of Ger-*

ontology 30 (1975): 584–95; Aaron Lipman, "Minority Aging from the Exchange and Structuralist-Functionalist Perspective" in Manuel, *Minority Aging,* 196–201; Weeks, *Aging Concepts and Issues,* 16–34; Cox, *Later Life,* 26–41; G. Homans, "Beneficence and the Aged" *Journal of Gerontology* 39 (1984): 102–8; G. Homan, "Social Behavior as Exchange," *American Journal of Sociology* 63 (1958): 597–606; A. W. Gouldner, "The Norm of Reciprocity," *American Sociological Review* 25 (1961): 161–78.

126. James D. Manney, *Aging in American Society: An Examination of Concepts and Issues* (Ann Arbor: The Institute of Gerontology—The University of Michigan—Wayne State University, 1975), 19; Robert C. Atchley, "Retirement: Continuity or Crisis," in *The Later Years: Social Application of Gerontology,* ed. Richard Kalish (Belmont California: Brooks, Cole Publishing Company, 1977), 136–41.

127. Owens, *This Species of Property,* 49.

128. J. W. Coleman, *Slavery Times in Kentucky* (Chapel Hill: The University of North Carolina, 1940), passim; For another study that makes a similar claim that occupations shaped the slaves' social outlook, see E. Ophelia Sette, "Social Attitudes during the Slave Regime: Household Servants versus Field Hands," *Racial Contacts and Social Research* 28 (December 1933): 95–98. See also C. W. Harper, "House Servants and Field Hands: Fragmentation in the Antebellum Slave Community," *N.C. Historical Review* XLV (winter 1978): 42–60.

129. Arnold Rose, "Perspectives on the Rural Aged," in *Older Rural Americans: A Sociological Perspective,* ed. E. Grant Youmans (Kentucky University Press, 1967), 8. For a contemporary discussion see Dean W. Morse, "Aging in the Ghetto: Themes Expressed by Older Black Men and Women Living in a Northern Industrial City," *Industrial Gerontology* 3 (winter 1976): 1–10.

130. Mark Messer, "Race Differences in Selected Attitudinal Dimensions of the Elderly," *The Gerontologist* 8 (winter 1968): 294; Joyce Ladner, *Tomorrow's Tomorrow: The Black Woman* (New York: Doubleday and Company, 1971), 72; Jacqueline Jackson, "Compensatory Care for the Black Aged," 15–23; The idea that Blacks tolerate mental peculiarities in their elderly can be found in Richard Shader and Martha Tracy, "On Being Black, Old and Emotionally Troubled: How Little is Known," *Psychiatric Opinion* 10 (December 1973): 30; Wylie, "Attitudes Toward Aging and the Aged Among Black Americans," 69; A. D. Gaines, "Alzheimers Disease in the Context of Black Southern Culture," *Health Matrix* 64 (winter 1989): 33–38.

131. Rey, "Attitudes Toward Aging and the Aged Among Black Americans," 192. See also Percil E. Stanford, "Theoretical and Practical Relationships among Aged Blacks and Other Minorities," *The Black Scholar* (January–February 1982): 49–59.

Chapter 2: "What Charity More Pure and Sweet": The Development of African American Old Age Homes With Special Emphasis on the Home for Aged and Infirm Colored Persons (HAICP)

The Home for Aged and Infirm Colored Persons referred to as HAICP throughout this study is presently the Stephen Smith Multi-Service Center. The word *Home* is capitalized to distinguish it from a private institution, and where reference is made to the title of the Home, the original word *infirm,* rather than the correct *infirmed,* is maintained. Since the following chapters of this study focus on the HAICP and its operation, much of the information about the background of the Home is included here.

1. James H. Carter, "Health Attitudes/Promotions/Preventions: The Black Elderly," in *The Black Elderly: Research on Physical and Psychological Health,* ed. James S. Jackson (New York: Springer Publishing Company, 1988), 292; Black American's fear of racist institutions was well founded, but in an integrated society this position needs to be reevaluated to make institutions responsive to their needs. Jacquelyne Jackson, *Minorities and Aging,* 181–84; Hobart Jackson, "The Current Nursing Home Crisis," *NCBA News* (December 1973): 4–5; Butler, *A Resource Guide on Black Aging,* 16–19.

2. Jane Riblett Wilkie, "The Black Urban Population of the Pre–Civil War South," *Phylon* 37 (fall 1976): 252; See also David Goldfield, "Black Life in the Old South Cities," in *Before Freedom Came: African American Life in the Antebellum South* (Charlottesville: The University of Virginia Press and the Museum of the Confederacy, 1991), 123–53.

3. U.S. Department of Commerce, Bureau of the Census, *Negro Populations, 1790–1915* (Washington, D.C.: Government Printing Office, 1918; Reprinted by Arno Press and *The New York Times,* 1968), 162–68. Includes documentation for parts of last paragraph. The number of centenarians here has been disputed.

4. Robert Taylor and Willie Taylor, "The Social and Economic Status of the Black Elderly," *Phylon*: 295. Hill, "A Demographic Profile of the Black Elderly," 2–9; Reynolds Farley, "The Urbanization of Negroes in the United States, in *Search of the Promised Land: Essays in Black Urban History,* ed. Theodore Kornweibel (Port Washington, N.Y.: Kinnekat Press, 1981), 10.

5. Farley, "Urbanization of Negroes," 12–14.

6. U.S. Dept. of Commerce, Bureau of the Census, *Negro Populations, 1790–1915,* 311; U.S. Department of Commerce, Bureau of the Census, *The Social and Economic Status of the Black Population in the United States: An Historical View, 1790–1978* (Washington, D.C.: U.S. Government Printing Office, 1978; Current Population Reports, Special Studies Series P-23, No. 80), 117; U.S. Department of Health and Human Services, Administration on Aging/National Clearinghouse on Aging, *Characteristics of the Black Elderly—1980* (Washington, D.C.: DHEW Publication No. [OHDS] 80–20057, April 1980), 16; Hill, "A Demographic Profile of the Black Aged," 3–4.

7. U.S. Dept. of Commerce, Bureau of the Census, *Negro Pupulations, 1790–1915,* 54.

8. Ira Berlin, *Slaves without Masters: The Free Negro in the Antebellum South* (New York: Pantheon Books, 1974), 176–77.

9. In 1976 Blacks made up about 7 percent of the aged population, but constituted over 14 percent of the centenarians. Manney, *Aging in American Society,* 105; Herbert Morais, *The History of the Afro-American in Medicine* (Cornwell Heights, Penn.: The Publishers Agency, The Association for the Study of Afro-American Life and History, 1967), 32–33; Achenbaum, *Old Age in the New Land,* 14.

10. Leon Litwack, *North of Slavery: The Negro in the Free States, 1790–1860* (Chicago: University of Chicago Press, 1961), passim; Richard Wade, "The Negro in Cincinatti, 1800–1830," *Journal of Negro History* 34 (January 1954): 43–57; Farley, "Urbanization of Negroes," 11.

11. Theodore Herschberg, "Free Blacks in Antebellum Philadelphia," in *The Peoples of Philadelphia: A History of Ethnic Groups and Lower Class Life, 1790–*

1940, ed. Allen F. Davis and Mark Hallen (Philadelphia: Temple University Press, 1973), 114-8, 131; Russell Weigley, *Philadelphia—A 300 Year History* (New York: W. W. Norton and Company, 1982), 309; Eric Foner, "The Battle to End Discrimination against Negroes on Philadelphia Streetcars: (Part 1) Background and Beginning," *Pennsylvania History* 40 (July 1973): 261-80; "The Battle to End Discrimination against Negroes on Philadelphia Streetcars: (Part 2) The Victory," 40 (October 1973): 353-79; Elizabeth Geffen, "Violence in Philadelphia in the 1840s and 1850s," *Philadelphia History* 36 (October 1956): 381-410.

12. John Hope Franklin, *From Slavery to Freedom: A History of Negro Americans* (New York: Alfred A. Knopf, 1974), 150-63; Woodson, 249-251; Berry and Blassingame, *Long Memory*, 33-69.

13. For a comprehensive analysis of African American property holders in the South see Loren Schweninger, *Black Property Owners in the South, 1790-1915* (Urbana: University of Illinois Press, 1990); John Hope Franklin, "The Free Negro in the Economic Life of Antebellum North Carolina," *North Carolina Historical Review* 19 (October 1942), 369. See also Leonard P. Curry. *The Free Black in Urban America, 1800-1850: The Shadow of the Dream* (Chicago: University of Chicago Press, 1981); Orville Vernon Burton, *In My Father's House are Many Mansions: Family and Community in Edgefield, South Carolina* (Chapel Hill: University North Carolina Press, 1985).

14. Michael Katz, *In the Shadow of the Poorhouse: A Social History of Welfare in America* (New York : Basic Books, 1986), 9-10; Walter Trattner, *From Poor Law to Welfare State: A History of Social Welfare in America* (New York: The Free Press, 1974), passim.

15. David Rothman, *The Discovery of the Asylum: Social Order and Disorder in the New Republic* (Boston: Little Brown and Company, 1971), 188; Katz, *In the Shadow of the Poorhouse*, 22-23.

16. The Quakers had operated an almshouse but abandoned the practice in the antebellum period in favor of placing their poor in families and boardinghouses. See David Forsythe, "Friends' Almshouse in Philadelphia," *Bulletin of Friends' Historical Association* 16 (spring 1967): 16-25.

17. Negley K. Teeters, "The Early Days of the Philadelphia House of Refuge," *Pennsylvania History* 27 (April 1960): 165-87; Cecile P. Frey, "The History of the House of Refuge for Colored Orphans,"; *Journal of Negro History* 66 (spring 1981): 10-25; Robert Pickett, *House of Refuge: Origins of Juvenile Reform in New York State* (Syracuse: Syracuse University Press, 1969); Rachel B. Marks, "Institutions for Dependent and Delinquent Children; Histories, Nineteenth-Century Statistics, and Recurrent Goals," in *Child Caring: Social Policy and the Institution*, ed. Donnell M. Pappenport, Dee M. Kilpatrick, and Robert Roberts (Chicago: Aldine Publishing Company, 1973), 9-67. Katz, *In the Shadow of the Poorhouse*, 103-9.

18. Alice Felt Tyler, *Freedom's Ferment: Phases of American Social History from the Colonial Period to the Outbreak of the Civil War* (New York: Harper and Row Publishers, 1962), 294-99; Gerald Grob, *The State and the Mentally Ill: A History of Worcester State Hospital in Massachusetts, 1830-1920* (Chapel Hill: The University of North Carolina Press, 1966), 12; Katz, *In the Shadow of the Poorhouse*, 30.

19. See chapter 1. Quakers had founded Friends Hospital in Pennsylvania in 1813 and were intricately involved in the movement to establish private asylums. Grob, *The State and the Mentally Ill*, 11-12.

20. Tyler, *Freedom's Forment*, 294-99.

21. Amos Warner et al., *American Charities and Social Work*, 4th ed. (New York: Thomas Y. Crowell, 1894), 92; Barry Kaplan, "Reformers and Charity: The Abolition of Public Outdoor Relief in New York City, 1870–1898," *Social Services Review* 52 (June 1978): 210.

22. U.S. Dept of Commerce, Bureau of the Census, *Negro Populations, 1790–1915*, 454–55; Alfred J. Kutzik, "American Social Provision of the Aged: An Historical Perspective," in *Ethnicity and Aging: Theory, Research, and Policy*, eds. Donald Gelfand and Alfred Kutzik (New York: Springer Publishing Company, 1979): 58. This figure of 46,000 reflects a reduction of about 5,500, which Kutzik attributes to the development of old-age Homes and beneficial associations.

23. Kutzik, "American Social Provisions for the Aged," 50. For a discussion of the transformation of poorhouses to old folks' Homes, see Katz, *In the Shadow of the Poorhouse*, 85–109; Haber, "Old Age, Public Welfare, and Race," 82.

24. David H. Fischer, *Growing Old in America* (Oxford: Oxford University Press, 1978), 12–13.

25. Ollie Randall, "Some Historical Developments of Social Welfare Aspects of Aging," *The Gerontologist* 5 (March 1965): 40; John Higham, *Strangers in the Land: Patterns of American Nativism, 1869–1925* (New York: Atheneum, 1972), passim.

26. Ethel McClure, *More Than A Roof: The Development of Minnesota Poor Farms and Homes for the Aged* (St. Paul: Minnesota Historical Society, 1968), 281, 108–124.

27. Jacob G. Gold and Saul Kaufman, "Development of Care of Edlerly: Tracing the History of Institutional Facilities," *The Gerontologist* 10 (winter 1970): 271–72; Kutzik, "American Social Provisions for the Aged," 56. Gari Lesnoff-Caravaglia, ed., *Values, Ethics, and Aging* (New York: Human Sciences Press, 1985), 123–25.

28. John T. Gillard, *The Catholic Church and the American Negro* (Baltimore: St. Joseph's Society Press, 1929; reprint Edition Johnson Reprint Corporation, 1968), 206; There are no statistics to corroborate this conclusion, but the Bureau of the Census, 1910 survey of benevolent institutions reported unanimous acceptance of Blacks by the Homes administered by the Little Sisters of the Poor. Generally, White Homes excluded African Americans, but some, the Salvation Army Homes, for example, merely stated that there were no rules against accepting them. Department of Commerce and Labor, Bureau of the Census, *Benevolent Institutions* (Washington, D.C.: U.S. Government Printing Office, 1910), passim.

29. William L. Andrews, *Three Black Women's Autobiographers of the Nineteenth Century* (Bloomington: Indiana University Press, 1986), 172–73, 188–205. The practice observed here was described by Douglass among the slaves in chapter 2. Foote claims that Blacks were taught to treat the aged with "great respect," but ironically the elderly criticized her attempt to preach to them as a violation of the respect for old age. One minister admonished her "to remember that you are too young to read and dictate to persons older than yourself, and many in the church are dissatisfied with the way you are talking and acting." On occasion some "elder sisters" tried to get ministers to allow her to preach.

30. Marilyn Richardson, ed., *Maria W. Stewart, America's First Black Woman Political Writer: Essays and Speeches* (Bloomington: Indiana University Press, 1987), 36. Stewart's liberation not only led her outside the boundaries of the "Cult of True Womanhood," but also led her to admonish the old to throw off their

yoke of fear and complacency. In 1833 in an address to the African Masonic Lodge, she claimed that Blacks were considered "dastards, cowards, faint-hearted wretches; and on this account (not because of our complexion) many despise us . . . I would ask, is it blindness of mind, or stupidity of soul, or the want of education that has caused our men who are 60 or 70 years of age, never to let their voices be heard, nor their hands be raised in behalf of their color? Or has it been for the fear of offending the Whites? If it has, o ye fearful ones, throw off your fearfulness, and come faith in the name of the Lord, and in the strength ot the God of justice, make yourselves useful and active members of society." Maria Stewart respected old age, but she danced to a higher authority.

31. Linda M. Perkins, "Heed Life Demands: The Educational Philosophy of Fanny Jackson Cappin," *Journal of Negro Education* 51 (summer 1982): 186. Coppin was not one to preach what she did not practice. Her students were often in and out of the HAICP, where they often entertained the old people, and where she served on the Board of Managers for three decades.

32. The average age of CME bishops today is about fifty, and age does not seem to play an independent role, that is, it does not operate independent of other qualifications. Methodist churches often waged their elections from two camps—those who favored traditonal leadership and those who advocated education as prerequisite to officeholding. Daniel Payne, the leading Black theologian in the nineteenth century, was a staunch advocate of trained leadership. Joseph Coles et al., compilers, *Discipline of the CME Church* (Memphis: General Board of Publication, CME Church, 1982), 443–47; Charles S. Smith, *A History of the African American Episcopal Church* (Philadelphia: Book Concern of AME Church, 1922); Daniel Payne, *A History of the African Methodist Episcopal Church* (Nashville: Publishing House of the AME Church Sunday School Union, 1891; reprint ed., New York: Johnson Reprint Corp.), 318–9; C. H. Phillips, *The History of the Colored Methodist Episcopal Church in America: Comprising Its Organization, Subsequent Development and Present Status* (Jackson Tennessee: Publishing House, CME Church, 1898: reprint edition New York: Arno Press, 1972); R. R. Wright, comp., *Encyclopedia of African Methodism* (Philadelphia: The Book Concern of the AME Church, 1947).

33. Grace King, *New Orleans, the Place and the People* (New York: The Macmillan Company, 1928), 349; Gillard, *The Catholic Church and the American Negro,* 141; Edward D. Smith, *Climbing Jacob's Ladder: The Rise of Black Churches in Eastern American Cities* (Washington, D.C.: Smithsonian Institution, 1988), 97–100.

34. Ibid., 353; Because of Lafon's "broad humanitarianism and true-hearted philanthropy" the state recognized him by displaying a bust of his likeness in New Orleans; the only Black so honored.

35. Curry, *The Free Black in Urban America,* 124–33.

36. This statement is not to be construed to mean that old slaves did not welcome freedom, but is meant merely to reflect the harsh realities they faced after the war. These difficulties are described in a study of the period. For an analysis of the issues surrounding the postwar years, see Peter Kolchin, *American Slavery, 1619–1877* (New York: Hill and Wang, 1993), 200–37.

37. John Hope Franklin, "Public Welfare in the South during Reconstruction, 1865–1880," *Social Service Review* 44 (December 1970): 379–92; William S. McFeeley, "Unfinished Business: The Freedmen's Bureau and Federal Action in Race Relations," in *Key Issues in the Afro-American Experience,* ed. Nathan Huggins et al. (New York: Harcourt Brace and Jovanovitch, 1971): 5–25; Joel

Williamson, *After Slavery: The Negro in South Carolina during Reconstruction, 1861–1877* (Chapel Hill: The University of North Carolina Press, 1965).

38. August Meier, *Negro Thought in America, 1880–1915; Racial Ideologies in the Age of Booker T. Washington* (Ann Arbor: The University of Michigan Press, 1970), passim; C. Vann Woodward, *The Strange Career of Jim Crow* (New York: Oxford University Press, 1974), passim; Franklin, *From Slavery to Freedom*, 244–64.

39. Floyd Appleton, *Church Philanthropy in New York: A Study of the Philanthropic Institutions of the American Episcopal Church in the City of New York* (New York: Thomas Whittaker, 1906), 95.

40. Brochure, "Lemington Home for Aged," 7081 Lemington Avenue, Pittsburgh, Pennsylvania, obtained from Mrs. Delores Cureton, Administrator, 28 October 1974 (formerly the Home for Aged and Infirmed Colored Women). For a history of Homes founded for African Americans during the Progressive period see Iris Carlton-Laney, "Old Folk's Homes for Blacks Founded during the Progressive Era," *Journal of Sociology and Social Welfare* 16 (September 1989): 43–60.

41. Brochure (1890–1970), "Eighty Years of Service in One Building on One Street," 45 East Transit Street, Providence, Rhode Island, 1970; Presently named the Bannister House. The Brooklyn Home is also still in existence and has completed an eighty-unit addition to care for the elderly and handicapped. Booklet, "The Brooklyn Home for Aged People, 91st Anniversary," 27 February 1982, obtained from Mrs. Zelean Quick, Brooklyn, New York; for descriptions of particular Black and White Homes see Norris Lewis, "The Old Folk's Homes of Chicago," *The Colored American Magazine* 2 (March 1901): 329–34; Ethel McClure, "The Protestant Home of St. Paul: A Pioneer Venture in Caring for the Aged," *Minnesota History* 38 (June 1962); H. C. Bittner, *A History of the Lutherans Orphans and Old Folks Home at Toledo, Ohio* (Toledo: Toledo Lutheran Publishing Co., 1923); L. M. Bowes, *A History of the Norwegian Old People's Home* (Chicago: 1940); Dorothy B. Lee, "A Study of the Development and Services of the Happy Haven Home for the Negro Aged in Atlanta, Georgia, March 1947 to May 1950," (master's thesis, School of Social Work, Atlanta University, 1951).

42. McClure, *More Than a Roof*, 118. See also Fannie King, "The Hard Beginning of Attucks Industrial School and Home at St. Paul, Minnesota," *Colored American Magazine* 16 (May 1909): 290–93.

43. Du Bois, "Efforts of Social Betterment," 77; Inabel Lindsey disagrees with this statement. She claims that orphanages outnumbered old folks Homes and must be considered the most characteristic charity, but for many who founded these institutions, the issues were reconciled by accepting the needy on both ends of the life cycle. Two of the Homes in Table 2 had 105 children, and about 15 percent of all Black Homes for the aged accepted children. See Inabel Lindsay, "The Participation of Negroes in the Establishment of Welfare Services, 1865–1900," (Ph.D. diss., University of Pittsburgh, 1952).

44. Samuel Denny Smith, *The Negro in Congress, 1879–1901* (Chapel Hill: The University of North Carolina Press, 1940), 14; Denny calls this proposal "two most chimerical schemes," but reparations is an idea that still fascinates some people. For a more recent examination of this idea, viewed as "keeping the faith with the old ex-slaves," see Mary Berry, "Reparations for Freedom, 1890–1916: Fraudulent Practices or Justices Deferred," *The Journal of Negro History* 56 (July 1972): 230. Japanese Americans who were interred during World War II

received reparations in a bill passed by Congress and signed by Presidnt Reagan on 10 August 1988, so the idea is not totally farfetched.

45. Robert W. Taylor, "An Appeal for the Harriet Tubman Old Folk's Home," *The Colored American Magazine* 3 (1903), 237-38.

46. Otey Scruggs, "The Meaning of Harriet Tubman," unpublished paper submitted to the Afro-American Bicentennial Corporation, (Syracuse University, Syracuse, New York, 15 August 1973), 18.

47. Ibid.

48. This was the formal name of the Association, but various other names were popular over the years. Among them were "The Home for Colored People," "The Colored Folk's Home," "The Old Colored People's Home," and "The Home for Colored People." Quakers called it the" Old Colored Home," newspapers preferred "The Colored People's Home," except the *Philadelphia Tribune*, a Black paper, which used no racial designation in its preference for "The Old Folk's Home." At first the Home only admitted women, and many referred to it as "The Old Women's Home." The HAICP's emphasis on keeping the elderly out of almshouses was typical of Black Homes and some, like the Chicago Old Folks Home, were modeled after the HAICP.

49. Thomas E. Drake, *Quakers and Slavery* (New Haven: Yale University Press, 1950), 78, 153; Drake claims, however, that the treatment of Indians "was liberality itself compared to their attitude toward Negroes," 10. See also Sydney James, *A People Among Peoples: Quaker Benevolence in 18th Century America* (Cambridge: Harvard University Press, 1963), passim. Many of those who supported the HAICP were involved in relief efforts for freedmen in the South. Oliver Hickman, "Pennsylvania Quakers in Southern Reconstruction," *Pennsylvania History* 12 (October 1946): 240-61; Youra Qualls, "Successors of Woolman and Benezet: The Beginnings of Philadelphia Freedmans' Associations," *The Bulletin of Friends Historical Association* 45 (autumn 1954): 82-105.

50. Sarah Douglass, "I Believe They Despise Us for Our Color," in *Black Women in White America,* ed. Gerda Lerner ed. (New York: Vintage Books, 1972), 362.

51. See Henry J. Cadbury, "Negro Membership in the Society of Freinds," *Journal of Negro History* 21 (April 1936): 151-212. A later section considers Quaker attitudes in the late nineteenth century.

52. Hershberg, 114-6; Curry, 52-53; The Black population actually declined from 19,833 in 1840 to 19,761 in 1850 and from 22,185 in 1860 to 22,147 in 1870.

53. Weigley, *Philadelphia,* 352.

54. Gary B. Nash, *Forging Freedom: The Formation of Philadelphia's Black Community, 1790-1840* (Cambridge: Harvard University Press, 1988), 246-47. Nash's work is an excellent analysis of the formation of the Phliadelphia Black community. Another work that has usefulness far beyond its title is Roger Lane, *Root's of Violence in Black Philadelphia* (Cambridge: Harvard University Press, 1986). See also W. E. B. Du Bois, *Philadelphia Negro,* passim.

55. The biracial tradition has continued up through the Jackson administration discussed in chapter 7. Women have also served on the Board throughout the Home's history. "Highlights of 1953-1954," Administrator's Address and Founder's Day, 7 November 1954. Stephen Smith Home for the Aged, Philadelphia, Pennsylvania. The formal name was the Pennsylvania Society for the Abolition of Slavery, the Relief of Free Negroes Unlawfully Held in Bondage and for Improving the Condition of the African Race. Some of the other supporters who will be mentioned later include undertaker Henriette Duterte, caterer S. J. M.

Brock, Bishop Jabez Campbell and his wife Mary, William Forten, who became a resident of the HAICP and whose impact will be discussed in detail later, and others. Joseph Truman was considered a repository of local information and served as the Home's secretary, but the collection in his name at Swarthmore College contains only one item related to the HAICP. This was a small book "Purchases for the Home for Aged and Infirm Colored Persons."

56. Home for Aged and Infirm Colored Persons, "Minute Book of the Association," October 1865. Owned by Stephen Smith Home for the Aged, Philadelphia, Pennsylvania. Hereafter referred to as "Association Minutes."

57. William S. Jackson, "Social Services among Mutual Aid Systems and Emergency Health Services," in James Jackson, et al., *The Black Elderly,* 33, 55.

58. *Proceedings of the Fifth Annual Meeting of the Home for Aged and Infirm Colored Persons Located at 340 South Front Street. Organized September 28, 1864. Also, the Proceedings of the Third Annual Meeting Held January 11, 1869; with List of Officers* (Philadelphia: Merrihew and Sons, Printers, 1869), 7–8; *Constitution, By-Laws and Rules of the Home for Aged and Infirm Colored Persons, Located at 340 South Front Street. Organized September 28, 1864. Also, the Proceedings of the Third Annual Meeting Held January 11, 1867; with List of Officers* (Philadelphia: Merrihew and Sons, Printers, 1867), 6–7. The titles of Annual Reports varied as did the printers and information included in the reports, but generally they contained proceedings of the Association meetings, constitution, bylaws, treasurer's reports, list of donations and donors, list of Board Members and officers, rules and regulations of the Home, doctor's reports, dates and times of religious meetings, and other items of interest. Hereafter annual reports will be referred to as *HAICP, Annual Report,* with the appropriate year and pages.

59. *HAICP, Annual Report,* 1867, 6–7.

60. Ibid. See chapter 1.

61. See chapter 1 for Double Jeopardy.

62. *HAICP, Annual Report,* 1895, 6; *HAICP, Annual Report,* 1866, 4; Mary Ann Shaw's true relationship to the Home was revealed only in her memorial in the 1895 annual report. Before that time and afterward, she was referred to only as "an excellent woman," "a white lady," or a "worthy woman." Evidence indicates that she was among the Quaker poor, and publication of her name would have violated Quaker discipline. The 1866 annual report referred to her "as an excellent woman whose time is chiefly occupied in providing her own support." Extant brochures are products of the Jackson administration, and the 1895 annual report is not among their collection. It was located at the Pennsylvania Historical Society.

63. Hershberg, "Free Blacks in Antebellum Philadelphia," 116; Weigley, *Philadelphia,* 492; R. R. Wright, comp., *The Philadelphia Colored Directory: A Handook of the Religious, Social, Political, Professional, Business Activities of the Negroes of Philadelphia* (Philadelphia: Philadelphia Colored Directory Company, 1907), 11.

64. *HAICP, Annual Report,* 1865, 11. The accusation by Sarah Douglass that Quakers could not deal with Blacks on the basis of equality merits study. On this issue of domestics, they seem particularly vulnerable. The Shelter for Colored Orphans and the Home for Destitute Colored Children accepted the children of domestics at reduced rates and emphasized training domestics as one of their goals. Some thought the southern schools run by Quakers should have the same educational objective. In 1910, for example, one woman complained in the *Friends' Intelligencer* that there "is oft-repeated remark that the southern schools

do not improve the quality of the colored people we have to take into our homes as help." The manager of one of these institutions replied that many of the students settle in their hometowns and find occupations such as typing, bookkeeping, and teaching. She added that the servant problem was not geographical, and the readers "do not blame schools for helping them [Blacks] make the best of themselves," *Friends' Intelligencer,* 12 February 1910.

65. Franklin, *From Slavery to Freedom,* 198; Robert C. Smedley, *History of the Underground Railroad in Chester and Neighboring Counties of Pennsylvania* (New York: Arno Press, first published in 1883), 27-28. William Still's book *Underground Railroad Record* is an invaluable resource for those interested in this topic.

66. Martin R. Delany, *The Condition, Elevation, and Destiny of the Colored People of the United States, Politically Considered* (Philadelphia: By the author in 1852; reprint Arno Press, 1968), 96; William F. Worner, "The Columbia Race Riot," *Lancaster County Historical Society Papers* 26 (1922): 185; Brawley, *A Social History of the American Negro,* 244. William Whipper deserves a biography in his own right. He was one of Philadelphia's leading intellectuals and an extremely successful businessman. Probably due to his friendship with Stephen Smith Whipper also served as auditor of the HAICP and supported the Home until his death in 1876. See Richard McCormick, "William Whipper: Moral Reformer," *Pennsylvania History* XLIII (January 1976), 23-46.

67. Worner, "The Columbia Race Riot," 187. Carl D. Oblinger, "In Recognition of their Prominence: A Case Study of the Economic and Social Backgrounds of an Ante-Bellum Negro Business and Farming Class in Lancaster County," *Journal of the Lancaster County Society* 72 (1968): 70; William Wells Brown, *The Rising Sun: or, The Antecedents and Advancement of the Colored Race* (Boston: 1874; reprint ed., N.Y.: Johnson Reprint Corp., 1970), 546; HAICP, *Annual Report,* 1881, 11. These accounts vary somewhat, but I have chosen to follow the Worner account, which more closely conforms to the recollections in the annual reports.

68. Worner, "The Columbia Race Riot," 177. Dennis Clark," Urban Blacks and Irishmen: Brother's in Prejudice," in *Blacks in Philadelphia,* ed. Mirium Ershkowitz and Joseph Zikmund (New York: Basic Books, 1973), 15-20.

69. Amy Oakley, *Our Pennsylvania: Keys to the Keystone State* (Indianapolis: The Bobbs-Merrill Co., 1950), 325; Quarles, *Black Abolitionists,* 26; Still, *Underground Railroad,* 735. In 1867 Whipper himself moved to Philadelphia next door to Stephen Smith, who lived at 921 Lombard Street. Their partnership was dissolved, and they later took on new partners but remained close friends.

70. Benjamin Klebaner, "Employment of Paupers at Philadelphia Almshouse before 1861," *Pennsylvania Heritage* (April 1957), passim.

71. Carole Haber, "The Old Folks at Home: The Development of Institutionalized Care for the Aged in Nineteenth-Century Philadelphia," *The Pennsylvania Magazine of History and Biography* (April 1977): 241.

72. Stephen Smith died on 14 November 1873. His will divided his estate among his wife, Harriet, a niece, Anna Vidal, and her daughter, Mary, one individual of undetermined relationship (probably a housekeeper), the Home for Destitute Colored Children, the House of Refuge—Colored Department, the Moyemensing House of Industry, and the HAICP, which received the bulk of the estate. The dower bequeathed to Harriet Smith, who remained interested in the Home and at one time had a room fitted there for her purpose, was passed on to the Home when she died in 1878. There is no way to determine the exact worth

of the Smith gift, but estimates claim that property and investments accrued to about two hundred thousand dollars that went to the Home. Stephen Smith Will, 14 November 1873, copy Owned by the HAICP, "Association Minutes," 14 September 1870. HAICP, *Annual Report,* 1865, 11; HAICP, *Annual Report,* 1881, Passim.

73. HAICP, *Annual Report,* 1894, 56; "Board Minutes," 12 August 1891; Edward Paxson to George W. Hancock, 18 February 1893. Letter owned by HAICP.

74. Residents were referred to as "inmates" from 1865 to 1938, when the management committee chose the term *residents.* During the 1940s and 1950s, the terms *residents* and *guests* were used interchangeably, with more than an occasional reference to them as "inmates." In January 1952 the Board of Directors adopted the term *residents* because the Committee on Sheltered Care of the National Social Welfare Assembly had chosen this designation.

75. This paragraph was constructed from numerous minutes and annual report that will not be listed here; see "lists of Inmates of the Home for Aged and Infirm Colored Persons," 1865 to 1904, owned by Stephen Smith Home for the Aged, Philadelphia, Pennsylvania. Hereafter referred to as "List of Inmates," 1865–1904; also "Entrance, Deaths, and Events," owned by Stephen Smith Home, Philadelphia, Pennsylvania. Hereafter referred to as "Entrance, Death, and Events."

76. Boarders are more fully discussed in chapter 7. HAICP, *Annual Report* 1880, 8; "Cash Book No. 2," 13 November 1884; "Cash Book, No. 2," 14 November 1884; Home for Aged and Infirm Colored Persons," Minutes of the Board of Managers," 10 July 1888, owned by Stephen Smith Home, Philadelphia, Pennsylvania. Hereafter referred to as "Board Minutes"; "Board Minutes," 4 February 1896; "Board Minutes," 8 February 1893.

77. Chapter 4 discusses beneficial associations. For the kind of benefits residents owned see HAICP, "Cash Book No. 2," December 1884, Owned by Stephen Smith Home for the Aged, Philadelphia, Pennsylvania. Hereafter referred to as "Cash Book, No. 2"; "Cash Book No. 2," 2 April 1888; "Cash Book No. 2," 8 October 1889. Occasionally, a resident had a pension from the U.S. Army; see "Cash Book N. 2," 10 June 1886.

78. When Hobart Jackson came in 1948, he outlawed the life care system, but without it in the pre–Social Security era, many would have been deprived of institutional care because a monthly payment was beyond their means. Boarder-to-inmate conversion testified to that fact. Today's private support to public assistance conversion is similar. See Jane L. Barney, *Patients in Michigan's Nursing Homes: Who Are They? How Are They? Why Are They There?* (Ann Arbor: Institute of Gerontology, University of Michigan—Wayne State University, 1973), 25–27. HAICP, *Annual Report,* 1880, 8.

79. Cadbury, "Negro Membership in the Society of Friends," 154. According to Benjamin Schuyler, Friends "feared and avoided debt like the plague" because "so intertwined was the Quaker business ethic with traditional success that the Friends who met failure carried their disgrace from the counting house to the meeting house." See Benjamin Schuyler, "The Philadelphia Quakers in the Industrial Age, 1865–1920," (Ph.D. diss., Columbia University, 1967).

80. The Home was listed as "partly" managed by Quakers in Philadelphia Yearly Meeting, *List of Organizations Managed by Wholly, or in Part by Members of the Society of Friends in Philadelphia Yearly Meeting* (Philadephia: Yearly Meeting, 1903);

81. As a matter of fact, Hobart Jackson claimed that one of his reasons for

accepting the administrator's position in 1948, when the HAICP was on the verge of collapse, was that he "did not want to see the Smith gift lost to history." Hobart Jackson, interview held at the Stephen Smith Home for the Aged, 6 October 1975, Philadelphia, Pennsylvania. See chapter 7.

82. *Christian Recorder,* 19 June 1890. Managers of the Home, Black and White, felt that the Black community should have contributed more to the Home. Black educator Fanny Coppin, in 1891, lamented that the Home was not primarily supported by Blacks. She had "hoped the time would come when the Colored people would be able to sustain and support this noble institution themselves without the aid now so generously contributed by others," *HAICP, Annual Report* 1891, 6; "Board Minutes," 8 July 1891. Quakers as a group were dwindling. Philadelphia Quakers, Hicksite and Orthodox, decreased by as much as 40 percent between 1827 and 1900, so fewer had to carry on the charitable work. Additionally, during the age of Booker T. Washington, their attitudes were increasingly reflective of the social assumptions of the times. Schuyler, "The Philadelphia Quakers in the Industrial Age," passim. According to Lane, Quakers "saw no more value in contemporary [antebellum] black culture than did other whites," and when the Civil War was over their "concern tended to recede." This may be true on a broad basis, but there was no diminution of Quaker support in the HAICP until the old guard passed from the scene. Roger Lane, *Roots of Violence in Black, 1860–1900* (Cambridge: Harvard University Press, 1986), 24.

83. William L. Pollard, *A Study of Black Self-Help* (San Francisco: RJE Research Associates, 1978), 65. See also Gerda Lerner, "Early Community of Black Club Women," *The Journal of Negro History* 59 (April 1974): 159; Carlton-Laney, "Old Folks Homes for Blacks During the Progressive Era," 50–52.

84. Du Bois, "Efforts of Social Betterment," 73.

84. Lerner, "Community Work," 163; Darlene C. Hine, *When the Truth Is Told: A History of Black Women's Culture and Community in Indiana, 1875–1950* (Indianapolis: The National Council of Negro Women, 1981), 41; Robert Warner, *New Haven Negroes: A Soial History* (New Haven: Yale University Press, 1949), 97, 284.

86. W. P. Burrell, "The True Reformers," *The Colored American Magazine* 7 (April 1904): 268; " The True Reformers," *The Colored American Magazine* 7 (May 1994): 340–46; Burrell at the time was General Secretary of this organization.

87. Ibid.

88. Howard Rabinowitz, "From Exclusion to Segregation: Health and Welfare Services for Southern Blacks 1865 to 1890," *Social Service Review* 48 (September 1974): 331, 340, and 343; Kaplan, 209–; Julia Rauch, "Quakers and the Founding of the Philadelphia Society for Organizing Charitable Relief and Repressing Mendicancy," *Pennsylvania Magazine of History and Biography* 98 (October 1974): 438–55; chapter 7 includes a more detailed discussion of medical developments in the HAICP. See Morais, *The History of the Afro-American in Medicine,* 59–74; Hobart Jackson, "The Current Nursing Home Crisis," *NCBA News* 1 (December 1973), 4–5; Eliot Rudwick, "A Brief History of the Mercy-Douglass Hospital," *The Journal of Negro Education* 20 (winter 1951): 51–54; Gamble, *The Black Community Hospital,* passim.

89. Lenwood G. Davis, *The Black Aged in the United States: An Annotated Bibliography* (Westport, Conn.: Greenwood Press, 1980), xii, 183–88.

90. W. E. B. Du Bois, *Economic Cooperation among Negro Americans* (At-

lanta: Atlanta University Press, 1907), 128–30; "Efforts for Social Betterment," 73.

91. "Benevolent Institutions," Department of Commerce and Labor, Bureau of the Census (Washington, D.C.: Government Printing Office, 1910), passim.

92. Kutzik, "American Social Provisions for the Aged," 57.

93. Haber, "Old Age, Public Welfare, and Race," 268.

94. Dubois, "Efforts of Social Betterment," 101–2, 73, passim. For a related discussion see Martha Chickering, "An Early Experiment in State Aid to the Aged, California, 1883–1895," *Social Service Review* 12 (March 1938): 41–50.

95. "Homes for Aged Colored Persons," *Monthly Labor Review* 29 (August 1929): 284–88; "Care of Aged in Old People's Homes," *Monthly Labor Review* 50 (May 1940): 1046–47; Florence Parker et al., compilers, *Care of Aged Persons in the United States* (New York: Arno Press, 1976); Davis, 183–88; North East: Volume of the Directory of Nursing Home Facilities (Rockville, Maryland: National Center for Health Statistics, DHEW Publication No. HRA 76-2001, U. S. Government Printing Office, 1975), passim. See also volumes for the South, North Central, and West, DHEW Publications HRA 76-20003, HRA 76-20002, and HRA 76-20004.

CHAPTER 3: "BETTER OFF THAN POOR WHITE PEOPLE": THE BENEFICIAL SOCIETY, THE HAICP, AND THE BLACK ELDERLY

1. Robert L. Harris, Jr., "Early Black Benevolent Societies, 1780–1830," *The Massachusetts Review* 20 (autumn 1979): 612.

2. The following works have taken various positions in regard to the origin of beneficial associations. Melville Herskovits, *The Myth of the Negro Past* (Boston: Beacon Press, 1941), 158–67; Du Bois, "Efforts for Social Betterment," passim. Carter G. Woodson, *African Background Outlined or Handbook of the Study of the Negro* (New York: 1971; first published in 1936), 168–69; Lerone Bennett, *The Shaping of Black America* (Chicago: Johnson Publishing Company, 1975), 114. Bennett claims that the benevolent society was the result of "grafting western political and social forms onto the conscious and unconscious body of the African legacy," 114; Herskovits describes several African mutual aid organizations among the Dahomeans and Yorubas and claims that among Dahomeans there are actually "permanent insurance societies . . . far removed from the type of organization customarily conceived as existing in nonliterate cultures," 116; while the argument for direct descendance may be unconvincing, the parallel is arresting. See the discussion of the Pro Esosu and Egbe and their functions among the Yoruba in N. A. Fadipe's, *The Sociology of the Yoruba* (Nigeria: Ihadan University Press, 1970), 243–61. Margaret Peil points out that many West African associations are ethically based and "attract mainly older people," 230. See Margaret Peil, *Cities and Suburbs: Urban Life in West Africa* (New York: Africana Publishing Company, 1981), 217–40.

3. This definition follows one similar to that of Leonard Curry. Curry, *The Free Black in Urban America,* 197; Goldfield makes a distinction between mutual aid and benevolent associations rather than benevolent and beneficial societies. He says: "Benevolent societies dispensed donations from affluent blacks to the black poor, while mutual aid societies collected funds to support any members who were unemployed, ill, or unable to afford decent burial." This distinction

Notes to Chapter 3

uses mutual aid associations the way I use beneficial associations. See David Goldfield, "Black Life in Old South Cities," in *Before Freedom Came: African American Life in the Antebellum South,* ed. Edward D. C. Campbell (Charlotteville: The University of Virginia Press, 1973), 147.

4. Gerda Lerner, ed., *Black Women in White America: A Documentary History* (New York: Pantheon Books, 1972), 438.

5. Ibid. For some of the other purposes see Harris, "Early Black Benevolent Societies:" 611; Dorothy Porter, "The Organized Educational Activities of Negro Literary Societies, 1828–1846," *The Journal of Negro Education* 5 (October 1936): 556–69; Anne Firor Scott, "Most Invisible of All: Black Women's Voluntary Associations", LVI *The Journal of Southern History* (February 1990): 3–22.

6. Henry C. Black, *Blacks Law Dictionary,* rev. 4th ed. (St. Paul: West Publishing Company, 1968), 200; sometimes this distinction was not clear to members of the legal profession as in the case of *Commonwealth v Equitable Beneficial Association* (1890) in which the distinguishing characteristics of insurance—profit, indemnity, or security against loss—were delineated from the features of beneficial association whereby benevolence and mutual aid are derived from a fund contributed by members; see *Atlantic Reporter* 18 (1893): 1112–14.

7. Herbert Aptheker, *A Documentary History of the Negro People in the U.S.* (New York: Citadel Press, 1915), 112.

8. E. Franklin Frazier, *The Negro Church in America* (New York: Shocken Books, 1963), 36.

9. In 1907 these companies were valued at $175,000 by Dr. Du Bois. Olive Cemetery had been purchased by Stephen Smith and bequeathed to the Home for Aged and Infirm Colored Persons (HAICP); Worner, "The Columbia Race Riot," 186; W. E. B. Du Bois, *Economic Cooperation among Negro Americans* (Atlanta: Atlanta University Press, 1907), 132–34. For an excellent overview of northern segregation see Leon Litwack, *North of Slavery: The Negro in the Free States, 1790–1860* (Chicago: University of Chicago Press, 1961), 279.

10. Berlin, *Slaves Without Masters,* 317; Genovese, *Roll Jordan, Roll,* 199–202; Woodson, *African Background,* 170.

11. Howard Rabinowitz, *Race Relations in the Urban South 1865–1890* (New York: Oxford University Press, 1978), 141.

12. Morais, *The History of the Afro-American in Medicine,* 21–34.

13. Savitt, *Medicine and Slavery,* 126–217.

14. Ibid.

15. George F, Bragg, *History of the Afro-American Group of the Episcopal Church* (Baltimore: Church Advocate Press, 1922), 97.

16. Savitt, *Medicine and Slavery,* 126.

17. Alfred J. Kutzik, "American Social Provision for the Aged: A Historical Perspective," in *Ethnicity and Aging: Theory, Research, and Policy,* ed. Donald Gelfand and Alfred Kutzik, eds. (New York: Springer Publishing Company, 1979): 41.

18. See endnote 1.

19. William H. Robinson, ed., *The Proceedings of the Free African Union Society and the African Benevolent Society* (Newport, R.I.: Published by the Urban League of Rhode Island, Providence, 1976); These minutes were turned over to the Newport Historical Society in 1963 by the Colored Union Congregational Church, which had held them since 1844. Hereafter referred to as "Proceedings, FAUS."

20. Ibid., 28. Rule V is referred to here: "That whenever there shall be the

money in the Treasury, and not immediately wanted for more necessary and important use, and any member of the society shall, by sickness or other misfortune, be in want of present relief, the major part of the Committee of said Society, may order such a sum of money to be paid him out of said sum of money for his relief, shall be under obligation to repay said Sum of Money into said Treasury, if he shall live to recover from his sickness or distressed condition." Additionally, the minutes that show amounts that are drawn from the Treasury do not indicate typical, routine or any kind of payments to the sick.

21. Ibid., 50, 160; Harris, "Early Benevolent Societies," 609; In 1802 the Free African Union Society became the African Society, and in 1807 it merged with the African Benevolent Society to operate the African Charity School and to dispense monies to the Black poor, though there is no evidence of activities relating to the latter objective. The society ceased to exist in the 1840s; see also Julian Rammelkamp, "The Providence Negro Community, 1820–1842," *Rhode Island History* 7 (January 1948): 20–33.

22. William Thornton to Free African Union Society, Providence, Rhode Island 6 March 1787, "Proceedings, FAUS,": 17.

23. Ibid.

24. For a related discussion see Lawrence Jones, "They Sought a City: The Black Church and Churchmen in the Nineteenth Century," *Union Seminary Quarterly Review* 26 (Spring 1977): 259.

25. Charles Coleman, "the Emergence of Black Religion in Pennsylvania, 1776–1850," *Pennsylvania Heritage* 4 (December 1977): 25. The African American's African consciousness, religious affiliation, as well as his dedication to the antislavery struggle were reflected in the names chosen for these organizations such as the Angolian, Society of Bethel, Female Benezet, Wilberforce, Angola Beneficial, and others; Curry, *The Free Black in Urban America*, 199.

26. Du Bois, *Philadelphia Negro*, 20.

27. James Browning, "The Beginning of Insurance Enterprise among Negroes," *The Journal of Negro History* 22 (October 1937): 418–9; Carter G. Woodson, "Insurance Business among Negroes," *The Journal of Negro History* 14 (April 1929): 212; Du Bois, *Philadelphia Negro*, 23; Constitution and Rules to be observed and kept by the Friendly Society of St. Thomas African Episcopal Church of Philadelphia, printed by W. W. Woodard, 1797, 1–6. Hereafter referred to as "Constitution and Rules . . . Friendly Society of St. Thomas."

28. Work, "Secret Wocieties as factors in the Social and Economic Life of the Negro," 343; Kutzik, "American Social Provisions for the Aged," 41; Benjamin Brawley, *A Social History of the American Negro* (London: 1970; first published, 1921), 241. The poor tended to have larger memberships in beneficial societies than did the affluent. Herschberg found that as wealth increased membership declined from 92 percent to 81 percent. Nevertheless, these organizations were culturally based, and their importance seem to transcend social class. Herschberg, "Free Blacks in Antebellum Philadelphia," 122.

29. Daniel Perlman, "Organizations of the Free Negro in New York City, 1800–1860," *The Journal of Negro History* 56 (July 1971): 184–86.

30. Samuel R. Scottron, "New York African Society for Mutual Relief—Ninety-Seventh Anniversary," *Colored American Magazine* 9 (December 1905): 689.

31. Ibid., 690; Perlman, "Organizations of the Free Negro in New York City," 184–86.

32. Ibid.

33. Herschberg, 116; *Negro Populations, 1790–1910,* 147–56.
34. Perlman, "Organizations of the Free Negro in N.Y. City," 187; Browning, "The Beginning of Insurance Enterprise Among Negroes," 421; Curry, *Free Blacks in Urban America,* 201; There is no way to be exact about the number of men's or women's organizations nor about which were purely beneficial in their activities. Aptheker, *A Documentary History of the Negro People in the U.S.,* 113–14. See Anne M. Boylan, "Women in Groups: An Analysis of Women's Benevolent Organizations in New York and Boston, 1794–1840," 71 *Journal of American History* (December 1984): 497–523.
35. "Proceedings, FAUS," 154, 171.
36. Curry, *Free Blacks in Urban America,* 202.
37. One reason for the popularity of this society among historians was its presumed intraracial exclusiveness, accepting only light-skinned Blacks and reflecting, thereby, the color consciousness of the White majority, mirroring the tripartite racial system of New Orleans or that imported to Charleston from Santo Domingo. See E. Horace Fitchett, "The Traditions of the Free Negro in Charleston, South Carolina," *The Journal of Negro History* 25 (April 1940): 139–52; Berlin, *Slaves Without Masters,* 58; For a refutation of this view see Robert L. Harris, Jr., "Charlestons Free Afro-American Elite: The Brown Fellowship Society and the Humane Brotherhood," *South Carolina Historical Magazine* 82 (October 1981): 289–310; For other northern societies see, Curry, *Free Blacks in Urban America,* 197–203; John Daniels, *In Freedom's Birthplace: A Study of Boston Negroes* (Boston: Houghton, Miflin Company, 1941), 206–5; Ann G. Wilmouth, "Toward Freedom: Pittsburgh Blacks, 1800–1870," *Pennsylvania Heritage* 4 (December 1977): 16.
38. This observation is most interesting in light of the position taken by the Free African Union Society of Providence ten years earlier. The FAUS members maintained that God had put them in a "Calamitous State," and destined them to "wretched meniality." Brown Fellowship members obviously felt that they had more control over their destiny. "Proceedings, FAUS, 8, 24, 153; "Minutes—Brown Fellowship Society," 7 January 1689—2 November 1893. Brown was succeeded by Century Fellowship Society 7 December 1793—November 1914, 1 June, 6 July 1916 with *Rules and Regulations* of the Brown Fellowship Society, Charleston, 1844," Robert S. Small Library, College of Charleston, Charleston, South Carolina. Hereafter referred to as "Minutes," Brown Fellowship or *Rules and Regulations,* Brown Fellowship, as appropriate.
39. Kutzik, "American Social Provision for the Aged," 35–36. The earliest society mentioned by Kutzik is the Scots Charitable Society organized in Boston in 1659.
40. Rules and Regulations, BFS, 9–10.
41. "Minutes, Brown Fellowship," 4 December 1843; "Minutes, Brown Fellowship," 6 November 1873.
42. Browning, "The Beginning of Insurance Enterprise Among Negroes," 428; Harris, "Charleston . . . Elite," 296.
43. Monroe Work, "Secret Societies as Factors in the Social and Economic Life of the Negro," in *Democracy in Earnest,* ed. James E. Mccullough (Washington, D.C.: Southern Sociological Congress, 1918): 344–45.
44. Du Bois, "Economic Cooperation," 97; For documentation of the rest of the paragraph see James M. Wright, *The Free Negro in Maryland, 1634–1860* (New York: Columbia University, 1921); 250–51; Work, "Secret Societies as factors in the Social and Economic Life of the Negro," 344; Rabinowitz, "From

Exclusion to Segregation," 338; Harris, "Early Black Benevolent Societies": 617; Browning, "The Beginning of Insurance Enterprise Among Negroes," 429–31; Kutzik, "American Social provisions for the Aged," 41. Philip A. Howard, "Afro-Cuban Mutual Aid Societies in 19th Century Cuba," paper presented at the Annual Meeting of the Southern Association of Historians, Atlanta, Georgia, 7 November 1992.

45. Howard Rabinowitz, "From Exclusion to Segregation: Health and Welfare Services for Southern Blacks, 1865–1890," *Social Service Review* 48 (September 1974): 327–54; Franklin, *From Slavery to Freedom*, 201–64; W. E. B. Du Bois, *Black Reconstruction in America* (New York: Atheneum Publishers, 1969, first published, 1935).

46. *Atlanta Constitution*, 13 November 1883; Du Bois, *Philadelphia Negro*, 186; Browning, 429–31; George B. Tindal, *South Carolina Negroes, 1877–1900* (Columbia: University of South Carolina Press, 1952), 284; Vernon Wharton, *The Negro in Mississippi, 1865–1890* (New York: Harper and Row Publishers, 1947), 270–71; Rabinowitz, "Exclusion to Segregation," 339; Frazier, 35.

47. Du Bois, *Philadelphia Negro*, passim.

48. John W. Blassingame, *Black New Orleans, 1860–1880* (Chicago: The University of Chicago Press, 1973), 167–69; Harry J. Walker estimated that there were as many as six hundred beneficial and benevolent societies in New Orleans before the Depression. Harry J. Walker "Negro Benevolent Societies in New Orleans," (Masters thesis, Department of Sociology, Fisk University, June 1937).

49. Ibid.

50. Walker, "Negro Benevolent Societies in New Orleans" 46. Walker studied eighty-three societies—interviewing members, doctors, druggists, and undertakers. Eighteen of his sample were founded before 1880, forty-seven before 1900; 72 percent were established before 1910.

51. Work, "Secret Societies as Factors in the Social and Economic Life of the Negro," 343.

52. Browning, "The Beginning of Insurance Enterprise Among Negroes," 422.

53. August Meier and Eliot Rudwick, *From Plantation to Ghetto* (New York: Hill and Wang, 1976), 91–92; August Meier, *Negro Thought in America, 1890–1915: Racial Ideologies in the Age of Booker T. Washington* (Ann Arbor: The University of Michigan Press, 1970), 142; Loretta J. Williams, *Black Free Masonry and Middle-Class Realities* (Columbia: University of Missouri Press, 1980), passim; J. H. Harmon, Jr., et al., *The Negro as A Businessman* (Washington, D.C.: The Association of Afro-American Life and History, 1928), 87–100.

54. Kutzik, "American Social Provisions for the Aged," passim; Burrell, "The True Reformers," passim; Du Bois, "Economic Cooperation," 109–10.

55. Kutzik, "American Social Provisions for the Aged," 45.

56. Ibid. Du Bois's figures show that there were 196 Black paupers in the almshouse in 1847, which represents a much smaller reduction than Kutzik claims. Du Bois, *Philadelphia Negro*, 270.

57. Benjamin Klebaner, "The Home Relief Controversy in Philadelphia, 1783–1861," *The Pennsylvania Magazine of History and Biography* 78 (October 1954): 418–21. In 1897 home relief was outlawed in Philadelphia except for medicine.

58. James M. Wright, *The Free Negro in Maryland 1634–1860* (New York: Columbia University, 1921), 248–49.

59. Daniels, *In Freedom's Birthplace*, 214.

60. Bracket, 49; also Abram Harris, *The Negro as Capitalist* (Philadelphia: American Academy of Political and Social Science, 1936), 20–21; Browning, "The

Beginning of Insurance Enterprise Among Negroes," 419; Work, "Secret Societies as Factors in the Social and Economic Life of the Negro," 343; Perlman, "Organizations of the Free Negro in New York City," 187.

61. Work, "Secret Societies as Factors in the Social and Economic Life of the Negro," 347.

62. Rabinowitz, "Exclusion to Segregation," 339.

63. Blassingame, *Black New Orleans,* 168.

64. Work, "Secret Societies as Factors in the Social and Economic Life of the Negro," 347.

65. Constitution *and Bylaws of the Colored Men's and Women's Protective Association No. 4* (Columbus, Ga.: Thos. Gilbert Printing, Bookbinding, Paper Boxes, 1890), 6. This organization was brought to my attention by Todd Savitt.

66. Rawick, *The American Slave,* 1704.

67. William Pollard, *A Study of Black Self-Help,* 73.

68. Rawick, *The American Slave,* 1893; Walker, "Negro Benevolent Societies in New Orleans," 253.

69. Much of this discussion was published in Leslie J. Pollard, "Black Beneficial Societies and the Home for Aged and Infirm Colored Persons: A Research Note," *Phylon* (September 1980): 230–34.

70. Home for Aged Colored Women, *Forty-Seventh Annual Report of the Directors of the Home for Colored Women,* (Boston, Home for Aged Colored Women, 1907). See Davis, *The Black Aged,* 46.

71. *HAICP, Annual Report,* 1865, 9. Rules and regulations for the Home may be found in the appendix.

72. These organizations were identified in a variety of records but primarily in the treasurers reports. The associations listed were founded between 1877 and 1890.

73. Du Bois, "Efforts for Social Betterment," 67–68.

74. The figures in the narrative are from the 1877 to 1891 annual reports.

75. Home for Aged and Infirm Colored Persons, "Applications, 1898–1918," Philadelphia, Pennsylvania, owned by Stephen Smith Home for the Aged.

76. "Minutes of the Committee on Management," Home for Aged and Infirm Colored Persons, Philadelphia, Pennsylvania, 13 November 1872. Hereafter referred to as "Management Minutes."

77. These figures were calculated from the annual reports for 1877 to 1891. It should be noted that Mary Campbell collected the largest amount from the society that carried her husband's name, the Jabez P. Campbell Society.

78. "Management Minutes," 19 January 1871; "Management Minutes," 14 July 1871; "Management Minutes," 10 January 1872; "Management Minutes," ? 1875. There is no evidence that any society paid more than twenty-five dollars for funeral expenses during this time. Thus the conclusion that benefits came from two organizations.

79. Disallowances were not said to be due to the number of weeks the residents were ill, but long-term care was not the goal of beneficial associations.

80. "Management Minutes," 14 April 1880; "Management Minutes," 5 May 1880; Board Minutes, 14 December 1887. The Pennsylvania Commonwealth sought to regulate charities in 1874, but there was no attempt to put these organizations out of business by imposing insurance restrictions on them; as they explained, "the character of their business was a matter of common knowledge." *Atlantic Reporter,* 1113; Work, "Secret Societies as Factors in the Social and Economic Life of the Negro," 348.

81. According to the late Hobart Jackson, the Home's chief administrator from 1948 to 1978, Pennsylvania allowed payments based on individual assessment. Hobart Jackson, interview held at Stephen Smith Home for the Aged, 6 October 1975, Philadelphia, Pennsylvania. According to Du Bois, St. Thomas had eighty members in 1896 and paid $416 in sick relief. Du Bois, *Philadelphia Negro*. 225.

82. "HAICP, Management Minutes," 12 February 1873.

83. "HAICP, Management Minutes," 14 February 1880; "HAICP, Management Minutes," 8 October 1902.

84. Woodson, *African Background*, 171. A recent uncovering of a slave burial ground in New York City by construction workers points out the significance of African American burials. Of twenty-thousand graves found to date there have been no mass burials, and each death carefully laid out despite the large number of graves. In other words, the Home's burial policies struck at the heart of the purpose of beneficial association. *The New York Times*, Sunday, 9 August 1992; *The New York Times* Saturday, 12 September 1992.

85. Walker, "Negro Benevolent Societies in New Orleans," 41; Tindall, *South Carolina Negroes*, 282–83; Harmon, et al., *The Negro as a Business Man*, 92–93; Abram Harris, *The Negro as Capitalist*, 20–21; Woodson, "Insurance," 208. See also John S. Haller Jr., "The Physician and the Negro: Medical and Anthropological Concepts of Race in the Late Nineteenth Century," *The Bulletin of the History of Medicine* 44 (March–April 1970): 154–67.

86. Robert Harris, "Charleston's . . . Elite," 301.

87. "Minutes, Brown Fellowship," 5 November 1891; "Minutes, Brown Fellowship," 3 November 1892; "Minutes, Brown Fellowship," 6 April 1893; "Minuets Brown Fellowship," 5 October 1893; "Minutes, Brown Fellowship," 2 November 1893.

88. Browning, "The Beginning of Insurance Enterprise Among Negroes," 426.

89. "Proceedings, FAUS," 2 October 1794; "Proceedings FAUS," 6 November 1794; "Proceedings, FAUS," 4 December 1794.

90. "Public Pensions for Aged Dependent Citizens," *Monthly Labor Review*, 28 (March 1929): 449–51. Pennsylvania's pension law was on the books for one year but was repealed in 1924.

91. Walker, "Negro Benevolent Societies of New Orleans," passim; *Friends' Intelligencer*, 25 May 1935; By 1910 only six states had failed to provide for relief of CivilWar veterans while only Illinois, Ohio, and Wisconsin had provided aid to the needy blind by that time. Generally, aid to blind, old, and children emerged after the first decade of the twentieth century. California was an exception, but its early attempt to aid needy elderly failed. By 1914 five states had provided for the blind, but the response toward children was much more rapid since twenty states by 1914 and thirty-nine by 1919 had provided for them. Pennsylvania provided aid to the blind in 1933. See Ann E. Geddes, *Trends in Relief Expenditures, 1910–1935* (New York: Cacapo Press, 1971; first published, 1937), 2–4, 91. For California, see Chickering, "An Early Experiment in the Care of the Aged," passim.

92. Bennett, *The Shaping of Black America*, 311.

93. William J. Trent, "Development of Negro Life Insurance Enterprise" (master's thesis, University of Pennsylvania, Philadelphia, 1932) 37–38; Walter Weare, *Black Business in the New South: A Social History of the North Carolina Mutual Life Insurance Company* (Urbana: University of Illinois Press, 1973), 12–4; Woodson, "Insurance," 211. Metropolitan Life Insurance Company contin-

ued to insure Blacks but at higher costs for less insurance, see Trent, 15–16. The seven existing Black Insurance companies that were founded during the period are Afro-American Life (1901), American Woodman's Life (1901), Southern Aid Life (1893), Atlantic Life (1905), North Carolina Mutual Life (1898), the Pilgrim Health and Life (1898), and Winston Mutual Life (1907). Pilgrim was purchased by Atlanta Life (1988) and no longer exists as an independent company.

94. Arthur Raper, *Preface to Peasantry: A Role of Two Black Belt Counties* (Chapel Hill: The University of North Carolina Press, 1936), 373. See also Hortense Powdermaker, *After Freedom, A Cultural Study in the Deep South* (New York: The Viking Press, 1939), 121–24; Having grown up with "cieties," in rural Georgia, I never quite appreciated the importance of these organizations. An investigation of my home county of Columbia (about fifteen miles west of Augusta, Georgia) showed that some churches still had beneficial organizations, though they are fewer and of less importance than they used to be. I can remember the 1950s, when the "ciety" meeting would be held about twice a year at my father's store for the disbursement of foodstuff—meal, flour, sugar, lard, soap, and so on. The name "Zack Pollard" would be called, and the man on the truck would holler "15 times," which was one item of food for each of my thirteen brothers and sisters and my parents. This is an indication of how societies cared for members in ways other than insurance or had by the 1940s and 1950s transformed their purposes.

95. The Rosemont Association still had substantial assets, particularly land holdings, but interest in it as well as the other organizations seems to lie primarily with a few old folks. Much of this information came from an interview with Mr. George Dent, an officer of the Rosemont Association and a member of Second Mt. Carmel. Interview, George Dent, Augusta, Georgia, 1 September 1983. For a more detailed view of the present-day workings of mutual aid societies see Bruce Ergood, "The Female Protection and the Sun Light: Two Contemporary Negro Mutual Aid Societies," *Florida Historical Review* 50 (July 1971): 25–38.

CHAPTER 4: "BUT SHE WAS WHITE": RACE, GENDER, AND RESIDENCY IN THE HAICP

1. Organizations are designed to achieve a particular purpose such as the care of old people, but they are inevitably subject to environmental pressures. See for example Philip Selznick, "Foundations of the Theory of Organization" *American Sociological Review* 13 (February 1948): 25–35. See also M. Powell Lawton, "Institutions for the Aged: Theory, Content and Methods in Research," *The Gerontologist* 10 (winter 1970): 302–12.

2. In 1938 the committee on management decided to drop the term *inmates* and use the term *residents*. During the 1940s and early 1950s, the terms *residents* and *guests* were used interchangeably, with more than an occasional reference to them as *inmates*. In January 1952 the Board of Directors (themselves called Board of Managers until the 1950s) adopted the term *residents* as the Committee on Sheltered Care of the National Social Welfare Assembly had chosen this term. The nomenclature used to refer to those living in institutions for the aged reflected the negative attitudes toward them and their inferior social position in American society.

3. HAICP, *Annual Report*, 1872, 6; *Friend's Review*, 26 August 1871; *Christian Recorder*, 8 July 1871.

4. *HAICP, Annual Report,* 1972, 6; *HAICP, Annual Report* 1871, 6–7; *Friends' Intelligencer,* 19 August 1871.

5. Edward Parker is discussed in chapter 3. *HAICP, Annual Report,* 1894, 49–56; "Board Minutes," 8 July 1891; "Board Minutes," 12 August 1891. Edward Paxson to George W. Hancock, 18 February 1893, on file at Stephen Smith Home for the Aged, Philadelphia, Pennsylvania. Paxson, executor of the Parker estate, here described his intention to the secretary of the Board.

6. *HAICP, Annual Report* 1884, 6; *HAICP, Annual Report,* 1901, 7.

7. *HAICP, Annual Report,* 1891, 9.

8. How the HAICP survived the hardships of the depression is the story of chapter 7.

9. See "List of Inmates of the Home for Aged and Infirm Colored Persons," Philadelphia. Owned by the Stephen Smith Home for the Aged; First entry, 5 March 1865, last entry, 29 April 1804. See also "Book of Admissions and Deaths, Home for Aged and Infirm Colored Persons," Philadelphia. Owned by the Stephen Smith Home for the Aged. *HAICP, Annual Report,* 1922, 4–5.

10. Home for Aged and Infirm Colored Persons, "Entrance, Deaths, and Events," Philadelphia. Owned by the Stephen Smith Home for the Aged. Hereafter referred to as "Entrance, Death, Events." Visitors, for example, on 6 October 1898 and 4 January 1898 expressed an interest in modeling a Home after the HAICP. It should be noted that the Quaker presence might have attracted potential Home builders because of expected contributions from wealthy Friends. See *Friends' Intelligencer,* 14 October 1893; "Board Minutes," 13 July 1892.

11. "Board Minutes," 24 September 1952.

12. The 1933 annual report accurately showed, 1,975 residents to date. Records for the years 1933 to 1939 are sporadic, and thereafter disappear altogether. The average rate of admission was 19 per year, which would give a combined figure of 2,355 when computed for years 1933 to 1953 and added to the figure in the 1933 report; the estimate of 2,200 was offered in consideration of the HAICP's decline during the 1940s.

13. "Rules and Regulations," *HAICP, Annual Report,* 1865, 8.

14. "Board Minutes," 10 July 1888; "Board Minutes," 9 February 1886; "Board Minutes," 20 November 1895; "Board Minutes," 4 February 1896.

15. See for example Jane L. Barney, *Patients in Michigan's Nursing Homes: Who Are They? How are They? Why Are They There?* (Ann Arbor: Institute of Gerontology, University of Michigan—Wayne State University, 1973): 25–27.

16. "Board Minutes," 8 February 1893.

17. Hobart Jackson, interview held at Stephen Smith Home for the Aged, 6 October 1975, Philadelphia, Pennsylvania, "Board Minutes," 14 June 1938. The life care concept has been revised as a way to care for old people in communities with essentially the same features as the HAICP practice. If there is a lesson here, it is that cost may outstrip operations, and people will have no place to go after exhausting all their resources. See Jane Bryant Quinn, "Life Care Centers for the Elderly," *Augusta Focus* (24 May 1984): 5.

18. *HAICP, Annual Report,* 1902, 7–8.

19. Those who listed more than one relative were counted only once, in the category of the most intimate kin. For example, an applicant who listed a son or daughter and a niece or nephew was counted only in the category of a son or daughter. The Stephen Smith Home owns 370 applications for the years 1898 to 1918. The sample was chosen by randomly selecting the first one and listing for analysis every fifth application thereafter. Applications averaged 17 per year and

ranged from 8 in 1898 to 28 in 1905. The sample included 57 females (78 percent) and 16 males (22 percent), almost the exact sex ratio of all residents served between 1865 and 1910.

20. *HAICP, Annual Report,* 8.

21. "Rules and Regulations," *HAICP, Annual Report,* 1865, 7.

22. Stephen Smith Home for the Aged, "List of Inmates of the Home for Aged and Infirm Colored Persons," 1865–1904, Philadelphia, Pennsylvania. Hereafter referred to as "List of Inmates," 1865–1904.

23. Ibid.

24. "Management Records," 20 October 1886; "Management Records," 4 June 1885; "Management Records," 19 January 1900; "Management Records," 3 April 1883; "Management Records," 19 October 1897; "Management Records," 11 February 1914.

25. At one time in the late nineteenth century, members in the Association must have reached a thousand or more with life members accounting for about half that number. It was this group of Quakers and Blacks that through their contributions and legacies provided for the economic success of the HAICP. Unfortunately, when these people died, they were rarely replaced by new supporters.

26. There is some discrepancy between the number of committees published in the annual reports and the minutes of the Association. The remarks here follow the minutes because they could not have functioned until they showed up in the minutes of the Association or Board of Managers. In addition to the three committees created in 1864, others included a committee on religious meetings in 1866, a committee on interments in 1867, an admissions committee in 1872, a committee on discipline in 1892, a distinct finance committee in 1901, and an auditing committee in 1907. A reading committee was created in 1864, but voluntarism soon obviated its continuation.

27. "Association Minutes," 3 November 1864; other Homes made a similar dichotomy between the duties of men and women; see Appleton, 95. While this distinction seems to contradict notions of Quaker liberalism, this is not necessarily the case. See for example Julia Rauch, "Women in Social Work: Friendly Visitors in Philadelphia, 1880," *Social Service Review* 49 (June 1975): 241–59; L. M. Bowes, *A History of the Norwegian Old People's Home* (Chicago: No publisher, 1940), 21. In his discussion about hospitals Rosenberg writes: "Society reconstructed itself within the hospital, mirroring in microcosm those values and relationships that prevailed outside its small stage." Charles E. Rosenberg, *The Care of Strangers: The Rise of America's Hospital System* (New York: Basic Books, 1987), 39–40.

28. *Christian Recorder,* 28 June 1894. Still's involvement spanned over thirty-seven years, and he was said to have visited the Home every Sunday for over a quarter of a century. He was also on the Board for Destitute Colored Children, the Shelter for Colored Orphans, Stover College, and the Black YMCA, which he helped to found. See Alberta Norwood, "Negro Welfare Work in Philadelphia, Especially as Illustrated by the Career of William Still, 1875–1930," (master's thesis, University of Pennsylvania, 1931). See also Larry Gara, "William Still and the Underground Railroad," *Pennsylvania History* 28 (January 1961): 34–44.

29. Irwin, "HAICP: Report to the Board," 99–102. There was no title to this report which was submitted to the Board of Managers in February, 1938. Chapter 7 discusses the report in detail.

30. Quakers enjoyed a reputation of fair treatment and honest dealings among

Black Americans, and it does not seem to have been a major concern that they served in the important positions. See Cadbury, "Negro Membership in the Society of Friends," 154.

31. Home for Aged and Infirm Colored Persons, "Records of the Committee on Management," 30 May 1884. Owned by Stephen Smith Home for the Aged, Philadelphia, Pennsylvania. Hereafter referred to as "Management Records."

32. *HAICP, Annual Report,* 1875, 11; "Board Minutes," 9 December 1894. See Rauch, "Women in Social Work," 244.

33. "Board Minutes," 9 January 1907.

34. "Board Minutes," 28 May 1908; *HAICP, Annual Report,* 1908, 6.

35. *HAICP, Annual Report,* 1884, 8.

36. "Board Minutes," 19 February 1897.

37. *HAICP, Annual Report,* 7.

38. "Board Minutes," 13 June 1883. These remarks about her duties are scattered throughout the reports, and the committee on management often noted that "she has too much for *any one person* [their emphasis] to carry in the management of so large an institution" or a similar remark. "Management Records," 7 September 1885. In 1901 the responsibilities of matron and assistant were more clearly delineated to avoid conflicting overlap of their duties. See "Management Minutes," 10 July 1901.

39. "Management Records," 21 December 1892; "Management Records," 10 August 1892; "Management Records," 6 September 1893; "Management Records," 10 October 1894; "Management Records," 16 June 1896; "Management Records," 9 June 1897; "Management Records," 10 August 1905; "Board Minutes," 9 January 1901; "Board Minutes," 27 March 1903; "Board Minutes," 9 June 1909.

40. "Management Records," 1 April 1885; "Management Records," 13 January 1897; "Management Records," 10 May 1905.

41. "Board Minutes," 9 September 1885; "Management Minutes," 9 September 1885.

42. "Management Records," 19 May 1909. In addition to room and board, domestics in 1890 earned about two dollars to four dollars a week. Lane, *Roots of Violence in Black Philadelphia,* 41.

43. "Management Minutes," 10 July 1901; "Management Minutes," 10 February 1909; "Management Minutes," 13 August 1902; "Management Minutes," 14 October 1909; "Management Minutes," 13 August 1902; "Management Minutes," 30 January 1909; "Management Minutes," 10 May 1905; "Management Minutes," 10 November 1909; "Management Minutes," 8 December 1909; "Management Minutes," 10 May 1905; "Management Minutes," 11 November 1908; "Management Minutes," 14 April 1909; "Management Minutes," 19 May 1909; "Management Minutes," 8 June 1910. See chapter 7 endnote 38 salary examples.

44. The annual reports for the HAICP for 1903 and 1904 are not available, therefore, the figures are not provided for corresponding years. The figures were obtained merely by dividing the cost of supplies (all expenditures except repairs) by the number of residents for the years given. *HAICP, Annual Report,* 1880, 10; *HAICP, Annual Report,* 1890, 13; *HAICP, Annual Report,* 1910, 8.

45. "Management Records," 16 June 1896; "Management Records," 2 June 1890; See "Management Records," 10 October 96. See also "Management Records," 14 February 1912.

46. "Board Minutes," 1 April 1885. The nature of the charges are more specifically outlined in chapter 7.

47. "Board Minutes," 9 September 1885.
48. "Management Minutes," 9 April 1890.
49. "Board Minutes," 9 September 1885.
50. "Management Records," 26 September 1884. Esther Barnes did not seem to be without compassion. In 1885 Anne Hollingsworth, a homeless woman showed up at the Home. She was cleaned, fed, and clothed. After a week, the matron, still refusing to turn her out, "took her to William Hill's house since she was homeless and broke." Milliscent Parvin, who was the first matron, coming to the Home in 1865 from her position as assistant matron at Pennsylvania Hospital, was also White.
51. "Board Minutes," 9 January 1889; "Board Minutes," 10 October 1888.
52. "Management Minutes," 9 April 1890.
53. Comilda Weinstock and Ruth Bennett, "Problems in Communication to Nurses among Residents of a Racially Heterogeneous Nursing Home," *The Gerontologist* 8 (summer 1968): 72–75.
54. *HAICP, Annual Report*, 1893, 9–10.
55. Interview, Hobart Jackson, Stephen Smith Home for the Aged, Philadelphia, Pennsylvania, 18 March 1977.

Chapter 5: "Complaint to the Lord": Social Structure in the HAICP

1. These two paragraphs were constructed from a variety of sources, including annual reports, minutes of the management committee, records of the committee, and so on. "Rules and Regulations," *HAICP, Annual Report*, 1865, 10. See appendix E.
2. "Board Minutes," 5 May 1875; "Board Minutes," 13 September 1871; "Board Minutes," 12 December 1906; "Board Minutes," 14 September 1892; "Board Minutes," 10 July 1878; "Management Records," 13 August 1884; "Management Records," 5 September 1884; "Management Records," 12 December 1906; "Board Minutes," 13 August 1884.
3. "Management Records," 26 June 1885. Ignorance was the most frequent explanation that residents used for infractions. It was not until 1951, when the House Council was established, that the residents were given input into the decision-making process.
4. "Management Records," 6 January 1885.
5. "Management Minutes," 10 October 1885.
6. "Board Minutes," 12 October 1892.
7. "Board Minutes," 11 November 1874; "Management Minutes," 4 March 1884. Making the decision to serve two meals in winter, managers noted that "inmates are old and do not care to rise early, and breakfast and dinner come too close together. "See "Management Minutes," 30 January 1906; "Management Minutes," 12 April 1895.
8. "Management Records," 7 August 1885.
9. The menus of the HAICP compared favorably with other institutions. The Home for the Blind in New York in 1906 had a diet that consisted of cereal, meat, coffee, and bread and butter for breakfast; roast or fish and two vegetables for dinner, hash or beans and cake or fruit for supper. The House of Mercy of the same city did not serve a meat for breakfast but served the other items, and for dinner there was one vegetable and one meat, with a cake or fruit added for

supper. Appleton, *Church Philanthropy in New York,* 186. For a discussion of nutritional needs of elderly Blacks in both an institutional and a historical context, see Maxine Willi, "Nutritional Needs of Black Adults and How They Relate to Life Expectancy," in *The Black Elderly in Long-Term Care Settings* (Oakland: Ethel Percy Andrus Gerontology Center, University of Southern California, 1974), pp. 5–9; June Abbey, "Health Care of the Aged Based on Physiological Concerns," in the same volume.

10. "Management Records," 24 March 1888. For other remarks see "Management Records," 10 March 1897. "Management Records," 14 April 1897.

11. "Management Records," 3 March 1891.

12. "Management Records," 21 September 1888.

13. "Management Records," 10 July 1878; "Board Minutes," 11 September 1878; "Management Records," 25 December 1885. These problems persisted through the years. Maria Pitts in 1934 was so dissatisfied that she sent for the food inspector, who was evidently somewhat sympathetic because he found things only "fairly satisfactory" and instructed the managers that oleomargarine could not be used by institutions. The use of butter evidently failed to improve the meals because Pitts left a year later. It is conceivable that she was in such disfavor with the managers that she no longer found life tolerable in the HAICP. "Management Records," 13 March 1934; "Management Records," 9 April 1935.

14. "Management Records," 26 January 1883; "Management Records," 23 May 1890; "Management Records," 26 November 1883 "Management Records," 29 October 1897.

15. "Management Records," 13 April 1898. Shoes were more difficult too obtain and orders sometimes dragged on for months. "Management Records," 26 November 1883; "Management Records," 14 August 1907.

16. "Management Records," 19 July 1897.

17. "Management Records," 27 October 1897. See also "Management Records," 14 February 1906.

18. "Management Records," 13 May 1903; "Management Records," 26 February 1889; "Management Records," 29 February 1889.

19. "Management Records," 13 December 1893; "Management Records," 9 January 1916; "Management Records," 9 May 1917.

20. "Management Records," 13 November 1895. Boarders were sometimes distinguished by an asterisk in the annual reports. In 1934 it was suggested that residents who were prone to run away have the Home's name stamped on their clothing, but it is not known whether this suggestion was carried out.

21. Alice Pennock, for example, was a Board member for over fifty years, 1885 to 1938, and was never seen without her white scarf, which symbolized her temperance beliefs.

22. "Rules and Regulations," *Annual Report,* 1865, 10.

23. "Management Minutes," 14 April 1897.

24. "Management Minutes," 5 May 1897.

25. "Board Minutes," 8 February 1881. "Board Minutes," 14 January 1885.

26. "Management Minutes," 5 May 1897. For a discussion of the sale and use of alcohol in the Philadelphia African American community see Lane, *Roots of Violence in Black Philadelphia,* 112–16.

27. "Board Minutes," 14 January 1885; "Board Minutes," 12 April 1893; "Board Minutes," 12 December 1906; "Board Minutes," 11 August 1909.

28. "Management Records," 8 January 1890.

29. "Management Records," 8 February 1881; "Management Records," 14

January 1886; "Management Records," 14 January 1885. The problem was not peculiar to the HAICP. See also Judith Cetina, *A History of Veterans Homes in the United States, 1811–1930* (Ph.D. diss., Case Western University, 1977: 442–56).

30. "Board Minutes," 11 November 1884. "Board Minutes," 14 December 1884. "Management Records," 14 August 1888. "Management Records," 3 February 1897.

31. "Management Records," 1 January 1890.

32. "Management Records," 18 January 1895; "Management Records," 21 January 1896; "Management Records," 31 January 1896; "Management Records," 11 March 1899.

33. "Management Records," 14 August 1888; "Board Minutes," 12 September 1906.

34. Each new infraction was counted to determine the most persistent problem that the matron and managers encountered. When the general categories of disobedience and insubordination (used when the label was attached or the exact problem was undetermined) are eliminated, leaving without permission and "hiring out" ranked, respectively, first and second, probably in that order since one had to leave without permission in order to hire out. This says nothing, however, about the gravity of the problems. For example, violence carried the weight of almost certain dismissal, whereas one might throw trash from the window for the duration of one's stay in the institution. Examples can be found in "Management Records," 1 January 1890. "Management Records," 12 March 1884; "Management Records," 5 January 1894; "Management Records," 12 February 1896; "Management Records," 7 February 1896.

35. *HAICP, Annual Report,* 1913, 19. Three couples were in the Home in 1913. As early as 1911 the management committee had recommended this policy. "Management Records," December 1911.

36. "Management Records," 23 December 1878.

37. "Board Minutes," 11 June 1873. As late as 1935 the Board's policy was unchanged. In one case women managers consented to a request for marriage, noting that there was a vacant apartment for couples, but their decision was reversed by the Board. The management committee noted that the proposed marriage "was thoroughly discussed," but the Board concluded that it was "inadvisable to allow them to proceed." This was the last instance in which a problem of management was manifested in terms of gender. This rule was changed by Hobart Jackson in 1949, but remaining in the Home after marriage, as the management committee had assumed in 1935, was a question of space and convenience. "Management Minutes," 10 December 1935; "Board Minutes," 14 January 1936; "Board Minutes," 22 December 1960.

38. William S. Young, *A History of Hollenbeck Home* (Los Angeles: 1934), 176.

39. Ibid.

40. "Management Records," 2 April 1911; "Management Records," 13 February 1907; "Management Records," 12 April 1911; "Management Records," 26 February 1892.

41. "Management Records," 8 January 1902. See also "Management Records," 12 September 1888.

42. "Board Minutes," 13 September 1876.

43. "Management Records," 13 November 1889; "Management Records," 6 November 1889.

44. "Management Records," 8 January 1890; "Management Records," 10 February 1890.
45. Hobart Jackson, Stephen Smith Home for the Aged, Philadelphia, Pennsylvania, interview 6 October 1975.
46. "Rules and Regulations," *HAICP, Annual Report,* 1865, 9.
47. *HAICP, Annual Report,* 1875, 8.
48. *HAICP, Annual Report,* 1876, 6.
49. *HAICP, Annual Report,* 1877, 5.
50. *HAICP, Annual Report,* 1901, 6–7.
51. "Board Minutes," 8 June 1881.
52. "Klebaner, "Employment," 139.
53. *HAICP, Annual Report,* 1881, 8.
54. "Management Records," 6 December 1883; "Management Records," 19 July 1890; "Management Records," 14 November 1900; "Management Records," 9 January 1901; "Management Records," 8 November 1916.
55. "Board Minutes," 12 April 1893.
56. "Board Minutes," 10 January 1894.
57. "Management Records," 12 October 1910.
58. "Board Minutes, 13 February 1895.
59. Emily Campbell to Management Committee, 9 February 1901, Stephen Smith Home for the Aged files, Philadelphia, Pennsylvania. *HAICP, Annual Report,* 1922, 8.
60. Dean W. Morse, "Aging in the Ghetto: Themes Expressed by Older Black Men and Women Living in a Northern Industrial City," *Industrial Gerontology: Studies of Work and Age* 3 (winter 1976): 4–5; Jacquelyne Jackson, "The Negro Aged," passim.
61. "Management Records," 14 February 1900. Graham lived sixteen years in the Home from 1892 to 1908.
62. "Management Records," 10 January 1911.
63. *Charter and By-Laws of the Home for Aged and Infirm Colored Persons, S. W. Corner Girard and Belmont Avenues," Philadelphia, 1867.* Owned by Stephen Smith Home for the Aged, 6. Although there are no records of residents' ability to read, the agreement books and applications reveal something about reading and writing skills. About 21 percent of the residents signed the property transfer books between 1888 and 1905, and about 22 percent of the applicants from 1898 to 1918 signed their own names. It cannot be assumed that those residents who were capable of writing their names could read, but perhaps some correlation existed. Many scribbled their names with great effort. "Book of Assignment and Agreement," Home for Aged and Infirm Colored Persons, First Entry 1888 and Last Entry 1905. Owned by Stephen Smith Home for the Aged.
64. "Management Records," 1 September 1882.
65. "Management Records," 16 November 1800; "Management Records," 8 January 1902; "Management Records," 12 March 1902.
66. "Management Records," 31 August 1897.
67. "Management Records," 13 May 1903.
68. *HAICP, Annual Report,* 1885, 6.
69. *HAICP, Annual Report,* 8.
70. *HAICP, Annual Report,* 1876, 10.
71. *HAICP, Annual Report,* 1893, 8.
72. The Concept of "total institution" is discussed by Erving Goffman, *Asylums: Essays on the Social Situation of Mental Patients and Other Inmates* (Gar-

den City: Doubleday and Company, 1961): 1–125. For a discussion of the concept and how it relates to Homes for the Aged, see Ruth Bennett, "The Meaning of Institutional Life," *The Gerontologist* (September 1963): 112–20; Morris Zelditch, "The Home for the Aged—A Community," *The Gerontologist* (March 1962): 37–41. For a related discussion that attempts a scheme to determine the degree of totality of Homes for the aged, see Allen Pincus, "The Definition and Measurement of the Institutional Environment in Homes for the Aged," *The Gerontologist* 8 (autumn 1968): 207–10. See E. A. Pollard, *Black Diamonds*, preface.

73. *HAICP, Annual Report,* 1883, 8.

74. *HAICP, Annual Report,* 1885, 12; "Board Minutes," 29 April 1885. See also "Management Records," 19 January 1886; *HAICP, Annual Report,* 1898, 7.

75. "Management Records," 16 September 1891.

76. "Management Records," 21 September 1888.

77. "Management Records," 16 September 1891.

78. On several occasions between 1904 and 1905 men were referred to as "boys," but that seemed to have been the habit of a single individual. *HAICP, Annual Report,* 1881, 11; *HAICP, Annual Report,* 1883, 10; *HAICP, Annual Report,* 1888, 13; See also *HAICP, Annual Report,* 1911, 7.

79. "Management Records," 16 May 1894.

80. "Management Records," 13 April 1898. See Lane, *Roots of Violence in Black Philadelphia,* pp. 55–61.

81. "Management Records," 5 April 1899.

82. *HAICP, Annual Report,* 1909, 11; "Management Records," 8 January 1911.

83. "Management Records," 30 April 1896.

84. Ibid.

85. "Management Records," 8 April 1885; "Management Records," 8 April 1903. Residents felt a special need to leave items to family or friends, and by the 1930s the Board allowed such items to be purchased at a nominal fee. See "Management Records," 10 October 1933; "Management Records," 13 December 1935.

86. "Management Records," 10 October 1894; "Management Records," 18 March 1895.

87. "Management Records," 10 October 1897; "Management Records," 18 May 1898.

88. "Management Records," 25 February 1910; "Management Records," 9 March 1910.

89. "Board Minutes," 9 January 1878; "Entrance, Deaths, Events," 1 November 1911; "Entrances, Deaths, Events," 13 December 1911. There is some indication that services were allowed, denied, and restarted after the protest.

90. The records were replete with inconsistencies. See "Management Minutes," 10 July 1895; "Management Minutes," 14 August 1895; "Management Minutes," 10 November 1897; "Management Records," 18 May 1898; "Management Records," 14 June 1899; "Management Records," 14 February 1900; "Management Records," 10 December 1890. To some extent, what seemed to have been favorite treatment was actually the result of preentrance negotiation, but it does not change the above contention. Between 1888 and 1905, there are five notations in the property books showing the articles residents were allowed to bequeath. For example, Mary A. Scott signed 1 January 1888, "I reserve the privilege of giving my watch and chain to my niece"; Richard Parker signed 30 November 1888, "I reserve the right to give my watch and chain to my son; Lavinia Snead

signed 29 December 1891, "I wish to give my daughter's photo to my grandchild." The last entry demonstrates the completeness with which property was relinquished.

91. "Management Records," 2 July 1884; "Board Minutes," 13 August 1884; "Management Records," 29 January 1886. This practice continued well into the twentieth century. See "Management Records," 12 October 1937.

92. "Management Records," 13 October 1886.

93. "Management Records," 8 December 1886.

94. Ibid.

95. "Management Records," 13 October 1886. This was the only reference to this position in the records. Evidently no one preceded or followed him in his job.

96. "Management Records," 10 December 1890.

97. "Management Records," 18 February 1891; "Management Records," 13 July 1892; "Management Records," 5 January 1894; "Management Records," 5 December 1894; "Management Records," 12 December 1894; "Management Records," 7 February 1896.

98. "Management Minutes," 8 April 1896; "List of Inmates," 8 April 1896. Harmon evidently took long reprieves from his troublesome ways since he disappeared from the records in 1893 and 1895. In 1896 he was expelled from the Home.

99. There are no data that separate categories in the annual reports until 1919 when "left" and "dismissed" are separated. According to the 1919 report six "left" and one was "dismissed." Ann Frazer "left" in 1922, Susan Baily "left" in 1925 and Margaretha Harris and Loretta Jones were "discharged" in 1924. After 1925 there are no data on departures except a passing reference to two individuals who withdrew between 1933 and 1939. *HAICP, Annual Report,* 1919, 12; *HAICP, Annual Report,* 1922, 11; *HAICP, Annual Report,* 1924, 12; *HAICP, Annual Report,* 1925, 12.

100. *HAICP, Annual Report,* 1878, 11.

101. *HAICP, Annual Report,* 1886, 14.

102. *HAICP, Annual Report,* 1893, 15; "Management Records," 18 May 1893.

103. "Management Records," 28 January 1887.

104. This information was compiled from all available records.

105. "Board Minutes," 10 November 1886; "Board Minutes," 10 May 1893; "Board Minutes," 8 February 1910; "Board Minutes," 10 October 1906; "Board Minutes," 13 October 1886.

106. "Management Minutes," 26 May 1884; "Entrance, Death, Events," 17 July 1903.

107. *HAICP, Annual Report,* 1920, 6.

108. *HAICP, Annual Report,* 1888, 8.

109. The stereotype here conforms to the traditional interpretation of Black religion. See E. Franklin Frazier, *The Negro Church in America* (New York: Shocken Books, 1964), passim. Ruby Johnstone, *The Development of Negro Religion* (New York: Philosophical Library, 1954), 1–2.

110. *HAICP, Annual Report,* 1887, 10.

111. *HAICP, Annual Report,* 1886, 11.

112. *HAICP, Annual Report,* 1888, 6–7.

113. *HAICP, Annual Report,* 1889, 10.

114. *HAICP, Annual Report,* 1894, 10.

115. "Management Minutes," August 1914.

116. For discussion of this view of Christianity and the attitude toward death in which it gave birth, see Gerald R. Wilson "The Religion of the American Negro

Slave: His Attitude toward Death and Dying," *The Journal of Negro History* 8 (January 1923): 41–71.

117. *Friends' Intelligencer,* 2 February 1920.

118. For a while after 1898, night services were discontinued because the management committee thought it was "a great tax on the oldsters," "Events," 9 October 1898. "Entrance, Death, Events," 1 November 1911 and 24 December 1911.

119. "Rules and Regulations," *Annual Report,* 1865, 1. It is worthy of mention that around the turn of the century, George Alexander McGuire, pastor of St. Thomas Episcopal Church, often favored the residents with his "practical" sermons, as managers called them. It was McGuire who became Chaplain-General of Garvey's Universal Negro Improvement Association and founded the African Orthodox Church in 1922. See "Events," 26 November 1902.

120. "Entrance, Death, Events," 22 February 1900. See Du Bois, *Philadelphia Negro,* 205, for religious denominations in the city. The baptist were conspicuously absent from the pattern of services in the Home, but they perhaps preferred to attend churches in the city.

121. "Management Records," 3 April 1883; "Management Records, 4 April 1883; "Management Records," 11 February 1914, "Management Records," 12 November 1919; "Management Records," 8 November 1938; "Management Records," 1911; "Management Records," 9 March 1935.

122. See appendix for the rules.

123. "Entrance, Death, Events," 6 April 1899. See *HAICP, Annual Report,* 1899, 9.

124. "Management Records," 23 September 1903.

125. Cadbury, "Negro Membership in the Society of Friends," 167–68; *HAICP, Annual Report,* 1884, 6; *HAICP, Annual Report,;* 1885, 9; *HAICP, Annual Report,* 1873, 6; *HAICP, Annual Report,* 1925, 19.

126. The Quaker role in the underground railroad has been overemphasized. See Charles Blockson, *The Underground Railroad: First Person Narratives of Escapes to Freedom in the North* (New York: Prentice Hall Press, 1987), 3–4. For the rest of paragraph see "Management Records," 11 June 1891.

127. *HAICP, Annual Report,* 1905, 5.

128. *HAICP, Annual Report,* 1892, 8.

129. *HAICP, Annual Report,* 10.

130. The Quaker sisters, Mary Johnson and Sarah Marshall, sponsored the West Indian celebration. They died before the end of the nineteenth century, and the celebration became a sporadic event.

131. "Entrance, Death, Events," 5 March 1896. The slide lecture or magic lantern lecture was most popular during the 1890s, "Entrance, Death, Events," 28 April 1898; "Entrance, Death, Events," 2 November 1897; "Entrance, Death, Events," 11 December 1899; "Entrance, Death, Events," 17 February 1900.

132. "Entrance, Death, Events," 6 May 1898. Children were virtually a part of the daily routine, judging from the records. See any of the annual reports. See also "Entrance, Death, Events," 29 November 1899. "Entrance, Death, Events," 2 April 1898. "Entrance, Death, Events," 20 May 1899.

133. "Entrance, Death, Events," 23 December 1898.

CHAPTER 6: "THE RUGGED PATH OF FALTERING AGE":
HEALTH CARE IN THE HAICP

1. The title of this chapter was taken from the Harper poem.
2. "Board Minutes," 2 June 1878.

3. *HAICP, Annual Report,* 1883, 18. See chapter 5.

4. "Management Records," 13 November 1889. See chapter 5 for fuller discussion of the point.

5. "Board Minutes," 10 March 1866; "Board Minutes," 28 February 1883; "Management Minutes," 28 January 1883; "Management Minutes," 9 July 1890; "Management Minutes," 12 November 1902. See also William Heffner, *History of Poor Relief Legislation in Pennsylvania, 1682–1913* (Cleone, Pa.: Holzaffel Publishing Co., 1913), 220–39.

6. "Management Minutes," 31 December 1871; "Board Minutes," 13 March 1872.

7. "Management Records," 4 December 1895; "Board Minutes," 4 December 1895.

8. *HAICP, Annual Report,* 1902, 6; "Management Minutes," 11 December 1901; "Management Records," 12 March 1902.

9. "Management Minutes," 8 August 1906. It seems that the typhoid case was introduced into the Home by an employee who had to be quarantined with the rest of the family.

10. In 1891 the doctor had fifty patients with the grippe, but no quarantine was imposed. See "Management Records," 15 December 1891; "Management Records," 22 December 1891.

11. "Management Records," 10 January 1917. *HAICP, Annual Report,* 1932, 1.

12. *HAICP, Annual Report,* 1876, 61.

13. *HAICP, Annual Report,* 1881, 7.

14. Ibid.

15. *HAICP, Annual Report,* 1883, 7. *HAICP, Annual Report,* 1884, 10.

16. "Board Minutes," 12 October 1892.

17. *HAICP, Annual Report,* 1902, 9; "Management Records," 10 April 1901.

18. "Management Records," 10 April 1901.

19. "Association Minutes," 13 January 1865. *HAICP, Annual Report,* 1868, 6.

20. "Board Minutes," 19 February 1872; "Board Minutes," 14 March 1880; *HAICP, Annual Report,* 1881, 12. These dates were constructed from a variety of sources and there is the distinct possibility that they are not always for continuous service.

21. "Management Records," 13 November 1895; "Management Records," 11 March 1896.

22. The first one hundred dollar salary was split between Dr. Jessie Thatcher, who received eighty dollars and Dr. Caroline Anderson, who received twenty dollars for expenses. *HAICP, Annual Report,* 1881, 12; "Board Minutes," 10 April 1878; "Board Minutes," 28 May 1903.

23. "Board Minutes," 14 March 1880.

24. "Management Minutes," 14 October 1896. This practice continued until the 1930s, when drugs were purchased from Smith, Kline and French Inc., by the nurse, who at that time was responsible for stocking the drug room. Prescriptions, however, were filled in the name of individual patients. See Irwin, "HAICP: Report to the Board," 49.

25. George B. Wood, *The Dispensatory of the U. S. of America,* 19th ed., 1907, passim; See also John Parascandola, "Patent Medicines in Nineteenth-Century America," *Caduceus* (spring 1985): 1–39. Any standard American history textbook will describe legislation resulting from the Progressive Movement.

26. See Judith Cetina, *A History of Veterans Homes in the U.S.* (Ph.D. diss.

Department of History, Case Western Reserve, 1977), 295–96; Irwin, "HAICP: Report to the Board," 50.

27. "Board Minutes," 9 March 1892. These minutes claim that managers were "fitting up a medicine room for the doctor," but evidently it was moved to the third floor of the infirmary, when it was completed in 1902. For earlier references see "Board Minutes," 11 June 1873; "Board Minutes," 9 July 1873. As stated, the drug room was stockpiled with an even larger number of tablets, ointments, mixtures, oils, and powders in later years. Examples include a variety of sulphur ointments and creams, chlorides, potassiums, sodiums, hypodermic tablets (e.g., nitroglycerine), bicarbonates, and others. See Irwin, "HAICP: Report to the Board," 51–55.

28. Wood, *The Dispensatary of the U.S. of America,* passim. J. Grier, *A History of Pharmacy* (London: The pharmaceutical Press, 1937), 59, 61, 184–85; R. C. Wren, *Potters New Encyclopedia of Botanical Drugs and Preparations* (Health Sciences Press, 1975, first published, 1907), 22, 64, 76, 198–99; John Clarke *A Dictionary of Materia Medica,* vol. 1 (Health Sciences Press, 1960) 203, 256. See Charles E. Rosenberg, "What It Was Like to Be Sick in 1884," *American Heritage* (October–November 1984): 23–31.

29. Parascandola, "Patent Medicines in 19th Century America," 11–12. Residents evidently bought patent medicines from visitors because managers expressed concern over the issue. See "Management Minutes," 8 January 1908.

30. "Management Records," 3 October 1888; See also "Management Records," 21 October 1887; Irwin, "HAICP: Report to the Board," 48.

31. HAICP, *Annual Report,* 1872, 7; "Management Records," 9 October 1878.

32. "Board Minutes," 9 August 1902; "Board Minutes," 11 February 1903; This was probably the first employee to complete a nurses training program whereas others were apprenticed or had acquired practical experience. "Management Records," 10 October 1883. The first approved Black nurses training school in Philadelphia was opened in 1895 at Douglass Hospital (founded the same year), which was supervised by Mrs. Minnie Clemons, who was said to be the first and only Black graduate of the University of Pennsylvania Nurses Program at that time. Mercy Hospital also started a school for Black nurses in 1907 when it opened. There was certainly not a large supply of trained Black nurses available for employment. See Estelle G. Massey-Riddle, "The Training and Placement of Negro Nurses," *The Journal of Negro Education* 4 (January 1935): 42–48. See also Russell J. Minton, "The History of Mercy-Douglass Hospital," *The Journal of the National Medical Association* 43 (May 1951): 153–59; In 1880 there were fifteen nurses schools for Whites. Rosenberg, *The Care of Strangers,* 31.

33. "Management Minutes," 9 September 1896; "Management Minutes," 13 January 1897.

34. "Management Records," 14 November 1898.

35. "Management Records," 1 April 1885; "Management Records," 16 November 1887; "Management Records," 1 April 1888; "Management Records," 18 May 1893. Chapter 5 discusses employee turnover.

36. "Board Minutes," 29 April 1885.

37. Irwin, "HAICP: Report to the Board," 47; Hobart Jackson, interview held at Stephen Smith Geriatric Center, Philadelphia, Pennsylvania, 6 October 1975; "Board Minutes," 24 October 1875.

38. "Management Records," 10 February 1897; "Management Records," 9 November 1898; "Management Records," 8 March 1911; "Management Records," 12 April 1911; Wills Eye Hospital, "the first hospital in the western Hemisphere

specially devoted to the eye," was opened in 1832 and started accepting Blacks five years later. See John F. Marion, *Philadelphia Medica* (Harrisburg: Smithlike Corporation, 1975): 47–48.

39. "Management Records," 13 December 1905; "Management Records," 9 November 1898; "Management Records," 8 March 1913; "Management Records," 12 April 1913.

40. "Management Records," 13 September 1881; "Management Records," 13 July 1910.

41. "Management Records," 23 September 1881.

42. "Management Records," 8 March 1911; "Management Records," 12 April 1911; Rosenberg, *Care of Strangers,* 302; The poor continue to be the "teaching material" for hospitals; See Rosemary Stevens, *In Sickness and in Wealth: American Hospitals in the Twentieth Century* (New York: Basic Books, 1989), 9–10.

43. "Management Records," 8 June 1898; "Management Minutes," 13 August 1898; It was formal ties that were disallowed.

44. "Management Records," 26 July 1885. See also "Management Records," 22 March 1882; "Management Records," 31 March 1882.

45. *HAICP, Annual Report* 1881, 8. See also *HAICP, Annual Report,* 1875, 7; *HAICP, Annual Report,* 1878, 8.

46. *HAICP, Annual Report,* 1900, 6–7.

47. "Management Records," 26 March 1897.

48. *HAICP, Annual Report,* 1878, 20.

49. "Board Minutes," 22 March 1892; "Board Minutes," 31 March 1882. "Board Minutes," 12 May 1897.

50. See for example Ernst Noam, *Homes for Aged: Supervision and Standards—A Report on the Legal Situation in European Countries* trans. John S. Monks (Washington, D.C.: DHEW Publication No [OHO] 75–20104, 1975), 60.

51. Martin Kaufman, *Homeopathy in America: The Rise and Fall of a Medical Heresy* (Baltimore: The Johns Hopkins University Press, 1971), 1; Leo J. O'Hara, *An Emerging Profession: Philadelphia Doctors, 1860–1900* (New York: Garland Publishing Co., 1989), 232–83.

52. Kaufman, *Homeopathy in America,* 25. Some aspects of this discussion were published earlier. See Leslie J. Pollard, "Allopathy and Homeopathy: Medical Clash in a Philadelphia Home for Aged Blacks," *Pennsylvania Heritage* 4 (September 1978): 22–24. William G. Rothstein, *American Physicians in the 19th Century: From Sects to Science* (Baltimore : The Johns Hopkins University Press, 1985), 152–74.

53. The first Black to be admitted to a medical society was John V. De Grasse of Bowdoin College, Class of 1849, who was admitted to the Massachusetts State Medical Society the same year. The first woman, Mary Willets, and the first Black, Nathan Mossell, an 1882 graduate of Pennsylvania University Medical School and founder of Douglass Hospital, were admitted to the Philadelphia City Medical Society in 1888. In 1895 Blacks founded the National Medical Association (NMA) in Atlanta because of the racially exclusionary policies of the American Medical Association (AMA). In 1900 Philadelphia's Black physicians, dentists, and pharmacists, led by Mossell, formed the Philadelphia Academy of Medicine and Allied Sciences, a branch of the NMA, "There seem to be three problem groups in medicine: Jews, women and Negroes," wrote M. O. Bousefield in 1945, "and the greatest of these is Negroes." M. O. Bousefield, "An Account of Physicians of Color in the United States," *Bulletin of the History of Medicine* 17 (January 1945): 62; See also James L. Curtis, *Blacks, Medical Schools, and Society* (Ann Arbor:

University of Michigan Press, 1971): 15; H. A. Callis, "The Need for and Training of Negro Physicians," *The Journal of Negro Education* 4 (January 1935): 32; John F. Marion, *Philadelphia Medica* (Harrisburg: Smith-Kline Corporation, 1975): 52; John H. Sanders, *100 Years after Emancipation: History of the Philadelphia Negro 1787–1963.* (no publisher): 101–2; R. R. Wright, comp., *The Philadelphia Colored Directory: A Handbook of the Religious, Social, Political, Professional, Business, and Other Activities of the Negroes of Philadelphia* (Philadelphia: Philadelphia Colored Directory Company, 1910): 69; Carter G. Woodson, *The Negro Professional Man and the Community* (Washington, D.C.: The Association for the Study of Afro-American Life and History, 1934): 10; Herbert M. Morais, *The History of the Afro-American in Medicine* (Cornwell Heights, Pa.: The Publishers Agency, 1976), 21–38; Only two Black medical schools have survived, Howard (1868) and Meharry (1876); See James Summerville, *Educating Black Doctors: A History of Meharry Medical College* (Birmingham: University of Alabama Press, 1983); and Walter Dyson, *Howard University: The Capstone of Negro Education: 1867–1940* (Washington, D.C.: Howard University Press, 1941).

54. "Board Minutes," 19 January 1877.
55. "Board Minutes," 14 September 1877; *Public Ledger,* 17 August 1877; Kaufman, *Homeopathy in America,* 118.
56. *Sunday Dispatch,* 19 August 1877.
57. Ibid.
58. *Sunday Dispatch,* 9 September 1877.
59. *Sunday Dispatch,* 30 September 1877.
60. *Sunday Dispatch,* 7 October 1877.
61. "Board Minutes," 13 March 1878; "Board Minutes," 10 April 1878. Contemporaries used the term *bigotry.* See Rothstein, *American Physicians In the 19th Century,* 323.
62. "Board Minutes," 11 September 1878; *HAICP, Annual Report,* 1880, 2. Some well-respected Black doctors were homeopaths, hydropaths, and eclectics. See Leslie A. Falk, "Black Abolitionists Doctors and Healers," *Bulletin of the History of Medicine* 54 (summer 1980): 260; Bousfield, "An Account of Physicians of Color in the U.S." 4. Morais, *The History of the Afro-American in Medicine,* 23–24. As stated in the text Caroline Anderson rendered the most important service. Two other Black physicians who provided medical service and were involved in the management of the HAICP were Cornelius Shafer, a graduate of Jefferson Medical College, chairman of the Board from 1891 to 1896, and homeopath Thomas Creigh Imes, who was Chairman in 1903 when he died. As far as can be determined Imes and Shafer served as only on an on-call basis. "Management Minutes," 13 July 1898; "Board Minutes," 10 August 1898; "Board Minutes," 8 September 1898; "Board Minutes, 22 April 1900; "Board Minutes," 13 June 1900; "Board Minutes," 9 September 1900; See also H. H. Wayman, "The Quaker City," *Colored American Magazine* 6 (December 1903): 887–96; Callis, "The Need for and Training of Negro Physicians," 33. Graduating from Women's College in 1869, Rebecca Cole was the first Black woman to receive a medical degree. Of the 3,409 Blacks in medicine in 1910, 57 were women. For the status of White Women physicians see Mary R. Walsh, *Doctors Wanted: No Women Need Apply: Sexual Barriers in the Medical Profession, 1835–1975* (New Haven: Yale University Press, 1977): 83–84.
63. *Friends' Intelligencer,* 12 October 1867.
64. Falk, "Black Abolitionists Doctors and Healers," 260.

65. *Friends' Intelligencer,* 20 December 1879; *Friends' Intelligencer,* 6 August 1878; *HAICP, Annual Report,* 1882.
66. "Board Minutes," 15 August 1885.
67. "Board Minutes," 9 September 1885. See also chapter 5.
68. Ibid.
69. "Board Minutes," 14 October 1885.
70. "Board Minutes," 11 November 1885; "Board Minutes," 17 November 1885; "Management Minutes," 20 November 1885.
71. "Board Minutes," 8 September 1885.
72. "Board Minutes," 9 December 1885; "Management Minutes," 9 December 1885.
73. "Management Minutes," 13 January 1886.
74. Rothstein, *American Physicians in the 19th Century,* 245, 325; Kaufman, *Homeopathy in America,* 173; See "Homeopathic Remedies: These 19th-Century Medicines Offer Safety Even Charm: But Efficacy is Another Matter," *Consumer Reports* (January 1987): 60–62; Chuducoff, *How Old Are You,* 54–57.
75. There was never an attempt to remove residents to Kirkbride's Asylum or Friends' Asylum because these were private institutions. Dr. Thomas Kirkbride, a leading figure in the treatment of mental illness in the latter half of the nineteenth century, practiced at the Pennsylvania Hospital, where his policy was a strict segregation of the races. Given the interest wealthy Quakers showed toward some of their former domestics, it was a bit surprising, however, that none were removed to the Quaker asylum. For a study of Kirkbride see Nancy Tomes, *A Generous Confidence: Thomas S. Kirkbride and the Art of Asylum Keeping* (London: Cambridge University Press, 1984).
76. These cases were discerned from all available records. Only eleven additional cases were found between 1910 and 1937, but that was due undoubtedly to an increasing paucity of records rather than a lowered incidence of mental deterioration. The cases found after 1910 conform to the conclusions in the text.
77. "Management Minutes," 10 March 1886.
78. "Management Records," 16 July 1889.
79. "Management Records," 8 October 1905.
80. "Management Records," 23 February 1894.
81. "Board Minutes," 14 July 1886; "Board Minutes," 11 August 1886. In 1909 the doctor requested that the Board hire a night watchman, but the Board found it "inexpedient." "Board Minutes," 10 February 1909.
82. The search for proper restraint led in 1936 to the development of a jacket (probably like a straightjacket), designed by the seamstress, to keep the wearer from hurting himself or others. "Management Minutes," 13 October 1936.
83. *Friends' Intelligencer,* 2 February 1865.
84. *Friends' Intelligencer,* 2 February 1872.
85. *Friends' Intelligencer,* 4 March 1876.
86. "Management Records," 10 January 1911.
87. During the late nineteenth century, according to Achenbaum, the term *senility* was transformed from a mere indication of old age as a stage of life to a pathological condition. It is significant that the term is completely absent from all HAICP's records, including the doctors' reports. Achenbaum, *Old Age in the New Land,* 43; Chudacoff, *How Old Are You,* 54–57; For discussion of cure rates at Pennsylvania Hospital see Tomes, *A Generous Confidence,* 324–27. See also Gerald Grob, *The State and the Mentally Ill: A History of Worcester State Hospi-*

tal in Massachsetts, 1830–1920 (Chapel Hill: The University of North Carolina Press, 1966), 252–58.

88. "Board Minutes," 11 December 1912. The Home's policy to remove the violent or troublesome remained throughout most of the Home's history. See "Board Minutes," 25 September 1956.

89. "Management Records," 26 February 1885.

90. "Management Minutes," 11 March 1908; "Management Minutes," 8 July 1908; *HAICP, Annual Report,* 1909, 11.

91. "Management Records," 3 July 1894.

92. "Cash Book No. 2," 11 December 1884. Entry for this date shows payment to Howard Davis for expenses incurred for getting Catherine Robinson into the insane hospital at Norristown. See also "Management Records," 12 June 1889 for relationship between insanity and discipline. Refund patterns showed that insanity sometimes occurred soon after admission into the Home. See for example, "Board Minutes," 11 May 1875.

93. "Management Records," 17 August 1888.

94. "Management Records," 10 May 1899; "Management Records," 12 November 1890; "Management Minutes," 10 May 1899; "Management Records," 8 November 1911.

95. "Management Minutes," 8 January 1913; "Management Minutes," 12 February 1913; "Management Minutes," 9 April 1913.

96. Morton Kramer, Carl A. Taube, and Richard W. Redick, "Patterns of Use of Psychiatric Facilities by the Aged: Past, Present, and Future," in *Psychology of Adult Development and Aging,* ed. Carl Eisdarter and M. Powell Newton (American Psychological Association, 1973), 433.

97. Lawrence Colb, "The Mental Hospitalization of the Aged: Is It Being Overdone?" *American Journal of Psychiatry* 8 (February 1956): 627–36; "Mental Hospitals: The End of the Road for Aged Blacks," *NCBA NEWS* (February–March 1974), 3; Grob concludes: "By 1950 mental hospitals were serving as a final home for aged persons." Gerald Grob, *From Asylum to Community: Mental Health Policy in Modern America* (Princeton: Princeton University Press, 1991), 159–60. For related comments on the birth of the boardinghouse industry, see U.S. Senate Subcommittee on long-term care of the special Committee on Aging. *Nursing Home Care in the United States: Failure in Public Policy, Supporting Paper No. 7, The Role of Nursing Homes in Caring for Discharged Mental Patients (and the Birth of for-Profit Boarding Home Industry)* (Washington, D.C.: Government Printing Office, March, 1976).

98. *HAICP, Annual Report,* 1923, 7.

99. This statistic was computed by comparing entrance dates to death dates in "List of Inmates of the Home for Aged and Infirm Colored Persons." The first entry is 1865, the last is 1904.

100. "Board Minutes," 14 March 1877. The classic explanation for the cause of death was "exhausted vitality from advanced age and past physical taxation." See *HAICP, Annual Report,* 1884, 11.

101. *HAICP, Annual Report,* 1884, 20; The leading causes of death in the HAICP from the doctor's reports from 1907 to 1920 were heart disease, brain disease, arteriosclerosis, nephritis, cancer, anemia, and so on. The principal cause of deaths of Blacks outside the Home was tuberculosis, but those individuals were denied entrance or removed from the institution. For a discussion of causes of deaths of Blacks around the turn of the century see *The Social and Economic Status of the Population in the United States: An Historical View, 1790–1978,* 118.

102. Agreement signed by Patience Johnson, 15 October 1903. On file at Stephen Smith Home for the Aged, Philadelphia, Pennsylvania.
103. Agreement signed by Eliza Bryan Bucknell, 15 October 1903. On file at Stephen Smith Home for the Aged, Philadelphia, Pennsylvania.
104. "Entrance, Deaths, Events," 27 November 1906.
105. "Management Records," 8 May 1889.
106. "Board Minutes," 9 December 1903; "Board Minutes," 11 February 1903; "Board Minutes," January 1903.
107. "Management Minutes," 14 April 1915; "Management Minutes," 13 March 1918; "Management Minutes," 13 February 1918; "Management Minutes," 10 March 1915. "Management Minutes," 27 May 1911; "Management Minutes," 13 July 1911; "Management Minutes," 14 August 1912; "Management Records," 10 January 1900; "Management Minutes," 10 January 1906.
108. *HAICP, Annual Report,* 1867, 12.
109. "Board Minutes," 1 September 1981; "Board Minutes," 13 March 1872; "Association Minutes," 14 September 1879. Smith willed about three-fourths of the cemetery company to the Home when he died in 1873.
110. See chapter 4 on beneficial associations for a discussion of burial preferences of Blacks and problems with the Home's burial practices. As stated there African Americans do not bury in mass graves.
111. "Board Minutes," 14 January 1903; "Board Minutes," 11 May 1903; It was not until 1910 that Olive was closed to private lot holders, and in 1923 the bodies were removed from the premises of the Home.
112. Board Minutes," 20 May 1908.
113. "Board Minutes," November 1914.
114. Cadbury, "Negro Membership in the Society of Friends," 160–61. For burial in Friends' cemeteries see "Management Minutes," 30 August 1886; "Board Minutes," 8 September 1886; "Board Minutes, 9 September 1907; "Management Records," 1910.

CHAPTER 7: HOBART JACKSON: THE FATHER OF BLACK GERONTOLOGY

1. As Stated in the introduction, Jacquelyne Jackson is the leading authority on elderly Blacks. Her publications are cited throughout this manuscript. Some of those not cited are: Jacquelyne Jackson, "Negro Aged and Social Gerontology," *Journal of Social and Behavioral Sciences" 13 (1968): 42–47;* "Aged Negroes: A Potpourri towards the Reduction of Racial Inequities," *Phylon* 32 (1971), 260–80; "Negro Aged: Toward Needed Research in Social Gerontology," *The Gerontologist* 11 (spring 1971), 52–57; "The Plight of Older Black Women in the United States," *The Black Scholar* 7 (1976), 47–55; "Myths and Realities about Aged Blacks," in *Readings in Gerontology,* ed. Mollie Brown (St. Louis: C. V. Mosby, 1978), 95–113. In addition to numerous other publications Jacquelyne Jackson has intensely involved herself as an advocate of the Black aged. She was also a founder of the NCBA and conceived the idea of the National Center. These impressive facts do not disclaim the above assertion that Hobart Jackson earned the designation the Father of Black Gerontology. A major portion of this discussion has been published elsewhere. See Leslie J. Pollard, "Around the Verge of Parting Life," *Journal of Gerontological Social Work,* 9 (summer 1986): 21–38;

Also published in Rose Dobrof's, *Ethnicity and Gerontological Social Work* (New York: Haworth Press, 1987), 21–38.

2. For examples of such visitors see chapter 4.

3. The major financial support came from the Society of Friends, but the size of the Quaker population had been shrinking for years. According to Schuyler, between 1827 and 1900 the decline of the number of Quakers, Hicksite and Orthodox, was 40 percent. Schuyler, "Philadelphia Quakers in the Industrial Age," 103–4. See also Lane, *Roots of Violence in Black Philadelphia,* 24–25.

4. "Management Minutes," 9 January 1933. The Association had pretty much lost its earlier meaning by this time, and the Home was run entirely by the Board. There were still some families that had maintained continuous membership on the board since the Home's founding. There were over five hundred life members by 1900, but no more than a one hundred by 1930, and there is no way to determine how many of them were alive or still supported the institution.

5. Based on the annual reports, contributions (excluding special gifts, legacies, and so on) reached an all-time high in 1875 of about $7,500, declined until about 1895 to about $1,000, and reached the nadir in 1920 of about $500. Broader appeal during the 1920s led them to rise again to about $2,000, but they never approached the level of the early years until Hobart Jackson became administrator. Yields from investments (all large gifts, legacies, and bequests were put into a permanent fund), which I estimated at about $325,000 in 1920, reached an all-time high in that year of approximately $17,500 and a low in 1940 of about $2,000. One explanation for the HAICP's decline was a rumor that the treasurer embezzled $150,000 between 1930 and 1940 and that the Society of Friends covered it up to protect their good name. Meta Howell, who served on the Board from 1935 to 1969, had heard the rumor but was convinced that it had no basis in fact and that the failure of investments caused the loss of funds. In the Home's records there is an anonymous paper (letter) alleging wrongdoing by the treasurer, who was not bonded. It also pointed out that there had not been any audits, except a partial audit in 1902, between 1895 and 1905 and that only the treasurer knew the Home's exact worth. This letter may be the basis for the rumor, but the paper was written in 1907. While the treasurer was accused of wrongdoing, the paper led to the exposure of improprieties by the secretary, who was said to have "hampered and delayed" the investigation. It turned out that he had deposited about $3,000 of the Home's money into his personal account. "Board Minutes," 11 March 1908; "Board Minutes," 8 April 1908; "Board Minutes," 20 April 1908; "Board Minutes," 20 May 1908; "Board Minutes," 9 June 1909; "Board Minutes," 8 June 1908; "Board Minutes, 8 June 1910; Board Minutes," 12 June 1912. Interview, Meta Howell, residence at 201 North Fifty-eighth Street, Philadelphia, Pennsylvania, 14 October 1975.

6. Irwin, "HAICP: Report to the Board." This was an impressive report that thoroughly examined almost all aspects of the Home's operation, but its recommendations were only halfheartedly implemented.

7. Dorothy Warrick, "A Quarter of a Century," Founders Day address at Stephen Smith Home for the Aged, October 1971, 2. Obtained from Mrs. Angeline Smith, Stephen Smith Towers, Philadelphia, Pennsylvania, 9 October 1975. Warrick's mother served from 1908 to 1946, and she served on the Board of Directors from 1946 to 1971.

8. Interview, Howell, 14 October 1975. Howell was on the Board from 1935 to 1969.

9. Shippen Lewis to Urwin Underhill, 9 April 1947, Stephen Smith Home

for the Aged, Philadelphia, Pennsylvania. Lewis was chairman of the Board at the time and Underhill was a Board member. In 1956 the Conshochocken property was sold because Jackson convinced Board members that only in the city could the Home find needed services and an infirmary, he maintained, that was more clearly responsive to the residents' changing conditions.

10. Warrick, "A Quarter of a Century," Founders Day Address, October 1971, 1.

11. Elliott M. Rudwick, "A Brief History of Mercy-Douglass Hospital," *Journal of Negro Education* 20 (winter 1951), 51–54.

12. Interview, Hobart Jackson, Stephen Smith Home for the Aged, Philadelphia, Pennsylvania, 10 October 1975; between October 1975 and March 1977, I held three lengthy interviews and numerous brief discussions with Hobart Jackson. In addition we talked several times on the telephone and communicated through the mail. To help with the interviews, Jackson prepared a brief paper for me, "Some observations for the Period 1940–1953." More recently (June 1993) I have had conversations with his widow, who has helped me with the biographical information.

13. This information is compiled from interviews with Hobart Jackson as well as a paper he prepared for me, "Hobart Jackson: Biographical Data and Information."

14. Jackson, "Biographical Data and Information." Indeed, in 1949 when Jackson's career in gerontology began, the field had not matured into a full-fledged academic discipline and lacked any significant theories or conceptual frameworks. The major theory, disengagement, was not posed until 1961 with the publication of Elaine Cumming and William Henry's *Growing Old* (New York: Basic Books, 1961); it is somewhat ironic that one of the earliest frameworks for understanding the aged was Milton Barrow's 1953 publication "Minority Group Characteristics of the Aged in American Society," in the *Journal of Gerontology* that posed race as a context for understanding aging, even though the Black aged were not yet considered a group with distinctive problems. *Philadelphia Tribune,* 15 February 1949.

15. Interview, Jackson, 18 March 1977.

16. Jackson, "Some observations about the period, 1940–1953," 1.

17. Jackson continued to study, taking courses in social work at Temple University and the University of Pennsylvania. He became a licensed nursing Home administrator and lectured on elderly care in institutions. In 1982 Black colleges organized the Association for Gerontology and Human Development at Historically African American Colleges and Universities to train minority gerontologists and disseminate information on the African American elderly. A recent study complained that minority content is still not included in gerontology curriculum. See David Satcher, "The Role of Black Universities in Research on Aging Black Populations," in James Jackson, 17–25. Also M. S. Harper, ed., *Minority Aging: Essential Curricula Content for Selected Health and Allied Health Professions,* Health Resources and Services Administration, Department of Health and Human Searvices, DHHS Publication No. HRS (P-DV9004). (Washington D.C.: U.S. Government Printing Office, 1990), 193–222.

18. Warrick, "A Quarter of a Century," 2–3.

19. For a related discussion see Donald E. Gelfand, "Visiting Patterns and Social Adjustment in an Old-Age Home," *The Gerontologist* 8 (winter 1968): 2, 40–41; Ruth Benedict, "The Meaning of Institutional Life," *The Gerontologist* 3 (September 1963): 112–20.

20. Home for Aged and Infirm Colored Persons, "Minutes of the Board of Directors," Philadelphia, Pennsylvania, 26 December 1950. Hereafter referred to as "Board Minutes."

21. "Board Minutes," 23 January 1951.

22. "Board Minutes," 26 December 1950; "Board Minutes," 2 December 1950.

23. "Board Minutes," 26 September 1952.

24. Interview, Jackson, 18 March 1977; The National Committee on Aging, *Standards of Care for Older People in Institutions Section, I: Suggested Standards for Homes for Aged and Nursing Homes* (New York: The National Committee on the Aging, 1953).

25. Interview, Jackson, 10 October 1975.

26. Hobart Jackson, "Our Newest Generation," Stephen Smith Home for the Aged, Philadelphia, Pennsylvania, 1954, 1.

27. Ibid. Interview, Jackson, 6 October 1975.

28. Jackson, "Our Newest Generation," 1.

29. See Murray Wax, "The Changing Role of the Home for the Aged," *The Gerontologist* 2 (September 1962): 128–33. Here Wax describes how institutions like the HAICP responded to changing conditions.

30. "Board Minutes," 26 June 1951; "Board Minutes," 24 February 1953; "Board Minutes," 27 January 1953; "Board Minutes," 14 March 1953; Warrick, "A Quarter of a Century," 4.

31. "Board Minutes," 24 February 1953.

32. "Highlights of 1953–1954," administrator's address on Founder's Day, 7 November 1954, Stephen Smith Home for the Aged, Philadelphia, Pennsylvania, p. 2.

33. The rule requiring permission to leave was in effect from 1864 to 1952, but it was violated with impunity, and accidents still occurred. Besides, the reason for the rule was the risk of epidemics, which had been greatly reduced by this time.

34. "Board Minutes," 2 September 1951; "Board Minutes," 23 February 1954.

35. Interview, 6 October 1974, Stephen Smith Home, Philadelphia, Pennsylvania.

36. For an overview of the services of the Home and an examination of the social participation of the Stephen Smith residents see Azelia Upshaw, "Differential Uses of Time," in *Community Services and the Black Elderly,* ed. Richard David (Los Angeles: Ethel Percy Andros Gerontology Center--University of Southern California, 1972), 17–19.

37. Hobart Jackson, "A Social Worker-Administrator Defines Successful Aging," *Clinical Medicine* 79 (August 1972), 20.

38. Ibid., 21. As seen in chapter 4, there was no system of remuneration and promotion. The matron at the time of Irwin's study in 1938 was paid one hundred dollars a month, the same salary she had started with nine years earlier. The baker started in 1903 at a salary of seventy-five dollars a month, and thirty-five years later he still earned that amount. The engineer was employed in 1906 at one hundred dollars, and in 1938 he earned the same salary. The assistant matron had been employed for eight years and had gotten a ten dollar raise, from sixty-five dollars to seventy-five dollars. Irwin, "HAICP: Report to the Board," 73.

39. Jackson obtained an extension of time from the city to repair the institution. Since 1942 the Chest had provided an annual appropriations to the HAICP of fifteen thousand to twenty thousand dollars. "Board Minutes," 24 June 1952 ; "Board Minutes," 28 October 1952; *Friends' Intelligencer,* 15 April 1950; *Philadel-*

phia Tribune, 11 November 1952; *Philadelphia Tribune* 26 May 1953; *Philadelphia Tribune,* 12 May 1953. "Landmark of Service for over 101 Years," Stephen Smith Home for the Aged, Philadelphia, Pennsylvania, 1965, 1. Hereafter referred to as "Landmark," 1965.

40. "Board Minutes," 24 October 1953.

41. Hertha Kraus, "Housing Our Older Citizens," in *The Annals of the American Academy of Political and Social Science, Social Contributions by the Aging,* ed. Clark Tibbits (Philadelphia: American Academy of Political and Social Science, l952), 126.

42. Edna Nicholson, "Nursing and Convalescent Homes," in *Housing the Aging,* ed. Wilma Donahue (Ann Arbor: University of Michigan Press, 1954): 124.

43. "Board Minutes," 24 October 1950.

44. "Landmark, "1965, 2. Handicapped persons in good health were now given a priority rating.

45. "Recent Highlights," report submitted by Hobart C. Jackson, administrator, Centennial Day, 25 October 1964. Stephen Smith Home for the Aged, Philadelphia, Pennsylvania, 2.

46. Rehabilitation of the elderly actually became popular in the 1940s. See McClure, *More than a Roof,* 211.

47. "Recent Highlights," report submitted by Hobart C. Jackson, administrator, Centennial Day, 25 October 1964: Stephen Smith Home for the Aged, Philadelphia, Pennsylvania, 2 (hereafter referred to as "Highlights"); "Highlights of 1969–1970," 8 November 1970, 3; "Board Minutes," 16 January 1964; "Board Minutes," 24 February 1976; "Board Minutes," 6 January 1976; interview, Jackson, 18 March 1977; Wax, "The Changing Role of the Home for Aged" passim.

48. "Landmark of Service for More than 109 Years," Stephen Smith Home for the Aged, Philadelphia, Pennsylvania, 1971, 2. The structure and objectives of the Tower's Corporation are outlined in "Board Minutes," 16 January 1967.

49. "Highlights of 1969–1970," report of the administrator, Founders Day, 8 November 1970, Stephen Smith Home for the Aged, Philadelphia, Pennsylvania, 3.

50. Information obtained from sources at the Stephen Smith Multi-Service Center, Philadelphia, Pennsylvania, and provided by James J. Wilson, who compiled the following document for my use. "Organization Summary: Stephen Smith Multi-Service Center," June 1990, 1–4.

51. National Urban League, *Double Jeopardy,* frontispiece. See introduction.

52. Beattie, "The Aging Negro," 131–35. See introduction.

53. Inabel Lindsay, "The Multiple Hazards of Age and Race: The Situation of Aged Blacks in the United States," A report by the Special Committee on Aging, United States Senate (Washington, D.C.: Government Printing Office, 1971); included in the publication is Hobart Jackson's, "Information about the National Caucus on the Black Aged," 55–63; see also Hobart Jackson, "National Caucus on the Black Aged; A Progress Report," *Aging and Human Development* 2 (1971), 226–31.

54. It is a noteworthy coincidence that the *Philadelphia Tribune* on 14 November 1970 on the ninety-seventh anniversary of Stephen Smith's death carried the news of the Caucus's organizational meeting and a telegram to the President of the United States that requested him to correct past injustices to the Black aged.

55. Hobart Jackson, "On the Opening of the NCBA Center," *Stephen Smith Geriatric Center Newsletter* 6 (January 1974): 4.

56. Jacquelyne Jackson, "The National Center on Black Aged: A Challenge

to Gerontologists," *The Gerontologist* 14 (June 1974): 194, 196; see also," NCBA on the Move: Center Open and Operating," *NCBA News* 1 (December 1973): 17; Since Black life expectancy was about seven years less than that for Whites and because Social Security legislation excluded domestic and agricultural workers until 1954, the NCBA recommended lowering the eligibility requirements for Social Security to make up for these discrepancies. See Dr. Davis-Wong's testimony before the Senate Special Committee on Aging on behalf of the NCBA entitled "Social Security and Older Blacks," *Urban Research Review* 7 (1981): 1–13. Already Black aged draw smaller checks because of their work histories, they opt for the sixty-two eligibility, and the cost of living increases are percentage based.

57. Hobart Jackson, "Housing and Geriatric Centers for Aging and Aging Blacks," in *Proceedings of Black Aged in the Future,* Jacquelyne Jackson, compiler (Durham: Duke University Press, 1973); see also Jacquelyne Jackson, "Family Organization and Ideology," 436.

58. Hobart Jackson, "The Current Nursing Home Crisis," *NCBA News* 1 (December 1973): 4–5.

59. Jackson often began his lectures with the story of an errant baseball player. On several occasions the manager had screamed at his shortstop for bobbling the baseball when making a play. With the next opportunity the player again failed to come up with the ball. The manager, now unable to control himself, ran onto the field and snatched the glove from the player, instructing him to watch closely as the master showed him the proper way to handle shortstop. When the ball arrived the manager himself erred. Throwing the glove onto the ground, the manager explained that the player had so messed up the position that nobody could play it correctly. Hobart Jackson concluded that the field of gerontology had become so messed up that nobody could straighten it out. One would be strained to argue that Hobart Jackson was a charismatic or spellbinding lecturer, yet one felt a kind of Jackson mystique that grew out of his strong sense of mission, a feeling that one had entered the presence of an individual with greatness or great authority. At various times Hobart Jackson held memberships in, served on the boards of, or was an officer of the following organizations: The Academy of Certified Social Workers, National Association of Social Workers, Federal Council on Aging, American Association of Homes for the Aging (vice president), Board of Examiners of Pennsylvania Nursing Home Administrators, International Association of Gerontology, International Committee on Social Welfare, Pennsylvania Board of Public Welfare, Board of directors of Pennsylvania Association of Nonprofit Homes for the Aging, among others. He presented papers or served on annual meeting programs of many of these organizations as well as the National Urban League, United Negro College Fund, Gerontological Society, National Conference on Aging—University of Michigan, White House Conference on Aging, and more. He served on the editorial board of *CONCERN* (publication of American Association of Homes for the Aging), *International Journal of Aging and Human Development, The Gerontologist,* and others. He was married to the former Elaine Bethel, a supervisor with the Philadelphia Department of Public Welfare. His children are Hobart, Jr., a professor at the University of Kansas, Dale, an IBM systems engineer in New Orleans, and Marlene, a research chemist with a firm in Wilmington, Delaware. Jackson was Ruling Elder at Calvin United Presbyterian Church at the time of his death.

60. Hobart Jackson, "National Goals and Priorities in the Social Welfare of the Aging," *The Gerontologist* (spring 1971): 89; Jackson's published works, not already mentioned, include Hobart Jackson, "Responsibilities and Functions of

the Administrator," *Nursing Homes* (March 1964); "National Goals and Priorities in the Social Welfare of the Aging," *The Gerontologist* 11 (spring 1971); "The Black Elderly: Jeopardized by Race and Neglect," *Geriatrics* (June 1972); "Easing the Plight of the Black Elderly," *Perspective on Aging* 4 (1975): 21–22. For some present problems confronting the Black elderly see Morgan W. F. Dickerson, "Problems of Black High-Risk Elderly," *Journal of Black Studies* 4 (December 1983): 251–59.

Note on Sources and Selected Bibliography

In 1967 Jacquelyne Jackson lamented the dearth of studies on the Black elderly in a comprehensive review in *The Gerontologist*. Since that time the sociological literature on African American and minority elderly has substantially increased because the research of such people as Wilbur Watson, E. P. Stanford, Roy Manuel, and James Jackson as well as Jacquelyne Jackson. There is no monograph on the history of Black aging however, and little of the existing research has focused on the valuable perspective history can bring to policy discussions of contemporary gerontological problems.

The major historical literature, David Fischer's *Growing Old in America* (1978), W. Andrew Achenbaum's, *Old Age in the New Land* (1978) and *Shades of Gray* (1983), Carole Haber's *Beyond Sixty-five* (1983), William Graebner's *A History of Retirement* (1980), Brian Gratton's *Urban Elders* (1986), and Howard Chudacoff's *How Old Are You? Age Consciousness in American Culture* (1988) contribute somewhat to our understanding of the history of Black aging. Richard Calhoun's *Aging Since 1945* (1978) ignores the Black gerontology movement and Judith Hushbeck's *Old and Obsolete* (1991) is focused on White males, while Terri Premo's *Winter Friends: Women Growing Old In the New Republic, 1785–1835* (1990) is devoted to White women. Little is known about Homes for the elderly despite Fischer's claim that a "large literature has grown up on this subject." In fact, except for Ethel McClure's *More than a Roof* (1968), the works cited by Fischer are obscure, nonscholarly tracts that certainly cannot realistically be said to constitute a "large literature." As far as Black old-age Homes are concerned, there is still little published about them.

Generally, the historical works agree that American society moved from veneration of the old during the early years of America's history to an ageist society that disesteemed the aged. When and why this transition occurred is not part of the consensus. David Fischer (noting such changes as language that began to scorn the old, seating patterns in churches that discontinued old-age preference, and dress and portraits that no longer flattered the old) claims that changing ideas about the elderly because of the egalitarianism of the American Revolution dragged the aged down from their esteemed status. However, the culprit behind the change is most often regarded as industrialization following the Civil War, as older workers were devalued, society became more bureaucratic, people crowded into cities, families became more nucleated, and the country entered the period Achenbaum has called the "obsolescence of old age." These two positions are not necessarily mutually exclusive as some have pointed out. While the ideas of the Revolution may have pulled the elderly down from their privileged position, it was perhaps the Industrial Revolution that moved them to scorn. For our discussion it is not clear where Black Americans fit into this scheme of things because they had different cultural traditions, the egalitarian ideas of the American Revolution did not apply to them, and they remained tied to the soil many years after industrialization.

All the sources used in writing *Complaint to the Lord* are cited in the endnotes. The first chapters rely substantially on secondary sources, the most significant of these appears in the selected bibliography that follows. Although numerous visits to libraries and historical collections were required to complete this project, much of the manuscript information used in the study was preserved by the Stephen Smith Home. Particularly during the early years of the Home's history, history-conscious Quakers and their African American colleagues kept meticulous records and jotted down their thoughts and actions on all kinds of material. Most of the Annual Reports are preserved, but gaps had to be filled from information found at such places as the Pennsylvania Historical Society, the Library Company of Philadelphia, Temple University, Lincoln University, Haverford College, and Swarthmore College. They are available from 1865 to 1936 but are piecemeal from 1903 to 1907.

The most important manuscripts are the minutes of the Board of Managers, the minutes of the Management Committee, and the comments of subcommittees on management (Visiting, House, and Clothing), which are referred to as records. The minutes of the Board (recorded as part of the Association Minutes from 1865 to 1874 and called the Board of Directors after 1954) are available from 1864 to 1893, 1902 to 1914, and after 1950. The Management Committee Minutes were preserved from 1881 to 1924 and 1933 to 1939. The records of the subcommittees are extant from the period 1885 to 1920. It important that one does not assume that these are the titles of any of these manuscripts or that the first entries begin in January and end in December or that the dates are inclusive. In reality there are frequent apertures in the information that vary from minor lapses to chasmic omissions.

The Home also preserved some brochures, pamphlets, letters, applications (1898–1918), several cash books, a list of inmates (1865–1904), admissions and death records, events books, and a donation book. There are also some scattering of notes on the backs of papers and other miscellany. The exact usage of these items can be determined from the endnotes. The Home preserved more material than I expected, and the information seemed to follow the pattern of the Home's prosperity and decline. All the Home's collection was made available to me by Hobart Jackson. We spent many hours together and visited on numerous occasions via the telephone. He also wrote several papers for my use as I have previously indicated. The dates and places for the formal interviews as well as those of other people interviewed are in the endnotes.

Beginning in the 1890s, there were many references to a room in the Home that housed a repository of antislavery materials named in honor of Robert Adger, a Black postal worker, who donated his collection of portraits and relics of the abolitionist movement to the Home. In 1898 the Board of Managers created a Committee on Library and Anti-slavery Repository chaired by the Quaker, Joseph Truman, an authority on local information. Harriet Henderson, a resident of the Home who was appointed caretaker, gained somewhat of a reputation for her "animated" accounts of these materials. During the 1930s managers began to express concern for the preservation of their collection and started a search for a place to store it while making it accessible to students. Eventually, the Quaker-related materials were donated to Swarthmore College, and the remaining materials were given to Horace Mann Bond for Lincoln University, but the books, relics, and portraits, regrettably, have not survived as a separate collection at either of these institutions, and there is little among the surviving materials related to the history of the Home. See, for example, chapter 2, endnote 56.

Selected Bibliography

BOOKS

Achenbaum, W. Andrew. *Old Age in the New Land: The American Experience Since 1790.* Baltimore: The Johns Hopkins University Press, 1978.

American Association of Homes for the Aged, 1966. *The Social Components of Care.* New York: American Association of Homes for the Aged, 1966.

Aptheker, Herbert. *A Documentary History of the Negro People in the U.S.* New York: Citadel Press, 1915.

Atchley, Robert C. *The Social Forces in Later Life: An Introduction to Social Gerontology.* Belmont, Calif.: Wadsworth Publishing Company, 1972.

Bacon, Margaret. *The Quiet Rebels: The Story of the Quakers.* New York: Basic Books, 1969.

Bass, Scott A., et al. *Diversity in Aging.* Glenview, Ill.: Scott, Foresman and Company, 1990.

Bassett, Sharon A. *Residential Care for the Elderly: Critical Issues in Public Policy.* New York: Greenwood Press, 1989.

Berlin, Ira. *Slaves without Masters: The Free Negro in the Antebellum South.* New York: Pantheon Books, 1974.

Billingsley, Andrew. *Black Families in White America.* Englewood Cliffs, N.J.: Prentice Hall, 1968.

Blassingame, John W. *The Slave Community: Plantation Life in the Antebellum South.* New York: Oxford University Press, 1972.

Brown, William Wells. *The Rising Sun: Or, the Antecedents and Advancement of the Colored Race.* Boston: 1874; reprint ed., New York: Johnson Reprint Corp., 1970.

Butler, Freida. *A Resource Guide on the Black Elderly.* Washington, D.C.: Institute of Urban Affairs—Howard University, 1981.

Campbell, Edward, ed. *Before Freedom Came: African American Life in the Antebellum South.* Charlottesville, Va.: Museum of the Confederacy, Carter Printing Company, 1991.

Chudacoff, Howard. *How Old You Are: Age Consciousness in American Culture.* Princeton: Princeton University Press, 1989.

Cowgill, Donald and Lowell Holmes, eds. *Aging and Modernization.* New York: Appleton-Century-Crofts, 1972.

Cromwell, Otelia. *Lucretia Mott.* Cambridge: Harvard University Press, 1958.

Curry, Leonard. *The Free Black in Urban America, 1800–1850: The Shadow of the Dream.* Chicago: The University of Chicago Press, 1981.

Delany, Martin R. *The Condition, Elevation, and Destiny of the Colored People of the United States, Politically Considered.* Philadelphia: by the author, 1852; reprint ed., New York: Arno Press, *The New York Times,* 1968.

Davis, Allen and Mark Hallen. *The People of Philadelphia: A History of Ethnic Groups and Lower Class Life, 1790–1940.* Philadelphia: Temple University Press, 1973.

Davis, Lenwood. *The Black Aged in the United States: An Annotated Bibliography.* Westport, Conn.: Greenwood Press, 1980.

Douglass, Frederick. *My Bondage and My Freedom.* New York: Miller, Orton, and Mulligan, 1855; reprint ed., New York: Arno Press, 1968.

———. *Narrative of the Life of Frederick Douglass: An American Slave.* New York: Signet Books, 1968; first published in 1845.

Drake, Joseph. *The Aged in American Society.* New York: The Ronald Press, 1958.

Drake, Thomas E. *Quakers and Slavery in America.* New Haven: Yale University Press, 1950.

Du Bois, W. E. B. *The Philadelphia Negro: A Social Study,* with an introduction by E. Digby Baltzell. New York: Shocken Books, 1967; first published in 1899.

Escott, Paul. *Slavery Remembered: A Record of Twentieth-Century Slave Narratives.* Chapel Hill: The University of North Carolina Press, 1979.

Fischer, David Hacker. *Growing Old in America.* Oxford: Oxford University Press, 1978.

Fisk Project. *The Underwritten History of Slavery.* Nashville: Social Science Institute, 1954.

Fogel, Robert and Stanley Engerman. *Time on the Cross: The Economics of American Negro Society.* Boston: Little, Brown, and Company, 1974.

Franklin, John Hope. *From Slavery to Freedom: A History of Negro Americans.* New York: Alfred A. Knopf, 1974.

Frazier, E. Franklin. *The Negro Church in America.* New York: Schocken Books, 1964.

Gamble, Vanessa N. *The Black Community Hospital: Contemporary Dilemmas in Historical Perspective.* New York: Garland Publishing Company, 1989.

Gelfand, Donald and Alfred Kutzik, eds. *Ethnicity and Aging: Theory Research and Policy.* New York: Springer Publishing Company, 1979.

Genovese, Eugene. *Roll, Jordan, Roll: The World the Slaves Made.* New York: Pantheon Books, 1974.

Gillard, John T. *The Catholic Church and the American Negro.* Baltimore: St. Joseph's Society Press, 1929; reprint edition, Johnson Reprint Corporation, 1968.

Goffman, Erving. *Asylums, Essays on the Social Situation of Mental Patients and Other Inmates.* Garden City, N.Y.: Doubleday and Company, 1961.

Gratton, Brian. *Urban Elders: Family, Work and Welfare among Boston's Aged, 1890–1950.* Philadelphia: Temple University Press, 1986.

Gutman, Herbert. *The Black Family in Slavery and Freedom, 1750 to 1925.* New York: Pantheon Books, 1976.

Haber, Carole. *Beyond Sixty-Five: The Dilemma of Old Age in America's Past.* Cambridge: Cambridge University Press, 1983.

Harel, Zev, et al., eds. *Black Aged: Understanding Diversity and Service Needs.* Newbury Park, Calif.: Sage Publications, 1990.

Herkovits, Melville. *The Myths of the Negro Past.* Boston: Beacon Press, 1941.

Hill, Robert. *The Strength of Black Families.* New York: Emerson Hall Publishers, 1971.

Hushbeck, Judith. *Old and Obsolete: Age Discrimination and the Antebellum Worker, 1860-1920.* New York: Garland Publishing, 1989.

Huyck, Margeret H. *Growing Older: What You Need to Know about Aging.* Englewood Cliffs, N.J.: Prentice Hall, 1974.

Jackson, James S., ed. *The Black American Elderly: Research on Physical and Psychological Health.* New York: Springer Publishing Company, 1988.

Jackson, Jacquelyne. *Minorities and Aging.* Belmont, Calif.: Wadsworth Publishing Company, 1980.

James, Sydney. *A People among Peoples: Quaker Benevolence in 18th-Century America.* Cambridge: Harvard University Press, 1963.

Jones, Jacqueline. *Labor of Love, Labor of Sorrow: Black Women, Work, and the Family from Slavery to the Present.* New York: Basic Books, 1985.

Johnstone, Ruby. *The Development of Negro Religion.* New York: Philosophical Library, 1954.

Katz, Michael. *In the Shadow of the Poor-House: A Social History of Welfare in America.* New York: Basic Books, 1986.

Kaufman, Martin. *Homeopathy in America: The Rise and Fall of Medical Heresy.* Baltimore: The Johns Hopkins University Press, 1971.

Kent, Miller and Ralph Dreger. *Comparative Studies of Blacks and Whites in the United States.* New York: Seminar Press, 1973.

Killion, Ronald and Charles Walker, eds. *Slavery Time when I Was Chillun Down on Marster's Plantation.* Savannah, Ga.: Beehive Press, 1973.

Ladner, Joyce. *Tomorrow's Tomorrow: The Black Woman.* New York: Doubleday and Company, 1971.

Lane, Roger. *Roots of Violence in Black Philadelphia, 1860-1900.* Cambridge: Harvard University Press, 1986.

Litwack, Leon. *North of Slavery: The Negro in the Free States, 1790-1860.* Chicago: University of Chicago Press, 1961.

Magdol, Edward. *A Right to the Land: Essays on the Freedmen's Community.* Westport, Conn.: Greenwood Press, 1977.

Manney, James D. *Aging in American Society: An Examination of Concepts and Issues.* Ann Arbor: the Institute of Gerontology—The University of Michigan—Wayne State University, 1975.

Martin, Elmer and Joanne Martin. *The Black Extended Family.* Chicago: University of Chicago Press, 1978.

Morais, Herbert M. *The History of the Afro-American in Medicine.* Cornwell Heights, Pa.: The Publisher's Agency, 1976.

McClure, Ethel. *More than a Roof: The Development of Minnesota Poor Farms and Homes for the Aged.* St. Paul: Minnesota Historical Society, 1968.

McNeeley, R. L. and John Cohen, eds. *Aging in Minority Groups.* Beverly Hills, Calif.: Sage Publishing, 1983.

Meier, August. *Negro Thought in America, 1880-1915: Racial Ideologies in the Age of Booker T. Washington.* Ann Arbor: The University of Michigan Press, 1966.

Nash, Gary B. *Forging Freedom: The Formation of Philadelphia's Black Community, 1720–1840*. Cambridge: Harvard University Press, 1988.

Oakley, Amy. *Our Pennsylvania: Keys to the Keystone State*. Indianapolis: The Bobbs-Merrill Company, 1950.

Parks, Arnold. *Black Elderly in the Rural America: A Comprehensive Study*. Bristol: Wyndham Hall Press, 1988.

Payne, Daniel A. *A History of the African Methodist Episcopal Church*. Nashville: Publishing House of the AME Sunday School Union, 1891; reprint ed., New York: Johnson Reprint Corporation, 1968.

Perdue, Charles, et al. *Weevils in the Wheat: Interviews with Ex-Slaves*. Charlottesville: University of Virginia Press, 1976.

Pickett, Robert. *House of Refuge: Origins of Juvenile Reform in New York State*. Syracuse, N.Y.: Syracuse University Press, 1969.

Quarles, Benjamin. *Black Abolitionists*. New York: Oxford University Press, 1969.

Rawick, George. *The American Slave: A Composite Autobiography*. Westport, Conn.: Greenwood Publishing Company, 1972.

Richards, Leonard. *Gentlemen of Property and Standing: Anti-Abolition Mobs in Jacksonian America*. London: Oxford University Press, 1970.

Rothman, David. *The Discovery of the Asylum: Social Order and Disorder in the New Republic*. Boston: Little Brown and Company, 1971.

Rothstein, William G. *American Physicians in the Nineteenth Century: From Sects to Science*. Baltimore: The Johns Hopkins University Press, 1985.

Savitt, Todd. *Medicine and Slavery: The Disease and Health Care of Blacks in Antebellum Virginia*. Urbana: University of Illinois Press, 1978.

Schneider, Robert L. and Nancy P. Kropf, eds. *Gerontological Social Work: Knowledge, Service Settings, and Special Populations*. Chicago: Nelson Hall Publishers, 1992.

Sharf, J. Thomas and Westcott, Thompson. *History of Philadelphia*. 4 vols. Philadelphia: L. H. Everts and Company, 1884.

Smedley, Robert C. *History of the Underground Railroad in Chester and Neighboring Counties of Philadelphia*. New York: Arno Press, 1969; first published in 1883.

Smith, Charles S. *A History of the African Methodist Episcopal Church*. Philadelphia: Book Concern of the AME Church, 1922.

Stampp, Kenneth. *The Peculiar Institution: Slavery in the Ante-bellum South*. New York: Alfred A. Knopf, 1956.

Starland, Gwendolyn. *Voices of Elderly Black Women: A Historical Perspective*. Bessemer, Ala.: Colonial Press, 1988.

Stuckey, Sterling. *Slave Culture, Nationalist Theory, and the Foundations of Black America*. New York: Oxford University Press, 1987.

The Civic Club. *A Directory of the Charitable, Social Improvement, Educational and Religious Association, and Churches of Philadelphia. Together with Legal Suggestions, Laws Applying to Dwellings, etc.* 2d ed. Philadelphia: The Civic Club, 1903.

The National Committee on Aging. *Standards of Care for Older People in Institutions. Section 1: Suggested Standards for Homes for the Aged and Nursing Homes*. New York: The National Committee on Aging, 1953.

Trattner, Walter. *From Poor Law to Welfare State: A History of Social Welfare in America*. New York: The Free Press, 1974.

Turner, Edward R. *The Negro in Pennsylvania—Slavery— Servitude—Freedom, 1639–1861*. Washington: The American Historical Association, 1911.

Twining, Mary A. and Keith Baird, eds. *Sea Island Roots: African Presence in the Carolinas and Georgia*. Trenton, N.J.: Africa World Press, 1991.

Tyler, Alice Felt. *Freedom's Ferment: Phases of American Social History from the Colonial Period to the Outbreak of the Civil War*. New York: Harper and Row Publishers, 1962.

Warner, Amos. *American Charities*. New York: Thomas Crowell Company, 1894.

Webber, Thomas L. *Deep Like the River: Education in the Slave Quarter Community, 1831–1865*. New York: W. W. Norton and Company, 1978.

Week, John. *Aging Concepts and Social Issues*. Belmont, Calif.: Wadsworth Publishing Company, 1984.

White, Deborah. *Ar'nt I a Woman? Females Slaves in the Plantation South*. New York: W. W. Norton and Company, 1985.

Wright, R. R., compiler. *The Philadelphia Colored Directory: A Handbook of Religious, Social, Political, Professional, Business, and Other Activities of the Negroes in Philadelphia*. Philadelphia: Colored Directory Company, 1910.

Zilversmit, Arthur. *The First Emancipation: The Abolition of Slavery in the North*. Chicago: The University of Chicago Press, 1967.

ARTICLES

Abbey, June. "Health Care of the Aged Based on Physiological Concerns." In *The Black Elderly in Long-Term Care Settings*, 10–14. Oakland: Ethel Percy Andrus Gerontology Center—University of Southern California, 1974.

Aptheker, Herbert. "The Quakers and Slavery." *Journal of History* 25 (July 1940): 331-62.

Arth, Malcolm. "Aging: A Cross-Cultural Perspective." In *Research Planning and Action for the Elderly: The Power and Potential of Social Science*, 362–65. Edited by Donald Kent, Robert Kastenbaum, and Sylvia Sherwood. New York: Behavioral Publications, 1972.

———. "Ideals and Behavior: A Comment on Ibo Respect Patterns." *The Gerontologist* 8 (winter 1968): 242–44.

Barome, Joseph. The Vigilant Committee of Philadelphia." *Pennsylvania Magazine of History and Biography* 92 (July 1968): 321–51.

Barrow, Milton. "Minority Group Characteristics of the Aged in American Society." *Journal of Gerontology* 8 (October 1957): 477–482.

Beattie, Walter. "The Aging Negro: Some Implications for Social Welfare Services." *Phylon* 21 (summer 1960): 131–35.

Bennett, Ruth. "The Meaning of Institutional Life." *The Gerontologist* 3 (September 1963): 112–20.

Browning, James. "The Beginnings of Insurance Enterprise among Negroes." *Journal of Negro History* 21 (April 1936): 417–32.

Cadbury, Henry J. "Negro Memberships in the Society of Friends." *Journal of Negro History* 21 (April 1936): 151–212.

Carlton-Laney, Iris. "Old Folks' Homes for Blacks during the Progressive Era." *Journal of Sociology and Social Welfare.* 16 (September 1989): 43–60.
Coggan, Blanche. "Gerontologic Reviews: A Review of Facilities Available for Older People." *Journal of Gerontology* 6 (1951): 394–97.
Calloway, Nathaniel. "Medical Aspects of the Aging American Black." In *Proceedings of Black Aged in the Future.* 53–56. Compiled by Jacquelyne Jackson. Durham, N.C.: Duke University Press, 1973.
Colb, Lawrence. "The Mental Hospitalization of the Aged: Is It Being Overdone?" *American Journal of Psychiatry* 8 (February 1956): 627–36.
Douglass, Sarah. "I Believe They Despise Us for Our Color." In *Black Women in White America.* Edited by Gerda Lerner. New York: Vintage Books, 1972.
Forsythe, David H. "Friends Almshouse in Philadelphia." *Bulletin of Friends' Historical Association* 16 (spring 1967): 16–25.
Geffen, Elizabeth. "Violence in Philadelphia in the 1840s and 1850s." *Pennsylvania History* 36 (October 1956): 381–410.
Gelfand, Donald. "Visiting Patterns and Social Adjustment in an Old Age Home." *The Gerontologist* 8 (winter 1968): 272–75.
Gold, Jacob and Saul Kaufman. "Development of Care of Elderly: Tracing the History of Institutional Facilities." *The Gerontologist* 10 (winter 1970): 262–74.
Haber, Carole. "The Old Folks at Home: The Development of Institutionalized Care for the Aged in Nineteenth-Century Philadelphia." *The Pennsylvania Magazine of History and Biography* 101 (April 1977): 240–57.
Hill, Robert. "A Profile of the Black Aged." In *Minority Aged in America.* Occasional papers in Gerontology, University of Michigan—Wayne State University, 1972.
Jackson, Hobart. "A Social Worker—Administrator Defines Successful Aging." *Clinical Medicine* 79 (August 1972): 19–31.
———. "Housing and Geriatric Centers for Aging and Aged Blacks." In *Proceedings of Black Aged in the Future.* 23–33. Compiled by Jacquelyne Jackson. Durham, N.C.: Duke University Press, 1973.
———. "Social Policy Which Facilitates Health Services." In *Community Services and The Black Elderly,* 28–38. Edited by Richard Davis. Los Angeles: Ethel Percy Andrus Gerontology Center—University of Southern California, 1972.
———. "The Current Nursing Home Crisis." *NCBA News* 1 (December 1973): 4–5.
Jackson, Jacquelyne. "About Black Aging." *Black Aging* 1 (October 1973): 1–2.
———. "Help Me Somebody! I's an Old Black Standing in the Need of Institutionalizing." *Psychiatric Opinion* 10 (December 1973): 6-16.
———. "Negro Aged: Toward Needed Research in Social Gerontology." *The Gerontologist* 11 (spring 1971): 52–57.
———. "The Blacklands of Gerontology." *Aging and Human Development* 2 (1971): 156–71.
———. "Social Gerontology and the Negro: A Review." *The Gerontologist* 7 (September 1967): 168–78.
Kelody, Ralph. "Ethnic Cleavages in the U.S.: A Historical Reminder to Social Workers." *Social Work* 14 (January 1969): 13–24.

Selected Bibliography

Kent, Donald P. "Changing Welfare to Serve Minority Aged." In *Minority Aged in America*. Occasional papers in Gerontology, 10, 25–37. Ann Arbor: Institute of Gerontology, University of Michigan—Wayne State University, 1972.

King, Fannie. "The Hard Beginning of Attucks Industrial School and Home at St. Paul, Minnesota." *The Colored American Magazine* 16 (May, 1909): 290–93.

Klebaner, Benjamin. "Employment of Paupers at Philadelphia Almshouse before 1861." *Pennsylvania History* 24 (April 1957): 137–48.

———. "The Home Relief Controversy in Philadelphia, 1782 to 1861." *The Pennsylvania Magazine of History and Biography.* 78 (October 1954): 418–21.

———. "American Manumission Laws and the Responsibility for Supporting Slaves." *Virginia Magazine of History and Biography.* 43 (1955): 443–53.

Kraus, Hertha. "Housing our Older Citizens." In *The Annals of the American Academy of Political and Social Science. Social Contribution by the Aging,* 126–38. Edited by Clark Tibbitts. Philadelphia: The American Academy of Political and Social Science, 1952.

Kutzik, Alfred, "American Social Provision for the Aged: An Historical Perspective." In *Ethnicity and Aging: Theory, Research, and Policy.* Donald Gelfaud and Alfred Kutzik eds. New York: Springer Publishing Co. 1979.

Lewis, Norris. "The Old Folk's Home of Chicago." *The Colored American Magazine* 2 (March 1901): 329–34.

Marks, Rachel B. "Institutions for Dependent and Delinquent Children: Histories, Nineteenth-Century Statistics, and Recurrent Goals." In *Child Caring: Social Policy and the Institution,* 9–67. Edited by Donnell Pappenport, Dee Morgan Kilpatrick, and Robert Roberts. Chicago: Aldine Publishing Company, 1973.

McCormick, Richard P. "William Whipper: Moral Reformer." *Pennsylvania History* 43 (January 1976): 23–46.

"Mental Hospitals: The End of the Road for Aged Blacks." *NCBA News* 2 (February–March 1974): 3.

Messer, Mark. "Race Differences in Selected Attitudinal Dimensions of the Elderly." *The Gerontologist* 8 (winter 1968): 245–49.

Morton, Thomas. "The Pennsylvania Hospital: Its Founding and Functions." In *The Age of Madness,* 12–17. Edited by Thomas Szasz. Garden City, N.Y.: Anchor Press, 1973.

Oblinger, Carl D. "In Recognition of Their Prominence: A Case Study of the Economic and Social Backgrounds of an Ante-Bellum Negro Business and Farming Class in Lancaster County." *Journal of the Lancaster County Historical Society* 72 (1968): 65–83.

Pincus, Allen. "The Definition and Measurement of the Institutional Environment in Homes for the Aged." *The Gerontologist* 8 (autumn 1968): 207–10.

"Public Pensions for Aged Dependent Citizens." *Monthly Labor Review of U.S. Bureau of Labor Statistics* 28 (March 1968): 449–58.

Randall, Ollie. "Some Historical Developments of Social Welfare Aspects of Aging." *The Gerontologist* 5 (March 1965): 40–49.

Rudwick, Elliott. "A Brief History of Mercy—Douglass Hospital in Philadelphia." *Journal of Negro Education* 20 (winter 1951): 50–66.

Shelton, Austin. "Ibo Aging and Eldership: Notes for Gerontologists and Others." *The Gerontologists* 5 (March 1965): 20–23.

Wax, Murray. "The Changing Role of the Home for the Aged." *The Gerontologist* 2 (September 1962): 128–33.

Weinstock, Comilda and Ruth Bennett. "Problems in Communication to Nurses among Residents of a Racially Heterogeneous Nursing Home." *The Gerontologist* 8 (summer 1968): 72–75.

Wilson, Gerald R. "The Religion of the American Negro Slave: His Attitude toward Death and Dying." *The Journal of Negro History* 8 (January 1923): 41–71.

Woodson, Carter. "Insurance Business among Negroes." *Journal of Negro History* 14 (April 1929): 202–26.

Worner, William Frederic. "The Columbia Race Riot." *Lancaster County Historical Society Papers* 26 (1922): 175–87.

Wylie, Robert. "Attitudes toward Aging and the Aged Among Black Americans: Some Historical Perspectives." *Aging and Human Development* 2 (1971): 60–69.

Zelditch, Morris. "The Home for the Aged—a Community." *The Gerontologist* 2 (March 1962): 37–41.

Dissertation, Theses, and Other Sources

Barber, Janet. "Old Age and the Life Course of Slaves: A Case Study of a Nineteenth-Century Virginia Plantation." Ph.D. Diss., University of Kansas, 1983.

Department of Commerce. Bureau of the Census, *Negro Populations, 1790–1915.* Washington D.C.: Government Printing Office, 1918; reprinted by Arno Press and *The New York Times,* 1968.

Department of Commerce and Labor. Bureau of the Census. *Benevolent Institutions.* Washington D.C.: Government Publications, 1910.

Dill, Augustus. *Morals and Manners among Negro Americans.* Atlanta: Atlanta University Publication, 14 Number 1914.

DuBois, W. E. B. *Efforts of Social Betterment among Negro Americans.* Atlanta: Atlanta University Publication, no. 10, 1910.

Irwin, Emma Mae. "The Home for Aged and Infirm Colored Persons." Report submitted to the Board of Managers, 17 February 1938. Philadelphia, Pennsylvania.

Lee, Dorothy B. "A Study of the Development of the Happy Haven Home for the Negro Aged in Atlanta, Georgia, from March 1947 to May 1950." Masters thesis, School of Social Work, Atlanta University, Atlanta, Georgia, 1951.

[Lindsay, Inabell]. "The Multiple Hazards of Age and Race: The Situation of Aged Blacks in the United States." A report by the Special Committee on Aging, United States Senate, Washington, D.C.: Government Printing Office. 1971.

———. "The Participation of Negroes in the Establishment of Welfare Services, 1865–1900." Ph.D. diss., University of Pittsburgh, 1952.

National Urban League. *Double Jeopardy: The Older Negro in America Today.* New York: The National Urban League, 1964.

National Caucus on Black Aged. "The Status of the Black Elderly in the United

States." Select Committee on Aging, House of Representatives. Washington, D.C.: U.S. Government Printing Office, 1987.

Norwood, Alberta. "Negro Welfare Work in Philadelphia, Especially as Illustrated by the Career of William Still, 1775–1930." Masters thesis, University of Pennsylvania, 1931.

Philadelphia Yearly Meeting. *List of Organizations Managed Wholly or in Part by Members of the Society of Friends in Philadelphia Yearly Meeting.* 1903.

Schuyler, Benjamin Phillip. "The Philadelphia Quakers in the Industrial Age, 1865–1920." Ph.D. diss., Columbia University, 1967.

Warrick, Dorothy. "A Quarter of a Century." Founders Day Address, October 1971. Stephen Smith Home for the Aged. Philadelphia. Obtained from Mrs. Angeline Smith.

Index

Note: Page references to photographs are in italics.

Abbott, Edith, 148
Abyssinian Benevolent Daughters of Esther Association, 95
Achenbaum, Andrew, 19
activities program, HAICP, 146–50
activity theory of aging, 55
Africa, 160
African American Female Intelligence Society of Boston, 87
African Association, 95
African Benevolent Society, 95, 97
African Clarkson Society, 94; sick benefits and, 105
African Friendly Society, 105
African Insurance Company, 93
African Methodist Episcopal Zion (AMEZ) Church, 70
Age Discrimination in Employment Act (ADEA), 42
Aged Men and Women's Home (Baltimore, MD), 68, 84
aging: beneficial societies and, 87–109; and family care, 21–24, 115; historical perspective, 19–27, 202; post–Civil War, 67–69; and poverty, 24, 63; segregation and, 20; in slavery, 31–58; theories of, 53–58. *See also* beneficial societies; gerontology; life expectancy; slavery
Alexander, Lucretia, 41
Alfa Society, 103, 104
Allen Chapel Bands, 161
Allen, Richard, 93
allopathic medicine, 173–77
almshouse, 63–65, 77, 100, 155
Alpha Home Association, 69, 81, 84, 86
AME Church, 76; bishops, 67
American Colonization Society, 46
American Medical Association, 173
American Missionary Association, 67

American Tract Society, 68
Anderson, Caroline, 166, 169, 175, 182
Anderson, Elizabeth, 154
Anderson, Phyllis, 182
Appleton, Floyd, 68
Ashley River Asylum, 83–84
Attucks Home, 69
Attwell, Cordelia, 159–60
Augustus, Peter, 72

Baker and Company, 167
Baltimore Mutual Aid Society, 99
Bannister House, 86
Barber, Janet, 33, 53
Barnard, Sarah, 79
Barnes, Esther, 124, 177
Beattie, Walter, 19
Beatty, Robert and Elizabeth, 144–45, 183
Becket, Ester, 127
beneficial societies, 87–109, 203; burial and, 87, 90–92, 94–96, 102, 105–6, 109; demise of, 106–9; female/male, 94–95; friendly visiting and, 87, 94, 96; HAICP and, 103–6; outside United States, 97; post–Civil War, 97–100; pre–Civil War, 92–97; sick benefits and, 87, 93, 101–5
Beneficial Society of Freemen of Color, 97
benevolent associations. *See* beneficial societies
Benevolent Daughters of John Wesley, 103
Benezet, Anthony, 71
Bennet, Ruth, 125–26
Benson, Hannah, 156, 169
Berlin, Ira, 46, 61
Best, W. L., 39
Bethel Church, 93

Index

Beven, Elizabeth, 182
Billingsley, Andrew, 51
Blassingame, John, 48–49
Blockley Almshouse, 100, 174, 178
boarding system, 113–14
Board of Managers, HAICP, 111, 117–26, 186, 196–97
Boles, John, 49
Boltwick, Elizabeth, 156
Bond, Horace Mann, 160
Boude, General Thomas, 75
Braddick, Henry, 145
Breeden, James, 38
Briscoe, Alma, 120
Brock, S. J. M., 117
Brooklyn Home for the Aged, 69
Brooklyn Tompkins Association, 94
Brooklyn Woolman Benevolent Society, 94
Brown Fellowship Society (BFS), 96, 107
Brown, H. J., 160–61
Brown, John, 35
Brown, Joshua, 102
Brown, Malinda, 124, 176
Brown, Mary, 79
Brown, Rachel, 183
Brown, William, 35
Brown, William Wells, 91
Browne, Reverend W. W., 81
Browning, James, 108
Bucknell, Eliza, 183
Bureau of Refugees, Freedmen and Abandoned Lands, 68
burial: and beneficial societies, 87, 90–92, 94–96, 102, 105–6, 109; HAICP and, 106, 184–85
Burke, Emily, 33, 36, 41, 46
Burr, Elmira, 155
Butler, William, 112

Cadbury, Henry, 159
Caldwell, Charles, 61–62
Calloway, Nathaniel, 25
Campbell, Bishop Jabez, 104, 116, 155, 160
Campbell, Emily, 148
Campbell, Mary, 104, 116
Carson, Mary, 78
Carter, James, 43, 59
Carter's Old Folk's Home, 69
Cassy, Joseph, 63

Catterall, Helen, 35
Catto, Octavius V., 76
Catto School, 139, 161
Caution, Ann, 188
census, 1840, 44
centenarians, 61–62, 78–79, 128–30
Century Fellowship Society, 107
charity, 59–86
Charity Organization Society, 65
Charles Crittenton and Company, 167
Chatters, Linda, 23
Childs, Ann, 154
Christian Benevolent Society, 97
Christian Recorder, 76
Civil War, 34; black population at the time of, 60–61
Coates, Edwin, 74, 176
Coates, Elizabeth, 176
Coleman, Charles, 93
Coleman, J. W., 57
Collins, Cato, 72
Collins, James, 166
Colored Aged Home (Irvington, NJ), 104
Colored Aged Home and Orphanage (Newark, NJ), 69, 84
Colored Benevolent Society (Nashville, TN), 97–98
Colored Men's and Ladies Protective Association, 101–2
Colored Old Folk's and Orphan Home (Mobile, AL), 69
Commonwealth vs Equitable Beneficial Association, 88–89
complaints, HAICP: clothing, 142–43; food, 141–42; liquor, 143–44
"Complaint to the Lord", 140–41
Conard, Rebecca, 140
Consolation, 97
Conway, Mary, 170
Coppin, Fanny Jackson, 66–67, 160, 161
Council of Auxilliaries, 191
Cowgill, Donald, 53–54
Craft, William and Edna, 35
Crawford's Old Men's Home (Cincinatti, OH), 69, 83
Cropper, Isaiah, 114
Cuff, Margaret, 114, 182
Cummings, Elaine, 55
Curry, Leonard, 95

Daniels, John, 101
Daughters of Cornish, 103
Daughters of Jerusalem, 97
Daughters of St. Paul, 103
Davis, Elijah, 180
Davis, Elise, 43
Davis, Frances, 157
Davis, Lenwood, 82, 85
death, 55; in the HAICP, 182–85; in slavery, 52; West African views, 48. *See also* burial
Delaney, Martin, 76, 91
Delille, Henriette, 67, *137*
demographics. *See* population
Derrickson, Mary, 78, 183
Dickerson, W. F., 22
discipline: in the HAICP, 150–51, 154–58
discrimination, 24, 62, 71–74, 100; and civil rights legislation, 34. *See also* racism
disengagement theory of aging, 55
Dix, Dorothea, 64
Dixon, Mary, 120
domestics, 74–75, 116
Double Jeopardy, 20, 198
Douglas, Sarah, 71, 73
Douglass, Frederick, 31, 37, 51–52
Douglass, Robert, 72
Doyle, Bertram, 38
drugs. *See* medicines
DuBois, W. E. B., 36, 69, 82–83, 90, 160
Duncan, Catherine, 78
Duterte, Henrietta, 116

Eaton, Frances, 166
Edwards, Mary, 128
Elijah Society, 103
Elks, 99
Emlen, Samuel, 150
employment, in the HAICP, 118–26
Engermann, Stanley, 40
epidemics, 164
Equal Rights League, 152
Eustis, Frederick, 41–42
Evans, William, 166, 180
exchange theory of aging, 55–57

Faith Home, 69
family care, 21–23, 26–27, 59, 113; HAICP and, 115, 171, 185, 204; and mental illness, 178–79; in slavery, 31–32, 50–52
Father of Black Gerontology, 60, 186–201. *See also* Jackson, Hobart; HAICP since 1949
Faucette, Lindsey, 39
Feldstein, Stanley, 52
Female Assistant Benefit Society, 95
Female Benevolent Society of Troy, New York, 95
First African Baptist Church (Baltimore), 91
Fischer, David H., 34, 65
Fogel, Robert, 40
Food and Drug Act, 167
Foote, Julia, 66
Ford, Nellie, 172
Forten, James, 63, 72, 152–53
Forten, William, 115–16, 130–31, 152–53
Fountain, Julia, 182
Fox, George, 71
Franklin Slaughter Insurance Co., 35
fraternal orders, 88, 99–101, 106. *See also* beneficial societies
Frazier, E. Franklin, 90
Frederick Douglass Memorial Hospital and Training School, 82, 189
Free African Society (FAS), 79–80, 93
Free Africa Union Society (FAUS), 92–93, 95, 107–8
Freedmen's Aid Associations, 68, 77, 97–98
Freedmans Hospital (Washington, DC), 82
Freedmen's Bureau, 68, 97–98
Friendly Society of St. Thomas, 93
funeral, 103. *See also* burial, death

Galilean Fisherman, 99
Gallaudet, Thomas, 64
Garrison, William Lloyd, 46
Gaudin, Juliette, 67, *137*
gender: HAICP and, 118–26
Genovese, Eugene, 36, 37, 51
George, Phillis, 182
Gerocomeia, 65
Gerontological Society, 192, 198
gerontology: cultural considerations and, 19–27, 43, 202–5; and the HAICP, 161–62; historical perspective, 19–58; and Hobart Jackson,

Index

186–201; slavery and, 53–58; theories of aging, 53–58. *See also* aging
Gillard, John, 66
Godwin, Samuel, 150
Good Samaritans, 99, 101
Gordon, Henry, 80
Governor's Advisory Committee on Aging, 198
Graham, Nancy, 149
Gram, Hans, 173
Grand Fountain of the United Order of True Reformers, 99
grandmothers: role of, 21–22, 51
Green, Edward, 80
Greenfield, Elizabeth, 111
grievance policies: in the HAICP, 122, 194
Guardians of the Poor, 77, 100, 174
guilt, 23, 27, 59, 115, 203
Gutman, Herbert, 50, 51

Haber, Carole, 77
Hagen, Margaret, 178
Hahnemann, Samuel, 173
Hahnemann Medical College, 175
HAICP (Home for Aged and Infirm Colored Persons): activities in, 146–50, 157, 180; beneficial societies and, 103–6; boarding system in, 113–14; death in, 106, 182–85; departures from, 156, 177–81; development of, 59–86; discipline in, 150–51, 154–58; employment practices in, 119–22; family support in, 115, 171, 185, 204; gender in, 118–26; gerontology theory and, 161–63; grievances in, 122, 132, 140–43; health care in, 163–85; life care system in, 105–6, 113–14, 194–95; management of, 111, 117–26, 186, 194–98; racial issues in, 110–11, 118, 124–26; religion in, 138–39; 158–60; residents of, 84, 112–14, 127–31; since 1949, 186–201; social structure of, 138–162. *See also* HAICP, health care and; HAICP, since 1949
HAICP: health care and, 163–85; allopathy vs. homeopathy, 175–78; diseases, 183–85; medicines used in, 167–69; mental illness in, 178–80; nursing care in, 169–70, 187; physicians, 166–70
HAICP: since 1949, 186–201; decline of, 187–90; Hobart Jackson and, 186–201; integration of, 193–94; as nursing home, 166–67, 196–98; self-government and, 194. *See also* Jackson, Hobart
Hall, Maurice, 75, 77
Hall, Prince, 99
Hancock, George W., 174
Hannah Gray Home, 81
Harmon, Patrick, 155–56
Harper, Frances, 73, 160; poetry of, 19, 59, 138, 163, 186
Harvey, Hettey, 80
Hasan, Robert, 160
health care, 21, 163–85; allopathic vs. homeopathic, 173–78; diseases, in the HAICP, 164, 183–85; mental illness, 44, 178–81; of slaves, 42–44. *See also* medical care; medicines; HAICP: health care and
Hebrew Benevolent Society, 96
Henderson, Harriet, 154
Henszey, Samuel, 166, 177
Herbra Gemilot Hasidim, 96
Herschberg, Theodore, 72
Hill, Leslie P., 160
Hill, Ruth, 183
"hiring out": HAICP and, 146
historical perspective, 19–87
Hoffman, Frederick, 107
Hogwood, Phyllis, 128
Hollenbeck Home, 145
Home for Aged Colored Women (Boston) 67, 103
Home for Aged Colored Women (Cleveland), 81
Home for the Aged Colored Women (Providence), 69, 84, 86
Home for the Aged and Infirm (New York), 65
Home for Aged and Infirm Colored Persons. *See* HAICP
Home for Aged and Infirmed Colored Women, (Pittsburgh) 69, 84, 86
Home for Aged and Infirm Israelites (St. Louis, MO), 65–66
Home for Aged Men (Springfield, MA), 69, 83
Home for Destitute Colored Children (Philadelphia, PA), 139, 161

Home for Incurables (Philadelphia, PA), 113, 183
Homeopathic College of Cleveland, 175
homeopathy, 173–78
Homes: development of, 59–86; during immigration, 65. *See also* nursing homes
Homes for the Aged and Nursing Homes, 192
House of Representatives Select Committee on Aging, 24
Houses of Refuge, 64, 161
Howard, Martha, 172
Howe, Samuel Gridley, 64
Humane Brotherhood, 96, 97, 108
Humphries, Solomon, 63
Hunts magazine, 62
Hurt, William, 146
Hushbeck, Judith, 41

identity crisis theory of aging, 57–58
Imes, T. Creiah, 166, 175
independent living, 196–97
Independent Order of St. Luke, 99
Indigent Widows and Single Women's Home, 77
infirmary, 165, 196
"The Influence of Climate Upon Longevity," 62
Institute for Colored Youth, 66–67, 139, 161
institutionalization, 22, 63–67; and Hobart Jackson, 200; and slavery, 20
insurance, 88–89, 108–9; and beneficial societies, 100, 106–7; in slavery, 34–35
Irwin, Emma, 167, 188

Jabez B. Campbell Society, 105
Jackson, Belinda, 120
Jackson, Hobart, 24, 25, 60, 70, *137*, 146; career, 189; and HAICP, 186–201; and life care contracts, 114, 194–95; medical care under, 195–96; national importance of, 191–92, 198–200; philosophy, 192–95. *See also* HAICP, since 1949
Jackson, Jacquelyne, 20,22, 25, 199
Jackson, Mary, 182
Jacobs, Harriet, 37
Jeanes, Anna, 116
Jeanes, Mary, 116

John Cornish Society, 103
Johnson, Catherine, 189
Johnson, George, 72
Johnson, Israel, 73, 123, 125, 176
Johnson, James Weldon, 160
Johnson, Mary, 116
Johnson, Patience, 183
Johnson, Power and Weighman, 167
Johnson, William, 63
Jones, Absalom, 93
Jones, J.C., 176
Jones, Jehu, 63
Jones, Margaret, 116
Jordan, Mary, 124, 195
Jordan, Wilbert, 43
Joseph Parrish Society, 103
Joshua Woodland Society, the, 103, 104
Jugan, Jeane, 66
Jungle, The, 167
Juvenile Daughters of Ruth, 94

Keystone Beneficial Society, 103
kinship systems, 31, 47, 50, 202. *See also* family care
Kirkbride, Thomas, 179
Klebaner, Benjamin, 46
Knights of Jericho, 99
Knights of Pythias, 99, 103
Knights of Tabor, 99
Kutzik, Alfred, 65, 92, 100

LaConcorde, 98
Ladies Benevolent Society, 98
Ladies Union Benevolent Society, 97
Lafon Homes, 83, 86
Lafon, Thomy, 63, 67
Laing Building, 163
Laing, Henry, 73, 104, 123
Laws, Ann, 120, 182
Laws, Mary Ann, 182
Lay, Benjamin, 71
Layton Home, 84, 86
Leach, Robert B., 175
Lebanon Cemetery Company, 90
Lee, Marie, 182
Lee, Mary, 158
Lemington Home, 86
Les Jeunes Amis, 98–99
Lewis, Shippen, 188
Liberator, 66
life care residency, 79, 105–6, 113–14, 194–95

life course theory of aging, 53
life expectancy, 25, 61; in slave population, 33
Lindsay, Inabel, 199
Little Sisters of the Poor, 66
Longfellow, Henry Wadsworth, 202
Lucas, James, 39

MacDonald, Mary, 79
Magdol, Edward, 47
manumission, 33, 44–45, 56, 61
marriage: at HAICP, 144–45
Marshall, Andrew, 63
Marshall, Sarah, 116
Martin, I. Maximillian, 193–94
Martin, Elmer, 22
Martin, Joanne, 22
Masons, 99
Mastion, Louisa, 183
Maxfield, Alexander, 173–75, 178
McClure, Ethel, 65, 118
McCollin, S. Mason, 175, 176
McCook, Rev., 158–59
McDonald, Mary, 130
medical care: herbal, 43; through beneficial societies, 102; of slaves, 42–44; in the HAICP, 163–85, 195–97. *See also* HAICP: health care and; health care
medical schools, 82
medical training: antebellum, 91
medicines, 167–69
mental health: of slaves, 44
mental illness: HAICP and, 178–81
Mercy-Douglass Center, 191, 197
Mercy Hospital, 82
Metropolitan Life, 107
Miles, Sarah, 154
Miller, Lucretia, 161
Miller, T. E., 70
modernization theory of aging, 53–54
Monthly Labor Review, 85
Morgan, Sarah, 180
Morris Brown Society, 104
Morris, Francis, 146
Morris, Sarah, 155
mortality, 25, 61; crossover, 25, 33; in slaves, 33. *See also* death
Mosaic Templars, 99
Mossell, N. F., 82
Mother Bethel, 77
Mott, Lucretia, 71, 73–74, 111

Mt. Airy Plantations, 33
Mueller, 166–67
Mugler, Nathan, 178
"The Multiple Hazards of Age and Race: The Situation of Aged Blacks in the United States," 199
Murphy, Emmareta, 127–28
mutual aid, 31, 88, 202; in HAICP, 171–172. *See also* beneficial societies; kinship systems
Mutual Union Aid and Beneficial Association, 105

National Association of Colored Women (NACW), 70
National Caucus and Center on Black Aged (NCBA), 24, 25, 42, 70, 187, 198–201
National Committee on Aging, 192
National Council on Aging, 198
National Social Welfare Assembly, 192
Negro Convention Movement, 93
National Mental Health Act, 181
Needs, Julia, 185
Negro Population, 1790–1915, 61
New York African Society for Mutual Relief (NYASMR), 94
New York Benevolent Branch of Bethel, 95
Nightingale Association, 171
Norristown State Hospital, 113, 120, 178–81
North Carolina Mutual Life Company, 35
nursing care: through beneficial societies, 98, 101; in the HAICP, 169–70; after 1953, 195–96. *See also* health care; HAICP, health care and
Nursing Home Bill of Rights, 204
nursing homes: accessibility, 22–27; HAICP, transition to, 166, 196–97; as problematic system, 200. *See also* Homes

Oakes, James, 36
Odd Fellows, 99, 101
Ogden, Peter, 99
Old Folks and Orphan's Home, 69
Old Men's Association, 98
Olive Cemetery Company, 90
ombudsman, 26, 116

outdoor relief, 100–103
Owens, Leslie, 57

Parker Annex, 78, 111–12, 165–66
Parker, Edward, 78, *132, 136,* 165–66
Parrish, Dillwyn, 72, 104, 117, 176
paternalism, 71; in slavery, 36–39, 47, 58; in domestic-employer relations, 74–75; HAICP and, 116, 138, 151–52
Paxson, Justice Edward, 78
Payne, Daniel Alexander, 96
Peck, David J., 91
Pennock, Alice, 181
Pennock, Lydia, 148
Pennock, Sarah, 124–25
Pennsylvania Abolition Society, 72
Pennsylvania Hospital, 178
pensions, 98–99, 102, 108
People's Relief Association, 102
Perseverance Benevolence and Mutual Aid Association of New Orleans, 93, 98
Perry, Eliza, 74
Phillips, Catherine, 140
Phillips, Ulrich, 37–38
Phyllis Wheatley Home, 81, 84
Platt, William, 63
Plessy v. Ferguson, 68
policy, 26, 202–5
Pollard, Edward, 36
population, 60–61; in African American Homes, 84–85; of domestics, 74–75
Postell, William, 44
Presidential Task Force on Aging, 198
Preston, Ed, 147
Provident Hospital, 82
Prudential Insurance Company, 107

Quakers, 71–86; and Black relations, 73–75, 138; and burial, 184–85; and charity, 73–74; declining involvement, 187–88; and HAICP, 73–80, 111, 117, 159–60
Quann, Esther, 178

Rabinowitz, Howard, 91
Race Traits and Tendencies of the American Negro, 107
racial issues: in aging, 19–27; HAICP and, 70–77, 124–26, 193–94; and Quaker-Black relations, 73–75

racism, 68, 77, 102; and *Double Jeopardy,* 20, 198; in insurance practices, 107; Irish attacks, 76. See also discrimination, paternalism, racial issues, segregation
Rainwater, Lee, 22
Raper, Arthur, 109
Reason, Rebecca, 172
Reid, Ira De A., 160, 192
relief: indoor, 103; outdoor, 100–103
religion: in slavery, 52; at HAICP, 138–39; 158–60; Seventh Day Adventists, 154
Resolute Beneficial Society, 97
Rev. Henry Davis Society, 103
Rev. Jabez Campbell Society, 103
Rev. R. Moore Society, 103
Rev. R. Robinson Society, 103
Rev. William Moore Society, 103
Reynolds, John P., 91
Rhone, JoAnne, 49
Ricaud, Cyprian, 63
Riker, Charlotte, 120
Robinson, Catharine, 181
Rock, John, 91
Roselle, David, 166, 173
Rosemont Association, 109
Rosengarten Sons, 167
Ruggles, David, 91
Rush, Benjamin, 179

St. Andrew's Society, 96
St. Cecilia Society, 95
St. Francis Home, 66
St. James Male Beneficial Society, 91
St. Thomas Episcopal Church, 93
Saulsbury, Temperance, 157
Savitt, Todd, 41, 42, 91
Scarborough, 38
Schick, Tom, 46
Scott, Mary Ann, 172
secret societies, 88, 99–100
segregation: after Reconstruction, 68; effect on aging, 20; in Homes, 83–85; late nineteenth century, 82–83. See also discrimination, racial issues, racism
Seven Wise Men, 101
Shafer, C. T., 166
Shaw, Mary Ann, 74, 77
Shelter for Colored Orphans, 161
Short, Elmira, 181

Index

Shyrock, Richard, 43–44
sick benefits. *See* beneficial societies, medical care
Silvey, Susan, 103, 112
Simmons, Leo, 21
Simpson, Martha, 183
Sims, Bill, 37
Sinclair, Upton, 167
Sisterhood of St. Phillip's, 68
Sisters of the Holy Family, 67, *137*
slavery, 20, 21, 31–59; apologists, 36–38; gerontological theory and, 53–58; manumission, 33, 45–46, 56, 61; medical care, 42–44; mental health, 44; neglect of elderly, 46; old slaves, selling of, 35–36; religion, 52; slave community, 47–58; slave system, 32–47; social status, 48–49, 57; social services, 49–50
Sleeper, Sarah, 104
Smith-Cunningham Personal Care Facility, 197–98
Smith, James McCune, 62, 91, 175
Smith-Pinn Center, 197–98
Smith, Sarah, 176
Smith-Shepherd Centers, 197–98
Smith, Stephen, 63, *136;* HAICP and, 75–79, 111, 117, 160; celebrations for, 193
Smothers, Louise, 183
Social Security Act, 108, 113–15
social services: in slave community, 49–50. *See also* beneficial societies
Society of Friends, 71, 159. *See also* Quakers
Society for Relief of Worthy Aged Paupers, 67
Sons and Daughters of John Wesley, 103
Sons of St. Thomas Society, 103, 105
South Carolina Society, 96
Southeby, William, 71
spiritual life. *See* religion.
sponsors, 116
Staat, Maria, 154
Stampp, Kenneth, 32, 36
Stanford, E. Percil, 20
Star in the East Association, 97
Stephen Smith Geriatric Center, 197
Stephen Smith Home for the Aged (SSHA), 78, 132–35, 193–201; *See also* HAICP
Stephen Smith Multi-Service Center (SSMSC), 197
Stephen Smith Towers, 196
Stewart, Maria, 66
Still, James, 91
Still, William, 73, 75, 78, 104, 116, 117, *136, 160;* in HAICP management, 123–27, 176
Stokes, William, 176
Stout, Annie, 129–30
Strand, Abram, 149–50
Striker, William, 145
Stuckey, Sterling, 48
Sudarkasa, Niara, 50
Sydnor, Charles, 33

Taylor, Lucy, 79, 80, 129
Taylor, Robert, 23
Teague, Catherine, 80
Tent Sisters, 81
Thatcher, Jessie, 166, 173–77
Thompson, Thomas and Anna, 156
Tillotson, M., 104
Time on the Cross, 40
Todd, Hannah, 129, 176
True Reformers, 99–101, 109
True Reformers Homes, 81–82
Truth, Sojourner, 70
Tubman, Harriet, 70
Tubman Home, 70
Turner, Nat, 45, 49; Nat Turner Revolt, 62

Union Benevolent Society, 97
United Brothers of Friendships, 99
Unity and Friendship Society, 97
Urban League, 20

visiting, friendly: and beneficial societies, 87, 96–98, 101–2, 109; in the HAICP, 26
voting rights, 62, 68

Wacamaw Plantation (SC), 40
Walker, Harry, 99
Wallace, Maria, 183
Warner, Amos, 65
Warner and Company, 167
Warrick, Dorothy, 188, 190, 193

Warrick, Marie, 181, 188
Washington, Booker T., 68
Watson, Wilbur, 22, 26, 43
Wayland, Rev. H. L., 160
Webb, Harrison H. 91
Webster, Amelia, 103, 104, 112
Weinstock, Comilda, 125–26
Wells, Ida B., 160
West Africa: cultural traditions of, 27, 47–48, 50, 59, 66, 87
Whipper, William, 73, 75–76
White, George H., 160
White House Conferences on Aging, 198
White, Jacob, 73
Wilberforce Philanthropic Society, 94

Willets, Mary, 178
Williams, Madame Selika, 115
Williamsburg Asylum, 64
Wilson, G. R., 52
Wilson, James, 166
women: role in Homes, 80–81; at HAICP, 118–26
Women's Loyal Union, 81
Women's Twentieth-Century Club, 81
Work, Monroe, 99
Woodson, Carter, 106
Woolman, John, 71
Wright, R. R., 160
Wylie, Robert, 21

Zimmerman, William, 170–71